CONCEPTUAL STRUCTURE, DISCOURSE and LANGUAGE

CONCEPTUAL STRUCTURE, DISCOURSE and LANGUAGE

edited by
Adele E. Goldberg

CENTER FOR THE STUDY OF
LANGUAGE AND INFORMATION
STANFORD, CALIFORNIA

Copyright ©1996
CSLI Publications
Center for the Study of Language and Information
Leland Stanford Junior University
Printed in the United States
05 04 03 02 01   5 4 3

Library of Congress Cataloging-in-Publication Data

Conceptual structure, discourse, and language / edited by Adele E. Goldberg
       p.   cm.
  Based on papers presented at the 1st Conceptual Structure, Discourse, and
Language Conference, which was held Oct. 1995, University of California, San
Diego.
  Includes bibliographical references and index.
  ISBN 1-57586-041-4 (alk. paper). – ISBN 1-57586-040-6 (pbk : alk. paper)
  1. Grammar, Comparative and general–Congresses. 2. Semantics–Congresses.
3. Linguistic change–Congresses. 4. Discourse analysis–Congresses. 5. Meta-
phor–Congresses. I. Goldberg, Adele E. II. Conceptual Structure, Discourse, and
Language Conference (1st : 1995 : University of California, San Diego)
P201.C66 1996   96-14206
415–dc20   CIP

♾ The acid-free paper used in this book meets the minimum requirements of the American National Standard for Information Sciences—Permanence of Paper for Printed Library Materials,
ANSI Z39.48-1984.

Contents

Preface

This collection of papers is the outcome of the first Conceptual Structure, Discourse and Language conference (CSDL) held at the University of California, San Diego in October 1995. CSDL was organized by Ron Langacker, Gilles Fauconnier and myself with the intention of bringing together researchers from both "Cognitive" and "Functional" approaches to linguistics.

The papers in this volume span a variety of topics, but there is a common thread running through them: the claim that semantics and discourse properties are fundamental to our understanding of language. Several recurrent themes can be recognized in the following collection. These include an emphasis on the dynamic nature of language, both diachronically and synchronically, the relevance of a notion of viewpoint in grammatical analyses, the role and nature of metaphor and cognitive blends, the possibility of non-derivational ways to capture relationships among constructions, and the importance of detailed lexical semantics. Other papers provide detailed and illuminating analyses of particular constructions.

Many of the articles stress the dynamic nature of ongoing discourse. Chafe's article builds on his earlier work providing a non-linear model of understanding discourse structure. Ono and Thompson discuss how interlocutors jointly construct meaningful discourse in a dynamic way. Van der Leek suggests that the lexicon be viewed as dynamically interacting with various constructions. Liu suggests that the semantics of the *de* complement in Mandarin is determined by dynamic aspects of speakers' construals.

Other articles stress the importance of a diachronic view of language, noting that the diachronic facts often have synchronic repercussions. Carey offers a detailed analysis of how the English and Spanish perfect tenses evolved from resultatives, by providing specific links in the grammaticalization chain. Gerdts and Hinkson discuss lexical suffixes in Salish languages as the end of a grammaticalization process involving noun incorporation, thereby positing a cline between lexical and grammatical elements. Israel provides a detailed analysis of the history of the *way* construction that helps motivate the verb clusters that appear in the construction today. Huang and Chang provide an analysis of the Mandarin *-quilai*, relating its directional, inchoative and completive meanings.

The importance of establishing a viewpoint is another theme that is echoed in several papers. Epstein stresses the importance of viewpoint in his analysis of the definite article in English, as does Laury in her discussion of demonstratives in Finnish. Poulin discusses the way that shifts in viewpoint are captured in ASL by subtle bodily shifts. The viewpoint-related notions of Figure and Ground are discussed by Polinsky, who argues that these notions are independent of thematic roles, and grammatical or discourse functions. Forrest's contribution provides some experimental data suggesting that a change in viewpoint and the attendant reconstrual occurs in real time.

Another group of papers breaks new ground in the theory of conceptual metaphor and the related process of *blending*. Grady, Morgan and Taub argue that conceptual metaphors should be broken down into component parts, each experientially grounded and capable of interacting with other parts to yield more complicated mappings with emergent properties. Anticipating this suggestion, Hines offers an illuminating look into the metaphorical uses of dessert terms to refer to women. She suggests that several component metaphors conspire to motivate these uses. Also anticipating the relevance of considering independent components of metaphorical schemas is Lakoff's contribution concerning the experiential grounding of our various conceptual schemas for morality. Fauconnier and Turner explore the idea of grammatical blending as a cognitive process that includes metaphor and grammatical fusion as special subcases. Coulson provides a case study making use of this mechanism.

Several contributions address the nature of relationships among families of constructions. Ward and Birner look at the discourse function of three constructions involving rightward movement in English; Lambrecht considers the partially analogous rightward anti-topic (A-TOP) position in various French constructions, particularly vocatives. The contribution of Michaelis & Lambrecht analyzes a family of constructions defined by their exclamative semantic/pragmatic function.

Quite rich lexical semantic properties are shown to be relevant in various ways. Countering the recent claim that only aspect is relevant to syntactic expression, Filip argues that detailed lexical semantics also must be taken into account, particularly for psychological predicates in English and Czeck. Ackerman and Goldberg argue that detailed lexical semantics together with general pragmatic principles can explain why certain adjectival past participles require modification when used pre-nominally (*?baked cake, half-baked cake*).

Other contributions explore the properties of particular constructions. Langacker offers a Cognitive Grammar analysis of a variety generic constructions. Sheffer provides a Cognitive Grammar analysis of deictic adjectives such as *previous, former*. Dancygier and Sweetser analyze conditional constructions. Matsumoto distinguishes and analyzes two types of fictive motion constructions, exemplified by the directional phrases in *The highway goes from LA to NY* and *The bike is parked across the street*. Kemmer and Barlow discuss the discourse properties of the emphatic -*self* construction. The role of motivation in analyses of modal verbs is explored in two papers. Wilcox argues that the grammatical form of modal verbs in ASL is motivated as opposed to arbitrary. Achard makes a similar point for the various complement types of modals in French.

French Modals and Speaker Control

MICHEL ACHARD
University of Florida

1. INTRODUCTION

A modal system is usually composed of a small class of verbs which exhibit certain structural and semantic characteristics. For example, the English modals do not have infinitive forms, they do not agree with their subject, and they do not have participial forms. The French modal class is by no means as distinctive. The verbs traditionally considered as modals are generally included in the broader class of auxiliaries because they are followed by infinitival complements, but they are not morphologically different from other verbs. I argue elsewhere (Achard 1993) that *pouvoir* 'can', *devoir* 'must', and the capability sense of *savoir* 'know how' constitute the French modal class.[1] This paper focuses on the different modal senses illustrated in (1)-(4). Example (1) presents the capability sense of *savoir*. (2a) illustrates the ability sense of *pouvoir*, and (2b) illustrates the possibility sense of the same verb. Example (3) presents the necessity sense of *devoir*, and (4a) and (4b) respectively present the epistemic senses of *pouvoir* and *devoir*:

(1) *Marie sait nager*
    'Mary knows how to swim'
(2) a. *Marie est forte, elle peut soulever 100 kilos*
       'Mary is strong, she is able to lift 100 kilos'
    b. *Le docteur peut vous voir demain, elle n'a pas de rendez-vous*[2]
       'The doctor can see you tomorrow, she has no appointments'
(3) *Jean doit partir immédiatement*
    'John must leave immediately'
(4) a. *Je ne vois pas de lumière, il peut ne rentrer que demain*
       'I don't see any light, he may only come back tomorrow'
    b. *Il a laissé la porte ouverte, il doit revenir bientôt*
       'He left the door open, he must be coming back soon'

---

[1] In Achard (1993), I argue that the conceptualizing role of the main clause subject with respect to the complement scene allows us to differentiate between different classes of verbs which take infinitival complements. The subject of cognition or volition verbs such as *espérer* 'hope' and *vouloir* 'want' acts as a conceptualizer towards the complement scene (Langacker 1991), whereas the subject of modals has little (if any) conceptualizing role. According to that analysis, *savoir* is a polysemous verb, and its capability (modal) sense presented here is to be kept separate from its cognition 'know that' sense.

[2] *Pouvoir* also has a sense of permission which will not be considered here. See Achard (1993) for further details.

1

The analysis of sentential complements has been a very prolific area of research in Romance linguistics, but very little has been said about the specific forms the complement of modals might take. In this paper, I am specifically concerned with the possible presence of the grammatical markers of aspect and voice on the infinitival complement following the different senses of the modals presented in (1)-(4). I will show that the distribution of those markers with a given modal is a direct manifestation of the conceptual structure evoked by that modal. The paper is structured in the following fashion: Section 2 presents the problem. Section 3 provides a semantic/conceptual analysis of the French modals. Section 4 presents the analysis of the distribution of the markers with the different modals. Section 5 summarizes the results obtained in the paper.[3]

2. THE PROBLEM

Infinitival complements in French can usually combine with the grammatical markers of perfect aspect (auxiliary *être* 'be' or *avoir* 'have' + past participle of the main verb) and passive (*être* + past participle of the main verb). In control constructions for example, the infinitive freely combines with both aspect and voice markers, as illustrated in (5).

(5) a. *Jean espère finir à l'heure*
   'John hopes to finish on time'
   b. *Marie espère avoir fini à l'heure*
   'Mary hopes to have finished on time'
   c. *Marie espère être élue*
   'Mary hopes to be elected'

In (5a), the content verb *finir* is in the infinitive. (5b) is in the so-called past infinitive. The auxiliary *avoir* is in the infinitive, and *finir* is in the past participle. (5c) is a passive sentence. The auxiliary is *être*, and the main verb is in the past participle.

However, certain constructions place tighter restrictions on the presence of these markers on their complement structures. For example, in a causative construction, the infinitive can only be used in its bare form, as shown in (6a). It cannot be inflected by an aspect marker as in (6b), or a voice marker as in (6c):

(6) a. *Marie fait travailler Jean*
   'Mary makes John work'

---

[3] The analysis presented here makes use of the concepts developed within the theory of Cognitive Grammar (Langacker 1987, 1991). Throughout the paper, I will assume basic familiarity with the CG framework.

b. *Mary fait avoir travaillé Jean*
    'Mary makes John have worked'
c. *Marie a fait être élu Jean*
    'Mary made John be elected'

With the modals, the possible presence of grammatical marking on the infinitival complement varies depending on the sense of the verb considered. The distribution of the markers of aspect and voice with the different senses of the modals illustrated earlier is presented in (7)-(20).

2.1 The Data

The ability sense of *pouvoir* and *savoir* are both most felicitous when they are followed by a straight infinitive. This is illustrated for *savoir* in (7) and (8), and for *pouvoir* ability in (9) and (10).

(7) *Il sait avoir nagé*
     'He knows how to have swum'
(8) ??*Il sait être enfermé* [4]
     'He knows how to be locked up'
(9) *Il est très fort, il peut avoir soulevé la table*
     'He is very strong, he can have lifted the table'
(10) ??*Il peut être enfermé dans le placard*
     'He can be locked in the closet'

At first sight, the possibility sense of *pouvoir* seems similar to the ability sense. In (11) and (12), the infinitival complements cannot be marked for aspect or passive morphology:

(11) *Il peut avoir nagé à cinq heures ce soir*
     'He can have swum at five o'clock tonight'
(12) *Jean peut être frappé par la police*
     'John can be hit by the police'

However, in other cases, the presence of the perfect or passive markers on the complement is perfectly felicitous, as illustrated in (13) and (14):

(13) a. *Marie peut être revenue à six heures si vous voulez*
         'Mary can have returned at six o'clock if you'd like'
     b. *Jean peut avoir fini dans cinq minutes si c'est important*
         'John can have finished in five minutes, if it is important'

---

[4] Some speakers have found that sentence remotely possible, if *être enfermé* 'be locked up' represents a specific skill the subject possesses, as for example in the case of a magic act, or an experienced burglar who relies on his capacity of being locked up in different places to rob them. However, my consultants all point to the marginality of the sentence, and invariably favor constructions such as *Il sait se laisser enfermer* 'He knows how to get himself locked up' to describe such situations.

(14) a. *Paul pourra être raccompagné par un professeur si vous voulez*
'Paul will be (able to be) taken home by a teacher if you want'
b. *Votre voiture pourra être réparée dans deux heures*
"Your car will be (able to be) fixed in two hours'

The root sense of *devoir* (necessity) imposes no constraints on the following infinitival process, as illustrated in (15) and (16).

(15) *Il doit avoir étudié la leçon avant de faire l'exercice*
'He must have studied the lesson before doing the exercise'
(16) *Il doit absolument être libéré tout de suite*
'He must absolutely be released right away'

In their epistemic senses, neither *devoir* nor *pouvoir* places any constraints on the following complement process. This is illustrated in (17) and (18) for *devoir* and in (19) and (20) for *pouvoir*.

(17) *Il doit être parti, je ne vois pas sa voiture*
'He must have left, I don't see his car'
(18) *Il doit être enfermé, je l'entends crier*
'He must be locked up I hear him scream'
(19) *Il peut ne pas avoir compris, il faudrait répéter*
'He might not have understood, we should repeat'
(20) *Il peut être enfermé, il vaut mieux l'appeler*
'He might be locked up, we had better call him'

The distribution of the markers of aspect and voice with the different modals presented in (7)-(20) is summarized in Table 1.

Table 1: Distribution of Grammatical Markers after Modals

	Epist.		Root			
	Pouvoir	*Devoir*	*Devoir*	*Pouvoir* /po.	*Pouvoir*/ab.	*Savoir*
Aspect	+	+	+	+/-	-	-
Voice	+	+	+	+/-	-	-

Table 1 clearly shows that the modals divide into three natural classes with respect to the kind of grammatical marking each verb allows on its complement. The first one is composed of the epistemic modals and the root sense of *devoir*. The second one contains the possibility sense of *pouvoir*. The third one is composed of the ability sense of *pouvoir* and *savoir*. The goal of this paper is to explain the distribution presented in Table 1. In the following sections, I will now show that the constraints on the possible form of the complement are a direct manifestation of the conceptual configuration which constitutes the semantics of each modal.

3. SEMANTIC ANALYSIS OF THE FRENCH MODALS

It was Talmy (1976, 1988) who first recognized that modality partakes of the general semantic category of force dynamics (henceforth FD). Sweetser (1990:51) thinks that it is best understood "in terms of our linguistic treatment of force and barriers in general." The term "force" applies to the category of necessity. The notion of "barrier" applies to the category of possibility. The semantic characterization of French modal verbs involves making specific the different FD configurations of *devoir*, *pouvoir* and *savoir*.

In his analysis of modality, Langacker (1991) notes that the English modals historically come from main verbs which denoted capability or volition, but later developed into modals via semantic change. These verbs share important semantic characteristics. First, they make schematic reference to the process in their complement, and secondly, their subject is "the locus of some kind of potency directed at the landmark process, i.e. a physical or mental force that, when unleashed, tends to bring about an occurrence of that process" (Langacker 1991:270). The French modals are interesting because they present synchronically the whole range of modal uses analyzed diachronically for English by Langacker, namely main-verb constructions, root meaning, and epistemic modality. Consistent with Langacker's analysis, the term "locus of potency" (henceforth LP) will refer to the origin of the force responsible for the potential realization of the complement process. The ability sense of *pouvoir* and *savoir* represent the "main verb constructions".[5]

3.1 Main verb Constructions: *Pouvoir* (ability), *Savoir*

With the ability sense of *pouvoir* illustrated in (2a), the subject is construed as the locus of potency of the physical force required to perform the activity evoked in the complement, should the circumstances so require. Depending on the nature of the activity, the force can also be mental, emotional, or intellectual. The FD configuration of the modal is quite simple. The force stored in the subject allows the latter to overcome the resistance coming from the activity profiled in the complement, and therefore perform an occurrence of that process.

The difference between *pouvoir* and *savoir* illustrated in (1) mainly concerns the nature of the subject's potency. The subject of *savoir* has mastered the process evoked in the complement to the point that the latter has become a well-established routine. That mastery goes beyond the possible physical accomplishment of a process, and involves the mental

---

[5] The term main verb constructions is used specifically to refer to the ability sense of *pouvoir* and *savoir*. Importantly, these verbs do not have an epistemic sense. The technical use of the term should not overshadow the fact that all modals are main (i.e. content) verbs in French.

integration of what it takes for that process to be realized. This is true even when the process is very physical. For example, what is being evoked in (1) is the mental integration of the swimming routine. It is that integration which makes every instance of the physical realization of the infinitival process possible. In that sense, we can say that the ability sense of *pouvoir* presents a physical capacity, while *savoir* presents a more mental capacity. The meaning of *savoir* can also be analyzed in terms of force dynamics. The obstacles inherent to the activity profiled by the infinitive have been overcome once and for all, and the subject is capable of performing any random instance of that activity.

Notice that for both the capability sense of *savoir* and the ability sense of *pouvoir*, the obstacles to be overcome are part of the activity itself, and not due to outside circumstances. The FD configuration of the *pouvoir* (ability) and *savoir* is given in Figure 1:

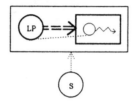

Figure 1. Main verb constructions

Figure 1 gives us an opportunity to present the notational system used throughout this paper. The sentence is represented by the larger rectangle. The speaker is indicated as S. The single arrow going from S to the sentence indicates that the sentence represents his/her conceptualization. The speaker's conceptualizing role is independent from his/her possible participation in the FD configuration of the modal. Its relevance will become clearer in the course of the analysis. The dashed double arrow represents the modal force directed at the infinitival process. The infinitival process is represented by the inner (heavy lined) rectangle. The subject of the modal is represented by the heavy lined circle.[6]

In Figure 1, the subject of the modal is identified with the locus of potency, therefore marked LP. It is the sole locus of the force which can produce an instance of the infinitival process. Notice, importantly, that the speaker does not partake in the FD configuration. It is a mere observer (a conceptualizer) of the potency displayed by the subject of the modal.

---

[6] Consistent with the conventions of Cognitive Grammar, the heavy lines in the diagrams represent the profiled entities, i.e. the focal entities within the base (Langacker 1987, 1991).

3.2 *Pouvoir* (possibility)

It was indicated earlier that possibility involves the notion of barrier (Sweetser 1990). A barrier represents any sort of external obstacle which might prevent the subject from performing the process evoked by the infinitive. The possibility sense of *pouvoir* profiles the absence of such obstacle. In (2b) for instance, the subject is able to perform the infinitival process, because no adversary outside circumstance (previous appointments) stands in her way. The kind of configuration illustrated in (2b) is given in Figure 2:

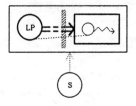

Figure 2. Possibility

The speaker points to the absence of a barrier (represented by the dotted rectangle), and thus to the fact that nothing prevents the subject from realizing the infinitival process. In (2b), that pointing to external favorable circumstances represents the extent of the speaker's participation in the FD configuration.

Note that Figure 2 looks quite similar to Figure 1. In particular, the subject of the modal is marked as the locus of potency in both cases. However, this merely illustrates a convenience of representation. In the possibility sense of *pouvoir*, the exact location of the locus of potency is not as clear as with the ability sense. The modal force directed towards the infinitival process is no longer concentrated in the subject alone. It is more diffuse, and incorporates the circumstances surrounding the possible occurrence of the infinitival process. For example, in (2b), the LP incorporates the doctor's daily schedule, which allows her to perform the activity evoked in the complement. Notice that the diffusion of the locus of potency away from the subject correlates with the involvement of the speaker in the FD configuration of the modal scene. His/her role is minimum, namely to point out the circumstances which surround the modal situation. S/he is nonetheless, in that limited way, associated with the locus of potency.

In spite of these differences in their FD configurations, I propose that in examples such as (2b), where it shows initial impulse towards the realization of the infinitival process (going to see patients is what doctors do), the subject is still most strongly associated with the locus of potency, precisely because of its intentionality. Consequently, for convenience of presentation, it will be identified as LP in the diagrams. It should be clear, however, that the semantic extension of *pouvoir* from the basic sense of ability to possibility involves the diffusion of the locus of potency away from a clearly delineated source (the subject) to incorporate the circumstances surrounding the modal situation. An important consequence of that diffusion is the change of role of the speaker. From a mere observer in the ability sense, s/he becomes in a minimal sense part of the FD pattern of the modal since s/he has access to the circumstances surrounding the complement process and can point to them.[7]

3.3 *Devoir* (necessity)

Necessity partakes of the category of force. The root sense of *devoir* illustrated in (3) profiles a relation of obligation, self-imposed or imposed by external elements, between a participant in the speech situation (usually the subject) and the complement process. Unlike the cases considered up to now, the locus of potency, i.e. the origin of the modal force, cannot be identified with the subject of the modal, but with the "target" (T) of that force, namely the entity in charge of bringing about the complement process. Notice that the target itself is not deprived of agentivity. It must be able to perform the infinitival process, but it lacks the initiative to provide the original impulse. The motivation for that force is with the locus of potency, and the target is treated like an instrument.

A situation of necessity can be represented by four different force-dynamic configurations which vary along two parameters, namely i) the role of the speaker vis-à-vis the LP, and ii) the role of the subject vis-à-vis the target of the modal force. The speaker can have a strong role, i.e. be identified with the locus of potency of the modal force, or a weak role, where s/he merely reports that force. Figure 3 presents the speaker's strong role, Figure 4 its weak role.

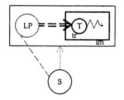 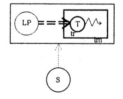

Figure 3. Necessity S=LP   Figure 4. Necessity S≠ LP

---

[7] Notice also that the possibility sense of *pouvoir* is different from the ability sense considered earlier, because it focuses on the adversary circumstances outside the process, and not on the force (resistance) coming from the activity itself.

In Figure 3, the subject (the trajector of the modal) is the target, therefore marked T. It is located downstream from the force emanating from the locus of potency which remains unprofiled (identified as the speaker). In Figure 4, the speaker is distinct from the source of obligation. This is simply indicated in the diagram by the absence of a correspondence line between S and LP. (Sweetser 1990) shows that there is no formal way to indicate the speaker's role. The example in (3) can be interpreted with a speaker's strong or weak role depending on pragmatic considerations .

The second area of variation concerns the relation between the subject of *devoir* and the modal force. In all the examples considered so far, the subject is identified with the target. It is the endpoint of the deontic force which forces it to perform the infinitival process. Talmy (1988) discusses examples such as (21), where the trajector of relation profiled by the modal verb is not the target. The latter remains an unprofiled part of the base.

(21) *La pizza doit aller au four à onze heures*
'The pizza must go in the oven at eleven o'clock'

The pizza in (21) is not capable of exercising any force or going anywhere. The target of the force of obligation is another participant which remains unprofiled. The configuration of (21) is given in Figure 5:

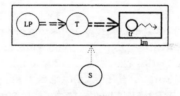

Figure 5. Necessity, Unprofiled Target

The target of the force of obligation is unprofiled in Figure 6. It must, however, perform the task of putting the pizza into the oven. In spite of its patient role, the relation profiled by the modal recognizes the pizza as the trajector. It is therefore profiled.

3.4 Epistemic Senses

In order to describe epistemic modality, Langacker (1991) presented the Dynamic Evolutionary Model, which incorporates as its components different ways we think about the world. First, that it is structured in a particular way, so that certain situations are possible, while others are precluded. Secondly, that it contains certain force dynamic properties, which yields the notion of "evolutionary momentum" when applied metaphorically to the model.

Even though reality is usually considered stable, it is conceived as evolving through time. Its evolution along the time axis yields a force-dynamic dimension to our conception of reality. Evolutionary momentum allows the future course of events to be predictable to some extent, because it constraints the elements which unfold within it. Some elements are seen as possible, while others are definitely excluded from the possible turn of events. Part of our conception of reality includes the understanding that the way it has already evolved leaves the potential for further evolution in constrained directions. These elements are illustrated in the Dynamic evolutionary Model presented in Figure 6 (from Langacker 1991:277):

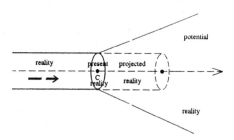

Figure 6. Dynamic Evolutionary Model

Reality is depicted by the cylinder, and C is a conceptualizer (identified as the speaker). The dashed double arrow represents evolutionary momentum, which tends to carry reality along a certain path and precludes it from taking others. Those paths which are not excluded are referred to as "potential reality". Reality is often constrained enough that the future course of events can be predicted with reasonable confidence. Such cases are referred to as "projected reality".

With respect to this model, *pouvoir* places the process in potential reality. In (4a) for example, the observation of certain elements of current reality (the absence of light) suggests to the speaker that the subject's coming back tomorrow is a possible occurrence. *Devoir* places the infinitival process in projected reality. In (4b), given the nature of current reality, namely the open door, the subject's imminent return can be considered with confidence, and therefore considered as an element of projected reality.

4. MARKING ON THE INFINITIVAL PROCESS: SPEAKER CONTROL

We are now in a position to provide an explanation to the issues considered in Table 1, namely: i) the grouping as a natural class of the root sense of *devoir* and the epistemic modals, ii) the variation observed in the case of *pouvoir* possibility, and iii) the absence of grammatical marking on the complement following *savoir* and *pouvoir* ability. The hypothesis I propose is the following: The possible presence of grammatical markers on the infinitival complement correlates with the "conceptual control" (to be defined shortly) of the speaker over that complement.

One of the key issues in any discussion about complementation concerns the respective roles of the main clause subject and the speaker in the conceptualization of the complement scene (Achard 1993, Langacker 1991). With modals, the subject has little (if any) conceptualizing role with respect to the complement process. In the following sections, I show that the presence of grammatical marking on the complement is a consequence of the speaker's direct conceptual relationship with the infinitival process (independently of his/her conceptualization of the whole sentence). I will call that direct conceptual relation the "control" of the speaker over the infinitival process. One can legitimately wonder why the speaker's conceptual control over the complement process should be reflected by the possible presence of grammatical markers on that process. The question cannot be answered without considering the semantic import of the grammatical markers themselves

4.1 Semantic Import of the Grammatical Markers

From a semantic point of view, an infinitive provides information regarding the core content of a process type (Langacker 1991). The addition of the markers of aspect and voice provides information relative to the internal structure of that process. The aspectual marker is traditionally analyzed as indicating, with respect to some temporal reference point, whether the process is completed or still in progress. Concerning the passive marker, Langacker (1991:197) writes that it "overrides the content verb with respect to one dimension of imagery, namely which processual participant assumes the status of trajector." In other words, the passive marker provides information concerning the specific coding of the participants in the complement process, i.e. their figure/ground organization.

These cursory observations do not do justice to the complexity of the problem of the semantic characterization of the grammatical markers concerned, but they should be sufficient for the purposes of this paper. The important point is that the addition of a specific grammatical marker (aspect or voice) to a process type imposes its own particular meaning on the conceptual content provided by the infinitival process. By doing so, the addition of a grammatical morpheme derives a higher-order process type, much in the same way that the addition of a plural marker to a singular noun stem derives a higher-order plural noun type (Langacker 1991). That higher-degree process type is quite different from the original (underived) process type, because it contains information about the inner-structure of the process which goes beyond its conceptual content. I will say that the creation of that higher-level type involves some "conceptual manipulation" of the original type. In that light, the speaker's ability to conceptually manipulate the complement process is the manifestation of his/her conceptual control over that process. The presence of grammatical marking on the infinitival complement can therefore be viewed as the morpho-syntactic manifestation of speaker control. The crucial point in the analysis consists in precisely determining the elements which facilitate the speaker's direct conceptual relationship with the complement process. In the following section, I show that the control of the speaker with respect to the complement process crucially depends on his/her role in the FD configuration evoked by the modal, and more specifically its relation to the LP of the modal force.

4.2 *Pouvoir*: Diffusion of the Locus of Potency

Pouvoir is the most interesting verb, because its three configurations (ability, possibility and epistemic modality) illustrate the three levels of restriction on the possible grammatical marking on the infinitival process. In light of the hypothesis presented above, we can speak of an increase in speaker control from the ability sense to epistemic modality. Crucially, that increase in speaker control correlates with the progressive diffusion of the locus of potency of the modal force, and therefore with the increasing participation of the speaker in the FD configuration of the modal. Let us briefly review the three stages in turn.

With the ability sense (this is also true for *savoir*), the LP is exclusively concentrated in the subject. The latter has total (physical) control over the complement process, and the speaker is a mere observer of the relation between subject and complement. The speaker's external position with respect to the FD configuration of the modal parallels his/her lack of control over the complement. The absence of any marking following *savoir* and the ability sense of *pouvoir* is fully consistent with our analysis, where such marking is imputable to the speaker's direct conceptual control over the complement process.

The sense of possibility is characterized by two different configurations. Recall that in the first one, illustrated in (11) and (12), marking on the infinitival process is impossible. In the second one, illustrated in (13) and (14), both aspectual and passive markers can appear on the infinitival complement. Consistent with our analysis, the difference in marking is imputable to the difference in the speaker's role in the two configurations. The first configuration is very similar to the ability sense. The speaker's role is merely to point out the absence of a barrier standing between the subject and its accomplishment of the complement process. The speaker has knowledge of the circumstances which enable the subject to perform that process, but s/he has no power to influence them. Crucially, in this configuration, the speaker is still only an observer of the modal force. Here again, the speaker's lack of control over the complement process is reflected by the impossibility of grammatical marking on that process. In the second configuration, the speaker's role in the FD configuration is more active. S/he takes responsibility for the occurrence of the complement. In (13) and (14), the speaker is in a position to impose a schedule on the subject, and can therefore easily be associated with the locus of potency of the modal force. (13a) for example is most natural uttered by the people in charge of a children's' party to the parents of one of the guests. The correlation between the speaker's proximity to LP and his/her control over the complement process is straightforward. In order to make a commitment relative to the occurrence of the infinitival process, the speaker must establish a direct conceptual relationship with that process. Consistent with the hypothesis formulated earlier, the speaker's control is manifested by the absence of restrictions on the complement.

The passage to epistemic modality involves the diffusion of the locus of potency to the point where the latter can only be identified with the evolutionary momentum of reality. The speaker's control over the complement process is obvious, because the appreciation of the evolutionary momentum is speaker internal by definition.[8]

4.3 *Devoir*. Necessity

The subject of *devoir* cannot be identified with the locus of potency of the modal force, because it lacks the initial impulse, or initiative towards the realization of the complement process. The control of the speaker in that case is obvious. In order for him/her to use the subject as an instrument to perform the complement process, s/he must have a direct conceptual relationship with that process. What necessity shares with epistemic modality, and therefore justifies their similar behavior considered in Table 1, is that under no circumstances can the subject be identified as the locus of potency of the modal force. The (conceptual) control over the complement process resides with the speaker.

5. CONCLUSION AND IMPLICATIONS

This paper was concerned with the restrictions placed on the complements of French modal verbs. It was shown that the distribution of the grammatical markers of aspect and voice with each individual modal is a manifestation of the conceptual organization evoked by that modal, and

---

[8] The total diffusion of the locus of potency is reflected by the absence of restrictions on the nature of the subject of epistemic modals. Impersonals and weather expressions can be main clause subjects, as in *Il doit faire du vent aujourd'hui* 'It must be windy today' for example.

more specifically, of the role of the speaker in its FD configuration. The closer the speaker is to the locus of potency of the modal force, the more control s/he has over the complement process. Control has been defined as a direct conceptual relationship between the speaker and the complement structure.

Much recent work in Cognitive Linguistics has shown that the form of a grammatical expression reflects the specific construal of the scene it describes. As a conclusion to this paper, I would like to briefly show how it contributes to the investigation of a specific dimension of construal, namely the "viewing arrangement" (Langacker 1985, 1990) existing between a conceptualizer and the entity s/he conceptualizes. We have seen that the loosening of the restrictions imposed on the complement of modals follows a gradual shift of control from the subject to the speaker. That shift can be expressed naturally, if we consider the process of diffusion of the locus of potency examined earlier in terms of the "subjectification" (Langacker 1985, 1990, 1991) of the modal force. The main-verb constructions present a maximally objective construal of the complement scene.[9] The locus of potency is a clearly identifiable and well-defined entity, and the modal force is also objectively construed. The externality of the speaker is representative of the maximally objective construal of the scene. Subjectification "involves some facet of the profiled relationship being reoriented from the objective axis [here from the subject to the complement process] to the subjective axis [here from the speaker to the complement process], so that it is no longer anchored by an objective participant (the subject) but rather by a reference point construed more subjectively, the default case being the ground itself" (Langacker 1991: 270 insertions in brackets mine). In the case of modality, the diffusion of the locus of potency can therefore be interpreted as a kind of subjectification of the modal force. It is quite natural that the speaker's control over the complement process should follow subjectification, because in that process, the modal force gets more and more associated with him/her. From maximally objective between well delineated elements, the modal force becomes maximally subjective and speaker internal.

The notion of viewing arrangement allows us to relate the behavior of the modals to that of other verbs which take infinitival complements. We saw in (6) that the causative verbs impose on their complements constraints similar to *pouvoir* ability and *savoir*.[10] It is interesting to note that both constructions present a maximally objective construal of the

---

[9] The terms "objective" and "subjective" are used here in the technical sense of Langacker (1985, 1990).

[10] The same analysis also holds for movement verb constructions such as *Marie court chercher le journal* 'Mary runs to get the paper' for instance.

In Figure 3, the subject (the trajector of the modal) is the target, therefore marked T. It is located downstream from the force emanating from the locus of potency which remains unprofiled (identified as the speaker). In Figure 4, the speaker is distinct from the source of obligation. This is simply indicated in the diagram by the absence of a correspondence line between S and LP. (Sweetser 1990) shows that there is no formal way to indicate the speaker's role. The example in (3) can be interpreted with a speaker's strong or weak role depending on pragmatic considerations .

The second area of variation concerns the relation between the subject of *devoir* and the modal force. In all the examples considered so far, the subject is identified with the target. It is the endpoint of the deontic force which forces it to perform the infinitival process. Talmy (1988) discusses examples such as (21), where the trajector of relation profiled by the modal verb is not the target. The latter remains an unprofiled part of the base.

(21) *La pizza doit aller au four à onze heures*
    'The pizza must go in the oven at eleven o'clock'

The pizza in (21) is not capable of exercising any force or going anywhere. The target of the force of obligation is another participant which remains unprofiled. The configuration of (21) is given in Figure 5:

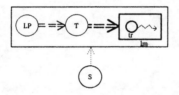

Figure 5. Necessity, Unprofiled Target

The target of the force of obligation is unprofiled in Figure 6. It must, however, perform the task of putting the pizza into the oven. In spite of its patient role, the relation profiled by the modal recognizes the pizza as the trajector. It is therefore profiled.

3.4 Epistemic Senses

In order to describe epistemic modality, Langacker (1991) presented the Dynamic Evolutionary Model, which incorporates as its components different ways we think about the world. First, that it is structured in a particular way, so that certain situations are possible, while others are precluded. Secondly, that it contains certain force dynamic properties, which yields the notion of "evolutionary momentum" when applied metaphorically to the model.

Constraints on Adjectival Past Participles

FARRELL ACKERMAN & ADELE E. GOLDBERG
University of California, San Diego

1   Introduction

In this paper, we examine certain distributions of deverbal adjectives based on past participles and used attributively, (hereafter, *APPs*). These distributions, although widely recognized, have not been sufficiently explained in the rather substantial literature on the subject of APPs (e.g., Lakoff 1965, Hirtle 1971, Wasow 1977, Bresnan 1982, Levin & Rappaport 1986, Langacker 1987, Grimshaw & Vikner 1993). [1] That is, certain types of contrasts are well-known and are accounted for in a fairly straightforwardly way by various approaches. These include the examples in (1):

(1)   a. * a worked man

    b. a frozen river

But less discussed are APPs which are sensitive to context: they are permitted only when modifying certain head nouns:

(2)   a. # paid physician[2]

    b. paid escort

---

[1] We would like to thank Tony Davis, Rich Epstein, Michael Israel, Laura Michaelis, Susanne Preuss, Ron Sheffer and members of the UCSD Cognitive Linguistics Working group for helpful discussion on this topic.

[2] Here and below, we use the # to indicate unacceptability in a 'neutral' context; the same APP can appear felicitously with other head nouns or with additional adverbs. We reserve *'s for cases which cannot be rescued by a changed context.

Finally, there is a third phenomenon that "...as is well known, some APPs sound peculiar unless qualified, for reasons that are not entirely clear" (Levin & Rappaport 1986:634, cf. also Wasow 1977). For example, certain verbs allow APPs only with the addition of adverbial modifiers or prefixes such as *un-*. This applies to (3) in contrast with (2a), as well as to the examples in (4).

(3) the highly paid physician

(4) a. # a built house

    b. a recently built house

While few attempts have been made to account for examples such as those in (2)-(4), one notable exception is a recent article by Grimshaw and Vikner (1993) which is discussed below.

The basic claim we will explore is that:

> APPs can only occur if they are construable as predicating an **informative** state of the head noun referent.

First we provide a brief overview of aspectual properties standardly assumed to be relevant. We then briefly discuss Grimshaw and Vikner's account of obligatory modification, and then we turn our attention to the main focus of this paper: addressing in more detail what allows a state to be considered sufficiently informative.

2   APPs must designate a state

Researchers from various theoretical perspectives have noted that the notion *resultant state* is a crucial characteristic of APPs. For example, relevant characterizations from Langacker and Parsons are given below:

> each [APP] derives a stative relation by confining the target's profile to the final, resultant state of the process that constitutes the standard. Observe that the profiled relationship is limited to the resulting condition of the entity undergoing the change of state. (Langacker 1991:202-203)

> PastP-Adj(Verb) is true of a state s if and only if s is the resultant state of an event of which the Verb is true. (Parsons 1990:236)

Aspectual distinctions such as these can help account for the distinct distributions of "unaccusative" vs. "unergative" predicates. For example, it is generally recognized that only unaccusative predicates make felicitous APPs. Notice that unaccusatives are conventionally analyzed as profiling or designating a state (e.g., Van Valin 1990):

(5) a. the frozen river

     b. a fallen leaf

     c. a broken spoke

Unergatives, on the other hand, as activity predicates, do not profile an endstate, and they are correspondingly unacceptable as APPs:

(6) a. *the run man

     b. *a coughed patient

     c. *a swum contestant

There is much more to say about the aspectual constraints on APPs (see Goldberg & Ackerman, forthcoming), but for present purposes we will simply assume that some notion relevantly like that of *statehood* is important in accounting for the English data. We also will not be discussing observations by Levin and Rappaport (1986) which are complementary to the present discussion.[3] In the remainder of this paper, we will concentrate on certain instances where APPs require modification.

3 An Event Structure Account

In a recent article, Grimshaw & Vikner (1993) point out that verbs of creation generally require some type of "obligatory adjunct" to form acceptable APPs. They provide examples such as those in 4, repeated below:

(7) a. # built house

     b. recently built house

and the contrasts in (8):

---

[3]In particular, we will leave aside whether all of the APPs must be interpretable as modifying OBJs at some level of representation, as well as the role of Levin and Rappaport's Sole Complement Generalization (see Hoekstra 1984 for observations foreshadowing this proposal.)

(8) a. # a created house

b. a carefully created house

They note that APPs based on verbs of creation correspond to *accomplishment* predicates which have two subevents, a process and a state. Extending a notion of "identification" in a new way, they claim that both subevents must be "identified" by some element in the sentence. They further claim that in APPs the head noun argument only serves to "identify" one subevent, the state. The process subevent is not identified. They claim that the adverbs serve the purpose of identifying the process component of the complex event. As they note, it would seem to follow from this idea that *all* APPs related to accomplishment verbs, and not only APPs corresponding to verbs of creation would require that the process aspect of the event be further identified with an adverbial of some kind. And yet change of state verbs such as *cool, broil* are fully acceptable as APPs without further qualification. For example:

(9) a. the cooled metal

b. the broiled potatoes

To account for related facts[4] they note that the role of the head noun is different in verbs of creation vis a vis other accomplishment verbs. They diagram the difference as follows:

The crucial thing to note is that the *y* variable is considered to "identify" the process part of the event in the case of *record* but not in the case of *create*, the rationale being that the theme argument does not exist until the building is completed. In what follows, we will refer to this as the "event structure" account.

---

[4] For some reason that is not clear to us, Grimshaw and Vikner do not make this point for change of state predicates such as *cool* or *broil* specifically. Instead they claim that predicates such as these are expected to require obligatory adverbs, and seem to imply that they do (1993:145). Since these examples are in fact fully acceptable to us and we see no reason why G & V need to classify all change of state verbs as "constructive accomplishments" we attempt to strengthen their argument by supposing that these cases can be accounted for in a way parallel to other acceptable APPs they do discuss.

4   Non-Redundancy

In this section, we propose an alternative account of these cases of obligatory adverbs which we argue has several advantages: 1) it accounts for a wider range of data, 2) it is motivated by general pragmatic principles, 3) it allows us to explain why it is that contrastive situations often alleviate the need for otherwise obligatory adverbs, and 4) it is not a constraint specifically on APPs, but holds of adjectives generally.

The event structure account does not generalize to other cases which we argue are related. Consider the contrasts in 10:

(10)   a. # served customer; but well-served customer

b. # fed child; but well-fed child

c. # sent letters, but recently sent letters

d. # married father; but recently married father

Notice that *serve, feed, send* and *marry* are not verbs of creation, and therefore the previous account does not explain why adverbs are necessary in these cases.

Notice that in each of the examples, the first APP designates a property that is implied by the frame semantics of the head noun. We expect customers to be served, children to be fed, letters to be sent, etc. At the same time, the second APP given in each example is *not* implied by the frame semantics of the head noun: the frame semantics associated with *customers* does not imply that the customers be *well* served. We claim that the following descriptive generalization holds:

Non-redundancy constraint

> If the referent of the head noun, N, implies a property P as part of its frame-semantic or encyclopedic knowledge, then an APP is not allowed to simply designate P; it must be further qualified.

That is, the APP must designate a property which is not already implied by the frame semantics associated with the head noun. This generalization also accounts for the contrasts in (2) repeated in (11), wherein the APP's acceptability is dependent on the choice of head noun:

(11)   a. #paid physician

b. paid escort

Notice we assume physicians are paid, whereas we do not automatically assume the same about escorts.

Returning to verbs of creation, notice that Grimshaw & Vikner's observation is in fact fairly robust. The following additional examples make the same point that verbs of creation generally require adverbs to be acceptable:

(12) a. # baked cake; but half-baked cake

b. # constructed furniture; but carefully constructed furniture,

c. # prepared feast; but well-prepared feast

d. # erected building; but recently erected building

We argue that these cases can be subsumed under the same non-redundancy constraint: the adjective must predicate a property which is not already implied by the frame semantics associated with the head noun. Predicating simple existence is not informative enough because this property is implied by the frame-semantic knowledge associated with the head noun. That is why verbs of creation are acceptable as APPs if some property in addition to existence is implied by the modified APP.

We predict then that when the method of creation is not the expected method, verbs of creation should be acceptable as APPs; indeed, we find that they are:

(13) a. manufactured diamonds

b. synthesized gold dust

c. microwaved brownies

In these cases the frame semantics associated with the head noun does not imply the property designated by the APP. We do not assume that diamonds are manufactured, gold dust is synthesized, or that brownies are microwaved.

Therefore on our account, it is not the event structure of verbs of creation which makes these verbs marginal as APPs, rather it is their lexical semantics. That is, verbs of creation satisfy the constraint of profiling an endstate; the problem is that the endstate in question, existence, is not sufficiently informative. Other change of state verbs such as those mentioned above: *cool, broil* etc. do designate an informative endstate, and are therefore predicated to be acceptable.

4.1   Motivating Non-Redundancy

Another reason to prefer the generalization in terms of non-redundancy to the event structure account is that while event structure account rests on the introduction of the assumption that all subevents be "identified," we argue that our account is motivated by two general pragmatic principles. The first is coincidentally labeled the Principle of Informativeness by Atlas and Levinson:

Atlas & Levinson's Principle of Informativeness (of Interpretation):
    Read as much into an utterance as is consistent with what you know about the world (Levinson 1983: 146-147)

The second is:
Horn's R-Principle:
    Make your contribution necessary; say no more than you must (Horn 1993)

The Principle of Informativeness encourages the listener to assume all of the frame semantic knowledge associated with the head noun. If the property, P, designated by the APP is already implied by the frame semantics associated with the head noun, it is not *necessary* to specify P unless P is qualified in some way. Therefore specification of P violates Horn's R-Principle: "say no more than you must," resulting in unacceptability.

4.2   Contrastiveness

Another advantage of the non-redundancy constraint is that it provides a principled account of why contrastive contexts are able to rescue APPs from unacceptability. For example, in the context of discussing several young doctors doing volunteer work under the direction of one medical director who is paid, it is perfectly natural to refer to the director as a *paid physician*. Or, in the context of a discussion about the merits of baking versus microwaving, one may felicitously contrast microwaved cakes with *baked cakes*. Notice that in any contrastive context, the APP serves the function of differentiating the head noun from other entities available in the discourse. Therefore, the R-Principle, "say no more than is necessary," is not violated, and as expected, acceptability results.

Finally, another reason why the pragmatic account is preferable to an account in terms of event structure, is the fact that the pragmatic account holds generally of all adjectives, including adjectives which are not deverbal and do not have any event structure.

4.3 Relation to Adjectives Generally

The basic non-redundancy generalization stated above for APPs parallels a generalization proposed by Hirtle (1969) for contrasts with de*nominal* adjectives with -*ed* suffixes:

(14) # headed boy; but red-headed boy

He notes, "The very notion underlying *boy* brings in the notion of *head* with no outside help."

Underived adjectives also have to be non-redundant. This fact may be obscured because sometimes seemingly uninformative or redundant adjectives are allowed for the purpose of evaluative emphasis. Examples of this include:

(15) a. stupid idiot

     b. dangerous murderer

     c. mischievous prankster

Our frame semantic knowledge tells us that idiots are stupid, murderers are dangerous, and that pranksters are mischievous, and yet the examples in (15) are acceptable. Notice, however, the adjectives involved are evaluative and serve the purpose of conveying an attitude towards the head noun referent. In this way, the APP is not simply redundant with the frame semantics associated with the head noun, but functions as an informative element.

When the adjective *is* truly redundant with the semantics of the head noun, it does sound odd:

(16) # dead corpse

The following examples show a similar contrast:

(17) a. # male doctor, but female doctor

     b. # female nurse, but male nurse

Note, of course, that in these cases, it is not the entailments of the head nouns that are relevant, but rather our frame semantic knowledge. As we saw was the case with APPs, contrastive contexts render the use of these adjectives fully felicitous:

(18) Would the *male* doctors stand on one side of the room, the female doctors on the other.

In fact it appears that modification relationships more generally are subject to the Non-Redundancy generalization. See Downing (1977) for discussion of a parallel constraint on English Noun-Noun compounds.

4.4 Cross-linguistic Applicability

Linguists working on APPs in languages other than English have observed that certain cases seem to resemble those of English in requiring modification (e.g., Zaenen 1993) The question arises to what extent the constraint just suggested operates cross-linguistically. The following representative data from German and Hungarian indicate that a relevantly similar constraint may in fact be at work:

German:

(19) # ein gebautes Haus
a built house

(20) ein kürzelich gebautes Haus
a recently built house

Hungarian

(21) # az épített ház
the built house

(22) a tegnap épített ház
Lit., the yesterday built house (cf. *the recently built house*)

In order to reliably claim that the same constraint is operative cross-linguistically, we need to do much more research. For example, we need to consider the role an imperfective/perfective contrast plays in examples (21)-(22). In any case, to the degree that the explanation of the English distributions relies on the general pragmatic principles, it is to be expected that they will also play a role in similar distributions of data elsewhere.

5 Paradigmatic Informativeness

Before concluding, we'd like to briefly discuss a separate constraint that appears to be grammaticalized, but is generally motivated by a pragmatic principle relevantly similar to Grice's Maxim of Quantity, or Horn's second conversational principle. Consider the following contrast:

(23) a. # taken item

b. stolen item

When a wider range of semantically related APPs is considered, we find that *taken* is the marked case in being unacceptable as an APP:

(24) a. shoplifted item

     b. smuggled goods

     c. pilfered money

It seems that the semantically less specific *taken* is noticeably dispreferred vis a vis the semantically richer APPs *shoplifted, smuggled, pilfered*. The relation between *taken* and the other members of its class can be characterized in terms of the *troponymic relation* proposed by Miller & Fellbaum (1991). According to them, V_1 is a troponym of V_2 if and only if to V_1 is to V_2 in some manner or fashion (1992:216).[5] On this account, e.g., *shoplift* is a troponym of the superordinate *take*, since to shoplift something is to take it in a certain manner. The follow data seem to exhibit a pattern similar to that found in 23 and 24:

(25) a. # given funds

     b. donated funds

     c. sacrificed funds

(26) a. # cut meat

     b. sliced meat

     c. chopped meat

(27) a. # told secret

     b. disclosed secret

     c. confessed secret

(28) a. # changed design

     b. altered design

     c. improved design

The well-known examples from Lakoff 1965 appear to be similar:

(29) a. # killed man

---

[5] Miller and Fellbaum coin the term *troponym* based on the Greek, *tropos*, "manner or fashion."

    b. murdered man

Note, as above, the following near-synonyms of *killed* are all fully acceptable:

(30) a. assassinated man

      b. slain man

      c. martyred man

We suggest the following constraint.
Paradigmatic Informativeness:

> An APP phrase is not felicitous if it is based on a superordinate verb which contrasts with semantically more specific predicates (i.e., with troponyms).

By *superordinate verb* we have in mind verbs which are semantically less specific than their troponymic or subordinate counterparts. What seems to disallow these verbs as APPs, is their relative lack of semantic specificity.

As expected, in each of these cases, the unacceptable APP can be rescued by the addition of an adverb, since the adverb serves to make the modification semantically more specific:

(31) a. surreptitiously taken item

      b. freely given funds

      c. thinly cut meat

      d. carelessly told secret

      e. intentionally changed design

      f. freshly killed chicken

The notion of paradigmatic contrast is important since many of these APPs are improved when they are used with meanings that do not stand in paradigmatic contrast to other APPs:

(32) a. taken seat

      b. killed e-mail messages (Laura Michaelis, personal communication)

      c. cut classes

While we do not claim that the Paradigmatic Informativeness constraint falls out of general pragmatic principles, it is interesting to note that it appears to be motivated by Horn's Q-Principle stated below:

Q-Principle (Horn 1984):

> Make your contribution sufficient, Say as much as you can
> (Horn 1984:13)

We do not claim that our generalization *follows* from Horn's principle because even in contexts in which the speaker knows no more than simply that an item was taken or a person killed, one still cannot felicitously describe the item as a *taken item* or the person as a *killed person*.

6 Conclusions

To conclude, we have considered a set of examples which have been widely acknowledged to exist, but rarely addressed. Our basic claim was that:

> APPs can only occur if they are construable as predicating
> an **informative** state of the head noun referent.

We proposed two generalizations, which can be interpreted as fleshing out this claim. The first, Non-redundancy generalization says that predicating the APP state of the head noun referent must be informative, i.e., that combining the meaning of the APP with that of the head noun cannot be redundant. This generalization was proposed to account for context sensitivity and the obligatory modification required for certain APPs. Our account was contrasted with a recent proposal to account for these cases in terms of the event structure of the corresponding verbs (Grimshaw and Vikner 1993). We argued that the present proposal is preferrable because the Non-redundancy generalization 1) accounts for a wider range of data 2) is motivated by general pragmatic principles 3) explains why acceptability is improved when the APP has a contrastive function in the discourse context 4) holds generally of prenominal adjectives.

We did not address the question of whether it is necessary to specify this generalization as a motivated, but non-predicted constraint on the modified noun construction. Because of its context sensitivity, and the straightforward way it seems to follow from pragmatic principles, we are inclined to believe that nothing special needs to be said in the grammar of English to account for this generalization; the constraint seems to follow from pragmatic principles that operate generally. However, if it turns out that languages differ in whether redundancy is tolerated in these situations, we may want to consider this generalization to be a conventionalized, although clearly motivated, part of the grammar. In that case, the generalization should be considered a pragmatic constraint on the modified noun construction.

We also proposed a second generalization, which we termed the Paradigmatic Informativeness constraint:

> An APP phrase is not felicitous if it is based on a superordinate level verb which contrasts with semantically more specific predicates (troponyms).

This generalization claims that an APP phrase is infelicitous if it is relatively uninformative given other choices of possible APPs. The second constraint is perhaps more surprising, and while it may be motivated by Horn's R-Principle: *say as much as you can*, it seems to be a grammaticalized constraint.

7 References

Atlas, J. and S. Levinson. 1981. *It*-clefts, informativeness and logical form. In Cole, ed. *Radical Pragmatics* New York: Academic Press. 1-61.

Bolinger, Dwight. 1967. Adjectives in English: Attribution and Predication. *Lingua* 18. 1-34.

Bresnan, Joan. 1982. *The Mental Representation of Grammatical Relations*. Cambridge, Mass: MIT Press.

Davis, Anthony. 1992. A fine-grained approach to "double-barrelled" adjectives. *BLS 18*.

Downing, Pamela. 1977. On the Creation and Use of English Compound Nouns. *Language 53*:810-842.

Grimshaw, Jane and Sten Vikner. 1993. Obligatory Adjuncts and the Structure of Events. In *Knowledge and language* eric Reuland and Werner Abraham (eds). Kluwer Academic Publishers.

Hirtle, W. H. 1969. -Ed Adjectives like *Verandahed* and *Blue-Eyed*. *Journal of Language* 6:19-36.

Hoekstra, Teun. 1984. Transitivity: Grammatical Relations in Government-Binding Theory. Foris Publications: Dordrecht, Holland.

Horn, Lawrence. 1984. Toward a New Taxonomy for Pragmatic Inference: Q-Based and R-Based Implicature. In D. Schiffrin, ed., *GURT '84: Meaning, Form and Use in Context*. Washington: Georgetown University Press. 11-42.

Lakoff, George. 1965/1970. *On the Nature of Syntactic Irregularity*. Indiana University dissertation. Published by New York, NY: Holt, Rinhard & Winston as *Irregularity in Syntax*.

Lakoff, George. 1987. *Women, Fire, and Dangerous Things*. Chicago: Chicago University Press.

Langacker, Ron. 1991. *Foundations of Cognitive Grammar*. Stanford University Press.

Levin, Beth and Malka Rappaport. 1986. The formation of adjectival passives. *Linguistic Inquiry 17*, 623-661.

Levinson, Stephen. 1983. *Pragmatics*. Cambridge University Press.

Miller, G.A. and C. Fellbaum. 1991. Semantic networks of English. *Cognition 41*:198-229.

Parsons, Terence. 1990. *Events in the Semantics of English: A Study in Subatomic Semantics*. MIT Press.

Van Valin, Robert. 1990. Semantic Parameters of Split Intransitivity. *Language 66*:221-260.

Wasow, Thomas. 1977. Transformations and the Lexicon. In P. W. Culicover, T. Wasow, and A. Akmajian (ed) *Formal Syntax*. New York, NY: Academic Press. 327-360.

Zaenen, Annie. 1993. Integrating Syntax and Lexical Semantics. In *Semantics and the Lexicon*. J. Pustejovsky, ed. Boston: Kluwer Academic Publisher.

From Resultativity to Current Relevance: Evidence from the History of English and Modern Castilian Spanish[1]

KATHLEEN CAREY

University of North Texas

The perfect tense has often been characterized as encoding "current relevance": an event marked with the perfect is judged by the speaker to have some present effect or consequences. Recent cross-linguistic research has demonstrated that current relevance of anterior constructions or perfects frequently develop from resultatives, claiming a close semantic and diachronic connection between the two categories. Several scholars who have investigated the development of the perfect in the history of Romance have noted that particular semantic-pragmatic contexts serve as stepping stones in the resultative -> perfect shift: (i) contexts with communication, cognition and perception verbs (cf. Pinkster 1987, Vincent 1982, and Benveniste 1968); (ii) iterative/durative contexts (cf. Harris 1982 and Alarcos-Llorach 1947). However, previous explanations of why these contexts should serve as catalysts for the resultative -> perfect shift have been somewhat limited in their scope, particularly in regard to the role of iterative/durative contexts. The present paper uses diachronic data from four periods in

---

[1] I would like to thank Aintzane Doiz-Bienzobas, Ricardo Maldonado, Errapel Mejías-Bikandi and Raúl Susmel for their grammaticality judgements and insights regarding the *tener* + past participle construction.

the history of English and synchronic variation data from Modern Castilian Spanish to demonstrate how these particular contexts play a crucial role in the development of a perfect.

1. Resultatives and Perfects

In characterizing the difference between a resultative and a current relevance of anterior (perfect), Bybee et al. (1994:65) note that "the resultative points to the state resulting from the action while the anterior [perfect] points to the action itself." As evidence for this claim, Bybee et al. cite the insightful observation put forth in Nedyalkov and Jaxontov (1988) that resultatives, but not perfects, are compatible with the adverb *still*. Consider the examples below taken from Bybee et al. (1994:65). The Modern English *be* + past participle construction is a resultative and is therefore compatible with the temporal sense of *still*, which indicates that a state persists at reference time, as is shown in example (1). In contrast, the perfect is not compatible with the temporal sense of *still*; the sentences in (2) are grammatical only if *still* is interpreted as meaning `nevertheless'.

(1a) *He is still gone.*
(1b) *The door is still closed.*
(2a) *He has still gone.*
(2b) *The door has still closed.*

Another semantic difference between resultatives and perfects pertains to the tightness of the semantic connection between the verb participle and the result (cf. Dahl 1985:135): in the case of a resultative, the state resulting from the past action derives directly from the verb participle itself, e.g., *John is gone* indicates that John is in the state of being gone at reference time. The semantic precursor to a `have' perfect is a particular type of resultative in which the objective result is necessarily present in the grammatical subject (cf. Langacker 1990 and Carey 1994 for further explanation.) The perfect, however, links a past situation to the present moment in a more subjective way. In the example, *Mary has gotten sick every time we have eaten at Ellington's, so we better not go there*, the perfect does not encode that the subject Mary bears the present resultant state of being sick, but rather that the past events of her being ill are relevant to the present decision to avoid Ellington's. Significantly, the result in the case of the perfect is not directly dependent of the semantics of the verb participle but rather on the intentions of the speaker in the particular discourse context. The locus of relevance for the past situation is not the subject but rather the current discourse situation, broadly construed.

These semantic differences between resultatives and perfects have grammatical consequences. Since resultative constructions require a resultant state in the subject at reference time, they are compatible only with situations that have an inherent goal or endpoint, that is, telic situations. The Modern English stative-perfect construction, a type of resultative, is compatible with the telic situation *fix the car* but not with the atelic situation *want a jaguar*: *I have the car fixed* vs. **I have the jaguar wanted*. Perfects, however, need not refer to an objective result tightly connected to the described situation: consequently, perfects may appear with atelic situations, e.g., *I have wanted a jaguar all my life*. A second grammatical difference between resultatives and perfects is that resultatives, but not perfects, are incompatible with dummy subjects. Since a resultative requires a present state in the subject at reference time, it cannot cooccur with a subject without objective semantic content. Collocations with the perfect do not require that the subject bear a state at reference time and therefore need not obey this constraint, e.g., *It has rained*.

The perfect, unlike the resultative, refers to the past action as well as the present state. In cognitive-semantic terms, the past event is salient in the conceptualization of a perfect construction but not salient in a resultative construction. A grammatical consequence of this seman-tic difference is that the perfect, unlike the resultative, may permit reference to the up-to-the-present time period in which the past event(s) occurred. Perfects can cooccur with up-to-the-present adverbials such as *since* and *before* whereas resultatives can not. (Compare the grammatical *I have seen her since Friday* with the ungrammatical ** He is gone since Friday*.) [2]

In the continuative use of the perfect, the perfect itself encodes that the situation extends *throughout* an up-to-the-present time period. The difference between *I have lived here for five years* (with the perfect) and *I lived here for five years* (with the past) is that the perfect-marked sentence can refer to a situation that extends through the present moment whereas the past-marked sentence can not. The Modern English perfect may also indicate that the situation occurred within an up-to-the-present temporal interval, e.g., *Have you ever been to Spain?* This type of use has been referred to as the experiential or indefinite past use of the perfect. (Cf. Comrie 1976, Leech 1971, Bauer 1970, Fenn 1987, Brinton 1988, McCoard 1978, and Michaelis 1993 for further discussion of the uses of the Modern English perfect.)

The differences between resultatives and perfects are shown in Table 1 below. The first two rows summarize the semantic differences between

---

[2] As has been often discussed in the literature, the Modern English present perfect cannot appear with definite past adverbials, e.g., ** I have eaten at three*.

the two constructions and the final three rows the grammatical consequences of these semantic differences. The next section will use these
grammatical differences to help determine when the resultative ->
perfect shift occurred in the history of English.

Table 1: Resultatives and Perfects

	Resultative	Perfect
Locus of relevance	subject	here-and-now of discourse context
Anterior event	not salient	salient
Atelic situations	not compatible	compatible
Dummy subjects	not compatible	compatible
Anterior adverbials	not compatible	compatible

2. The Historical Data

Data was collected from four periods in the history of English, separated
by approximately 200 year intervals. The Old English data were taken
from the Old English Concordance (Venezky and DiPaolo, 1980). For
the Alfred period (c. 850), examples were taken from Alfred's
translations of Boethius, Orosius and The Pastoral Care. For the Ælfric
period (c. 1050), examples were taken from the works of Ælfric: the first
and second series of homilies, the Catholic homilies, Lives of the saints
and his letters. Layamon's Brut (c. 1225) was used for the early Middle
English period and Sir Gawain and the Green Knight was used for
Middle English.
   An analysis of the data from the four historical periods in regard to the
grammatical indicators listed in Table 1 yields some striking results.
None of the 129 have + participle constructions from the early Old
English period occurred with atelic situations, dummy subjects or
anterior adverbials. Similarly, not a single example from the 104 have
+ participle constructions from late Old English occurred with either of
these three grammatical indicators. The early Middle English data,
however, contains examples with atelic situations, as is shown in (3)
below, anterior adverbials, as in (4) below, and dummy subjects, as in
(5) below.

(3) Lay. 7085

Lud king lette þane wal abuten þe burh of Lundene al.
þe auere yet haueð ilast & swa he wule yet wel longe.

`King Lud caused the wall to be laid all about the burgh of London,
that ever yet hath lasted and so it will yet well long.'

(4) Lay. 16311

betere beoð ure fifti þænne heore fif hundred.
þat heo feole siðen ifonded habbeoð.
seoðen heo an londe sodeden leoden.

`better are fifty of us, than of them five hundred.
that they many times have found.
since they in land sought the people.'

(5) Vsp. A. Hom 239 (1225) (M.E.D.)

þus hit hað ibi and is and wrð oft domesdei.
`Thus, it has been and is and will be often doomsday.'

3. The Shift from Resultative -> Perfect

The grammatical evidence strongly suggests that the *have* + participle construction first emerges as a true perfect during early Middle English: we would therefore expect that the transition from resultative -> perfect probably occurred during the late Old English period, and that data from the late Old English period would provide the strongest clues as to how this shift occurred. Table 2 provides a breakdown of the historical data by the semantic class of the verb participle and Table 3 indicates what percentage of the *have* + participle uses occurred in iterative/durative contexts.

Table 2: Frequency of Verb Participles by Semantic Class

	Alfred (c. 850) n=129	Ælfric (c. 1050) n=104	Lay. Brut (c. 1225) n=161	Sir Gawain (c. 1375) n=47
Mental State	50 (38.8%)	6 (5.8%)	4 (2.5%)	4 (8.5%)
Commun.	21 (16.3%)	30 (28.8%)	15 (9.3%)	1 (2.1%)
Perception	2 (1.6%)	25 (24.0%)	9 (15.6%)	3 (6.4%)
Other	56 (43.3%)	43 (41.4%)	133 (72.6%)	39 (83.0%)

Table 3: Frequency of Iterative and Durative Contexts

	Alfred (c. 850) n=129	Ælfric (c. 1050) n=104	Lay. Brut (c. 1225) n=161	Sir Gawain (c. 1375) n=47
Durative	1 (.8%)	0	26 (16.1%)	6 (12.7%)
Iterative	0	15 (14.4%)	15 (9.3%)	2 (4.3%)
Total	1 (.8%)	15 (14.4%)	41 (25.4%)	8 (17.1%)

3.1 The Role of Perception and Communication Verbs

Table 1 above reveals that mental state verbs are prevalent during the early Old English period, comprising 38.8% of the data set and relatively rare in the late Old English period, making up only 5.8% of the data. The reverse pattern occurs with perception verbs: they are extremely rare in the early Old English data, making up only 1.6% of the data but represent 24% of the data from late Old English. Carey (in press) argues that the difference in the historical frequency patterns between mental state and perception verbs is consistent with the following account of their respective roles in the grammaticalization process: mental state verbs play a role early on in the process by conventionalizing the resultative sense; perception verbs, on the other hand, help to bring about the first current relevance uses of the construction.

The different roles played by mental state and perception verbs in the grammaticalization process can be attributed to their differing semantic/pragmatic properties in regard to (i) the degree of salience of the event relative to the resultant state; (ii) the tightness of the link between the event and the resultant state. While mental events, such as understanding, discovering, planning and deciding, are typically internal, one-participant events that are not anchored to a particular spatio-temporal location, situations involving perception and communication necessarily involve two or more participants, external signs of the communication process (sounds, gestures, etc.) and are spatio-temporally anchored. Consequently, with mental events, the event is typically construed with a very low degree of salience in relation to the resultant state whereas the reverse is true with perception verbs. In the case of mental state verbs, the resultant knowledge state is tightly linked to the verb itself and is entailed by the completion of the event. With perception verbs, however, the resultant state is implicated rather than entailed by the anterior perception event and can be cancelled: *I have heard that argument, but I don't remember anything about it.*

As a consequence of these semantic/pragmatic differences, it is not surprising that mental state verbs are prevalent during an early stage in the grammaticalization process in which only a pure resultative interpretation is possible. Perception verbs, on the other hand, help bring about the first step in the resultative to perfect shift by (i) increasing the salience of the anterior event in the conceptualization; (ii) starting to widen the semantic distance between the anterior event and the resultant state. Importantly, these early uses with perception verbs are still not semantically well-formed current relevance uses: although there has been some widening of the distance between the event and the resultant state, the "result" is still restricted to the grammatical subject.

3.2 The Role of Iterative/durative Contexts

A comparison of Tables 2 and 3 demonstrates that the surge in perception verbs is concomitant with a surge in iterative uses of the *have* + participle construction. This correspondence is not accidental: 14 of the 15 iterative examples from the late Old English period occurred with verbs of communication or perception, as in example (6) below.

(6) ÆC Hom I 32 478.1 (c. 1050)

Nu hæbbe ge oft gehyred by his mæran drohtnunge...

`Now you have often heard about his distinguished life...'

The correlation between iterativity and perception and communication verbs can be explained in the following way; with these types of verbs, iteration strengthens the likelihood of a resultant state; the more times a proposition has been heard or communicated, the more likely it has been retained by the listener. In the case of typical event verbs such as *eat*, iterativity cancels the resultant state interpretation in which the subject bears some immediate physical state, e.g., feeling full. Perception verbs play a crucial role in the development of the perfect because they conventionalize a construal in which a series of anterior events produces a durative experiential state in the subject. Once this construal is conventionalized with perception verbs, it can extend to other event verbs in which an experiential, resultant state construal is less likely. By early Middle English, iteration has extended to other event verbs, as is shown in example (7) below:

(7) Lay. 6223

We habbeð ihaued moni burst moni hunger & moni þurst.
moni walc moni wind bi wilde þisse watere
Nu we biddeð þin ære ne maye we drien hit na mare.

`We have had may harms many hunger and many thirst
many tosses and many turns on this wild water
Now we pray thy favor; we may bear it no more.'

Previous work on the history of the perfect in Romance has claimed that semantically well-formed perfects emerge first in iterative/durative contexts and then later extend to single event contexts (cf. Harris 1982, Alarcos-Llorach 1947): however, none of these accounts have provided a comprehensive analysis of why this should be the case. I believe that the transitional role played by iterative/durative (imperfective) contexts can be accounted for in three ways (i) iterative/durative contexts facilitate the shift from resultative -> perfect by increasing event salience in a gradual way; (ii) iterative/durative contexts help establish the up-to-the-present temporal sense of the perfect; (iii) particular iterative/durative uses help shift the locus of relevance from the subject to the discourse context.

The link between imperfectivity and backgrounding has been well-established, most notably in Hopper and Thompson 1980. Other research has correlated foreground and background in narrative with figure/ground organization and the cognitive notion of salience (cf. Chvany 1985). Wallace (1982:215) elucidates the relationship between the perfective/imperfective distinction and figure/ground organization in the following way:

In terms of figure and ground, the principles of Gestalt psychologists would predict that the bounded, punctiliar perfective is more figure-like and the unbounded, linear imperfective more ground-like. The greater salience of the perfective figure in discourse as opposed to the lesser salience of the imperfective ground naturally follows from the perceptual principles involved.

It stands to reason that, in a period of time in which the anterior events are just beginning to become more salient in the conceptualization, the construction would first extend to iterative/durative contexts so that the shift to greater event salience can occur gradually.

Iterative-durative contexts also enable a gradual strengthening of the up-to-the-present temporal sense of the perfect. Although iterative examples necessarily involve a series of anterior events, the focus can remain on the final resultant state rather than on the up-to-the-present time span in which the events occurred. In the early iterative uses with verbs of perception, the frequency of the event is noted not to draw attention to the up-to-the-present time span in which they occurred but instead to emphasize the knowledge state of the subject. Recall that no examples from late Old English occurred with up-to-the-present adverbials. However, it is the fact that experiential resultant states are thought to be produced by up-to-the-present lifetime experiences that helps first associate up-to-the-present temporality with the construction. As the focus gradually shifts from the final resultant state to the up-to-the-present events that produced it, up-to-the-present adverbials begin to appear with the construction and, ultimately, continuative uses with atelic situations in which the perfect-marking itself encodes up-to-the-present temporality, as in examples (3) and (5) above.

Recall that one of the significant differences between a resultative and a perfect is that the subject is the locus of relevance for the past events in the case of a resultative (and therefore must bear some objective resultant state at reference time) whereas with the perfect, the locus of relevance is not the subject but rather the here-and-now of the discourse context; the "result" in the case of the perfect is any present effect that the speaker construes as related to the anterior events. While there is nothing inherent in the nature of iterative/durative contexts that helps bring about this shift, in many iterative/durative examples from early Middle English, the speaker implicates that a result/effect is present not only in the subject but also in the larger discourse context. In example (7) above, the speaker begins by describing what has happened to him and his people in the period leading up to the present moment, that is, the many harms, hunger, thirst, etc.. The use of the *have* + participle construction in this example can be construed as simply performing the resultative function of indicating the relevance of the past events to the subject who has experienced them. However, the speaker follows up these lines in the discourse with a request for a piece of land from the hearer, causally linking their past suffering with the present request for a piece of land to settle on, thereby implicating a current relevance interpretation. Carey (in press) argues that examples such as (7) help shift the locus of relevance from the subject to the discourse context.

4. The Modern Castilian *tener* `have' + past participle Construction

One considerable drawback of basing an analysis solely on frequency data from historical texts is that one never really knows to what degree the frequencies are driven by the particular author or discourse topic. Also, the absence of a particular semantic class of adverb or verb need not necessarily indicate that it was not permitted in the construction. One could argue that perhaps the high percentage of mental state verbs during Old English is driven by the fact that one of the main topics in Boethius is Boethius' own state of philosophical enlightenment. Similarly, the high percentage of perception and communication verbs in the late Old English period is somewhat suspicious since a great majority of the texts are sermons in which there are more likely to be overt references to the speaker and the listener.

The *tener* `have' + past participle construction in Modern Castilian Spanish provides an excellent source of data that can be used to test the analysis based on the historical English data. This construction is particularly interesting because different dialects of Spanish, and even speakers of the same dialect, seem to have grammaticalized the construction to different degrees. Data from different dialects and different speakers can therefore help test the grammaticalization stages posited above. Also, the analysis of a present day construction can benefit from native speaker intuitions---clearly not an option for the data from Old and Middle English.

The *tener* + past participle construction is not a new innovation by any means, having first arisen in the 12th or 13th centuries. Several works have treated the construction from a historical/descriptive standpoint, most notably, Pountain 1985, and more recently Harre 1991. The recent work by Harre is particularly useful for the present study because of its depth and scope, benefiting from both historical text studies and the present day judgements of eight native speakers from Valladolid and Zaragoza, Spain.

Taken together, they provide a substantial body of data with which to text the diachronic hypotheses presented above. Harre's data will be supplemented by my own data which incorporates native speaker judgements from two dialects of Spanish: Bilbao (Northern) Spain and Buenos Aires, Argentina.

Harre uses the grammaticality judgements of her eight consultants to categorize them along a cline of grammaticalization: examples accepted by all consultants were presumed to represent the lowest level of grammaticalization and the earliest diachronic stage: examples accepted by the fewest consultants represented the most grammaticalized stage. Ideally, this type of analysis involves an implicational hierarchy in which a consultant at stage (n) should also accept as grammatical all of the examples at stage (n-1).

All of the consultants accepted examples (8)--(10) below, each of which involves a durative mental state in the subject.

(8) *Tengo entendido que mañana no va a haber clase.*
`I have it understood that there isn't going to be class tommorrow.'

(9) *Tengo pensado ir al cine esta tarde.*
`I have it planned to go to the movies this afternoon.'

(10) *Tengo olvidado el libro.*
`I have the book forgotten=I can't remember anything about the book.'

Also, all of her consultants accepted examples (11)--(13), which appear with verbs of perception and communication.

(11) *Ya te tengo dicho no sé cuántas veces que no hagas eso.*
`I have told you I don't know how many times not to do that.'

(12) *Se tienen contadas muchas historias el uno al otro.*
`They have told each other many stories one to the other.'

(13) *Tengo oído que mañana no va a haber clase.*
`I have heard that there isn't going to be class tommorrow.'

These data correlate with the historical English data to a remarkable extent. The fact that the examples with mental state verbs are accepted without question by all consultants supports my analysis of the English historical data, in which the mental state examples from early Old English represent the least grammaticalized stage. Significantly, one of the consultants had doubts about (13), claiming that *Tengo entendido* `I have it understood' would be preferable. These intuitions concur with my analysis that examples with perception verbs are slightly more grammaticalized than examples with mental state verbs in that the anterior event is more salient in the conceptualization. The speaker's tendency to substitute *entender* `understood' for *oído* `heard' indicates the semantic closeness of the corresponding propositions, and the fact that these constructions with perception verbs still involve a high degree of resultant state focus.

Importantly, some consultants who accepted (11)--(13) did not accept sentences with *ver* `see' (and, in addition, iteration with other verbs.)

(14) *Tengo vistas muchas películas suyas.*
`I have seen a lot of his films.'

(15) *Tengo vistas muchas cosas raras.*
`I have seen a lot of strange things.'

These data suggest that verbs of communication and hearing are the first verbs to appear in the *tener* construction with the more perfect-like construal in which an anterior event produces a present resultant state. The notion of an anterior event producing a present resultant knowledge/experiential state later becomes extended to other event verbs in which this interpretation is inherently less pragmatically likely. Not surprisingly, the construction is first extended to another perception verb, *ver* `see', as in (14) and (15) above: verbs of seeing are also easily construed as producing a resultant knowledge state in the subject.

The following data is taken from my own interviews with a speaker from Buenos Aires, Argentina. In this dialect, the sense in which iterative past events are construed as producing a resultant experiential state in the subject has clearly become conventionalized: the *tener* construction imposes this construal on verbs that are not inherently pragmatically associated with a resultant knowledge state.

(16) *Tengo gastada mucha suela.*
`I have spent a lot of sole=I am an experienced dancer.'

(17) *Tengo visitado Portugal muchas veces.*
`I have visited Portugal many times=I know Portugal.'

(18) *Tengo conocida mucha gente.*
`I have met a lot of people=I know all kinds.'

(19) *Tengo sudadas muchas camisetas.*
`I have sweated a lot of shirts=I am an experienced soccer player.'

These examples can only have the resultative reading in which the subject bears an experiential state: (19) cannot be used in a single event current relevance sense in which the player has just sweated through ten shirts in a single game (and therefore must do laundry); similarly, (16) can not be used by an exhausted dancer who has been dancing non-stop for three hours (and therefore must take a rest). The speaker from Buenos Aires also accepted the following example:

(20) *Desde mi época en el congreso, tengo leídos millones de libros.*
`Since my time in the congress, I have read millions of books.'

Example (20) is significant because the `since' adverbial phrase indicates the ability to construe the situation as occurring within an anterior, up-to-the-present time span. Significantly, the first appearance of anterior, up-to-the-present adverbials occurs in iterative contexts. Some of Harre's speakers who accept iterative examples do not accept examples such as (21) below, which is iterative and contains the up-to-the-present adverbial phrase *durante estos últimos años* `during these last years'. These data indicate that the examples with up-to-the-present adverbials represent a slightly later diachronic stage. Importantly, none of the speakers would permit non-iterative up-to-the-present adverbials, such as *alguna vez* `ever' and *nunca* `never', as is shown in (22) and (23) below, providing further evidence that up-to-the-present temporality originates in iterative contexts.

(21) *Durante estos últimos años se tienen construidas muchas fábricas por la zona.*
`During these last years, many factories have been constructed in this region.'

(22) *Tienes vista esta película alguna vez?
    `Have you ever seen this movie?'

(23) *Nunca tengo vista esta película.
    `I have never seen this movie.'

None of the Castilian speakers permitted either atelic situations or dummy subjects with the *tener* construction, as is demonstrated in examples (24)--(26) below. The speakers of the most grammaticalized *tener* dialect therefore seem to be in an intermediate stage from resultative -> perfect: none of the speakers have a conventionalized perfect sense.

(24) *Te tengo amado durante muchos años.
    `I have loved you for many years.'

(25) *Tengo tenido un gato desde el marzo.
    `I have had a cat since March.'

(26) *Tiene llovido mucho.
    `It has rained a lot.'

The fact that there is a conventionalized resultative but not a conventionalized perfect sense of the *tener* construction is clearly indicated by the following sets of data. In each of the cases in (27)--(29) below, a metaphoric, mental state interpretation of the predicate is grammatical, as shown in the (a) sentences, but the corresponding achievement use, as shown in the (b) sentences is not grammatical. The mental state interpretation corresponds to a resultative construal whereas the achievement use corresponds to a single event current relevance construal.

(27a) Te tengo descubierto.
    `I have discovered you=I know what you are like.'

(27b) *Tengo descubierta una bomba.
    `I have discovered a bomb.'

(28a) Tengo encontrada la puerta de la felicidad.
    `I have found the door to happiness.'

(28b) *Tengo encontradas las llaves.*
       `I have found the keys.'

(29a) *Tengo perdida la esperanza.*
       `I have lost hope=I am in a state of hopelessness.'

(29b) *Tengo perdidas las llaves.*
       ʳI have lost the keys.'

5. Conclusion

Central to the analysis presented above are three theoretical notions regarding grammaticalization: (i) grammaticalization is a gradual process (cf. Lichtenberk 1991); (ii) grammaticalization/reanalysis occurs through repeated use in particular local contexts, and (iii) grammaticalization results from the conventionalization of conversational implicatures (cf. Traugott and König 1991). Perception and communication situations help facilitate the first step in the resultative -> perfect shift by increasing the salience of the anterior event in the conceptualization and by slightly widening the semantic link between the event and the resultant state. Importantly, the appearance with perception verbs indicates that only a small step toward a more perfect-like interpretation has taken place: these examples are still very similar to a pure resultative sense in that they involve considerable focus on the resultant state, even when they occur with iteration. Recall that some Modern Castilian speakers permitted iteration but not anterior adverbials with the *tener* construction, indicating that these early iterative uses do not involve focus on the anterior events. Iterative uses with perception and communication verbs help conventionalize a construal in which a resultant experiential state is produced by a series of up-to-the-present events; this experiential construal can then extend to other event verbs.

The first semantically well-formed perfects emerge in iterative/durative contexts because they involve the felicitous convergence of several semantic-pragmatic factors: (i) iterative situations involve lower event salience than single event situations, fostering a gradual extension of the more perfect-like interpretation to other event verbs; (ii) iterative/durative contexts that produce an experiential resultant state implicitly involve an up-to-the-present temporal span, facilitating the development of the up-to-the-present temporal sense of the perfect through a gradual shift in focus from the resultant state to the up-to-the-present events that produced it; and (iii) particular iterative/durative examples may implicate that the locus of relevance is not the subject but rather the discourse context.

In addition to articulating the nuts and bolts of the shift from resultative -> perfect, this paper has also hoped to demonstrate the utility of variation data for testing hypotheses regarding historical change. The *tener* data confirmed that mental state verbs would diachronically precede perception verbs and that iteration would precede anterior adverbials. Other recent studies have put forth diachronic hypotheses on the basis of variation data alone: Cukor-Avila and Bailey (to appear) use longitudinal data from an ethnographic study to argue that the past perfect in rural African American Vernacular English (AAVE) is grammaticalizing into a simple past; Schwenter (1994) uses variation data from the Alicante dialect of peninsular Spanish to determine the grammaticalization steps in the shift from perfect -> perfective. Recent cross-linguistic research by Bybee et al. (1994) has demonstrated that the original lexical source of a grammatical morpheme, e.g., *have* + past participle, determines the possible grammaticalization paths it can follow. The present study has shown that variation data can be used in conjunction with historical data to identify particular semantic-pragmatic contexts that serve as catalysts for a particular step along a grammaticalization path, thereby providing a much more complete picture of these universal pathways.

References

Alarcos Llorach, E. 1947. Perfecto simple y compuesto en español. *Revista de Filología Española* 31:108-39.

Bauer, Gero. 1970. *The English Perfect Reconsidered.* Journal of Linguistics, Vol 6 No. 2:189-98.

Benveniste, Emile. 1968. Mutations of Linguistic Categories. In W.P. Lehmann and Yakov Malkiel, eds., *Directions for Historical Linguistics*, 85-94. Austin: University of Texas Press.

Brinton, Laurel. 1988. *The Development of English Aspectual Systems.* Cambridge: Cambridge University Press.

Bybee, Joan; Revere Perkins and William Pagliuca. 1994. *The Evolution of Grammar: Tense, Aspect and Modality in the Languages of the World.* Chicago: Chicago University Press.

Carey, Kathleen. 1994. The Grammaticalization of the Perfect in Old English: an account based on Pragmatics and Metaphor. In William Pagliuca, ed., *Perspectives on Grammaticalization*, 103-117. Amsterdam:John Benjamins..

Carey, Kathleen. In press. Subjectification and the Development of the English Perfect. In Susan Wright and Dieter Stein, eds., *Subjectivity and Subjectivisation in Language*, 83-102.

Chvany, Catherine. 1985. Foregrounding, `Transitivity', Saliency (in Sequential and Non-sequential Prose). *Essays in Poetics* 10.1:1-27.

Comrie, Bernard. 1976. *Aspect*. Cambridge: Cambridge University Press.

Cukor-Avila, Patricia and Guy Bailey. Grammaticalization in AAVE. To appear in the *Proceedings of the 21st Annual Meeting of the Berkeley Linguistics Society*.

Dahl, Östen. 1985. *Tense and Aspect Systems*. Oxford: Basil Blackwell.

Fenn, Peter. 1987. *A Semantic and Pragmatic Examination of the English Perfect*. Tübingen: Gunter Narr Verlag.

Harre, Catherine. 1991. *Tener + past particple: A Case Study in Linguistic Description*. London: Routledge.

Harris, Martin. 1982. The `past simple' and `present perfect' in Romance. In Nigel Vincent and Martin Harris, eds., *Studies in the Romance Verb*, 42-70. London: Croom Helm.

Hopper, Paul and Sandra Thompson. 1980. Transivitity in Grammar and Discourse. *Language* 56: 251-299.

Langacker, Ronald W. 1990. Subjectification. *Cognitive Linguistics* 1: 5-37.

Leech, Geoffrey. 1971. *Meaning and the English Verb*. Longman: London.

Lichtenberk, Frantisek. On the Gradualness of Grammaticalization. In Elizabeth Traugott and Bernd Heine, eds., *Approaches to Grammaticalization*, Vol. I, 37-90. Amsterdam: John Benjamins.

McCoard, Robert. 1978. *The English Perfect: Tense Choice and Pragmatic Inferences.* Amsterdam: North-Holland Publishing Company.

Michaelis, Laura. 1993. *Toward a Grammar of Aspect: The Case of the English Perfect Construction.* University of California at Berkeley Ph.D. dissertation.

Nedyalkov, V.P. and S.J. Jaxontov. 1988. The Typology of Resultative Constructions. In V.P. Nedyalkov, ed., *Typology of Resultative Constructions*, 3-62. Amsterdam: John Benjamins.

Pinkster, Harm. 1987. The Strategy and Chronology of the Development of Future and Perfect Tense Auxiliaries in Latin. In Martin Harris and Paolo Ramat, eds., *Historical Development of the Auxiliaries*, 193-223. Berlin: Mouten de Gruyter.

Pountain, Christopher. 1985. Copulas, Verbs of Possession and Auxiliaries in Old Spanish: The Evidence for Structurally Interdependent Changes. *Bulletin of Hispanic Studies* 62: 337-55.

Schwenter, Scott. 1993. The Grammaticalization of an Anterior in Progress: Evidence from a Peninsular Spanish Dialect. *Studies in Language* 18:71-111.

Traugott, Elizabeth and Ekkehard König. 1991. The Semantics-pragmatics of Grammaticalization Revisited. In Elizabeth Traugott and Bernd Heine, eds., *Approaches to Grammaticalization*, Vol. I, 189-218. Amsterdam: John Benjamins.

Venezky, Richard L. and Antoinette DiPaolo Healey. 1980. *A Microfiche Concordance of Old English.* Dictionary of Old English Project, Center for Medieval Studies: University of Toronto.

Vincent, Nigel. 1982. The Development of the Auxiliaries *Habere* and *Essere* in Romance. In Nigel Vincent and Martin Harris, eds., *Studies in the Romance Verb*, 71-96. London: Croom Helm.

Wallace, Steven. 1982. Figure and Ground: The Interrelationships of Linguistic Categories. In Paul Hopper, ed., *Tense-Aspect: Between Semantics and Pragmatics*, 201-233. Amsterdam: John Benjamins.

Beyond Beads on a String and Branches in a Tree

University of California, Santa Barbara

There continues to exist a need for a model of natural discourse that pulls together the diverse cognitive and social factors responsible for the shape of language. Discourse is many-sided, and the limitations of any attempt to represent its patterning in one or two dimensions become increasingly evident as one explores it in depth. My plan here is to begin with a brief look at a representation that is essentially one-dimensional, and then move on quickly to a two-dimensional representation of a familiar kind. The inadequacies of the latter will suggest a more complex alternative whose ramifications will occupy us for the remainder of the paper.

As an illustration I am going to quote a short segment of a long conversation in which the principal speakers were three older Native American men who had attended the same Catholic boarding school when they were children. They were reminiscing about their experiences at the school, and particularly about punishments meted out for various infractions of the rules. These three men will be identified as speakers A, B, and C. Also present were a graduate student, identified as speaker D, and myself, speaker E. Acute and grave accent marks show primary and secondary accents respectively. Sequences of two and three dots show very brief and normal-length pauses. Square brackets show overlapping speech. The equals sign shows an expressively lengthened syllable.

1 C: Yeah I remémber gettin' a ... whìppin' with a blácksnake one
        time.
 2 A: <cough>

3 A: ... Get a whìppin' on a rùbber hóse?
4 C: Fàther Ál,
5 C: .. I ran óff,
6 C: .. when they càught me by Ríverside,
7 B: Uh,
8 C: and [took] took me báck to the schóol,
9 A: [<cough>]
10 B: were yóu–
11 C: .. took me to the= Fàther Ál,
12 C: and uh,
13 C: .. took me to his óffice,
14 C: and he had a ... blácksnake hàngin' up,
15 C: .. on the [...] wáll,
16 B: [Do yòu know what thát is?]
17 E: .. A a hóse?
18 A: <cough>
19 C: took took [ít] down and,
20 B: [Nó.]
21 B: Nó it 's a–
22 E: .. A whíp?
23 B: it's a yeah it's a bràided whíp;
24 B: for uh–
25 C: mhm,
26 B: like
27 D: .. Gód.
28 B: ... fór hórses,
29 B: or sómething like that [ányway.]
30 D: [Uh=.]
31 D: Uh=,
32 E: Mh.
33 B: It 's quíte a déal;
34 B: you know.
35 C: Yeah.
36 A: <cough>
37 B: <laugh>
38 C: Well hé tóok me uh=
39 C: ... from thére he took me to cláss,
40 C: .. and uh=,
41 C: ... took uh= that ... nu- uh nún hé was tàlking abòut,
42 C: ... Sis- Sìster Olívia,
43 C: ... she was [our] téacher in that ... in that uh ... cláss,

44 E: [Mhm,]
45 E: Uh huh.
46 C: ... and that uh Fàther Ál,
47 C: .. wàlked me ín there,
48 C: .. and uh,
49 C: ... and uh,
50 C: ... hè tòld hér that .. I had run óff,
51 C: a=nd that .. he 'd bròught me báck,
52 C: ... só=,
53 C: ... what did she dó;
54 C: the first thíng that–
55 C: .. was to òpen her dráwer,
56 C: ... and get a .. rúler out;
57 C: you know.
58 E: Mh.
59 C: ... She was gonna
60 A: <cough>
61 C: let me háve it;
62 C: háve it.
63 A: <cough cough>
64 A: <cough>
65 C: A=nd uh,
66 A: [<cough cough>]
67 C: .. [Father Ál] said I 've already .. whípped him.
68 C: ... So she put the .. rúler back.
69 E: Óh.
66 D: ... Glàd he sáid something.
67 C: .. [Yéah.]
68 D: [<laugh>]

Much that contributes to the shape of the language in this excerpt involves the flow of information into and out of the focal consciousnesses of the participants, the choice of starting points (determining grammatical subjects), decisions as to identifiability ("definiteness"), and the like. These are matters I have discussed with reference to data of this kind in Chafe (1994). Here I will concentrate on some points that were only touched on in Chapters 10 and 11 of that work.

The transcript above has the format of a series of lines, each representing an intonation unit, as identified through various prosodic criteria including pitch, duration, volume, and/or voice quality. It has proved fruitful to hypothesize that each intonation unit verbalizes the speaker's focus of consciousness at the moment of its utterance, the speaker's intention being that the listener acquire in his or her own consciousness something resembling what the speaker had in mind. If we were to ignore a number of factors that are evident from even a cursory inspection of this example, we might momentarily conceive of a discourse as a series of beads on a string as suggested in figure 1, consisting of nothing more than a succession of intonation units, each expressing a focus of consciousness.

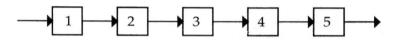

Figure 1. The Beads on a String Model

The need for something more is obvious in the first place from the observation that certain foci of consciousness cluster together more tightly than others. For example, the connection between the foci expressed in intonation units 6 and 8 was a close one:

6 C: .. when they càught me by Ríverside,
8 C: and [took] took me báck to the schóol,

For one thing, these two intonation units contained two clauses that shared the same grammatical subject. Moreover, so far as their content was concerned, the event verbalized in 8 followed immediately on that verbalized in 6; there was no temporal gap. In contrast, the immediately preceding intonation unit:

5 C: .. I ran óff,

had a different subject from that shared by 6 and 8, and there was no tight temporal connection between the running off and the being caught. The events in 5 and 6 were separated by an interval of time that was left vague and open. Observations like these suggest that varying degrees of tightness of connection need to be recognized between successive intonation units, as suggested in figure 2 where the heavier arrow is meant to show a closer link.

Figure 2. Varying Strengths of Connections
Between Beads on a String

An alternative way of representing the same relations would be in terms of a tree diagram, as in figure 3.

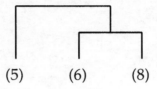

(5)   (6)   (8)

Figure 3. An Arboreal Version of Figure 2

Pursuing this tree model at a higher level, we can notice that the entire excerpt has three major parts, which we might call episode 1 (C's punishment by Father Al), a digression in which B clarified for D and E what was meant by the word *blacksnake*, and episode 2 (C's narrow escape from punishment by Sister Olivia). Thus, the initial branching of the tree might be shown as in figure 4.

C's Narrative

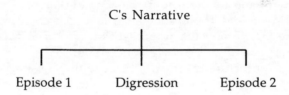

Episode 1   Digression   Episode 2

Figure 4. Initial Branching

Combining figures 3 and 4 and adding names to the lower branches would yield the tree diagram shown in figure 5. One could fill in the Punishment, Digression, and Episode 2 branches in a similar manner.

Doubtless the general appeal of this tree model is related to a universal human need to understand complexity in hierarchical

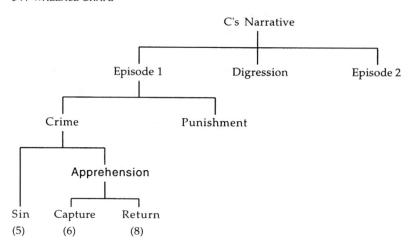

Figure 5. The Tree Model

terms, with larger systems composed of smaller ones. For linguists, trees have long been popular as models of sentence structure. They have also been the basis of the "story grammar" model that has seemed a natural way to capture the structure of narratives (e.g., Mandler 1984). With an important modification, they have also underlain "rhetorical structure theory" (Mann and Thompson 1988). The modification in question involves the recognition of explicit relations between sister nodes. For example, the relation between the Capture (6) and the Return (8) was one of *immediate temporal succession* (Mann and Thompson called it *sequence*). The relation between the Sin (5) and the Apprehension (6 and 8) was one of *temporal succession after an interval,* and so on.

Rhetorical structure theory has dealt with expository written prose, and not with spontaneous spoken language. Ease of hierarchical modeling surely bears a relation to the planned nature of expository writing, as opposed to the on-line, evanescent quality of ordinary speaking. There is a valid sense in which spoken language is produced "one idea at a time," even though that is not the whole story. Thus, there is a need to integrate the respective insights of the beads-on-a-string model with the branches-in-a-tree model, but in the end it will prove necessary to move beyond them both.

It is not always easy to apply the tree model unambiguously. When I have asked students to analyze a stretch of discourse in this way, I have often been surprised by the range of different interpretations that have emerged, each with some degree of justification. To suggest that the students had not yet learned to do this sort of thing, and that with more practice a consensus might have been reached, would be to ignore the fact that I too, in spite of some fairly clear ideas about what ought to go into such a hierarchy, and many opportunities over the years to apply those ideas, still find myself faced with uncertainties when confronting almost any piece of natural discourse.

I can cite the first line of the above excerpt as an example:

1 C: Yeah I remémber gettin' a ... whìppin' with a blácksnake one time.

The question is how best to fit this statement into the tree structure diagramed in figure 5. The function of 1 was evidently to introduce and summarize the narrative to come. From that point of view, perhaps figure 5 should be modified to show four rather than three major branches at the top, as in figure 6.

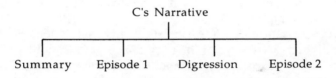

Figure 6. One Possible Location for the Summary

But one could also make a case for interpreting 1 as an entry into episode 1 alone, and not into the entire excerpt, since it introduced the idea of the whipping by Father Al but did not foreshadow C's escape from a second whipping by Sister Olivia. With that in mind we might prefer figure 7 on the next page.

The truth is that 1 simply functions as an entry into the topic to follow, and that trying to insert it into any structure that implies a high degree of prior planning is like supposing that a chess player who is making his first move already knows all the rest of the game. Years ago I wrote a piece called "The Flow of Thought and the Flow of Language" (Chafe 1979) in which I exemplified some of the problems for a strictly hierarchical model that result from the fact that people think and talk on-line. A tree diagram falls short of capturing the gradual development of ideas through time under

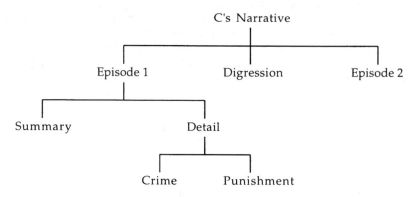

Figure 7. Another Possible Location for the Summary

the influence of both cognitive and social goals and constraints. People move from one thought to another, chunking certain thoughts together to be sure, but continually influenced by ongoing processes of memory as well as by the thoughts, language, and actions of others.

To return to the question raised by the competing figures 6 and 7, speaker C apparently began his topic in 1 with a relatively coherent story to tell. We can think of his first statement meta-phorically as activating a mental space within which there existed many incipient ideas, some semiactive, some probably inactive for him at that moment, a space within which it was now his goal to navigate in order to communicate something of its nature to his interlocutors. We can wonder how clearly, at the beginning, he had episode 2 in mind, or even whether he had it in mind at all. Intonation unit 19 was as far as he got with episode 1,

19 C: took took [it] down and,

at which point he surrendered to B's digression. When he later resumed his narrative in 38, the whipping by Father Al had already taken place. In spite of the fact that it was the climactic event of episode 1, it was masked by the digression. But neither C nor his interlocutors seem to have been bothered by that omission, and they probably did not even notice the truncation of what a tree-oriented analyst would have expected as the peak of a well-formed narrative.

As an improvement on both the beads and branches models, I am going to suggest what I will call the flow model. Its goal will be to combine linear development through time with the clustering of ideas into smaller and larger chunks, while allowing also for ideas that get nowhere, as well as for the contributions of other participants. I will introduce it one intonation unit at a time.

With the summary in 1, C was able to activate a new topic, most of whose content was at this moment in part semiactive, in part inactive in his consciousness. Only the climax was fully active. We can suggest C's entry into this topic as shown in figure 8.

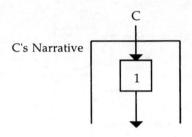

Figure 8. C's Entry into His Topic

Speaker A then coughed and inserted what seems to have been a rhetorical question:

3 A: ... Get a whìppin' on a rùbber hóse?

We can show his question as falling outside C's narrative proper in the manner suggested in figure 9.

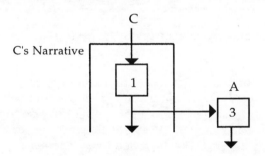

Figure 9. A's Rhetorical Question

C did not answer A's question, but moved directly from 1 to begin developing the details of the punishment episode. He first activated the idea of Father Al, who was to be an important player in that episode:

4 C: Fàther Ál,

This initial entry into the particulars of episode 1 is diagramed in figure 10.

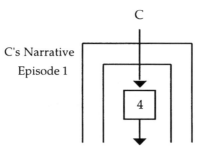

Figure 10. C Begins to Activate Particulars of Episode 1

At this point C had not completely decided how to organize his presentation, and he quickly chose to back up a little, saving the idea of Father Al, activated in 4, to be picked up later in what would eventually become intonation unit 11. He entered now into the sub-episode dealing with the crime, and specifically with the sin itself:

5 C: .. I ran óff,

Like 4, this statement was a successor to 1. The idea of Father Al was temporarily suspended, as suggested in figure 11.

The next section of the narrative, comprised of intonation units 5, 6, and 8, conformed rather nicely to the hierarchical model. As noted above, 6 and 8 were tightly bound together, not only through their sharing of the same grammatical subject but also through the tight temporal sequencing of the events they expressed, whereas 5 was set apart by a switch of subject and by an open-ended temporal interval separating the events:

5 C: .. I ran óff,

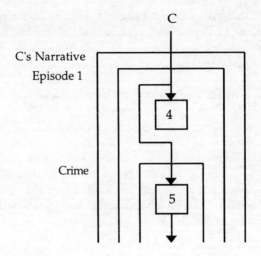

Figure 11. Replacing 4 with 5

6 C: .. when they càught me by Ríverside,
8 C: and [took] took me báck to the schóol,

The diagram can thus be continued as shown in figure 12.

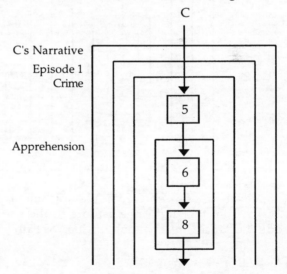

Figure 12. Addition of the Apprehension Sequence

But things did not progress in quite as straightforward manner as figure 12 suggests. In the middle of the 6 to 8 sequence speaker B attempted to take the floor by saying *uh*. He began to ask a question in 10, but never finished it:

6 C: .. when they càught me by Ríverside,
7 B: Uh,
8 C: and [took] took me báck to the schóol,
9 A: [<cough>]
10 B: were yóu–

This attempted digression, following on something said by C (although precisely what is not clear), can be added to the diagram as shown in figure 13.

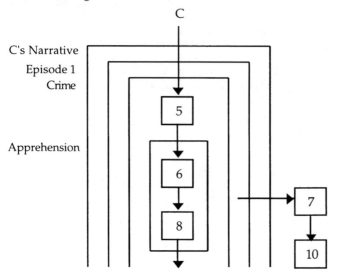

Figure 13. B's Attempted Digression

Speaker C now entered the punishment scene, switching spatially from the site of the capture to the site of the whipping and in the process reactivating the idea of Father Al:

11 C: .. took me to the= Fàther Ál,

Adding 11 to the diagram we now have figure 14, which is as far as we need carry the example here.

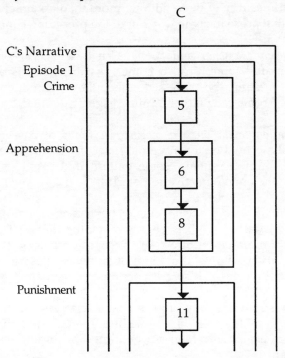

Figure 14. C's Entry into the Punishment Sub-episode

Although figures 8-14 are an improvement on the tree diagram in figure 5, they provide nothing more than a skeleton on which some important flesh still needs to be hung. Discovering the nature of this flesh constitutes, as I see it, a major task for future discourse research, and an area where great mysteries still lie. For each focus of consciousness expressed in an intonation unit, we need to discover how that focus is related to its environment within the larger ongoing discourse. Because the discourse environment itself is always multifaceted, a focus of consciousness necessarily bears a multiplicity of relations to it. Discourse relations fan out in various directions, among which are at least the following four:

(1) *A relation to what preceded.* Nearly every focus of consciousness bears some relation to ideas that were activated before it.
Ideas do not usually arise out of nothing. The relation may or

may not be to the immediately preceding intonation unit, and sometimes it may be to nothing more than a vaguely delimited idea that arose in some way out of the preceding context.

(2) *A relation to what will follow.* Usually a focus of consciousness anticipates something to come. Again, what is anticipated may sometimes be expressed in the following intonation unit, or may be something larger or more vaguely defined.

(3) *A relation to the current schema.* A focus of consciousness is usually located on a conceptual trajectory that is determined by some familiar schema, some pattern that provides a path to guide the ongoing activation of ideas.

(4) *A relation to the ongoing interaction.* The things people say have social as well as cognitive motivations. The need to specify the relation of a focus of consciousness to the ongoing interaction allows the kind of analysis described here to dovetail nicely with socially oriented concerns.

To illustrate how these four kinds of relations can be applied, I will show how they can link some of the initial intonation units in the present example to their surroundings, beginning with the first thing said:

1 C: Yeah I remémber gettin' a ... whìppin' with a blácksnake one time.

(1) *Relation to what preceded:* 1 added a new example to the ongoing supertopic, with only a broad relation to what had previously been talked about. The three men had been swapping memories of punishments at the boarding school, and at this point speaker C introduced an experience of his own to add to the collection.

(2) *Relation to what will follow:* 1 anticipated the development of this new topic. It would have been odd for 1 to have been the only thing said about this incident. There was an expectation by all concerned that C would provide specific details of his experience.

(3) *Relation to the schema:* 1 summarized the topic by presenting its climax. The schema customarily followed in the development of such a topic dictates an initial summary of some kind. While there are several options for what may be included in a summary, C chose to summarize by stating the climax.

(4) *Relation to the interaction:* 1 reinforced group solidarity. Evidently C's reason for introducing this topic was to add to the comfort derived from knowing that one's unpleasant experiences were shared with others. Misery, even ancient misery, loves company.

Speaker A then coughed. He was suffering from a respiratory illness that made coughing unavoidable, but his coughs were generally located at significant boundary points, as here between the summary and the development of details. He then asked:

3 A: ... Get a whìppin' on a rùbber hóse?

(1) *Relation to what preceded:* 3 (seemed to) request confirmation of 1. I say "seemed to" because A probably did not expect an answer.

(2) *Relation to what will follow:* 3 (seemed to) anticipate an answer. A question might seem to be a prime example of language that anticipates other language, but a rhetorical question is defined by the absence of such an anticipation.

(3) *Relation to the schema:* 3 encouraged development of the topic. By saying 3, speaker A encouraged C to elaborate on what he had just introduced.

(4) *Relation to the interaction:* 3 expressed A's empathy with C's experience, showing that he shared some knowledge of what it was like.

Instead of answering 3, C immediately said:

4 C: Fàther Ál,

(1) *Relation to what preceded:* 4 shifted from the summary to particulars. Whereas 1 provided a view of the entire topic from a more distant perspective, 4 zoomed in on detail.

(2) *Relation to what will follow:* 4 prematurely activated an important referent. By activating the idea of Father Al, C anticipated the latter's participation in the events to follow.

(3) *Relation to the schema:* 4 started episode 1.

(4) *Relation to the interaction:* 4 reinforced group solidarity. This, and most of what followed, continued the interactive function established in 1.

After no more than a slight break in timing C then said:

5 C: .. I ran óff,

(1) *Relation to what preceded:* Like 4, 5 shifted the level of discourse from the summary to particulars, zooming in on detail.

(2) *Relation to what will follow:* 5 anticipated 6 and 8, and more vaguely the rest of the topic. C used this focus to anticipate the consequences of his running off, in the first place his capture and return to the school, but eventually his punishment.

(3) *Relation to the schema:* 5 restarted episode 1.

(4) *Relation to the interaction:* 5 continued to reinforce group solidarity.

Space is lacking here to continue this exploration of ways in which each focus of consciousness was related to its surroundings, but these examples can at least suggest ways in which flesh can be added to the skeleton in figures 8-14. Further work should allow us to specify more fully the kinds of relations a focus may bear to what precedes it, to what is anticipated to follow it, to whatever schema guides topic development, and to interpersonal goals. Refinement of these relations will depend on the careful examination of large quantities of discourse. Although conversational language enjoys a certain priority in this endeavor, the effort needs also to be extended to other genres, written as well as spoken, and certainly to other languages as well, for there is no reason to believe that all languages shape discourse in the same way.

References

Chafe, Wallace. 1979. The Flow of Thought and the Flow of Language. In Talmy Givón, ed., *Discourse and Syntax*. New York: Academic Press.

Chafe, Wallace. 1994. *Discourse, Consciousness, and Time: The Flow and Displacement of Conscious Experience in Speaking and Writing*. Chicago: The University of Chicago Press.

Mandler, Jean Matter. 1984. *Stories, Scripts and Scenes: Aspects of Schema Theory*. Hillsdale, NJ: Lawrence Erlbaum.

Mann, William C., and Sandra A. Thompson. 1988. Rhetorical Structure Theory: A Theory of Text Organization. *Text* 8:243-281.

Menendez Brothers Virus: Blended Spaces and Internet Humor*

SEANA COULSON
University of California, San Diego

This paper concerns the interaction of frame semantics and the use of blended spaces (Fauconnier & Turner, 1994) in the meaning construction invoked to understand a joke about a computer virus which shares certain properties with Erik and Lyle Menendez. We suggest that the purpose of the analogical mappings in the virus joke is to highlight one particular construal of the controversial source domain and discuss how this occurs. Mechanisms include: (i) the importation of one particular framing of the source domain into the blended space; and (ii) the projection of structure from a well-developed blended space back onto the source. We argue that there is nothing inherent to the process of analogical mapping which mandates mapping from the source to the target, and suggest that the traditional emphasis on source to target mappings is a by-product of standard examples of analogy and metaphor. The analysis of the Menendez Brothers Virus joke suggests how the conceptual integration which occurs in blended spaces can afford the linguistic representation of a dynamic conceptual system.

1   Introduction

MENENDEZ BROTHERS VIRUS: Eliminates your files, takes the disk space they previously occupied, and then

*Thanks to Gilles Fauconnier for his many helpful comments on this analysis. Thanks also to Adele Goldberg for raising important objections to the blended spaces account of the MBV joke. Preparation of this document was facilitated by Seana Coulson's support from a Public Health Service (PHS) Institutional Training Grant (No. 5 T32 MH14268-19) to the Center for Human Information Processing (CHIP) at UCSD.

claims that it was a victim of physical and sexual abuse on
the part of the files it erased.

This description of the Menendez Brothers Virus (MBV) is a joke
which relies upon the reader's knowledge of the trial of Erik and Lyle
Menendez, two young men who confessed to murdering their parents.
The case achieved a certain degree of notoriety due to the brothers' legal
defense in which they claimed that their parents had repeatedly abused
them both physically and sexually since childhood, and, moreover, that
their actions against their unarmed parents were motivated by self-
defense. One way of explaining the process of meaning construction in
the MBV joke is as a metaphoric or analogical mapping of the event
scenario associated with the Menendez Brothers' trial onto the domain
of computer viruses.

American culture members with even passing familiarity with the
Menendez Brothers' affair will intuitively note the parallels which exist between the actions of the Menendez Brothers Virus and those of
Erik and Lyle Menendez. The Menendez Virus erases files, whereas
the Menendez brothers killed their parents; the Menendez virus takes
disk space once occupied by the erased files, whereas the Menendez
brothers acquired their parents' million dollar mansion; and, finally,
the Menendez Virus claims to be the victim of physical and sexual
abuse perpetrated by the erased files, whereas the Menendez brothers
pleaded self-defense motivated by years of physical and sexual abuse
on the part of their murdered parents.

The target domain of computer viruses thus shares a system of
relations with the source domain of the Menendez brothers. Moreover,
objects in the target have been placed into correspondence with objects
in the source, based on similar roles in their shared relational structure.
However, it is clear that whatever else it might be doing, the mapping
in the Menendez Brothers Virus example does not elucidate the target
domain by leading to productive inferences about computer viruses.
If anything, it leads to fallacious inferences about the target domain.
What then is the purpose of the analogical mapping done in the MBV
joke?

We argue that this puzzle stems from limitations in the current
conception of analogical mapping. These include: (i) the idea that
analogical mapping is one-way: from source to target; and, (ii) under-
estimation of the importance of frame semantics, especially the role
of alternative construals of the same objective scenario. Further, we
point to an alternative account of analogical mapping which involves
the construction of blended spaces (Fauconnier & Turner, 1994). Below
we discuss the interaction of frame semantics and the use of blended

spaces in the Menendez Brothers Virus joke. What follows is a short discussion of the nature of blended spaces, and a demonstration of the use of blended spaces in the meaning construction process invoked to understand the joke. We then contrast the blended space account with more traditional accounts of analogical mapping and explore the implications of blending for conceptual structure and analogical mapping.

2   Computer Viruses and Blended Spaces

Fauconnier and Turner (1994) suggest that metaphoric mappings are one manifestation of a more general mapping process which crucially involves the construction of blended spaces. Blended spaces are mental spaces (Fauconnier, 1994) which are built up on-line in order to incorporate elements from both generic frames and local contextual information. Because blended spaces can contain elements from a number of different domains, they often have a rich counterfactual feel to them. Although the structure of blended spaces contains information which would be inconsistent if incorporated into other spaces, blended spaces are internally consistent.

One example of a concept which results from a conceptual blend (Fauconnier & Turner, to appear) is that of the computer virus itself. Computer viruses are programs written for the express purpose of damaging other people's computational resources. The way a virus works is to attach itself to another program where it replicates and spreads to other programs. Although some viruses are relatively benign, interrupting processes and printing humorous messages to the user's screen, others are designed to destroy data and/or cause harm to the system.

As in conventional accounts of analogical mapping, counterparts map to distinct elements whose attributes are licensed by the structure of the inputs. For example, in the case of the computer virus, particular programs in the domain of computers are picked out as counterparts to viruses in the health domain. Moreover, the choice of counterparts is not arbitrary, but motivated by each element's role in abstract structural schemas. Fauconnier and Turner (to appear) note the generic schema common to both the computer virus and its biological counterpart. This is represented schematically below:

Invades (virus, host)
Infects (virus, host)
Unwanted (virus)
Replicates (virus)
    Resources-used (Belong-to (host))

Results ((More (viruses)) & (Diminished-capacity (host)))

The existence of integrated schemas which can be abstracted from both domains enables us to map elements from both source and target domains into the blended space. Schemas from the health domain of biological viruses are projected from the source space into the blend. Meanwhile, elements from the target space are projected into the blend in order to fill the slots of the virus schema.

Although the mapping which occurs is systematic, it is not comprehensive. There are many aspects of the health domain conceptualization of viruses which are not mapped into the domain of computer viruses. Further, although the blend receives only selected structure from its input spaces, the resultant blend can contain structure which was not present in either of the inputs. Properties unique to the blend emerge when background knowledge is activated in order to provide a coherent blending of projected aspects of the inputs. The resultant blend contains both more and less structure than the inputs: less, because only selected structure in the inputs is projected into the blend, and more, because the overall blend can contain novel structure which is unavailable from the inputs (Fauconnier & Turner, 1994).

3   Blended Spaces and the MBV

Earlier we noted the intuitive parallels between the actions of the Menendez Brothers Virus and those of the real Menendez brothers. However, in this section we discuss the mapping in terms of blended spaces in more detail. Table 1 lists the named elements in the source domain of the Menendez brothers and their corresponding elements in the target domain of the computer viruses. To say this is just to say that in the domain of the Menendez brothers' affair, three salient elements were the brothers, their parents, and the Menendez family's property. Similarly, in the target domain of computer viruses, common elements include viruses, affected files, and disk space.

As in conventional accounts, (e.g. Gick & Holyoak, 1980; 1983; Holland et al. 1986), the blended spaces account of analogical mapping includes a generic, or schematic, space which is structured by the abstract relational schemas common to both source and target spaces. In the case of the Menendez Brothers Virus, the generic space would contain the information represented in Table 2.

Given the existence of a shared relational schema a fourth space may be set up in which blending of the two input domains may occur.

Source	Target
Elements	*Elements*
• a' Menendez Brothers	• a Computer Virus
• b' Mr. & Mrs. Menendez	• b Affected Files
• c' Property	• c Disk Space

Table 1: Elements in Source and Target Spaces

Generic
Elements
• a" Agent
• b" Patients
• c" Transferred Entity
Relations
Eliminates (a",b")
Takes (a",c")
Previously Occupied (b",c")

Table 2: Elements and Relations in Generic Space

The blended space contains elements linked to counterparts in the other spaces (see Table 3).

Note that the blended counterpart of a and a' is not just an abstract computer virus, but a particular virus named the Menendez Brothers Virus. Because the Menendez Brothers Virus (aa) is linked to the Menendez brothers (a') in the source domain, the computer virus (a) in the target domain, and the agent (a") in the generic domain, it can inherit properties from any of these spaces. Moreover, the correspondence between the relational structures in the source and target spaces – the same correspondences which structure the generic space – are used to import structure from the target into the blend.

Table 4 lists the corresponding relations which exist between elements in each of the four spaces. We have tried to employ predicates

Blend
Elements
• aa Menendez Brother Virus
• bb Affected Files
• cc Disk Space

Table 3: Elements in Blended Space

Source	Blend	Generic	Target
Relations	*Relations*	*Relations*	*Relations*
Kill (a',b')	Erases (aa,bb)	Eliminates (a",b")	Erases (a,b)
Acquire (a',c')	Takes (aa,cc)	Takes (a",c")	Takes (a',c')
Owned- previously (c',b')	Occupied- previously (cc,bb)	Occupied- previously (c",b")	Occupied- previously (c,b)

Table 4: Counterpart Relations in Source, Blend, Generic, and Target

which are most appropriate to the domain in question. For example, the term *kill* is used to refer to the social source domain, while the term *erase* is used to refer to the technical target. However, the language user is not similarly constrained. Once elements in two or more domains have been linked, the access principle (Fauconnier, 1994) can be invoked to refer to corresponding elements in either of those domains. Similarly, predicates which are customarily associated with one particular domain can be applied to refer to counterpart relations in linked domains.

It is important to note that, out of the context of the joke, the predicates which have been equated involve quite disparate concepts. Objectively, killing people and erasing files have almost nothing in common. Acquiring property and taking disk space are markedly distinct actions. Moreover, the concept of property ownership in the social source is a very different thing from occupying disk space in the technical target. However, once the context of the joke has been set up, linking the disparate properties in the social source and the technical target proceeds quite naturally.

The text of the joke utilizes terms from the generic domain (viz. eliminates, takes, occupied) perhaps to facilitate mapping from the input domains into the blended space. The blended space itself concerns the Menendez Brothers computer virus and is structured by schemas from the target domain (viz. erasing files, taking over disk space) which are shared by counterparts in the other spaces. Moreover, the existence of links between the source and the blended spaces also enables the importation of structure from the source which has no counterpart in the target. The blended spaces framework is unique in its capacity to explain asymmetric projections which occur in the MBV joke.

In Table 5, we can see the projection of an entire event scenario from the source domain of the Menendez brothers' murder trial into the imaginary scenario associated with the blended space. Because the event is extended in time, the representation of the source domain includes three mental spaces: one for each of the relevant time periods.

A mental space is needed to represent each of the time steps (T0, T1, and T2) in Table 5. The base space in the source domain is the time at which the Menendez brothers have been accused of murder (T2). At this time they offer a claim about the events of their childhood. The content of this claim is represented in the structure of the claim space which occurs at T0. Moreover, the content of the claim space is offered as an explanation of the murder of Mr. and Mrs. Menendez, which occurred at T1: after the purported child abuse and before the accusation of murder. The entirety of this event scenario gets mapped into the blended domain. Because the target domain contains a counterpart relation for *killed*, *killed* maps onto it erased in the blend. However, because there are no target counterparts for the it abused and it victim predicates, these schemas are mapped directly into the blend, their slots filled by elements in the blended domain. The result is a blend in which the contribution of the inputs is particularly asymmetric.

Partial structures from the source and from the target have been integrated into a single structure in the blended domain. The blended space omits many salient aspects of both the source and the target domains. In particular, the familial relationship between the murderers and their victims was not imported into the blend. However, blending results in the local creation of a new concept of the computer virus. In this blended joke space, computer viruses can make excuses for their behavior – something which neither biological nor computer viruses ever do!

Further, the blended joke space motivates humor which is absent in both the source and the target input spaces. This exemplifies the point made by Fauconnier and Turner (1994) that one function of blended spaces is to enable different emotional responses to a given scenario. One might surmise that the humorous nature of the MBV joke is the result of linking disparate domains in the blended space. However, we argue below that the humorous nature of the MBV joke goes beyond the mere juxtaposition of disparate concepts. Rather, humor results from the way in which the fantastic world of the blended space accentuates a particular framing of the source domain in which the mitigating claims of the Menendez Brothers appear ridiculous.

4   Conventional Accounts of Mapping

Conventional accounts of analogy involve knowledge mapped from a relatively well-understood source domain onto a less well-understood

Source Event Scenarios	Blend Event Scenarios
Base TIME 2	**Base** TIME 2
Elements	*Elements*
• a' Menendez Brothers	• aa Menendez Brothers Virus
Accused (a')	Accused (aa)
Claim TIME 0	**Claim** TIME 0
Elements	*Elements*
• a' Menendez Brothers	• aa Menendez Brothers Virus
• b' Mr. & Mrs. Menendez	• bb Affected Files
Relations	*Relations*
Abused (b',a')	Abused (bb,aa)
Victims (a')	Victim (a)
Crime TIME 1	**Crime** TIME 1
Elements	*Elements*
• a' Menendez Brothers	• aa Menendez Brothers Virus
• b' Mr. & Mrs. Menendez	• bb Affected Files
Relations	*Relations*
Killed (a,b)	Erased (aa,bb)

Table 5: Parallel Event Scenarios in the Source and the Blend Domains. Each domain contains 3 mental spaces which correspond to three events, occurring at 3 different times. The earliest event (at TIME 0) concerns the Menendez Brothers' childhood, and is represented in the elements and relations of the Claim Space. The latest event (at TIME 2) is in the courtroom, and is represented in the Base Space. The event represented in the Crime Space occurred between TIME 0 and TIME 2.

target domain (see e. g. Gentner, 1980-90; Gick & Holyoak, 1980, 1983; Holland et al. 1986; Holyoak, 1985; Lakoff & Johnson, 1980; Lakoff, 1986). Mapping involves first, noticing a shared system of relations which hold in both source and target domains; and, second, placing objects from the two domains into correspondence with one another, based on common roles in the shared relational structure. In this way, reasoners can begin with a partial mapping of components which play similar roles, and later extend the mapping in order to import novel inferences from the source domain to the target.

Lakoff (Lakoff & Johnson, 1980; Lakoff, 1986) has demonstrated the generative capacity which these sorts of metaphoric mappings entail for language. Early work pointed to the pervasive and systematic nature of entrenched metaphoric mappings in everyday language, while later work has focused on the identification of idealized cognitive models (ICMs) which are mapped from the source domain to the target and the role which these ICMs play in reasoning about the target domain. Mapping is generative because linguistic constructions (lexical items, syntactic constructions, idiomatic expressions, etc.) used to describe the source domain can also be imported to describe the target domain. Moreover, inferences generated by schemas in the source domain can, after mapping, be generated by shared schemas in the target domain.

A key emphasis in mapping research, then, involves the implications which conceptual structure in the source domain have for the way in which the target domain will be conceptualized. Analogical or metaphoric mapping is chiefly done to structure a less well- understood target domain by importing schemas from a better-understood source domain. Occasionally, however, mapping is done purely to highlight a schema which is shared by both the source and the target domains.

Gentner, for example, contrasts it pure matching, mapping which occurs when the learner has knowledge of both domains, to it pure carryover, mapping which occurs when the learner is quite familiar with the source domain, but has little knowledge of the target. In carry-over, mapping systems of relations from the source to the target serves to produce novel information about the target domain. In pure matching, analogical mapping serves only to focus attention on the matching systems rather than to convey new knowledge.

4.1   Menendez Brothers Virus

However, the nature of the analogical mapping in the Menendez Brothers Virus is such that it undermines the distinction between matching and carry-over analogies. The point of mapping in the MBV example is neither to produce novel information about the target domain, nor to point to pre-existing similarities between the source and the target. Rather, the purpose of the mappings employed in computer virus jokes is to highlight a particular construal of the source domain.

This occurs in two ways: first, by importing one particular framing of the source domain into the blended domain; and, second, by projecting structure from a well-developed blended domain back onto the source. The blended joke space imports a framing of the source domain which accentuates the degree to which the Menendez brothers profited from their actions. Recall that the framing of the (real) Menendez brothers' actions in the source space was itself quite controversial . Besides being televised on Court TV, the brothers' trial was the subject of countless news reports, several books, and no less than three made-for-TV movies. Moreover, the outcome of the trial was a hung jury. At the center of the controversy was the issue of who played the role of the evil agents, and who the role of innocent victims. Below we sketch two contrasting framings of the Menendez brothers' affair: the first is labeled the conspiracy framing, the second is dubbed the victim framing.

- *Conspiracy Framing*

    1. Brothers plan to acquire parents' possessions by committing homicide.

    2. Brothers shoot parents and inherit their possessions.

    3. When arrested, claim long-term physical and sexual abuse as a mitigating factor.

- *Victim Framing*

    1. Kitty and Jose Menendez physically, sexually, and psychologically abuse their two sons.

    2. Brothers sense imminent escalation of parents' abuse.

    3. Brothers shoot parents in self-defense.

In order to further appreciate the extent to which the Menendez Brothers Virus joke involves a controversial framing of the source domain, one need only constrast the sequence of events stated explicitly in the joke with other possible sequences, given the same sort of mapping. The sequence in the MBV joke involves:

    (i) Elimination of files;

    (ii) Taking of disk space;

    (iii) Claim of physical and sexual abuse.

However, consider the following alternative 'joke' which employs a different mapping of relations from the source.

MENENDEZ BROTHERS VIRUS DOPPELGANGER:

Suffers for many years of physical and sexual abuse from the .com files on your hard drive; finally decides to get revenge and escape abuse by deleting the offending files.

Whereas in the original MBV scenario, the claim is an excuse whose validity was questionable, the same claim in the MBVD scenario serves as a justification whose validity is taken for granted. In the MBV scenario, the brothers themselves are framed in an agentive manner as agents motivated by greed. By contrast, the MBVD scenario frames the Menendez brothers as victims of their circumstances, motivated by fear, revenge, and/or self-defense. Thus the original joke relies upon the conspiracy framing of the source domain in which the Menendez brothers are (agentive) greedy conspirators in pursuit of their parents' multi-million dollar home and attendant riches.

Moreover, this framing of the source space is reinforced in the joke space by background knowledge imported from the target domain. Computer viruses are customarily construed as agentive and never as victims. Moreover, the suggestion that a computer virus could be the victim of physical and/or sexual abuse is patently absurd. The absurdity of the claim in the target domain thus reinforces the framing of the claim in the source domain as a highly questionable excuse.

Although the initial structuring of the blended space was quite consonant with the target domain of computer viruses (viruses often delete files, occupy disk space, and even have colorful names such as the Menendez Brothers Virus), the structure contributed by the social source domain is incoherent with respect to the technical target. The mapping in this instance cannot be said to structure the target domain. Nor can it be said to point to pre-existing similarities between the source and the target. While one might sensibly argue that the sequence of elimination of files/parents and subsequent confiscation of disk space/property is a pre-existing similarity, it is much harder to maintain the same for the virus's/brothers' claim of physical and sexual abuse.

The notion of an abused computer virus (in the sense intended) is incoherent in the target domain, and fantastic in the blended domain. The possibility of an abused virus arises only in the blended space where it enjoys a short-lived existence, confined to local purposes, forever forbidden access to the target domain of real computer viruses. However, its access is not similarly forbidden to the source domain. In particular, the inference that the virus's claim is ridiculous and false gets transferred back to the source domain where it triggers a similar inference for the MBV's source counterparts.

At this point, one might question why the MBVD joke, which imports the Victim Framing into the blend, does not project the construal of the Menendez brothers as innocent victims back onto the source. This is because the coherence of the blended domain ultimately depends upon how well the particular framing imported from the source resonates with the logic of the target space. In the case of the MBV joke, the construal of computer viruses as agentive reinforces the Conspiracy Framing which has been imported into the blend; however, in the case of the MBVD joke, the agentive construal of computer viruses actually undermines the Victim Framing imported into the blend. Consequently, the blended domain built to understand the MBV joke is structured in such a way as to promote the transfer of inference schemas regarding linked elements in the blend and the source. However, the blended domain built to understand the MBVD joke provides a context which makes the imported Victim Framing appear implausible. Besides blocking transfer of schemas, this might be why the MBVD joke is less funny.

5   Conclusions

The point of the mappings in the virus jokes is not to provide structure for the target domain – as in the conventional account of analogical mapping – but rather to highlight one particular construal of the source domain, perhaps over competing construals. According to traditional accounts of analogy, these virus jokes constitute instances of pure matching analogies. On the conventional accounts, the analogical mapping which occurs in the computer virus jokes would contrast with the sort of analogies deemed useful for problem solving (viz. that of the pure carry- over analogy), falling instead into the category of pure matching.

However, if we take seriously the import of accepting one framing of the source domain over other competing framings, then we must realize that the nature of the framing/construal process undermines any sharp distinction between matching and carry-over analogy. Because the mapping operation involves integrated frames as opposed to isolated predicates, the choice of one particular framing over another necessarily results in a different set of attendant inferences. Even in the pure matching cases, then, the choice of exactly which similarities are highlighted by the mapping has inferential ramifications.

The blending which occurs in the MBV joke is not isolated to jokes, but rather occurs in meaning construction more generally. The fantastic world of jokes such as the MBV often present clear instances of phenomena such as asymmetric mapping and conceptual blending. Just as the psychophycisist investigating vision concentrates on visual illusions in order to better elucidate the processes which underlie normal, veridical visual processing, the cognitive semanticist often concentrates on verbal flourishes to better elucidate the processes which underlie normal language processing.

Although the virus we examined is not real, people do employ names such as the Menendez Brothers Virus to serve ends which we usually talk about in the context of analogical mapping[1]. For example, suppose a Menendez Brothers Virus really did exist. We might use the name MBV in order to quickly access one of the schemas associated with the Menendez Brothers from our long term memory, and thereby quickly convey the nature of this particular virus's activities. However, independent of any functional utility the mapping might serve in the target domain, a blend of this nature will nonetheless reinforce the existence of a particular construal of the source domain.

We suggest that the emphasis in traditional accounts of analogical and metaphoric mapping on the mappings from source to target is a by-product of the examples of analogy and metaphor which have traditionally been examined. If your purpose in drawing an analogy is to map schemas from a well-defined source onto an ill-defined target, then it makes perfect sense to map schemas from the source to the target with minimal (or no) alteration in the blend. If, however, your purpose in metaphoric or analogical mapping is to say something nasty about the source domain, then it might make more sense to map schemas from the blend into the source.

There is nothing inherent to the process of analogical mapping which mandates mapping from the source to the target. The ability to link counterparts across disparate domains based on shared relational schemas is a fundamental cognitive process. Moreover, the mapping of inference schemas and the conceptual integration which can occur in the blend are similarly basic abilities which we actively exploit to suit our needs. Ultimately, it is the purpose of the mapping which determines the direction of the inference schema transfer.

Overall, one might question what it means to say that the source

---

[1] Viruses are often given colorful names by computer users based on the nature of the disruption they cause to the infected system. For example, the Stoned virus relocates and overwrites the PC's boot sector and partition table, and writes itself to floppies which are inserted into the drive. On startup, the infected computer will display the message, "Your PC is now Stoned."

domain structures the target in analogical and metaphoric mappings. For example, in the Menendez Brothers Virus joke, the source domain of the Menendez Brothers has been used to structure the target domain of computer viruses. The end result is to anthropomorphize the computer virus as an entity which commits crimes, and which feels the need to create excuses to escape responsibility and censure. Does the use of social schemas (take, for example, that associated with responsibility) to generate inferences about a technical target imply some sort of deep connection between conceptual structure in the social and target domains?

The blended spaces framework employed in the explication of the Menendez Brothers Virus joke suggests that the answer to this question is *no, not necessarily.* The blended space, like any other mental space, involves representations in working memory which are exploited in on-line interpretation of discourse. Thus the fact that shared schemas are exploited temporarily in the blended space need not have any ramifications for the organization of general knowledge in long- term memory. The conceptual integration which occurs in blended spaces may be used to form new concepts, or it might just as likely be employed to generate a disposable concept for some local, often rhetorical, purpose.

6   References

Chien, Phillip and Robert Bixby. (1993). The great virus scare. *Compute* 15:70-72.

Fauconnier, G. 1994. *Mental Spaces.* Cambridge, UK: Cambridge University Press.

Fauconnier, G. and M. Turner. 1994. Conceptual projection and middle spaces. La Jolla, CA: Cognitive science technical report 9401.

Gentner, D. 1982. Are scientific analogies metaphors? In D.S. Miall, ed. *Metaphor: Problems and perspectives.* Brighton, Sussex: Harvester Press.

Gentner, D. 1983. Structure-mapping: A theoretical framework for analogy. *Cognitive Science* 7, 155-170.

Gentner, D., and Donald Gentner. 1983. Flowing waters or teeming crowds: Mental models of electricity. In D. Gentner and A.L.. Stevens, eds. *Mental models*, 99-130. Hillsdale, N.J.: Lawrence Erlbaum.

Gentner, D., and A. L. Stevens, eds. 1983. *Mental models.* Hillsdale, N. J. : Lawrence Erlbaum.

Gick,M.L., and K.J. Holyoak. 1980. Analogical problem solving. *Cognitive Psychology* 12, 306-355.

Gick, M.L., and Holyoak, K.J. 1983. Schema induction and analogical transfer. *Cognitive Psychology* 15, 1-38.

Hofstadter, D.R. 1985. *Metamagical themas.* New York: Basic Books.

Holland, J.H., Holyoak, K.J., Nisbett, R.E., and Thagard, P.R. 1986. *Induction: Processes of inference learning and discovery.* Cambridge, MA: MIT Press.

Lakoff, G., and Johnson, M. 1980. *Metaphors we live by.* Chicago: University of Chicago Press.

Lakoff, G. 1987. *Women, fire, and dangerous things.* Chicago: University of Chicago Press.

Suls, Jerry. 1977. Cognitive and disparagement theories of humour: A theoretical and empirical synthesis. In Anthony J. Chapman and Hugh C. Foot., eds., *It's a funny thing, humour,* 11-30. Oxford: Pergamon Press.

Conditionals, Distancing, and Alternative Spaces

BARBARA DANCYGIER & EVE SWEETSER
University of California, Berkeley

1. Introduction.

There have been at least two quite distinct strands of research on the meaning and use of conditional forms, a logical strand and a pragmatic one. Philosophers and formal semanticists have seen *if-then* constructions as reflecting logical semantic structures such as material implication, or more recently as describing possible worlds; pragmatic analysts, on the other hand, have been interested in the ways that conditional forms reflect non-logical structures such as hedging on the social conditions of speech act appropriateness. Meanwhile, of course, descriptive and prescriptive grammarians have continued to tell students how to use correct verb forms in conditional constructions: one should say, *If it rains, they'll cancel the game* in English, rather than *If it will rain, they'll cancel the game.* In this paper, we bring together these divided aspects of the understanding of English conditionals, within a framework which we hope will be useful also to the analysis of similar constructions in other languages.

Specifically, we will argue that the framework of mental spaces (Fauconnier 1985/1994, in press) allows us to capture generalizations about both the logical and pragmatic aspects of conditional meaning. At the same time, a constructional analysis of conditional forms (cf. Fillmore 1990)[1] allows us to describe formal parameters such as choice of verb forms, and to map those formal choices directly onto semantic and functional aspects of conditional constructions.

---

[1] See Fillmore 1988 and Fillmore, Kay and O'Connor 1988 for exposition of the Construction Grammar framework.

We begin, then, with the idea that an *if*-clause sets up a *mental space* in Fauconnier's sense: a partial or local model of some aspect of mental content, in this case very possibly a model of some situation in the world, or (as we shall see) of some speech-act interaction or some reasoning process.[2] Mental spaces are different from possible worlds in a number of respects, most importantly in that they are not objective in nature, nor necessarily describable in terms of Boolean truth conditions; and also in being local rather than global. The claim that I set up a mental space in *If John had come to the meeting, I'd be happier* crucially does not mean that I'd be happier in a world just like the current one (complete with famines, wars, and AIDS); but neither does it mean that I have envisioned some definite better world in these global respects. I am simply concerning myself only with a limited bit of the world's structure, in setting up this alternative imagined state of affairs: I set up a space in which John came to the meeting, and other local structure (such as the time, place and other participants) probably remains the same. My reasoning does not take global issues into account.

2. Prediction and Reasoning.

One of the most important reasons for setting up mental spaces is to imagine alternatives: in a mental space where we imagine rain happening tomorrow, what do we imagine resulting from the rain? (Will the planned tennis game be cancelled? Or will it be played in the rain?) These imagined futures, and their imagined unfolding continuations, constitute the basis for an important human activity: *prediction* (cf. Dancygier 1993). If we never engaged in prediction, in the construction of (and commitment to) some future scenarios as more likely than others, we could never make decisions or take action at all.

Some predictions may be based on certainties: in saying, *When morning comes, it'll be light again*, we do not consider mental spaces wherein there won't be a morning. Fillmore (1990) remarks that *when* involves a *positive epistemic stance* towards the content on the part of the speaker. But perhaps the most interesting predictions are those that are based on alternatives: for example, an imagined rainfall tomorrow might allow us to predict cancellation of the tennis game, while some other state of affairs would have allowed us to predict some other result. In a sense, a prediction not based on alternatives is less valuable than an alternative-based one, even if it is true: it does not help us set up plans of action, or to choose ways of responding to events and situations, in the way that we are helped by comparing alternatives.

---

[2] cf. Sweetser (in press a) for a discussion of mental space structures and conditionality.

   A predictive conditional, then, sets up a correlation of parameters which structures alternative mental spaces. *If it rains tomorrow, they'll cancel the game* sets up two alternate mental spaces (both interpreted as potential futures of the speaker's Base space): one wherein it rains and they cancel the game, and another wherein it doesn't rain and they don't cancel the game (see Diagram 1, below).

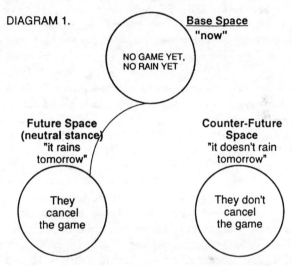

DIAGRAM 1.

Base Space
"now"

NO GAME YET,
NO RAIN YET

Future Space
(neutral stance)
"it rains
tomorrow"

Counter-Future
Space
"it doesn't rain
tomorrow"

They
cancel
the game

They don't
cancel
the game

"If it rains tomorrow, they'll cancel the game."

The essence of predictiveness is the correlation (here, between rain and game-cancelling) which allows conditional prediction of one event based on knowledge about the other. Normally, speakers and hearers assume a causal structure behind such a correlation: two events correlated with each other this strongly are correlated because of a causal relationship. This means that prediction normally invites a hearer to imagine what models of the world would lead the speaker to believe in the correlation mentioned in a conditional utterance. For example, in this case, the hearer might share with the speaker a belief that rain normally causes tennis matches to be canceled, and draw on this causal model to explain the correlation as part of a more general, causally motivated correlation with which he is already familiar. In this sense, prediction brings along a causal model into the speaker's and hearer's mental space structure.[3]

---

[3] Not all causal models involve direct causation of the event in the main clause by the event

This explains why predictive conditionals are normally interpreted as having "iff" or biconditional structures. Notice that the mental spaces in question are partially structured entities. Thus, if I tell you that *If it rains tomorrow, they'll cancel the game*, I really do mean "and if it doesn't, they won't" - in the limited world-structuring provided by these spaces. I am not concerned with the fact that they might also cancel the game if one of the two singles tennis players became ill - although I know that that is also true. And I don't even mean that conditions won't change, forcing players to play in the rain because of new regulations from the Tennis Association. If this happened (*after* my utterance), my uttered conditional prediction would still have been "true" (a valid prediction) at the time of utterance. Of course, it is true that a speaker or hearer can dream up many different causal scenarios which bring about the same result. Even if it does not rain, other things may cause the game to be cancelled: there may be an earthquake which destroys the town where the game is to take place, the authorities in charge of the game may change the schedule or the rules, or a comet could collide with the Earth. But in saying *If it rains tomorrow, they'll cancel the game*, a speaker is not considering those possible chains of events, rather she is considering the possibility of rain in contrast with the possibility of non-rain. The "iff" reasoning structure which normally seems to prevail in such cases (that is, the speaker seems to mean that the game will *only* be cancelled if it rains) is not a logical property of the formal semantics of the conditional sentence: if it were, one could not continue by saying something like *Of course, if it snows, they'll also cancel it.* However, the properties of mental space construction ensure that the IFF interpretation will be the normal one, since speakers and hearers will construct a minimally altered mental space, adjusting it locally as directed by the content of the *if* clause.[4]

Naturally, one of the two spaces is set up more saliently and directly than the other. In our example, this is the rain space, rather than the non-rain space. But neither *If it rains, they'll cancel the game* nor *If it doesn't rain, they won't cancel the game* is a reasonable mental-space-structuring

---

described in the *if*-clause: other relationships, such as enablement (*If I get funding, I'll go to the conference*), are also included in our understanding of causal models of the world and causal relationships between events.

[4] It is interesting to note that in fact, even when speakers consider multiple possible conditional causal scenarios, they do not do so cumulatively, but alternatively. Thus, a speaker who says, *If it rains, they'll cancel the game* and adds, *If there's an earthquake they'll cancel it too*, and *If there's a hurricane they'll cancel it too* is nonetheless not taken to be envisioning a world wherein rain, earthquake and hurricane all happen together, but three alternative possible scenarios, each of which has one of the same results. (Cf. Grice 1978, Karttunen and Peters 1979 for further discussion of some of the kinds of implicature structures which have been proposed to account for interpretations of conditionals).

utterance without the presence of both possible future spaces. We will be arguing that certain grammatical forms are characteristic of conditionals used in this way, to make predictions of this kind.

In particular, the apparently "past-tense" verb forms which are sometimes called *counterfactual* in English conditionals are limited to conditional sentences with two characteristics: (1) they are predictive, in the sense defined above, and (2) they are also treated by the speaker as unlikely predictions: they express a rejected future scenario, rather than the chosen alternative. Fillmore (1990) refers to this as taking a *negative epistemic stance* towards the content of the conditional. The speaker of *If it rained tomorrow, they'd cancel the game* thus takes a negative stance towards the mental space wherein rain occurs, while the non-past form in *If it rains* takes a *neutral* stance (see Diagram 2).[5]

DIAGRAM 2.

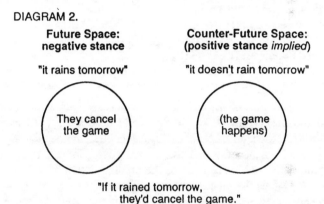

Future Space:
negative stance

"it rains tomorrow"

They cancel
the game

Counter-Future Space:
(positive stance *implied*)

"it doesn't rain tomorrow"

(the game
happens)

"If it rained tomorrow,
they'd cancel the game."

(Note: The favored scenario is the one *not* referred to, with a
game and no rain.)

We will use the term *distanced* verb forms to refer to these "past" (or

---

[5] We are unwilling to use the term *counterfactual* because it seems clear that such conditionals are by no means restricted to genuinely counterfactual uses; cf. Comrie's (1986) discussion of examples such as *If you got me a cup of coffee, I'd be very grateful.* We should note that the distanced verb forms used in conditional protases also occur in certain other environments marking negative epistemic stance (Fillmore 1990): *I hope I have enough money to go to the conference,* but *I wish I had enough money to go to the conference.*

It should also be noted that the "past tense" of negative stance and the past tense of temporal reference are not mutually exclusive. An example like the following apparently involves setting up a predictive relationship between the two clauses of the conditional construction, and taking a negative epistemic stance towards the whole. Since the whole is situated in the past, and therefore the speaker might be assumed to know the actual outcome of the "subjunctive") forms which mark the speaker's understanding that the conditional space is one towards which he or she has a negative epistemic stance, in contrast to some alternate conditional scenario towards which speaker stance is more positive. (Fleischman [1989] argues persuasively that there is a crosslinguistic connection between past tense form and various kinds of distancing, including epistemic distancing and "counterfactuality.") In order for a distanced form to be possible, there must not only be alternate scenarios, but the structure of the conditional must be the structure of the predictive relations that set up those scenarios.[6]

Thus far, we have only mentioned conditionals in which the two clauses describe (and indeed refer to) events or states of affairs in the world, and there is a causal relationship between those events or states. However, this is clearly not the case with all conditional sentences. Let us compare some examples:

(1) If Martin misses another staff meeting, he'll be fired.
(2) If Martin missed another staff meeting, he would be fired.
(3) If you're so smart, when was George Washington born?
(4) If he typed her thesis, (then) he loves her.
(5) My ex-husband, if that's the right word for him, was seen in Vegas last
    week.   (The divorce isn't final till next week.)

(1) and (2) are examples of the kind already discussed: Martin missing the staff meeting will cause his firing, in the world described. (1) leaves the speaker's attitude towards that mental space neutral, while (2) adopts a negative epistemic stance towards the mental space defined by Martin's missing the meeting, and hence towards the prediction that he will be fired. Sweetser (1990) labels these **content** level conditionals, because the dependency between the two clauses is at the level of the contents: the events described are in a causal and conditional relationship with each other. (3), however, is structured quite differently. *If you're so smart* bears no causal relationship to anything about George Washington's birth; rather the

---

scenario, the use of negative-stance verb forms is taken to mean counterfactuality.

(a) If Martin had missed another meeting, he would have been fired.

The pluperfect here is the result of superimposing negative epistemic stance on simple past reference, creating the need for a double layering of tense marking.

[6] It is worth noting, although we will not here discuss it further, that the "backshifting" of tense involved in the use of "present for future" in *if*-clauses is also specific to predictive structure: it occurs in *when*-clauses as well as in predictive conditional protases:

(a) If she arrives (#will arrive), we'll eat dinner together.
(b) When she arrives (#will arrive), we'll eat dinner together.

It appears to be characteristic, among other places, of backgrounds to prediction. For discussion of this backshifting, see Dancygier 1993.

speaker's assumption that the interlocutors have agreed on the addressee's smartness is in turn the justification for the speech act of asking the question about George Washington's birth. Such examples have been labelled *speech act conditionals* (Van der Auwera 1986, Sweetser 1990). In particular, it is important to note that (3) is not *predicting* either George Washington's birth or the act of asking questions about it; instead, it is conditionally performing the act of questioning.

Parallel problems arise with examples such as (4) and (5). Perhaps the likeliest interpretation of (4) can be glossed as "If I know (or believe) that he typed her thesis, then I can conclude that he loves her." This interpretation does not involve the typing (content of the *if*-clause) being construed as a cause of the loving (content of the *then*-clause). If anything, we prefer the opposite construal of the relationship between the contents of the clauses: perhaps he typed it because he loves her. But the causal relationship between the speaker's belief states is one wherein the knowledge about the typing causes or enables the conclusion about the loving. Sweetser (1990) labels such examples *epistemic conditionals*. Finally, in (5), there is no causal relationship between the choice of a "right word" (to refer to the husband who will be finally divorced from me next week, but isn't yet) and the event of his being seen in Las Vegas; the causal relationship, if any, is between the belief about rightness and the use of the single word *husband*. Dancygier (1986, 1992) and Sweetser (1990) refer to such cases as *metalinguistic* conditionals.[7]

With content conditionals, the story is fairly simple. The speaker sets up a hypothetical world or space wherein the protasis holds, and claims that the apodosis should also hold. Thus, *If it rains, they'll cancel the game*, predicts that the cancelling of the game will happen in the hypothetical future mental space where the rain happens. The *claim* of such a sentence is not that it will rain or that they will cancel the game, but that there is a predictive relationship between the two events. Such "neutral" epistemic stance examples don't allow me to decide whether or not the speaker has explicit other options in mind. Here, it seems likely from the content that the speaker thinks that the game will not be cancelled in a non-rainy world.

A distanced form such as *If it rained, they would cancel the game* brings the unexpressed alternate option into more prominence by clearly showing that the speaker doesn't think the described future world matches the real future. The more likely future world, then, must be the alternate conditional scenario, equally structured by the predictiveness defined above.

---

[7] Jespersen (1940) was, we believe, the first to remark on such usages of conditional forms.

DIAGRAM 3.   Metalinguistic: full alternative spaces
"If we were speaking Spanish, he'd be your uncle."

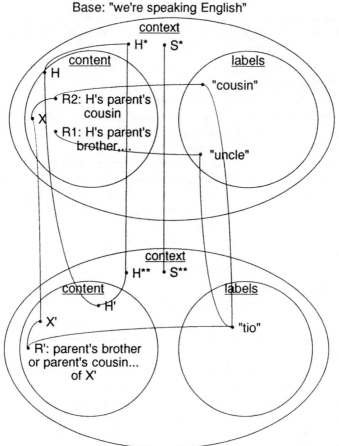

R1, R2, R' are *roles*.
H, H*, S *, H**, S**, H', X, X' are *individuals*;
use of the same letter to refer, e.g. to H, H*, H',
and H** indicates that the individuals referred to
are *counterparts* of each other in different spaces.

Content-level conditionals are not the only ones which engage in prediction based on alternative spaces. A metalinguistic space is a complex space consisting of a pairing of a content space and a language or code space. Certain metalinguistic conditionals (though not all) really set up two separate complete metalinguistic spaces - that is, two separate pairs of content and linguistic spaces, with independent mappings between them. Each context space includes a Speaker (S) and a Hearer (H), as well as the content and label spaces with which S and H are concerned. As well as *individuals* (such as S, H, and the unnamed X in Diagram 3), mental spaces include *roles*, such as *President*, or *S's father's brother*. In examples like *If we were speaking Spanish, he would be your uncle* (see Diagram 3), there is an English-speaking content-space where events of usage proceed in one way (the "base" space, the speaker's interpreted reality) and a corresponding space of English labels; let us say that the relative in question is actually the addressee's father's cousin, and the speaker knows that the role of parent's cousins standardly takes the label *cousin*, not *uncle*, in her English dialect. Contrasting with this pairing of spaces, there is a Spanish-speaking content-space where events of usage occur in another way, and are mapped onto a corresponding space of Spanish language labels: the speaker here imagines that the role of father's cousin receives the Spanish label *tio*, also used for a parent's brother. Both of these spaces are structured by predictive type relationships: on the basis of the correlation between language and labels, I can use the language being spoken as a basis for predicting the choice of labels.[8]

In other cases, however, metalinguistic conditionals do not set up two full alternate metalinguistic spaces. In *My ex-husband, if that's the right word for him, was seen in Vegas last week* (Diagram 4), there are not two separate content spaces (a space wherein that is the right word and he was seen in Vegas, and another wherein it's the wrong word and he was not seen in Vegas). No matter what the choice of words may be, the speaker intends to convey unconditionally that the man referred to was seen in Vegas. Only the judgement of vocabulary appropriateness allows for possible alternate scenarios - and even that is more of a comment on the speaker's part, rather than a serious attempt to evoke hypothetical states of affairs at any level (alternate choices of label for this role might include "husband" as opposed to "ex-husband"). The most we could say in constructing alternatives here would be that the speaker expresses an

---

[8] We are not here dealing with another interpretation of this example, the one where the speaker could mean that she thinks that in a Spanish-speaking world, *social relationships* between the hearer and his father's cousin or uncle or friend would be different, causing different labels to be chosen. This reading seems to involve a much closer, more unified cultural space, where relationships *and* labels are co-present in a single space.

essentially unconditional content and allows for an alternate way of expressing that content. There is surely no way in which the apodosis material is dependent on, predictable from, or caused by the protasis material, since the former operates at the content level and the latter at the metalinguistic level. Since there are neither two full alternate spaces, nor are the expressed claims predictive ones, it is natural that there is no "distanced" equivalent of this example.

DIAGRAM 4.   Metalinguistic: NOT full alternative spaces

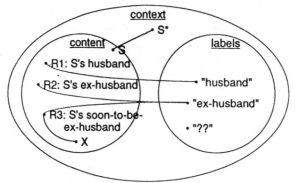

(X was seen in Vegas last week, and X and S are in the process of getting divorced.)

"My ex-husband, if that's the right word for him, was seen in Vegas last week."

Epistemic conditionals often resist distanced forms, but it is possible to get acceptable epistemic interpretations of some examples with distanced verb forms, e.g. *If she had taken only a one-hour oral, she'd be in the entering class of 1980* (Diagram 5). The example in Diagram 5 seems acceptable in a context where we assume that we just looked at her file, discovered that she had taken the 3-hour oral exam required of all students entering in 1981 or later, and deduced that she entered in 1981 (we had been debating whether she entered in '80 or '81). In such an example, the speaker is precisely setting up a scenario where the interlocutors discover that the student took a one-hour oral, and conclude that she entered in 1980; further, the speaker takes a negative stance towards this scenario, and a positive stance towards an alternate reasoning scenario. Both of these scenarios are predictive: that is, from the speaker's hypothesized discovery, or believed premise, she predicts the conclusion that she is likely to reach.

Although premises and conclusions don't stand in a causal relationship in most logicians' theories, it is clear that people's models of human minds see them as causally related, and base predictions precisely on such a causal theory of mind.

DIAGRAM 5.   EPISTEMICS

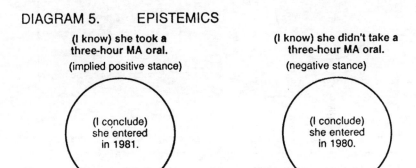

(I know) she took a
three-hour MA oral.

(implied positive stance)

(I conclude)
she entered
in 1981.

(I know) she didn't take a
three-hour MA oral.

(negative stance)

(I conclude)
she entered
in 1980.

"If she had taken only a one-hour oral, she'd be
in the entering class of 1980."

Interestingly, not all epistemic conditionals readily allow distanced interpretation, and most of the interpretations of such examples seem very hard to contextualize. Why should this be so? The answer lies again in the degree of genuine hypothetical space-building involved, and in the question of whether the conditional is really "about" the predictive relationship or about the expressed content of the clauses. A speaker who says, *If he typed her thesis, then he loves her* (Diagram 6), is most likely to be using this utterance to centrally express the conclusion that he loves her, and indeed may be doing so in a performative way: "I hereby conclude this, as I speak." The protasis content is evoked mostly as an explanation to the hearer for the speaker's behavior, or as a link to the context (perhaps it was the hearer who claimed that he typed her thesis). Rather than building a new mental space, it may evoke an already established one (a common assumption about the thesis-typing); and in any case, such a usage does not involve setting up alternatives or imagining worlds where the evoked background is not true.

DIAGRAM 6.   EPISTEMICS

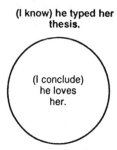

(I know) he typed her thesis.

(I conclude) he loves her.

"If he typed her thesis, then he loves her."

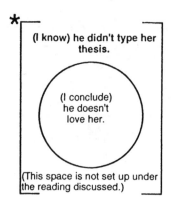

(I know) he didn't type her thesis.

(I conclude) he doesn't love her.

(This space is not set up under the reading discussed.)

In such an epistemic conditional, the central content is certainly not the conditional relationship itself: although the speaker might be willing to explicitly say "yes, thesis-typing is evidence for someone being in love," that is not the issue. Unlike *If it rains, they'll cancel the game*, where neither clause is asserted, but only the relationship, here the speaker is essentially asserting the apodosis and contextualizing that assertion by evoking the protasis and laying out the conditional relationship. Not surprisingly, such conditionals don't have distanced forms. They neither focus on predictive relations, nor genuinely bring up two alternative predictive scenarios in the relevant (epistemic) domain. They may in fact be more common than the distanceable (predictive) epistemic conditionals, perhaps because epistemic conditionals are really mostly used to contextualize newly asserted conclusions, rather than to compare reasoning scenarios at a truly meta-epistemic level. They still involve mental space structure: the *if*-clause still sets out a mental space (perhaps evoked rather than built), and hence the use of the conditional construction is appropriate. In many respects, then, we are adopting Haiman's (1978) point of view that conditionals are topics: one reason for using a space-builder is precisely to contextualize by indicating which already-available information is the background to what is being said.[9] The distanced verb forms, which belong to the domain of prediction rather than just to space-structure in general, are

---

[9] Traugott's (1985) observation that there is a crosslinguistic historical connection between conditional markers and topic markers is further evidence for the importance of the topic function in conditional meaning.

inappropriate for such use, and therefore not interpretable in such a context.

Speech-act conditionals almost never comfortably allow distanced verb forms, and this is also natural once we consider their normally non-predictive functions. In *If you need help, my name is Jeanie*, the speaker asserts the "apodosis" (or rather, engages in the speech act it represents) and contextualizes it with the protasis, which is an evoked and shared context (in this respect speech-act conditionals are similar to the epistemics just discussed above). There is no predictive relationship: not only does the speaker say that her name is Jeanie no matter what the hearer needs in the way of help, but her name *is* Jeanie no matter what. Performative status almost prohibits such a relationship, since (however hedged), a word once said really is said, and a speech act performed is performed. There are no alternate scenarios in the speech-act world here (although there may be some playing on scenario structure - politeness may once have consisted in pretense that you would "take back" an unacceptable protasis speech-act). The speaker just accesses a context in which it is possible that the hearer may need help (or, in the original Austin [1961] example *If you're hungry, there are biscuits on the sideboard*, a context in which he may be hungry), and sets it up as the background to an utterance. With no alternative scenarios or predictive relations between clause contents, there is no basis for marking distance.[10]

3. Conclusions.

The model we have presented treats *if* as a "space-builder" which sets up or evokes a mental space, with respect to which the main clause is understood. The spaces constructed with *if* are marked as not involving positive epistemic stance, but do not tell a listener whether the speaker's stance to the space is negative or merely neutral. In English, choice of verb forms marks negative versus neutral epistemic stance, for predictive conditionals.

Prediction is here treated (following Dancygier 1993) as a central function of conditionals: speakers often use conditional forms to express the relationship between alternative scenarios of events, and the correlated events which are predicted to result from the posited scenario. The importance of this function may to some extent explain the feeling of many speakers that the content predictive conditionals are somehow "basic" or

---

[10] Gilles Fauconnier points out to us that a parent leaving a babysitter in charge of children might say *If you needed any help, the emergency number would be 911*, as well as *If you need any help, the emergency number is 911*. In such a case, the speaker seems indeed to be distancing the whole performance of the informative speech act, and it is possible that it is a genuine predictive speech act conditional.

"good" examples of conditionals. However, *if*-clauses may engage in space building either as a basis for prediction (setting up alternative spaces and comparing scenarios), or simply for purposes of contextualization. In the latter case, normally the speaker's epistemic stance is not specifically marked, and in any case it is impossible to use the verb forms which indicate marked (negative) epistemic stance. The commonality between the more "logical" kinds of conditionals and the more "pragmatic" ones, then, lies precisely in their neutral space-building function, while the differences surface in divergent patterns of verb morphology connected with more specific functions.

Clausal connectives such as *if* are by no means alone in having a semantics involving mental space structure. Fauconnier (1985/1994, in press) has argued that such pervasive grammatical markers as definite and indefinite articles are equally engaged in mental-space construction. Fauconnier and Sweetser (in press) presents a set of studies of grammatical marking of mental space structure; Sweetser (in press [b]) suggests that the choice of a lexical or periphrastic predicate may also be one of the space-structuring grammatical markers. From these and other current work (such as Van Hoek 1992), set-up and structuring of mental spaces appears to be a central component of our production and interpretation of linguistic forms; it is therefore no surprise that grammatical markers and constructions often explicitly indicate aspects of mental space structure. The *If P, (then) Q* construction itself has been treated as a space-builder since Fauconnier 1985/1994, and the choice of verb forms to indicate epistemic stance fills a function similar to that proposed by Fauconnier for the French subjunctive. The point to be made here is that an analysis which treats these constructions as having mental-space semantics can make generalizations which would otherwise be missed about the use of the constructions, and about restrictions on their use.

References

Austin, John L. 1961. Ifs and Cans. In J. L. Austin, *Philosophical Papers*, eds. J. O. Urmson & G. J. Warnock (3rd edition, 1979), 153-180. Oxford: Oxford University Press.

Comrie, Bernard. 1986. Conditionals: a Typology. In Elizabeth Closs Traugott *et al.* eds., 77-99.

Dancygier, Barbara. 1986. Two Metalinguistic Operators in English and Polish. Paper presented at the Language Acquisition Research Symposium in Utrecht.

Dancygier, Barbara. 1992. Two Metatextual Operators: Negation and Conditionality in English and Polish. In *Proceedings of the Eighteenth Annual Meeting of the Berkeley Linguistics Society*, 61-75. Berkeley Linguistics Society, University of California at Berkeley.

Dancygier, Barbara. 1993. Interpreting Conditionals: Time, Knowledge and Causation. *Journal of Pragmatics 19*, 403-434.

Fauconnier, Gilles. 1985/1994. *Mental Spaces*. 2nd ed., Cambridge, England: Cambridge University Press.

Fauconnier, Gilles. In press. *Cognitive Mappings for Language and Thought*. Cambridge: Cambridge University Press.

Fauconnier, Gilles and Eve Sweetser, eds. In press. *Spaces, Worlds and Grammars*. Chicago: University of Chicago Press.

Fillmore, Charles J. 1988. The Mechanisms of 'Construction Grammar'. In *Proceedings of the Fourteenth Annual Meeting of the Berkeley Linguistics Society*, 35-55. Berkeley Linguistics Society, University of California at Berkeley.

Fillmore, Charles. 1990. Epistemic Stance and Grammatical Form in English Conditional Sentences. In *Papers from the Twenty-sixth Regional Meeting of the Chicago Linguistic Society*, 137-162. Chicago Linguistic Society, University of Chicago.

Fillmore, Charles J., Paul Kay, and Mary Catherine O'Connor. 1988. Regularity and Idiomaticity in Grammatical Constructions: the Case of 'Let Alone'. *Language* 63:3, 501-38.

Fleischman, Suzanne. 1989. Temporal Distance: a Basic Linguistic Metaphor. *Studies in Language 13:1*, 1-50.

Grice, H. P. 1978. Further Notes on Logic and Conversation. In Peter Cole, ed., *Syntax and Semantics, Vol. 9: Pragmatics*, 113-127. New York: Academic Press.

Haiman, John. 1978. Conditionals are Topics. *Language 54:3*, 564-589.

Jespersen, Otto. 1940. *A Modern English Grammar on Historical Principles, V: Syntax*. London: George Allen and Unwin.

Karttunen, Lauri and Stanley Peters. 1979. Conventional implicature. In Choon-Koy Oh and David A. Dinneen, eds. *Syntax and semantics 11: Presupposition*, 1-56. New York: Academic Press.

Sweetser, Eve. 1990. *From Etymology to Pragmatics*. Cambridge: Cambridge University Press.

Sweetser, Eve. In press (a). Mental Spaces and the Grammar of Conditional Constructions. In Fauconnier and Sweetser, eds. (in press).

Sweetser, Eve. In press (b). Mental Spaces, Roles, and English Change Predicates. In Jan Nuyts and Eric Pederson, eds., *Language and Cognition*. Cambridge: Cambridge University Press.

Traugott, Elizabeth Closs. 1985. Conditional Markers. In John Haiman, ed., *Iconicity in Syntax*, 289-310. Amsterdam/Philadelphia: John Benjamins.

Traugott, Elizabeth Closs, Alice ter Meulen, Judy Snitzer Reilly and Charles A. Ferguson, eds. 1986. *On conditionals*. Cambridge: Cambridge University Press.

Van der Auwera, Johan. 1986. Conditionals and Speech Acts. In Elizabeth Closs Traugott *et al.*, eds., 197-214.

Van Hoek, Karen Ann. 1992. *Paths Through Conceptual Structure: Constraints on Anaphora*. Ph.D. dissertation, University of California at San Diego.

Viewpoint and the Definite Article

RICHARD EPSTEIN

University of California, San Diego

1. Introduction[1]

All utterances present conceptual content as construed from some point of view. Ordinarily, the point of view is that of the speaker, but viewpoints may be shifted, and even intermingled, between the speaker, the addressees, and third persons. Linguists have investigated the way viewpoint is expressed in language by such formal means as pronouns and reflexives (e.g., Kuroda 1973, Cantrall 1974, Kuno 1987, Zribi-Hertz 1989, van Hoek 1992, Kemmer, in press), and tense/aspect (e.g., Kamp and Rohrer 1983, Fleischman 1990, Cutrer 1994); see also Langacker (1993). The aim of this paper is to contribute to this literature by exploring the distinct viewpoints that may be conveyed through the use of the definite article in English. I shall argue that the most well-known uses of the definite article reflect the common viewpoint of both speaker and addressee, insofar as they share knowledge of the referent designated by a nominal with *the* (§2). Less well-known, though, are uses of *the* designating referents which speaker and addressee do not share knowledge of (numerous examples can be found in Epstein 1994a). For instance, *the* sometimes reflects the sole viewpoint of the speaker, when it serves as a marker of prominence (§3). In other situations, *the* reflects the viewpoint of neither the speaker nor the addressee, but rather, of a third person referent (§4). To date, little work has been done on the interaction between viewpoint and the definite article; more broadly, the data presented below are intended to show that felicitous use of *the* depends on a wider range of factors—both referential and expressive—than is usually acknowledged.

2. Referential Function of the Definite Article

Nearly all theories of definiteness treat the definite article as an essentially referential element. Although the terminology employed in this area varies considerably—*the* has been described as a marker of "uniqueness" (Russell 1905, Kadmon 1990, Hawkins 1991, Birner and Ward

---

[1] I would like to thank Suzanne Fleischman and Michael Israel for their extremely helpful comments on a previous draft of this paper. All remaining errors are my own responsibility.

1994), "identifiability" (Chafe 1976, Du Bois 1980), "familiarity" (Christophersen 1939, Heim 1982), *inter alia*—the basic intuitions underlying these analyses are remarkably parallel. There is wide agreement that the definite article serves a referential function, that is, to pick out entities (discourse referents) in the universe of discourse. More precisely, referential theories of definiteness claim that the speaker selects *the* only when he/she assumes that the hearer is able to uniquely identify the referent in question. The principal bases on which unique identifiability is established are reviewed in (1):

(1) a. I bought a book ... **the book** was interesting.
     b. We bought a used car, but **the motor** is brand new.
     c. Pass me **the hammer**, please.
     d. Did you see **the President** on TV last night?

In (1a), the referent of *the book* is uniquely identifiable to the hearer because this same book has been previously mentioned in the discourse. In (1b), although *the motor* has not yet been explicitly referred to, it is nonetheless uniquely identifiable via its association with the previously mentioned car, thanks to the stereotypical assumption, "all cars have a motor" (cf. the "Inferrables" of Prince 1981). Other cases in which a definite article is felicitous even without explicit previous mention of the referent are given in (1c) and (1d). In the former, the presence of the hammer in the deictic situation can give rise to unique identifiability (if, say, it is the sole hammer visible to both speech act participants). In the latter, background knowledge shared by all members of the social/cultural groups to which the speech act participants belong allows certain referents to be routinely uniquely identifiable (e.g., *the President, the sun,* etc.).

An important aspect of the referential function of *the* is its "hearer orientation": "the speaker when referring must constantly take into consideration knowledge of various kinds which he assumes his hearer to have ... If he fails to be sensitive to the hearer's assumed knowledge and the shared situation of utterance, communication will generally break down" (Hawkins 1978:97).[2] In other words, felicitous use of the definite article is contingent not only on the speaker's knowledge and (referential) intentions,

---

[2]   Compare: "Definite reference is an example par excellence of something speakers and listeners achieve through coordination" (Clark and Marshall 1981:26-27). Also: "definite description is inherently about knowledge by one mind of the knowledge of another mind" (Givón 1989:206).

but also, crucially, on the speaker's assessment of the *hearer's* knowledge of the referent. The hearer's ability to successfully pick out (uniquely identify) a referent stems from that knowledge, which is acquired through previous mention, deictic presence, culturally salient shared background assumptions, etc. (see above).

In order to relate these well-known facts about definite reference to work on viewpoint, I shall employ some of the basic concepts of mental space theory (see Fauconnier 1994, Cutrer 1994, and references therein), according to which the production and comprehension of discourse involves the construction of hierarchically organized and interconnected cognitive domains (mental spaces). The starting point, or origin, of any discourse is the "base" space. This space anchors the interpretation of all deictic, referential, and evaluative relations. Canonically, the base is identified with speaker reality, but as a discourse unfolds, alternate base spaces may be set up (representing hearer reality, that of a third person, etc.). Within any mental space configuration, there is always a "viewpoint" space, the space from which other spaces can be accessed. Viewpoint is "the center of conceptualization and consciousness of the self to whom an utterance is attributed" (Cutrer 1994:73). The initial viewpoint coincides with the base space, but it can and often does shift to other spaces within the overall hierarchy.

How should the referential function of *the* be characterized in mental space terms? We have seen that this function is hearer oriented—definite reference crucially requires the speaker to take into account the hearer's knowledge of the referent. This means that the speaker's discourse model must include a mental space H modelling the hearer's assumed state of knowledge. In other words, felicitous referential use of *the* obliges the speaker to construct a representation of the hearer's point of view, at least with respect to the referent in question. More precisely, when referring with *the*, the speaker sets up, or must have previously set up, an element x (the intended referent) in a mental space R (in the default case, R is both base and viewpoint). In addition, an element y is set up in space H, on the assumption that the hearer too has knowledge of the referent. A conceptual connection is then constructed between x and y (see Fig. 1), which captures the fact that the two elements are identical and that the hearer's access to x arises from knowledge that is shared by both speaker and hearer. Two important points should be emphasized concerning the referential function of *the*. First, since knowledge of the referent is shared, counterpart (linked) elements must be set up in mental spaces for both speaker and hearer reality. Second, the speaker's own viewpoint is not sufficient for determining that the referent is uniquely identifiable—the speaker is also obliged to consider the hearer's viewpoint (hearer orientation of *the*). In this sense, referential use of *the* can be said to reflect the sharing of viewpoint between speaker and hearer.

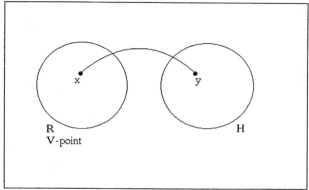

Figure 1. Referential function of *the*

The literature on definiteness has been confined almost exclusively to the discussion of reference. Epstein (1994a), however, presents extensive evidence showing that *the* has an expressive function, in addition to its referential function. The next section will examine some of these less well-known uses of *the*.

3. Expressive Function of the Definite Article

This section will examine the expressive function of the definite article in relation to viewpoint. I shall argue that these uses of *the* principally serve to convey the speaker's subjective attitude with regard to the referent of the definite nominal. In this sense, expressive *the* is "speaker oriented", rather than hearer oriented, and portrays a referent from the sole viewpoint of the speaker. Shared knowledge is not required, so these referents are often not uniquely identifiable.

Expressivity may be defined as "the foregrounding of a speaker's own involvement in an utterance, including subjective evaluation, special emphasis, surprise, admiration, etc." (Hanks 1992:49-50). In particular, *the* is often used expressively to indicate that the speaker construes a referent as highly prominent. To illustrate, let us first consider a clear case of prominence, too often overlooked in studies of definiteness:[3]

(2)   In other countries, soccer is *the* sport. If the national team loses, there could be a coup. [LAT 6/5/94 p.C9; italics in the original]

Stressed, or "emphatic *the*", frequently signals the prominence of a referent (Christophersen 1939:111), as in (2), where soccer is portrayed as a sport of great importance in other countries.

Stress is not necessary, though, for the definite article to convey a reading of prominence, as shown in (3), where *the* indicates that, according to Richard Ofshe, the recovered memory phenomenon is the paragon of 20th century psychiatric quackeries:

(3)   The recovered memory phenomenon "is going to go down as **the psychiatric quackery** of the 20th century," said Richard Ofshe, a social psychologist at UC Berkeley and author of an upcoming book on false memories. "If family members who are damaged by these irresponsible practitioners win the right to react in the legal setting, then maybe we can stop this epidemic." [LAT 4/6/94 p.A20]

Furthermore, although in (2)-(3) *the* occurs in attributive nominals, it can also be used expressively in referring nominals, as a means of inducing the addressee to accept the referent under a certain guise:

(4)   ... an American diplomat here pronounced himself perplexed by the "Alice in Wonderland quality" of Haitian politics, where words seem to mean only what their speakers want them to mean. Nor is he the first to feel confused. Citing **the phrase** coined by a former ambassador, diplomats here routinely counsel new arrivals that in Haiti it is best to believe "nothing you hear and only half of what you see." [NYT 10/16/94 sec.4 p.5]

In (4), the initial mention *the phrase* does not simply introduce a uniquely identifiable referent, since the task of introducing this referent into the discourse could equally well have been accomplished with an indefinite article. Instead, *the* also conveys the speaker's evaluation of *the phrase* as

---

[3]   Most data are drawn from the *Los Angeles Times* [LAT] and *The New York Times* [NYT]. See Epstein (1994a) for examples of expressive uses of the definite article in other discourse genres.

highly prominent amongst diplomats in Haiti, who consider it to be an extremely apt description of life in that country. In general, to fully understand the expressive function of the definite article, it is important to ask why speakers choose *the* when *a* is also possible. Potential contrast with *a* helps brings out the meaning of expressive *the* more clearly (see Epstein 1994b).

Epstein (1994a) describes several subtypes of prominence that may be conveyed by the definite article. One subtype, "paradigmatic importance", is illustrated by (2)-(4), where *the* indicates that a referent is a particularly important member of a category (a paradigmatic relation). For instance, in (2), soccer is construed as more important than other sports in other countries. A second kind of prominence is "syntagmatic importance", or discourse prominence, in which the prominence of the referent stems primarily from its role in the broader discourse context (a syntagmatic relation). For instance, in (5), the initial mention of the definite nominal *the rule* signals that the referent is about to become highly topical over the next stretch of talk:

(5)   There were boos coming from the paying customers, a rare sign of rancor during this upbeat American World Cup, now history. The boos were not for the warriors still standing on the grass of the Rose Bowl, and the boos were surely not for warriors like Franco Baresi and Roberto Baggio, bent over from stabbing cramps.

The boos were for **the rule**. The rule that transforms an endurance contest into a crap shoot. The rule that forced Brazil and Italy to take penalty kicks to decide the championship of the most popular sports tournament on the face of the earth. The rule that led to Brazil beating Italy yesterday, 3-2, in penalty kicks after 120 minutes of scoreless play. [NYT 7/18/94 p.B6]

The recurrence of *the rule* in this context supplies explicit evidence in support of the analysis of *the* as marking a highly topical referent.

Another example of syntagmatic importance is the well-known use of *the* to introduce a new referent at the beginning of a literary narrative in order to signal that the referent will be important later in the story (see Christophersen 1939:29). This strategy is not confined to literary texts, however:

(6)   ... most Los Angeles drivers regard the sight of a person standing in a crosswalk as an optional stop, not a required one. They *might* stop, but only if they are feeling especially gracious and aren't too busy putting on lipstick, checking their hair plugs in the rear-view

mirror or chatting on the car phone.

I have no idea what **the guy in the Mercedes** was doing when we entered the crosswalk.

On the day in question, we were plodding westward and were halfway across the intersection when a black southbound Mercedes seemed as if it were going to barrel right through the crosswalk, and—by extension—us.

At the last minute, the driver slammed on his brakes. The nose of his car came to a stop rather too close to our calves for comfort. [LAT 6/5/94 p.E1; italics in the original]

The definite articles in *the guy in the Mercedes* allow the writer to foreshadow the important role this driver will play in the subsequent discourse, a familiar dramatic device (which creates a high degree of reader involvement) made possible by the expressive function of *the* as a marker of prominence.

The expressive function of the definite article encodes viewpoint differently from the referential function. Whereas the latter is hearer oriented and depends on shared knowledge, the former conveys the speaker's subjective stance towards a referent—it is speaker oriented (expressive language in general is speaker oriented; Jakobson 1960:354). Expressive uses of *the* indicate that an element x has been set up in space R and is construed by the speaker as prominent. Crucially, the speaker's model of the discourse in these cases need not include a space H representing the hearer's knowledge of the referent, as in the referential cases. R is again the viewpoint space, but x is not linked to any counterpart in H. The hearer must simply accept the referent on the speaker's terms and await an explanation for its prominence (as well as its subsequent identification). Consequently, the expressive function reflects solely the viewpoint of the speaker. In expressive contexts, the speaker is not concerned with what the hearer may or may not know about the referent, because unique identifiability does not motivate these uses of *the*. Instead, the definite article in such cases conveys the speaker's personal attitudes, something the hearer normally does not share knowledge of.

4. Other Viewpoints Conveyed by the Definite Article

In this section, I shall argue that the definite article can indicate not just the viewpoint of the speaker or addressee, but also that of a third person, e.g., discourse protagonist, fictional narrator, etc.[4] In these cases, the speaker's model of the discourse includes a mental space M representing the reality of some third person. The definite article here indicates that an element x has been set up in M, and that it is only accessible in M. In other words, viewpoint must have shifted from R to M, which is now the viewpoint space (see Fig. 2). Once again, no space H need exist in the discourse model, because knowledge of the referent is not shared by speaker and addressee. In some cases, even the speaker may not be able to identify the referent (perhaps (10) below?). The function of *the* in these examples may be either referential or expressive.

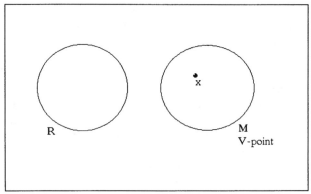

Figure 2. Third person viewpoint

The use of the definite article to mark a shift in viewpoint is well-known amongst literary theorists, who analyze these articles as encouraging readers to empathize with, or adopt the point of view of a narrator (e.g., Stanzel 1981:11), as in (7), the opening sentence of Hemingway's *A Farewell to Arms*:

(7)   In the late summer of that year we lived in a house in a village that looked across **the river** and **the plain** to **the mountains**.

---

[4]   The indefinite article is also used to mark shifts in viewpoint to a third person (see Du Bois 1980:264-265; Epstein 1994a:222, 229; Sanders and Redeker, forthcoming).

Cutrer (1994, Ch. 7) shows that a fictional narrator is associated with an alternate base space (representing the reality of the narrator rather than that of the speaker/writer), which is by the same token the new viewpoint space.

A non-literary occurrence of *the* that is justified by a viewpoint shift is given in the following example:

(8)   The young people working the potato fields ... seem to be learning the value of money.
        Jonah Alexander, 14, whose father is a doctor from Brooklyn, said picking potatoes was helping to pay for **the cow he bought** recently for $300. [NYT 10/7/94 p.A9]

The initial mention definite *the cow he bought* is consistent with the fact that this nominal occurs in reported speech. This definite article formally reflects the shift in viewpoint to Jonah, which is explicitly marked by the speech act verb *said* and the backshifted tense markers in the embedded clause.

A similar, though somewhat more complex case of viewpoint shift is shown in (9):

(9)   Barbara Wolfe, a 36-year-old mother of two, was so appalled by the anti-gay resolution that she joined the Cobb Citizens Coalition, a group organized to oppose it. But when she talks about life in Cobb County, she has mostly good things to say. She loves the hills and trees, the friendliness of the people, **the good schools**, the affordability of housing, even to a point **the Sunday-school manners** and well-scrubbed sensibilities. [NYT 8/1/94 p.A10]

Various grammatical markers in (9) again suggest that viewpoint has shifted to a third person referent, Barbara Wolfe (*she talks, she loves*). The definite articles in the final sentence of (9) further encourage readers to understand these referents as reflecting Wolfe's viewpoint, which is especially relevant for the interpretation of the evaluative adjectives *good* and *Sunday-school*.

The definite articles in (7)-(9) serve a referential function, that is, they introduce referents from the viewpoint of a third person without, however, marking those referents as prominent. The passage in (10), taken from a news item about the disastrous fires in Southern California in 1993, illustrates an expressive viewpoint shift marked by *the*:

(10)   Sierra Madre resident Andy Dotson might not have needed to breach security barricades to return to his threatened home. He had forgotten his tattered, 19-year-old blanket with **the distinctive**

penguin design.

"The kids and the animals are my security blanket, they come first," he said. "But my family didn't get [the blanket], so I went back there. It means something to me. I was gonna bust through the barricades if I had to ... [LAT 10/30/93 p.A10]

In (10), *the* marks two sorts of conceptual strategies. First, it signals that events are being related from the point of view of a discourse protagonist, Richard Dotson (cf. the "nonreportive narrative style" of Kuroda 1973). Second, it is used expressively to indicate the importance of this blanket to Dotson. Referentially inappropriate occurrences of *the*, such as the one in (10), provide striking evidence for the usefulness of viewpoint in accounting for the meaning and distribution of the definite article.

One final point worth mentioning is that under the analysis proposed in this paper, prominence is as much a part of the basic meaning of *the* as unique identifiability. It is not considered to be a secondary effect derived via some process of pragmatic accommodation. This way of analyzing *the* helps account for contrasts like the one in (11a):

(11)   a.   With lust in his heart for a Nobel Prize, Jimmy Carter undermined Bill Clinton's resolve and turned a triumph of American strength in Haiti into a fiasco of wimpish indecision ... Carter, with no authority, offered the junta a broker, then enlisted Sam Nunn and Colin Powell, then confronted **a (?the) President panicked by the prospect of using force**; the passive Clinton permitted the negotiation of major concessions while pretending he was permitting only "modalities" of eviction. [NYT 9/22/94 p.A19]

        b.   In supporting the positions of the Christian right, Bush seemed to be stepping out of character. It was hard for anyone to believe that **a (the) Connecticut-born, Yale-bred Episcopalian** wanted to wage religious war against fellow Americans. [LATmag 11/29/92 p.30]

In (11a), the nominal *a President panicked by the prospect of using force*, with an indefinite article, can be interpreted both as a "role" (a function) and as an instantiation of that role (a specific individual, or a "value"; see Fauconnier 1994 for detailed discussion of definite and indefinite descriptions that can designate both roles and values). The possibility of a role reading arises because *President* is presented here under the guise of a description conveying new information. At the same time, a value for the role is inferred from context because the past tense verb *confronted* designates a specific event with specific individuals. Under the value reading, the specific individual referred to by *President* is clearly Clinton, who is highly topical and has been previously mentioned several times. He is therefore a uniquely identifiable referent at this point in the discourse, and yet, surprisingly, if *a* were substituted by *the* in this nominal, the result would be strange. The reason is that the description designates a property that is not easily construed as a permanent, i.e., prominent, aspect of Clinton's character. Thus, it does not allow access to the counterpart of Clinton that has previously been set up in the discourse. The lack of prominence renders the description incapable of (directly) accessing a referent in this context, so the speaker must use an indefinite article in order to set up a new element.

It is important to point out that the fact that the description contains new information that makes a role reading possible does not, in and of itself, cause the definite article to be infelicitous. In (11b), the description *a Connecticut-born, Yale-bred Episcopalian* is compatible with both role and value readings but, unlike in (11a), *the* could perfectly well substitute for *a* in (11b), since this description represents a prominent aspect of Bush's character, thereby allowing access back to the counterpart of Bush previously set up in the discourse (if the speaker so chooses). If unique identifiability alone were a sufficient condition for the use of the definite article, then the constraint on the use of *the* illustrated in (11a) would be difficult to explain, since the condition is clearly fulfilled on the basis of previous mention.[5]

5. Conclusion

I have argued that the definite article in English should be analyzed as yet another formal means for marking viewpoint. In its referential function, it signals that a referent is accessible from the point of view of both speaker and hearer. In its expressive function, it marks the sole viewpoint of the speaker. Finally, it is also capable of reflecting shifts in viewpoint to third persons. The data presented here suggest that all uses of *the* convey some viewpoint—the notion of viewpoint must therefore be a part of any comprehensive theory of definiteness. More generally, the data

---

[5]   Epstein (1994a, §4.5 and §5.5; 1994b, §3) provides other evidence, both synchronic and diachronic, for considering prominence to be part of the basic meaning of *the*.

show that to simply analyze *the* as a referential marker of unique identifiability or familiarity does not do justice to the subtle nuances of interpretation it conveys, nor to the range and complexity of the cognitive work it accomplishes in the construction of discourse.

REFERENCES

Birner, Betty and Gregory Ward. 1994. Uniqueness, Familiarity, and the Definite Article in English. In *Proceedings of the Twentieth Annual Meeting of the Berkeley Linguistics Society*, 93-102. Berkeley, CA: Berkeley Linguistics Society.

Cantrall, William R. 1974. *Viewpoint, Reflexives, and the Nature of Noun Phrases*. The Hague: Mouton.

Chafe, Wallace L. 1976. Givenness, Contrastiveness, Definiteness, Subjects, Topics, and Point of View. In Charles N. Li, ed., *Subject and Topic*, 25-55. New York: Academic Press.

Christophersen, Paul. 1939. *The Articles: A Study of Their Theory and Use in English*. Copenhagen: Einar Munksgaard.

Clark, Herbert H. and Catherine R. Marshall. 1981. Definite reference and mutual knowledge. In Aravind K. Joshi, Bonnie L. Webber, and Ivan A. Sag, eds., *Elements of discourse understanding*, 10-63. Cambridge: Cambridge University Press.

Cutrer, L. Michelle. 1994. *Time and Tense in Narrative and in Everyday Language*. Doctoral dissertation, University of California, San Diego.

Du Bois, John W. 1980. Beyond Definiteness: The Trace of Identity in Discourse. In Wallace L. Chafe, ed., *The Pear Stories. Cognitive, Cultural, and Linguistic Aspects of Narrative Production*, 203-274. Norwood, N.J.: Ablex.

Epstein, Richard. 1994a. *Discourse and Definiteness: Synchronic and Diachronic Perspectives*. Doctoral dissertation, University of California, San Diego.

Epstein, Richard. 1994b. Variation and Definiteness. In *Papers from the 30th Regional Meeting of the Chicago Linguistic Society. Volume 2: The Parasession on Variation in Linguistic Theory*, 61-75. Chicago: Chicago Linguistic Society.

Fauconnier, Gilles. 1994. *Mental Spaces. Aspects of Meaning Construction in Natural Language*. Cambridge: Cambridge University Press.

Fleischman, Suzanne. 1990. *Tense and Narrativity. From Medieval Performance to Modern Fiction*. Austin, Tx.: University of Texas Press.

Givón, T. 1989. *Mind, Code and Context. Essays in Pragmatics*. Hillsdale, N.J.: Lawrence Erlbaum Associates.

Hanks, William F. 1992. The indexical ground of deictic reference. In Alessandro Duranti and Charles Goodwin, eds., *Rethinking context*, 43-76. Cambridge: Cambridge University Press.

Hawkins, John A. 1978. *Definiteness and Indefiniteness: A Study in Reference and Grammaticality Prediction*. London: Croon Helm.

Hawkins, John A. 1991. On (in)definite articles: implicatures and (un)grammaticality prediction. *Journal of Linguistics* 27:405-442.

Heim, Irene R. 1982. *The Semantics of Definite and Indefinite Noun Phrases*. Doctoral dissertation, University of Massachusetts, Amherst.

Jakobson, Roman. 1960. Concluding Statement: Linguistics and Poetics. In Thomas A. Sebeok, ed., *Style in Language*, 350-377. Cambridge, Mass.: MIT Press.

Kadmon, Nirit. 1990. Uniqueness. *Linguistics and Philosophy* 13:273-324.

Kamp, Hans and Christian Rohrer. 1983. Tense in Texts. In Rainer Bäuerle, Christoph Schwarze, and Arnim von Stechow, eds., *Meaning, Use, and Interpretation of Language*, 250-269. Berlin: Walter de Gruyter.

Kemmer, Suzanne. In press. Emphatic and Reflexive *-self*: Expectations, Viewpoint and Subjectivity. In Susan Wright and Dieter Stein, eds., *Subjectivity and Subjectivization in Language*. Cambridge: Cambridge University Press.

Kuno, Susumu. 1987. *Functional Syntax: Anaphora, Discourse and Empathy*. Chicago: Chicago University Press.

Kuroda, S.-Y. 1973. Where Epistemology, Grammar and Style Meet: A Case Study from Japanese. In Stephen Anderson and Paul Kiparsky, eds., *A Festschrift for Morris Halle*, 377-391. New York: Holt, Rinehart and Winston.

Langacker, Ronald W. 1993. Viewing in Cognition and Grammar. Ms., University of California, San Diego.

Prince, Ellen F. 1981. Toward a Taxonomy of Given-New Information. In Peter Cole, ed., *Radical Pragmatics*, 223-255. New York: Academic Press.

Sanders, José and Gisela Redeker. Forthcoming. Perspective and the Representation of Speech and Thought in Narrative Discourse. In Gilles Fauconnier and Eve Sweetser, eds., *Spaces, Worlds, and Grammar*. Chicago: Chicago University Press.

Stanzel, Franz K. 1981. Teller-Characters and Reflector-Characters in Narrative Theory. *Poetics Today* 2:5-15.

van Hoek, Karen. 1992. *Paths Through Conceptual Structure: Constraints on Pronominal Anaphora*. Doctoral dissertation, University of California, San Diego.

Zribi-Hertz, Anne. 1989. Anaphor Binding and Narrative Point of View: English Reflexive Pronouns in Sentence and Discourse. *Language* 65:695-727.

Blending as a Central Process of Grammar

GILLES FAUCONNIER & MARK TURNER
University of California, San Diego

Mental spaces are small conceptual packets constructed as we think and talk, for purposes of local understanding and action. They are interconnected, and can be modified as thought and discourse unfold. Fauconnier and Turner have recently proposed the existence of a general cognitive process—conceptual blending—that operates over mental spaces as inputs. In blending, structure from two input spaces is projected to a separate space, the "blend." The blend inherits partial structure from the input spaces, and has emergent structure of its own.

As an example of blending, consider a contemporary philosopher who says, while leading a seminar,

> I claim that reason is a self-developing capacity. Kant disagrees with me on this point. He says it's innate, but I answer that that's begging the question, to which he counters, in *Critique of Pure Reason,* that only innate ideas have power. But I say to that, what about neuronal group selection? And he gives no answer.

In one input mental space, we have the modern philosopher, making claims. In a separate but related input mental space, we have Kant, thinking and writing. In neither input space is there a debate. These two input spaces share frame structure: there is a thinker, who has claims and musings, a mode of expression, a particular language, and so on. This shared frame structure constitutes a third space, a generic space, connected to both input spaces. There is a fourth space, the blend, which has both the modern philosopher (from the first input space) and Kant (from the second input space). The blend additionally recruits the frame of *debate*, framing Kant and the modern philosopher as engaged in simultaneous debate, mutually aware, using a single language to treat a recognized topic. The debate frame comes up easily in the blend, through pattern completion, since so much of its structure is already in place in the two inputs. Once the blend is established, we can operate cognitively within that space, which allows us to manipulate the various events as an integrated unit. The debate frame brings with it conventional expressions, available for our use. We know the connection of the blend to the input spaces, and the way that structure or inferences developed in the blend translates back to the input spaces. We work over all four spaces simultaneously, but the blend gives us structure, integration, and efficiency not available in the other spaces.

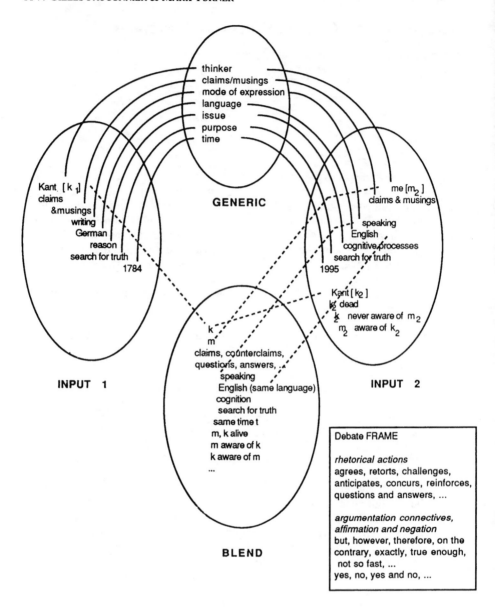

GENERIC

Kant [k₁]
claims
&musings
writing
German
reason
search for truth
1784

me [m₂]
claims & musings
speaking
English
cognitive processes
search for truth
1995

Kant [k₂]
k₂ dead
k₂ never aware of m₂
m₂ aware of k₂

INPUT 1

INPUT 2

k
m
claims, counterclaims,
questions, answers, ...
speaking
English (same language)
cognition
search for truth
same time t
m, k alive
m aware of k
k aware of m
...

BLEND

Debate FRAME

rhetorical actions
agrees, retorts, challenges,
anticipates, concurs, reinforces,
questions and answers, ...

argumentation connectives,
affirmation and negation
but, however, therefore, on the
contrary, exactly, true enough,
not so fast, ...
yes, no, yes and no, ...

thinker
claims/musings
mode of expression
language
issue
purpose
time

The "debate with Kant" has characteristic features of blending:

—Blending exploits and develops counterpart connections between inputs. Any two counterparts may or may not be fused in the blend. For example, in the debate with Kant some frame counterparts are fused (issues, languages used, modes of expression) while some are not (the two philosophers). Fused elements need not be counterparts as indexed by the generic space: Kant [k1] in input 1 and Kant [k2] in input2 are very different (k2, for example, has an international fame over two centuries and is the paragon of rational philosophers); but k1 and k2 are fused in the blend.

—Blending has many effects. They include the conceptual integration of related events into one complex event (for example, a debate), the use and evolution in the blend of frames not obligatory (or in many cases, not even conventional) for its inputs (the debate frame is not required for the inputs); and the development of novel conceptual structure (for example, in the debate blend, the time of the debate is a very unusual kind of time, neither the time of the inputs nor some fusion of them, but rather a special transcendent time—it would be odd to say, "Two years ago, Kant disagreed with me, when I thought reason was a self-developing capacity."

—Blended spaces are sites for central cognitive work: reasoning (the philosopher's intellectual inquiry into cognition takes place in the blend), drawing inferences (only in the blend can Kant beg the question put by the philosopher, and blamed for it), and developing emotions (the modern philosopher can feel excited and flattered to be debating Kant).

—Blending is usually not consciously perceived, but it can be highlighted, as in jokes, cartoons, puzzles, and poetry. As long as we are not pressed to engage the blend vividly (as when the modern philosopher dons a white wig to speak with Kant) or give it reference in ways we think to be false (as when we are asked to think that the modern philosopher has a time machine), then this particular blend is a normal and automatic way to conceive of doing philosophy in response to work by previous philosophers.

—Dynamically, input spaces and blends under construction recruit structure from more stable, elaborate, and conventional conceptual structures that may have conventional connections of various sorts: shared frame roles, connections of identity or transformation or representation, metaphoric connections. These conventional connections are fully available to the work of blending. Blending may exploit, simultaneously, more than one kind of counterpart connection (e.g., frame-role connection and identity connection). Through entrenchment, blending can influence conventional structures and their conventional connections. Blends can themselves become conventional.

—During blending, conceptual work may be required at any site in the conceptual array. Spaces, domains, and frames can proliferate and be modified. Blending can be applied successively during that proliferation. For local purposes, we seek to achieve useful counterpart structure and useful integration. Those goals can be fulfilled in various ways: by activating different input mental spaces, by changing the recruitment of structure to them, by seeking to establish different generic connections between them, by projecting different structure from the inputs to the blend, by recruiting different frames to the blend, by projecting different structure from the blend back to the inputs, by multiplying the blends, and so on.

The debate frame can structure less obvious blends, as in: "The bean burrito is California's answer to France's Croque Monsieur." In the Blend, regions of the world are debating. In reality, there need not even be any gastronomic competition between them. It is important in all of these cases to observe that although the blend may be centrally useful for cognitive work, that does not mean that we reify it, or are concerned with how the world would have to be different in order for it to be reified. The utility of the blend lies principally in its relation to input spaces; by itself the blend would do no effective work for us. The relation of the blend to possible existence is a different matter. We need not think that the debate with Kant or the culinary competition between France and California are real in order to find them extremely useful.

Many phenomena give rise to blends: inventive actions, analogy, dramatic performance, counterfactuals, integrated meanings, grammatical constructions. All of these have partial projection, emergent structure, counterpart mappings, and so on. Metaphor is one of the phenomena that give rise to blends. It has the appropriate features: partial projection from input spaces; emergent structure in the blend; counterpart structure between input spaces; projection of integration of events from the source, the unconscious status of the blend until it is highlighted; cognitive work specific to the blend, and so on.

In Turner and Fauconnier (1995), we showed how elaborate conceptual blending can be reflected by simple two word or one word expressions. We discussed the formation, meaning, and sometimes multiple potential meanings, of expressions like dolphin-safe, jail-bait, Mcjobs, boathouse vs. houseboat, Chunnel. More generally, we wish to say that grammatical patterns often reflect conceptual blends and integration of events. Language users feel that some grammatical forms present events as integrated, while others do not. For example, consider "Jack threw the napkin off the table." This integrates the physical motion by Jack, the manner in which he acted, the object he moved, the motion of that object, the manner in which the object moved, the original location of the object, and the direction of its motion. Now consider another sequence: "Jack sneezed. The napkin moved. It was on the table. Now it is off the table." This grammatical form signals an action by Jack, the manner in which he acted, the object he moved, the motion of that object, the original location of the object, and the direction of its motion. Speakers of the language feel that it presents the scene as a sequence of events rather than as an integrated event. But English can express the same content with a form that conveys event integration: "Jack sneezed the napkin off the table." This form is structurally similar to the form "Jack threw the napkin off the table" and conveys the same impression of the event as integrated rather than decomposed.

There is pressure to integrate conceptual structure. Sometimes, we like to think of events as integrated, and one way of doing this is by blending them with an already integrated event structure. Inversely, when we encounter a grammatical form typically used to express a certain kind of integration, we understand it as a prompt to perform blending.

The grammatical form

Noun-Phrase   Verb   Noun-Phrase   Prepositional-Phrase

expresses event integration of caused motion. It is the syntactic component of the caused-motion construction studied by Goldberg (1995). Some verbs, like *throw*, already specify caused-motion, and occur prototypically with the syntactic form NP V NP PP: *Jack threw the ball into the basket.* [Jack acts on the ball. The ball moves. The ball is in the basket.]

The verb *throw* in this case specifies Jack's action, the ball's motion, and the fact that they are causally integrated. But some verbs that do not themselves specify caused motion can be used in the caused-motion construction. Such verbs highlight different elements that play roles in caused motion:

—causal agent's action:
Gogol sneezed the napkin off the table. [Gogol sneezes. The napkin moves off the table.] The syntactic form is the same as before, but the verb corresponds only to the agent's action. Its frame semantics contains no object, and a fortiori no motion of such an object.

—object's motion:
Junior sped the toy car around the Christmas tree. [Junior presses remote control. Car speeds around tree.] Junior is not moving. The verb *speed* corresponds to the car's motion, specifically to the manner of that motion.

—causality:

Sarge let the tank into the compound. [Sarge signs a form or waves his hand or opens the door. The tank moves into the compound.] The verb *let* does not specify Sarge's action or the tank's motion. It focuses on the removal of restraint and enablement.

Many languages have a form analogous to NP V NP PP for verbs of caused motion like "throw", but only some of those languages, like English, have developed a caused-motion construction to express the more general integration of a causal sequence of action and motion. It is not a coincidence that the syntactic form used to express the general integration is the same as the one for prototypical caused-motion verbs like *throw*.

The point we wish to make is that Conceptual Blending motivates the emergence and main properties of such constructions. Specifically, we view the grammatical construction as a <u>conventional blend</u> of Input 1, a typical basic form for a fully integrated event (as for *throw*) with Input 2, an unintegrated causal sequence.[1]

Input 1 is the frame which structures typical cases (like *throw*). It includes an agent role **a**, an object role **o**, a role **e** that subsumes causal action, means, manner of the action, motion of the object, manner of that motion, and a direction role **dm**. In English, it is associated with the basic syntactic form NP V NP PP.

INPUT 1

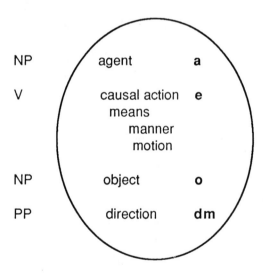

Input 2 is the unintegrated sequence containing an agent **a'** performing some action, an object **o'** undergoing motion and a direction **dm'** for that motion.

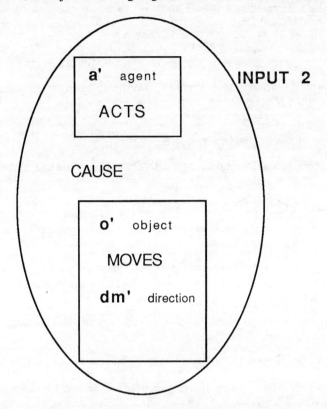

A blend of these two conceptual schematic spaces requires a partial mapping of counterparts. Agents of the causal action, **a** and **a'**, objects **o** and **o'**, directions **dm** and **dm'**, are natural conceptual counterparts. The general principle for the mapping between the integrated frame (**a, o, e, dm**) and the unintegrated sequence is to maximize the correspondence between the integrated complex of roles and subroles in one space and the unintegrated complex in the other space. Role **e** in the integrated input can be mapped in more than one way: to **a**'s action, to **o**'s motion, to the causal link between the events. This is because **e** shares relevant features with each of these roles in the causal sequence.

The purpose of the blend is to integrate the causal sequence. This is done by importing the conceptual roles, and the corresponding syntax, from Input 1. The Blend will have roles **a''**, **o''**, **e''**, **dm''**, mapped from Input 1. Content for those roles will be provided by Input 2. Agent, object, and direction map straightforwardly. But for **e''**, there is more than one possibility, because there is more than one way to map **e**.

If **e** is mapped onto the agent's action, the blend will inherit that action, and a verb expressing it will show up in the V position of the syntactic form NP V NP PP:

> Gogol *sneezed* the napkin off the table.
> The audience *laughed* the poor guy off the stage. [Goldberg 94]

If **e** is mapped onto the object's motion, a verb expressing that motion will show up in the V position:

> Andy *rolled* the drum into the warehouse.
> Junior *sped* the car around the Xmas tree.

If **e** is mapped primarily onto the causal link, an appropriate causal verb will be used:

> Sarge *let* the tank into the compound.

Blending allows other combinations from Input 2 to map onto **e"**, and to be reflected by a single verb form:

> He *forced* the tank into the compound. [*force* expresses causality, but also points to an unspecified action by the agent, and some resistance on the part of the object]

The mapping may also highlight different aspects of the counterpart relation chosen for **e**:

> He carted the drums into the warehouse. [vehicle used for motion of object]
> He muscled the boxes over the fence. [part of the body used for action]
> He ordered the tanks into the compound. [social action of giving orders]

It is worth noting at this point that there is no uniform way of obtaining the sentence forms shown here by means of a syntactic derivation from simpler clause types. For example,

NP_1 V + NP_2 (move) PP $\rightarrow$ NP_1 V NP_2 PP
would work for

> He sneezed + the napkin (move) off the table $\rightarrow$ He sneezed the napkin off the table

but not for the examples with *let, force, order, muscle*, because the input clauses are not independently well-formed: **He let. *He forced. *He ordered. *He muscled.*

A transitive simple clause is not the right source either for such cases, because either it is not well-formed, or it yields the wrong semantics:

*He let the tanks. *He forced the tanks. %He ordered the tanks.

For *rolling the drums*, a plausible source might be the simple transitive clause *He rolled the drums*, plus a direction, but this will not work in general for cases where the object's motion is highlighted, because of the ill-formedness of *Junior sped the car* or %He turned the tomatoes [for *He turned the tomatoes into spaghetti sauce*]

Consider also *Hunk choked the life out of him*, but not %Hunk choked, or *Hunk choked the life*. It is especially interesting in this example to see that conceptually the agent's action is indeed choking, and that the resulting motion, expressed through a conventional metaphor, is 'the life go out of him'. This fits the unintegrated causal sequence of Input 2, with 'choke' mapped to **e**, and 'the life' mapped to **o**. The syntactic form of the Blend is thus correctly predicted, even though what ends up in object position (*the life*) is not what gets choked in the unintegrated sequence of Input 2.

The same verb may be used to indicate the agent's action, or the object's motion. In *He trotted the stroller around the park*, it is the causal agent who is doing the trotting, and thereby making the stroller move around the park. In *The trainer trotted the horse into the stable*, the trainer could be walking, holding the horse's bridle, and the horse would then be trotting, but not the trainer. Or the trainer might be riding the horse, in which case technically only the horse is trotting, but one can also attribute the motion metonymically to the rider.[2]

The grammatical form that signals integration can now be used to express the blend, and therefore to express the (previously unintegrated) events. A speaker needs to achieve a conceptual blend in order to use the grammatical form associated with verbs like "throwing" to express more general causal sequences of events. A hearer takes the use of the grammatical form as a prompt to construct that conceptual blend. As shown by M. Israel (this volume), the conditions on such blends change through time. But they are part of the language. At the most schematic level, the blend is conventional, and the conceptual work is, so to speak, prepackaged. But there is room for innovation and creativity, in using a counterpart mapping between the inputs, and in building causal sequences in Input 2. Consider (i) *Max kicked the ball over the fence;* (ii) *The spy Houdinied the drums out of the compound;* and (iii) *So far, the people of this small textile town in northwestern Carolina have been unable to pray Mrs. Smith's two little boys home again.* [NY Times]. All three of these examples use the same caused-motion blend, but (ii) and (iii) stand out as more unusual integrations than (i).[3] All of these cases are instances of the general blending process, diagrammed below.

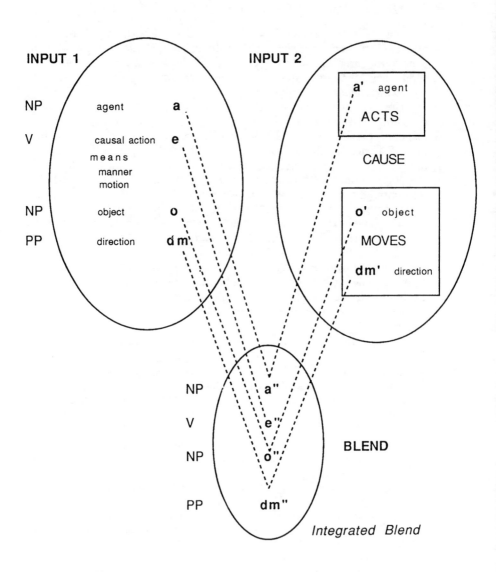

In the caused-motion construction, the syntactic component comes entirely from the input space of integrated caused motion, while lexical items come from the space of the events associated with the causal sequence. But there are other constructions in which the syntactic form used for the blend does not come entirely from one space, part of it comes from the other space, and part of it develops specifically for the blend. Consider causatives in French, which are formed using the verb *faire* ('do'):

Pierre nourrit Paul.	*Pierre fait manger Paul.*
NP V NP	NP V V NP
(Pierre feeds Paul.)	[Paul is the agent of 'manger']

Pierre expedie le paquet.	*Pierre fait envoyer le paquet.*
NP V NP	NP V V NP
(Pierre sends the package.)	['le paquet' is the object of 'envoyer']

Pierre donne la soupe à Paul.	*Pierre fait manger la soupe à Paul.*
NP V NP à NP	NP V V NP à NP
(Pierre feeds Paul the soup.)	[Paul is the agent of 'manger', 'la soupe' is the object]

It is apparent that the causative forms are superficially similar to basic transitive and ditransitive forms in the language. As Kemmer and Verhagen (1994) have pointed out, this is no accident: "Analytic causative constructions can best be described as extensions of simpler kinds of expressions, rather than as reductions from more complex underlying structures."

Kemmer and Verhagen argue that there are cognitive models of causation based on force dynamics and interactions between participants, and that these models relate to basic models, including transitive and ditransitive event structures. We think this view is exactly right, and that Blending is the cognitive operation which allows the basic models to serve as inputs to the conceptual integration of more elaborate causal sequences.[4]

Extension and conceptual mechanisms are not available to generative and relational theories of grammar, and the vast majority of analyses of causative constructions, in French and other languages, has attempted explanations based on reduction of underlying structure.[5]

Such analyses prove to be extremely complex. The French data is rich in apparent exceptions, odd distributions and constraints. Here are some well known examples:

(The semantics is roughly: CA (causal agent) CAUSE [EA (event agent) ACT (upon patient) (to recipient)])

Clitic pronouns show up in front of the *'faire V'* complex, except if the pronoun is a reflexive, anaphoric to EA:

(1) *Marie fait courir Paul.* *Marie le fait courir.* (pronoun = EA)

(2) *Marie fait envoyer le paquet. Marie le fait envoyer.* (pronoun = patient)

(3) *Marie fait envoyer le paquet à Paul. Marie lui fait envoyer le paquet.* (pro = recipient) "Marie has the parcel sent to Paul."

(4) *Marie fait manger la soupe à Paul. Marie lui fait manger la soupe.* (pro = EA)

(5) *Marie se fait envoyer le paquet.* (reflexive pronoun = recipient)

(6) *Marie fait se transformer Paul.* (reflexive pronoun = patient (= EA))

The event agent EA can be expressed by the form "par NP" or the form "à NP."

In the first case, the recipient can be cliticized, but not in the second:

(7) *Marie lui fait envoyer le paquet par Paul.* (lui = recipient)

(8) **Marie lui fait envoyer le paquet à Paul.* (with Paul sender of parcel)

(9) *Marie fait envoyer le paquet à Suzanne à Paul.* (Suzanne = recipient, Paul = EA)

The event agent EA can also be expressed by a bare NP, if there is no caused-action object O, but in that case too, the indirect object of the caused action cannot be cliticized:

(10) *Marie fait téléphoner Paul à Suzanne.* (Suzanne = recipient)

(11) **Marie lui fait téléphoner Paul.*

(12) *Marie fait téléphoner à Suzanne.* (Suzanne is recipient of phone call). "Marie has (someone) call Suzanne."

(13) *Marie lui fait téléphoner.* (lui = recipient). "Marie has (someone) call her."

Trying to account for this, and more, with a reduction of underlying forms leads to many ad hoc mechanisms. But there is a different way to conceive the entire problem. French, like English, has three basic constructions corresponding to integrated events involving causation:

Transitive: Syntax: NP   V   NP
             Roles: CA   E   O

[notation: O for "object," IO for "indirect object," E for an event or state.]

[example: *Marie nourrit Paul.* Does not admit an IO: **Marie nourrit Paul à Pierre.* E includes causal action and resulting event (Pierre eats)]

Transfer: Syntax: NP   V   NP   à NP
                Roles: CA   E   O   IO

[example: *Marie donne la soupe à Paul.*]

Optional Transfer: Syntax: NP   V   NP   (à NP)   (par NP)
             Roles: CA   E   O   (IO)   (EA, means)
[example: *Marie vend des livres (à Paul) (par un intermédiaire)*]
[a middle construction is also possible here, that doesn't express the CA: *Ces livres se vendent par un intermédiaire.*]

The causative (with *faire*) is a means for French of expressing integrated causal sequences that go beyond the basic types. This is achieved through a Blend of the extended causal sequences with the basic constructions. Because there are three Basic types, we find not just one, but three blends.

Transitive Blend: the conceptual causal sequence
[CA acts upon O]   CAUSE [EA event]   O = EA
blends with the Transitive Input [CA E O]

The counterpart mapping is straightforward: CA onto CA, O onto O, except for E which is mapped onto two counterparts, 'act' and 'event.' The blend inherits CA and O from integrated Input 1, and 'act' and 'event' from Input 2:

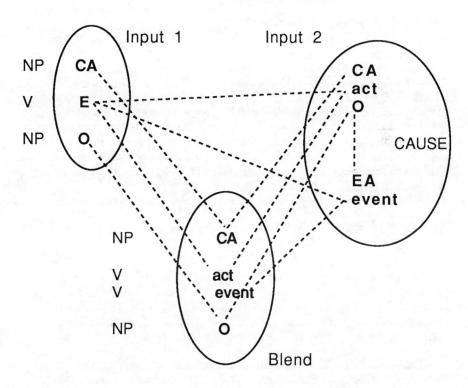

The double mapping from E to 'act' and to 'event' triggers double verb syntax specific to the blend because French has no morphological way of assigning a single verb form to the conceptual blend of the causal action and the resulting event.

Notice that if there happens to be an indirect object of the event in the causal sequence (e.g. *téléphoner à Suzanne*), there will be no IO for it to map onto in Input 1. Because the integrated role structure is projected to the Blend from Input 1, the Blend has no IO. This explains the impossibility of a clitic lui (always an IO) in example (11), without precluding the prepositional phrase *à NP* in (12), because prepositional phrases are not restricted to IO's. In other words, the Blend has no IO (and hence no clitic IO's), because it inherits its role structure from the Basic Transitive, which has no IO.

Now consider a second Blend: causal sequence with the Basic Transfer construction:

Transfer Blend: the causal sequence
[CA act] CAUSE [EA event O]
blends with the Transfer construction [CA E O IO]

CA and O have unproblematical counterparts CA and O. The counterpart of EA is the indirect object IO, simply because in the prototypical case, the IO is the agent of the caused event, e.g. *Bill feeds the soup to Mary* = [Bill acts] CAUSE [Mary eats]. And, as in the Transitive Blend, E maps both to 'act' and 'event.' The Blend therefore acquires the role structure [CA act event O IO] (ex. 4). 'Paul' this time is a true IO in the blend, and so the clitic 'lui' is possible. However, since the Blend, like the Basic Construction, has only one IO (this is independently a general constraint on role structures in French[6]), if the caused event in the causal sequence happens to have an indirect object of its own, it will have no position to map onto (IO is already taken), and a corresponding IO clitic pronoun will be excluded, as in the ungrammatical (8).[7]

Finally, the Optional Transfer Basic Construction allows a third Blend:

Optional Transfer Blend: the causal sequence
[CA act] CAUSE [event O (IO) (EA = means)][8]
blends with the Basic: [CA E O (IO) (means)]

The counterpart relations are straightforward, and the syntax for the Blend is *NP faire V NP (à NP) (par NP)*. This time, there is an IO position in the Blend, and furthermore it is mapped onto the IO position of the resulting event in the causal sequence. This predicts that corresponding clitic pronouns will be acceptable, as confirmed by examples like (7) and (13).

The preverbal position of the clitics and reflexives is inherited from the integrated Basic input. But the event in the causal sequence may already itself be reflexive conceptually, in which case it is mirrored by a reflexivized verb *se-V*. It then fits into the Blend according to its remaining number of roles. For example *transformer* has an object O, but *se transformer* does not. Hence the reflexive verb will fit the Transitive Blend, yielding example (6), with the reflexive superficially in between the two verbs (syntax specific to the Blend), and with NP (rather than "à NP") for the agent of the caused event.

It is important to see that the Blends are motivated by the existing Basic Constructions. Adele Goldberg (p.c.) asks the pertinent question: why not get the ungrammatical example (11) by blending the causal sequence [Marie act] CAUSE [EA event IO] with the Basic transfer construction? The interesting answer is that the language does not have this formally possible conventional blend because it has no basic transfer verb for which the IO is conceptually the IO of resultant event, and the O is conceptually its EA.[9] There is no verb "blurb" (in English or French) such that *Marie blurbs Suzanne to Paul* means something like "Marie makes Suzanne speak to Paul."

A nice contrast to French is provided by Nili Mandelblit's study of Hebrew causatives (Mandelblit (to appear)). Hebrew forms causatives by conceptual blending just like French, but in addition has a morphological process of formal blending, which allows a verb root to blend with a causative pattern into a single word. This allows Hebrew to transfer the integrated event syntax to the blend, just like English does with caused motion.[10]

In sum, the theory of blending provides a simple account of the superficially complex and counter-intuitive surface syntax of causatives: *faire* syntax is the result of three natural blends with the three basic causal grammatical constructions.[11]

Footnotes

[1] We adopt here Goldberg's general idea that constructions and specific verbs come together through a fusion process. Fusion is explored in Goldberg (1995). The account we propose below, however, is substantially different, as to what exactly gets blended, both from Goldberg (1995), and Fauconnier and Turner (1994).

[2] As suggested by A. Goldberg (p.c.).

[3] In order to be integrated, events have to be linked in certain ways. Researchers in construction grammar and cognitive grammar have pointed out a number of interesting defaults, regularities, and constraints that govern the conceptual integration of events as represented in various grammatical constructions. Adele Goldberg (1995) summarizes work by Talmy, Matsumoto, Deane, Croft, and herself as follows :
Let e_c be the event type designated by the construction, and e_v be the event type designated by the verb.
I. e_v must be related to e_c in one of the following ways:
(a) e_v may be a subtype of e_c
(b) e_v may designate the means of e_c
(c) e_v may designate the result of e_c
(d) e_v may designate a precondition of e_c
(e) to a very limited extent, e_v may designate the manner of e_c, the means of identifying e_c, the intended result of e_c.
So, in "They laughed the guy out of the room," e_c is the caused-motion and e_v is the event of laughing, and it is laughing that is the means of causing the motion out of the room. In another example cited by Goldberg, "I knitted my way across the Atlantic," e_c is the caused-motion, e_v is knitting, and knitting is a manner attached to that motion.

[4] In the same general spirit, Shibatani (to appear) offers an insightful integrational account of possessor raising and ethical datives.

[5] See Kayne (1975), Comrie (1976), Fauconnier (1983), Gibson and Raposo (1986).

[6] And perhaps more generally (stratal uniqueness in RG).

7 (8) of course is grammatical, if Paul is the recipient, and 'lui' is the sender of the parcel, because then lui corresponds to the IO position in the Blend.

8 The resulting event is construed as an 'unaccusative' structure, focusing on the effect of the causal action on object O. In this construal, the agent of the event is a conceived as a non-obligatory oblique argument (means).

9 If the event is unaccusative, however, it will fit the Optional Transfer Blend, and there will be a slot for IO: *Je lui ai fait venir des idees.* (Fauconnier 1983).

10 Mandelblit (to appear) argues persuasively however that the causative double accusative construction constitutes Blend-specific syntax.

11 Many other interesting properties follow, which space limitations prevent us from discussing here. Notice that the Blends motivate the use of *faire* (meaning "do"), and justify the absence of passive morphology in examples like (7) that "feel" like passives.

References

Comrie, B. 1976. The Syntax of Causative Constructions: Cross-language Similarities and Divergencies. In Shibatani, M., ed. *Syntax and Semantics 6: The Grammar of Causative Constructions*. New York: Academic Press.

Fauconnier, G. 1983. Generalized Union. *Communication and Cognition 16*, 3-37.

Fauconnier, G. and M. Turner. 1994. Conceptual Projection and Middle Spaces. UCSD Cognitive Science Technical Report 9401. Compressed (Unix) postscript version available from http: //cogsci.ucsd.edu or http: //www.informumd.edu/EdRes/Colleges/ARHU/Depts/English/englfac /MTurner/.

Gibson, J. and E. Raposo. 1986. Clause Union, the Stratal Uniqueness Law and the Chomeur Relation. *Natural Language and Linguistic Theory* 4, 295-331.

Goldberg, A. 1995. *Constructions*. Chicago: The University of Chicago Press.

Mandelblit, N. to appear. Blends in Hebrew Causatives. *Proceedings of the Fourth Conference of the International Cognitive Linguistics Association.*

Kayne, R. 1975. *French Syntax. The Transformational Cycle*. Cambridge, Mass.: MIT Press.

Turner, M. and G. Fauconnier. 1995. Conceptual Integration and Formal Expression. *Journal of Metaphor and Symbolic Activity*, vol. 10, no. 3.

Shibatani, M. to appear. An Integrational Approach to Possessor Raising, Ethical Datives, and Adversative Passives. *Berkeley Linguistic Society* 20.

Psychological Predicates and the Syntax-Semantics Interface

HANA FILIP

University of Illinois, Urbana-Champaign

1 Basic issues

The hypothesis of the autonomy of syntax makes special demands on one of the central issues in linguistic theory: the specification of correspondences between a lexical conceptual and syntactic structure. One strategy is to distinguish several layers of lexical representation and allow only one of them to be "visible" to syntactic and morphological processes (cf. Pinker 1989, Grimshaw 1990). A recent implementation of this strategy is the *Aspectual Interface Hypothesis (AIH)* advocated by Tenny since 1987. The AIH is driven by the assumption that there is a direct and uniform association between *telicity*, or what Tenny calls "aspectual measuring-out" of events, and the internal direct object argument in the d-structure.

The AIH has attracted considerable attention (see Pinker 1989, Grimshaw 1990, Jackendoff 1990, Pustejovsky 1991, Levin and Rappaport Hovav 1991, Gropen 1989, Gropen, Pinker, Hollander and Goldberg 1991, Dowty 1991, and others). Its appeal is understandable given that telicity and related semantic notions play an important role in the syntax-semantics interface in the domain of argument structures (see Van Valin 1987, 1990, 1991; Dowty 1988, 1991 and Zaenen 1988, 1993, for example). The AIH also promises to provide additional semantic support for the Unaccusative Hypothesis proposed by Perlmutter (1978) in Relational Grammar and adapted in GB Theory by Burzio (1981, 1986) (cf. Tenny 1989:18ff., 20-1).

Nevertheless, empirical evidence strongly suggests that the AIH should be rejected. As a case in point, I will take psychological predicates, as they occupy much of the current debates on theories of linking. Drawing on data from English and Czech I will argue that the syntax-semantics interface in the domain of psychological predicates cannot be based on telicity or the aspectual property of "event measuring", contrary to the AIH. I will contrast the AIH with an approach that relies on a monostratal syntax and a direct linking between the semantic and syntactic representations. The linking approach proposed here presupposes that the relevant classes of psychological predicates can be differentiated in terms of their thematic structures. To give a thematic characterization of verbal arguments I will adopt Dowty's (1991:571ff.) view of thematic roles as prototypes. Such a thematic characterization along with Dowty's Argument Selection Principle can account for all the observations which have been used in support of the AIH and multistratal syntax. The proposed linking approach has the advantage that it avoids some of the problems and ad hoc explanations that weaken linking approaches combined with multistratal syntactic accounts. It can also accommodate the full range of data, including those from languages with rich morphological case marking systems like Czech.

2 Aspectual Interface Hypothesis (AIH): Tenny (1987-1994)

2.1 Basic characterization

(1)   **Aspectual Interface Hypothesis** (Tenny 1994:115-6)

The universal principles of mapping between thematic structure and syntactic argument structure are governed by aspectual properties relating to measuring-out. Constraints on the aspectual properties associated with direct internal arguments, indirect internal arguments, and external arguments in syntactic structure constrains the kinds of event participants that can occupy these positions. Only the aspectual part of thematic structure is visible to the syntax.

The driving force behind the AIH is the claim that the internal direct object argument in the d-structure of verbs of change or motion is associated with the argument in the lexical conceptual structure (LCS) that aspectually delimits or "measures out" an event. Tenny uses the "measuring-out" property "in an informal sense, as a convenient metaphor for uniform and consistent change, such as change along a scale" (Tenny 1989:7); "the endpoint of the scale can be established in absolute rather than relative terms" (Tenny 1992:7-8). What is meant by this can be best illustrated by the following examples:

(2-a)   *I ate* **an apple.**
(2-b)   *John went* **to the post office.**
(2-c)   **The butter** *melted.*

The typical understanding of (2a) involves the knowledge that there was an eating event during which an apple was gradually consumed, part by part, until all its parts were consumed, at which point the eating event *necessarily* ended. In this sense the participant denoted by the NP *an apple* "measures out" the event. In (2b) the internal indirect object *to the post office* (Goal) introduces a terminus that delimits the denoted event and the implicit path measures the event (this complies with the *Terminus Constraint on Indirect Internal Arguments*). In (2c) the whole piece of butter undergoes a series of consecutive transformations until it becomes liquid. This marks the necessary end of the melting event. Change-of-state verbs like *melt* denote events whose part structure can be correlated with the degrees on some property scale associated with the changing participant.

Aspectual (or telic) properties of verbs are encoded with 'aspectual roles' assigned by a verb to its arguments. They are invariably linked to internal arguments (direct and indirect) in the d-structure. Hence, external and internal arguments are asymmetrical with respect to telicity (cf. also Verkuyl 1972, 1981, 1989). The privileged status of aspectual roles with respect to linking motivates the **modular** relationship between aspectual and non-aspectual (thematic) information in the LCS (cf. Tenny 1992:14, 1994:190ff.). Variations in the surface alignment of aspectual roles (cf. ex. (2c)) are accounted for by means of transformational movement.

2.2 Psychological predicates and the "measuring-out" of events

In terms of the expression of the Experiencer argument, two main classes are distinguished in English (cf. Chomsky 1965, Postal 1971, Lakoff 1970, Jackendoff 1990, Levin 1993), as is shown in (3).

(3-a)   **FEAR class: Experiencer-subject**
         admire, detest, enjoy, hate, miss, respect; marvel at.

(3-b)   **FRIGHTEN class: Experiencer-object**
         amuse, embarrass, irritate, worry; appeal to.

The linking in the domain of psychological predicates is problematic if we assume that there is a direct and uniform association between thematic (or lexical semantic) arguments and syntactic arguments (see the *Uniformity of Theta Assignment Hypothesis* by Baker (1988:46), for instance) and that psychological predicates of the *frighten* and *fear* type are analyzed as taking the same thematic roles, Experiencer and Theme, for example. The problem then arises, because psychological predicates differ in the way they map thematic roles into syntactic arguments. The AIH solution to this problem rests on the proposal that it is not thematic roles, but aspectual principles that govern linking. Only Experiencers of causative psychological predicates of the *frighten* type "measure out" the denoted event (cf. Tenny, 1987:294; 1988:13) and this justifies their realization as internal direct objects in the d-structure. Psychological predicates of the *fear* type are stative. The AIH implies that stative predicates in general have no aspectual roles. Consequently, Experiencer arguments of stative psychological predicates do not "measure" events and are realized as external arguments in the d-structure.

The main objection against this account has to do with the application of the "measuring-out" property to the Experiencer arguments of causative psychological predicates. Given that the "measuring-out" property is understood as entailing telicity (or delimitedness), and vice versa (cf. Tenny 1994:15-6), such predicates are by definition telic. However, a close look at the data reveals that only psychological predicates that partially overlap with Vendler's achievements, namely those denoting instantaneous changes from one mental state to another (e.g., *frighten, strike (as), astonish, shock, startle*), are telic. Although their Experiencer arguments can be said to "measure out" events, they do so only in a trivial way. What is more troubling is the analysis of causative psychological predicates that entail or allow for a gradual change in the Experiencer participant: *calm, disillusion, sadden, soothe, disarm*. The problem is that it is not the kind of change that can be measured "along a scale with an absolute end-point", because they are atelic. This observation can be illustrated by the co-occurrence restrictions with adverbs like *halfway*, as is shown in (4):

(4-a)   *?The music halfway saddened John.*
(4-b)   **The high-pitched noise halfway distracted her.*
          Van Voorst (1992:89)

In general, to make a felicitous assertion about a half of an event, one needs to know what state exactly constitutes the final stage of the event. Hence, the incompatibility of a predicate denoting an extended event with *halfway* indicates that the predicate in question is atelic. Although it is possible to monitor the process of John's becoming more and more sad, there is no point at which we can say that John is halfway sad and on his way to being completely sad. The reason is that we would need to know what state exactly constitutes the stage of somebody's being sad or distracted beyond which that person cannot be sadder or more distracted. However, predicates like *sadden* do not entail such a well-defined final stage, they are not telic.

The observation that causative psychological predicates denoting gradual changes are atelic can be also confirmed by the standard Vendler-Dowty tests. (For a detailed discussion of Vendler-Dowty tests and psychological predicates see Van Voorst 1992.)

Tenny (1987:291, 1988:13 and 1994:20) adduces two tests in support of the claim that the "measuring-out" property is inherent in the meaning of causative psychological predicates. The first exploits the observation that a resultative predicate can only be applied to the internal Experiencer argument of the *frighten* type predicates, but not to any argument of the *fear* type predicates. This is shown in (5) and (6) (examples are taken from Tenny 1988:13):

(5-a)   *The news frightened [John]$_i$ [to death]$_i$.*
(5-b)   **[The news]$_i$ frightened John [to the end]$_i$.*
(6-a)   **[John]$_i$ feared the movie [to death]$_i$.*
(6-b)   **/??John feared [the movie]$_i$ [to the end]$_i$.*

Although it holds that the resultative predicate can be applied to an argument that is entailed to undergo a change of state (cf. Goldberg 1992/1995), to an Incremental Theme argument to be more precise (cf. Filip 1993), the whole complex verbal predicate to which the argument in question belongs may be telic (*John broke the vase to pieces*) or atelic (*The horses dragged the logs smooth*). The compatibility of a complex verbal predicate with a resultative predicate does not provide any conclusive evidence about the telic or atelic nature of the complex verbal predicate.

The second test, the modification with "expressions referring to increments, such as *a little (bit)*" (Tenny 1994:20), does not work, because it concerns attenuation of events taken as whole entities and not their increments or proper parts. For example, *The music saddened John a little bit* does not express a part of a larger event expressed by *The music saddened John*, but rather it denotes a whole psychological event that is of low(er) intensity. Notice that attenuation of events can be also conveyed by derivational affixes on verbs: *spark* vs. *sparkle*.

The above objections strongly suggest that causative psychological predicates like *calm, disillusion, sadden, soothe, disarm* lack the "measuring-out" property, because they are atelic, just like stative predicates in the *fear* class. It is important to emphasize that such causative psychological predicates are by no means exceptional in this respect. There are other classes of predicates that entail a change in the referent of their internal direct object argument, but it is not the kind of change that falls under the universal *measuring-out constraint on the internal direct object argument*. Take, for example, atelic predicates like *stir (the soup)* and unaccusative predicates like *sweat, breath, shiver (from cold), suffer*. Their internal direct object is associated with a participant that does not (necessarily) change part by part or degree by degree in one of its properties and the denoted change cannot be measured on a scale with a definite end-point. Notice that the existence of atelic unaccusative predicates indicates that the 'telic-atelic' distinction is not co-extensive with the 'unergative-unaccusative' distinction, and hence the AIH cannot be said to explain the distribution of verb meanings across unergative and unaccusative classes.

In the light of the above observations we may conclude that the AIH applies to a smaller class of eventive predicates than it is intended to. The reason is that the notion of "measuring-out" on which it rests is not sufficiently constrained. This notion overlaps with the familiar and explicitly constrained notion of 'Incremental (Path) Theme' (cf. Dowty 1988, 1991 and proposals by Hinrichs 1985 and Krifka 1986). Furthermore, if a number of causative psychological predicates lacks the "aspectual measuring-out" property, then this property cannot serve to constrain the linking in the domain of psychological predicates.

In general, there is no uniform association between the internal direct object argument and an argument in the LCS that "measures out" the event or the narrower notion 'Incremental Theme'. Not only are there internal direct objects of eventive predicates denoting participants that do not "measure out" events, but also certain participants that "measure out" events are not invariably realized as internal arguments. Take, for instance, the following example: *The carnival procession was slowly crossing the street.* Here, the length of the procession "measures" the denoted event, yet the NP *the carnival procession* is clearly an external argument (cf. Filip 1990, 1993; Dowty 1991).

3 Czech psychological predicates

3.1 Data

With their tripartite division and case-marked arguments Czech psychological predicates non-trivially differ from English psychological predicates and thus provide good testing data for the AIH (and any other theory of linking for that matter). This is shown in (7). A similar tripartite division of psychological predicates as in Czech can be found in other Indo-European languages, Russian (Holloway-King 1993), Bulgarian (Slabakova 1994), Dutch (Zaenen 1988, 1993), Italian (Perlmutter 1984, Belletti and Rizzi 1988), French (Legendre 1989), and in South Asian languages (cf. Verma and Mohanan 1990), for example.

(7-a)

Václav	*miluje*	*Marii.*	**Nominative-Experiencer**
Václav-NOM	loves	Mary-ACC	

'Václav loves Mary.'

Other examples: *nenávidět* 'hate', *chtít* 'want', *bát se*+GEN 'fear', *divit se*+DAT 'wonder', *pohrdat*+INSTR 'despise', *toužit po* 'long for'.

(7-b)

Václav	*baví*	*Marii.*	**Accusative-Experiencer**
Václav-NOM	amuses	Mary-ACC	

'Václav amuses Mary.'

Other examples: *zlobit* 'anger', *přitahovat* 'attract', *překvapovat* 'surprise', *nudit* 'bore'.

(7-c)

Václav	schází	Marii.	**Dative-Experiencer**
Václav-NOM	lacks	Mary-DAT	

'Mary misses Václav.'

Other examples: *chybět* 'lack', *líbit se* 'like', *hnusit se* 'disgust', *vadit* 'annoy', 'harm', *svědčit* 'be beneficial to', *prospívat* 'do good to, benefit', *vyhovovat* 'comply, satisfy, please', *být vhod* 'suit', *škodit* 'harm', *nesedět* 'bother'.

3.2 The Aspectual Interface Hypothesis and Czech psychological predicates

The class of nominative-Experiencer predicates in Czech roughly corresponds to the class of Experiencer-subject predicates in English (e.g., the *fear* type) and the class of accusative-Experiencer ones to the class of English Experiencer-object predicates (e.g., the *frighten* type). In Slavic languages, the nominative argument of a predicate and the controller of verb agreement is the morphological subject. An argument in the accusative case is the basic morphological encoding of the direct object. The application of the linking principles determined by the AIH to Czech psychological predicates will be invalidated by the same objections as those brought forward in the case of English predicates. In addition, the question arises what to do with the dative-Experiencer class. The dative case is the basic morphological encoding of the indirect object. As is well-known the dative case is the typical exponent of three thematically related arguments: Goal, Recipient and Experiencer. Given this, one way to accommodate the dative-Experiencer within the AIH would be to extend the Terminus Constraint on indirect internal arguments to include also cases in which the Path and Terminus are transposed from the concrete spatial domain into the abstract domain of psychological events. It is doubtful whether such a move, which presupposes semantic properties motivated by the theory of metaphors (cf. Lakoff 1993) or some other extension of the syntax-semantics interface, could be accommodated within the AIH. Alternatively, we could motivate the assignment of the dative case to the Experiencer argument by language-particular linking rules or delegate it to idiosyncratic lexical rules. The latter has been proposed for comparable classes of psychological predicates in Italian by Belletti and Rizzi (1988) within Government and Binding Theory, in Dutch by Zaenen (1988, 1993) within Lexical-Functional Grammar and in Icelandic by

Foley and Van Valin (1984) and Van Valin (1991) within Role and Reference Grammar. Such proposals presuppose that no properties can be found that can be connected to the dative case of the Experiencer argument.

To account for the full range of data in English and other languages in an adequate way, I will sketch a linking proposal that pays close attention to the systematic semantic differences among the relevant classes of psychological predicates. This proposal crucially differs from Tenny's in assuming a monostratal syntactic representation and a direct mapping between the thematic and syntactic structure, hence there is no need for movement rules. Most importantly, it does not a priori restrict the kind and number of semantic properties that mediate between lexical semantics and syntax. In this respect, I follow a number of semantically-based studies devoted to the argument structure of psychological predicates in the past ten years or so (cf. Croft 1986; Kiparsky 1987; Pesetsky 1987, 1995; Van Valin 1987, 1990, 1991; Dowty 1988, 1991; Rozwadowska 1988; Zaenen 1988, 1993; Condoravdi and San Filippo 1990; Van Voorst 1992).

3.3 Semantically-based accounts

In particular, two proposals stand out, Dowty's (1988, 1991) and Pesetsky's (1987, 1995). Pesetsky suggests that the Experiencer-subject and Experiencer-object predicates differ in the thematic roles assigned to their respective co-arguments. The *frighten*-type predicates take Causer and the *fear*-type ones Target or Subject Matter of Emotion. "Causer is always associated with the *subject* position, and Target is associated with the *object* position" (Pesetsky 1995:56). This can be also represented in the following hierarchy: Causer > Experiencer > Target/Subject Matter. Without going into the details of Pesetsky's proposal, we notice that his linking generalization does not hold for Czech data. The argument that corresponds to what Pesetsky calls 'Target' can be realized as object (with nominative-Experiencer predicates) or as subject (with dative-Experiencer predicates), even though it is lower on the hierarchy than the Experiencer. We need a linking mechanism that can distinguish these two cases.

The most promising way to do just this appears to be within theories of linking that view thematic roles as clusters of semantic properties. Such theories have been advocated by Foley and Van Valin (1984), Van Valin (1987, 1990, 1991), Rozwadowska (1988), Zaenen (1988, 1993), Dowty (1988, 1991), Pinker (1989), Bresnan and Zaenen (1991), Pustejovsky (1988) and Jackendoff (1990). Given that Dowty's theory is the most explicitly articulated, let us consider how he accounts for psychological predicates.

In Dowty's framework, the linking between the semantic and syntactic representations is determined by clusters of verbal entailments, or Proto-Agent and Proto-Patient properties (8).

(8)   Dowty (1991:572)

Contributing properties for the Agent Proto-Role: a. volitional involvement in the event or state; b. sentience (and/or perception); c. causing an event or change of state in another participant; d. movement (relative to the position of another participant); (e. referent exists independent of action of verb).

Contributing properties for the Patient Proto-Role: a. undergoes change of state; b. incremental theme; c. causally affected by another participant; d. stationary relative to movement of another participant; (e. does not exist independently of the event, or not at all).

The Argument Selection Principle (9) determines the association of clusters of Proto-Agent and Proto-Patient properties with grammatical relations.

(9)   **Argument Selection Principle** (Dowty 1991:576)

In predicates with grammatical subject and object, the argument for which the predicate entails the greatest number of Proto-Agent properties will be lexicalized as the subject of the predicate; the argument having the greatest number of Proto-Patient properties will be lexicalized as the direct object.

Although the Experiencer argument of the *fear* and *frighten* classes are equal in Agent properties, they are unequal in that the Experiencer of the *frighten* class denotes an entity that undergoes a change in the denoted event, and hence it is a 'better' Patient. Therefore, it must be the direct object (cf. Dowty 1991:580).

In this connection it is important to notice that the notion of 'Incremental Theme', which partially overlaps with Tenny's argument that "measures out" the event, plays no role in Dowty's description of psychological predicates. Second, the Proto-Patient property 'Incremental Theme' is not privileged in any way, it is treated on a par with other verbal entailments.

3.4 Suggested analysis

In order to analyze Czech data within Dowty's framework, we need the notion of 'morphological case feature'. Case features are to be distinguished from case morphology. The main reason is that NPs with distinct case features may have the same case morphology, and vice versa. All references to 'case' in this paper, including the glosses, are to be understood as references to case features. The linking rules determine alignments between clusters of Proto-Agent (PA) and/or Proto-Patient (PP) properties and NPs specified with a given case feature or with PPs which govern NPs with a given case feature. The linking-to-cases in Czech can be formulated without recourse to grammatical relations (cf. also Van Valin 1991:192). This is justified by a fairly high correlation between morphological cases and semantic properties of thematic roles (cf. Langacker 1990 and Comrie 1981), which seems to be tighter than the correlation between thematic roles and grammatical relations (cf. Comrie (1981:73), for example).

For the three main classes of Czech psychological predicates the linking-to-cases is summarized in (10):

(10)

milovat 'to love'	zlobit 'to anger'		vadit 'to harm', 'to annoy'
<NOM, ACC>	<NOM, ACC>		<NOM, DAT>
PA:sentience	PA:cause	PA:sentience	PA:sentience
(PA:volition)	(PA:volition)	PP:change	PP: ?
		PP:causally affected	

As the above table shows, all three predicate types entail the Proto-Agent property 'sentience' in one of their arguments (Experiencer). However, only the Experiencer argument of such verbs as *milovat* 'to love', *bát se* 'to be afraid' can be also understood as a volitional Agent that instigates the denoted emotional event. This is reflected in the acceptability of the imperative formation:

(11-a)
$Neboj^1$ se   ho!
NEG-fear   REFL   him-ACC
'Don't be afraid of him!'

The two Proto-Agent properties 'sentience' and 'volition' clearly justify the lexicalization of the Experiencer as subject in the nominative case. By contrast, the dative-Experiencer and accusative-Experiencer denote participants that lack control or that have a very low degree of control and volitional involvement in the event.

The second distinguishing feature concerns the causal event structure. Only accusative-Experiencer predicates are eventive and causative. The referent of the nominative argument is the *cause* of the denoted change of psychological state in the Experiencer participant and it can also be construed as a volitional agent, as is shown in the imperative example (11b). 'Cause' and 'volition', two Proto-Agent properties, motivate the encoding of this argument as subject in the nominative case.

(11-b)

Nezlob[I]   *mě!*
NEG-anger   me-ACC
'Don't make me angry!'

On the side of the Experiencer argument the causal event structure is registered in terms of two Proto-Patient properties, 'causally affected by another participant' and 'undergoes a change of state'. This motivates the encoding of the Experiencer in the accusative case.

The above observations suggest that active clauses with accusative-Experiencer predicates are high on the transitivity scale (cf. Hopper and Thompson 1980). It is not surprising then that accusative-Experiencer predicates can freely occur in the passive. Clauses with dative-Experiencer predicates, on the other hand, are very low on the transitivity scale. One of their distinguishing features is the absence of Proto-Agent properties in their nominative subject argument. This is manifested in the lack of the imperative (11c) construction:

(11-c)

Nevaď[I]   *mi!*   *Nechyb*[I]   *mi!*
*NEG-annoy   me-DAT   *NEG-lack   me-DAT
'Don't annoy me!'   '*Don't lack me!'

It can be also seen as motivating the fact that dative-Experiencer predicates do not occur in the passive (although some can form impersonal passives), if we accept that (one of) the function(s) of the passive is the defocusing of an Agent(-like) subject.

The assignment of the dative case to the Experiencer argument may seem at first sight puzzling. Although the Experiencer argument of such predicates as *vadit* 'to annoy', 'to harm' seems to be more thematically prominent than its co-argument (it is associated with the Proto-Agent property 'sentience'), it is marked with the dative case, rather than in the nominative case. We cannot solve this puzzle by claiming that the dative-Experiencer nominal is a 'quirky' subject, because it does not exhibit properties typically ascribed to subjects in Czech. It does not determine verb agreement, for example.

Is it possible to motivate the puzzling dative case assignment to the Experiencer argument on semantic grounds? In general, psychological predicates can be classified along the 'good - bad' scale according to the evaluation of the emotional state or episode they express (cf. Jackendoff 1990). However, only dative-Experiencer predicates incorporate the evaluation along the more specific 'benefit - harm' scale, over and above the basic 'good - bad' scale, as their dominant semantic feature. In other words, dative-Experiencer arguments are typically entailed to be Beneficiaries or Maleficiaries, whereby the qualitative aspects of the emotional state or episode itself are backgrounded. This observation can be confirmed by the fact that dative-Experiencer verbs cannot be freely modified with manner adverbials like *příjemně* 'in a pleasant manner', *vášnivě* 'passionately', *hořce* 'bitterly', *horlivě* 'ardently', for example. However, they can be modified with degree and intensity adverbials like *hodně* 'a lot', *málo, trochu* 'a little', which are related to the expression of benefit or harm.

(12-a)

Ten výsledek   nás   nepříjemně   / hodně   překvapil.
the result-NOM   us-ACC   unpleasantly /a-lot   surprised
'The result surprised us in a pleasant way / a lot.'

(12-b)

Ten výsledek   nám   *nepříjemně / hodně   vadil.
the result-NOM   us-DAT   *unpleasantly /a-lot   annoyed
'The result annoyed us in an unpleasant way / a lot.'

The evaluation of the Experiencer's mental state along the 'benefit - harm' scale may be viewed as a kind of Proto-Patient entailment. Together with the observation that the Experiencer has low or no control over its mental state, such an additional Proto-Patient entailment may explain why the Experiencer of such predicates as *vadit* 'to harm', 'to annoy' is not encoded in the nominative case. This seems to have an interesting implication for the theory of linking. If it is the case that the evaluation of the Experiencer's mental state, as a Proto-Patient property, prevents the Experiencer from being encoded in the nominative case, then it has more weight than the Proto-Agent property 'sentience' in the linking-to-cases mechanism. This suggests that a possible modification of Dowty's system of mapping could involve the mapping of weighted clusters of properties to grammatical relations and/or morphological cases. I will leave this as a proposal for future research.

Having justified why the Experiencer argument of such predicates as *vadit* 'to annoy' is not encoded in the nominative case, how do we motivate the assignment of the dative case? The use of the governed dative-Experiencer is related to the interpretation of benefit or harm and modality often associated with optional or "free datives", as in *Jana mu koupila košili* (lit.: Jane him-DAT bought shirt-ACC) 'Jane bought a shirt for him', *Zemřel nám kanárek* (lit.: died us-DAT canary) 'Our canary died on us.' The notions of 'benefit' and 'harm' can be viewed as a transposition of the transfer schema from the concrete spatial domain into the psycho-physical domain of mental states. From this perspective, the Beneficiary and Maleficiary are Recipients of some good or favor and harm, respectively. Such observations dovetail nicely with the view that the Experiencer of psychological predicates is thematically a kind of Location (cf. Anderson's (1971) Localistic Theory of Case), related to both Goal and Recipient, and with the claim made by Kurylowicz (1949/64) that the origin of the IE dative is in a concrete locative inflection. Therefore, it does not come as a surprise that the dative case is the typical exponent of not only Goal and Recipient, but also of Experiencer.

4 Conclusion

It has been shown that the linking between the thematic argument structure and morphologically case-marked NPs in the domain of Czech psychological predicates is predictable, provided we make reference to the fine-grained properties of the thematic structure of the relevant classes of predicates and general linking principles along the lines suggested by Dowty (1988, 1991). The proposed analysis avoids postulating the assignment of the dative case to the Experiencer argument by idiosyncratic lexical rules.

The linking in the domain of Czech psychological predicates cannot be motivated by a *single* semantic property, regardless whether it is "aspectual delimitedness" (telicity) or some other property. Consequently, it cannot be covered by the AIH or any other universal linking hypothesis that assumes a direct and uniform association between a single semantic property and syntactic arguments. Of course, such hypotheses are not automatically invalidated by the existence of data like Czech psychological predicates. It is to be expected that linking of certain classes of predicates will be exempt from universal linking rules and follow specific language-particular rules. However, if it turns out that universal linking hypotheses like the AIH cannot account for a large number of classes of predicates in various languages, they will have to be rejected. By the same token, we will have to acknowledge that the syntax-semantics interface cannot be constrained by any single privileged semantic property or layer in the lexical representation 'visible' to syntax. To the extent that the thesis of the autonomy of syntax is defended by means of such a narrow interface as the AIH, there will also be reasons to doubt whether it can be upheld.

References

Anderson, J. M. 1971. *The Grammar of Case. Towards a Localistic Theory.* Cambridge: Cambridge University Press.

Baker, M. 1988. *Incorporation: A theory of grammatical function changing.* Chicago: University of Chicago Press.

Belletti, A. and L. Rizzi, 1988. "Psych-verbs and Theta-theory". *Natural Language and Linguistic Theory,* **6**, 291-352.

Bresnan, J. and A. Zaenen. 1991. "Deep Unaccusativity in Lexical Functional Grammar". Dziwirek, K., Farrell, P. and E. Mejias-Bikandi (eds.), *Grammatical Relations: A Cross-Theoretical Perspective.* San Diego: University of California.

Burzio, L. 1981. *Intransitive Verbs and Italian Auxiliaries.* Ph.D. Thesis. MIT.

Burzio, L. 1986. *Italian Syntax. A Government and Binding Approach.* Dordrecht: Reidel.

Chomsky, N. 1965. *Aspects of the Theory of Syntax.* Cambridge, MA: The MIT Press.

Comrie, B. 1981. *Language Universals and Linguistic Typology.* Chicago: University of Chicago Press.

Condoravdi, C. and A. Sanfilippo. 1990. Technical report ESPRIT BRA-3030 ACQUILEX WP NO.007, July 1990, The University of Cambridge.

Croft, W. 1986. "Surface Subject Choice of Mental Verbs". Paper presented at the Annual Meeting of the Linguistic Society of America, New York.

Dowty, D. R. 1988. "Thematic Proto-Roles, Subject Selection, and Lexical Semantic Defaults", ms. (Paper presented at the 1987 LSA Colloquium. The Twenty-Second Annual Meeting of the Linguistic Society of America, San Francisco; preliminary draft of January 1988).

Dowty, D. R. 1991. "Thematic Proto-Roles and Argument Selection". *Language,* **67**, 547-619.

Filip, H. 1990. "Thematic Roles and Aktionsart". *Proceedings of the Twentieth Western Conference on Linguistics,* Vol. **3**, B. Birch, K. Hunt and V. Samiian (eds.), pp. 88-99.

Filip, H. 1993. *Aspect, Situation Types and Nominal Reference.* Doctoral Thesis, Department of Linguistics, University of California at Berkeley.

Foley, W. A. and R. D. Van Valin, Jr. 1984. *Functional Syntax and Universal Grammar.* Cambridge: Cambridge University Press.

Goldberg, A. E. 1992/95 *Argument Structure Constructions.* Ph.D. Thesis. University of California at Berkeley. Published by the University of Chicago Press, Chicago. 1995.

Grimshaw, J. 1990. *Argument Structure*. Cambridge, MA: The MIT Press.

Gropen, J. 1989. *Learning Locative Verbs: How Universal Linking Rules Constrain Productivity*. Ph.D. Thesis, MIT.

Gropen, J., Pinker, S., Hollander M. and R. Goldberg. 1991. "Affectedness and Direct Objects: The Role of Lexical Semantics in the Acquisition of Verb Argument Structure". In Levin, B. and S. Pinker (eds.).

Hinrichs, E. 1985. *A Compositional Semantics for Aktionsarten and NP Reference in English*. Ph.D. Thesis, Ohio State University.

Holloway-King, T. 1993. "Russian Psych-Verbs and Refining the UTAH", ms. Stanford University.

Hopper, P. and S. Thompson. 1980. "Transitivity in Grammar and Discourse." *Language* **56**, 251-299.

Jackendoff, R. S. 1990 *Semantic Structures*. Cambridge, MA: The MIT Press.

Kenny, A. 1963. *Action, Emotion and Will*. London: Routledge and K. Paul; New York. Humanities Press [1963]. Series title: Studies in philosophical psychology.

Kiparsky, P. 1987. *Morphology and Grammatical Relations*, ms., Stanford University.

Kurylowicz, J. 1949/1964. *The Inflexional Categories of Indo-European*. Heidelberg: Carl Winter.

Lakoff, G. 1970. *Irregularity in Syntax*. New York: Holt, Rinehart and Winston.

Lakoff, G. 1993. The Syntax of Metaphorical Semantic Roles. Pustejovsky, J. (ed.). *Semantics and the Lexicon*. Dordrecht, The Netherlands: Kluwer Academic Publishers. pp. 27-36.

Langacker, R. W. 1990. *Concept, image, and symbol: the cognitive basis of grammar*. Berlin; New York: Mouton de Gruyter.

Legendre, G. 1989. "Inversion with Certain French Experiencer Verbs." *Language* **65**, 752-782.

Levin, B. 1993. *English Verb Classes and Alternations: A Preliminary Investigation*. Chicago: University of Chicago Press.

Levin, B. and M. Rappaport Hovav. 1991. "Wiping the Slate Clean: A Lexical Semantic Exploration". *Cognition*, **41**, 123-51.

Levin, B. and S. Pinker (eds.) 1991. *Lexical and Conceptual Semantics*. Amsterdam, The Netherlands: Elsevier Science Publishers, B. V.

Perlmutter, D. 1978. "Impersonal Passives and the Unaccusative Hypothesis". *Papers from the Fourth Annual Meeting of the Berkeley Linguistics Society*. Berkeley: Berkeley Linguistics Society, University of California at Berkeley, 157-189.

Perlmutter, D. 1984. "Working 1s and Inversion in Italian, Japanese and Quechua." Perlmutter, D. and C. Rosen (eds.).

Perlmutter, D. and C. Rosen (eds.). 1984. *Studies in Relational Grammar 2*. Chicago: University of Chicago Press.

Pesetsky, D. 1987. "Binding Problems with Experiencer Verbs". *Linguistic Inquiry*, **18**, 126-40.

Pesetsky, D. 1995. *Zero Syntax: Experiencers and Cascades*. Cambridge, MA: The MIT Press.

Pinker, S. 1989. *Learnability and Cognition: The Acquisition of Argument Structure*. Cambridge, MA: The MIT Press.

Postal, P. M. 1971. *Cross-Over Phenomena*. New York: Holt, Rinehart and Winston.

Pustejovsky, J. 1988. "The Geometry of Events". Tenny, C. (ed.), *Studies in Generative Approaches to Aspect*, Lexicon Project Working Papers 24, Center for Cognitive Science at MIT, Cambridge, MA.

Pustejovsky, J. 1991. "The Generative Lexicon". *Computational Linguistics* **17.4**.

Pustejovsky, J. 1993 (ed). *Semantics and the Lexicon*. Dordrecht: Kluwer Academic Publishers.

Rozwadowska, B. 1988. "Thematic Restrictions on Derived Nominals." *Syntax and Semantics 21: Thematic Relations*, Wilkins, W. (ed.). San Diego, CA: Academic Press, 147-66.

Slabakova, R. 1994. "Bulgarian Psych-Verbs"s, ms. McGill University.

Tenny, C. L. 1987. *Grammaticalizing Aspect and Affectedness*. Doctoral Dissertation, MIT. Cambridge: Mass.

Tenny, C. L. 1988. "The Aspectual Interface Hypothesis: The Connection between Syntax and Lexical Semantics". *Lexicon Project Working Papers*, **24**. Cambridge, MA: Center for Cognitive Science at MIT.

Tenny, C. L. 1989. "The Aspectual Interface Hypothesis". *Lexicon Project Working Papers*, **31**. Cambridge, MA: Center for Cognitive Science at MIT.

Tenny, C. L. 1992. "Aspectual Roles, Modularity, and Acquisition", ms.

Tenny, C. L. 1994. *Aspectual Roles and the Syntax-Semantics Interface*. Dordrecht: Kluwer Academic Publishers.

Van Valin, R. D. 1987. "The Unaccusative Hypothesis vs. Lexical Semantics: Syntactic vs. Semantic Approaches to Verb Classification". *Proceedings of NELS 17*, University of Massachusetts at Amherst, 641-661.

Van Valin, R. D. 1990. "Semantic Parameters of Split Intransitivity. *Language* **66**, 221-260.

Van Valin, R. D. 1991. "Another Look at Icelandic Case-Marking and Grammatical Relations". *Natural Language and Linguistic Theory*, **9**.

Van Voorst, J. 1992. "The Aspectual Semantics of Psychological Verbs". *Lingustics and Philosophy* **15**, 65-92.

Vendler, Z. 1957. "Verbs and Times". *Philosophical Review*, **56**, pp. 143-160.

Vendler, Z. 1967. "Verbs and Times". *Linguistics in Philosophy*. Ithaca, New York: Cornell University Press. pp. 97-121. Verkuyl, H. J. 1972. *On the Compositional Nature of the Aspects*. Foundations of Language, Supplementary Series, Vol. **15**. D. Reidel Publishing Co., Dordrecht, Holland.

Verkuyl, H. J. 1981. "Numerals and Quantifiers in X-bar-Syntax and their Semantic Interpretation". Groenendijk et al. (ed.) Part 2. pp. 567-599.

Verkuyl, H. J. 1989. "Aspectual classes and aspectual composition." *Linguistics and Philosophy*, Vol. 2, pp. 39-94.

Verma, K. M. and K. P. Mohanan. 1990. *Experiencer Subjects in South Asian Languages*. Stanford, CA: The Center for the Study of Language and Information.

Zaenen, A. 1988. "Unaccusative Verbs in Dutch and the Syntax-Semantics Interface". CSLI Report 123, Stanford, CA.

Zaenen, A. 1993. "Integrating Syntax and Lexical Semantics". Pustejovsky, J. (ed.), *Semantics and the Lexicon*. Dordrecht: Kluwer Academic Publishers.

Discourse Goals and Attentional Processes in Sentence Production: The Dynamic Construal of Events[1]

LINDA B. FORREST
University of Oregon

Intuitively, we know that things in the world attract our attention differentially, either because they are inherently salient to humans or because they are of special interest to a particular perceiver. This differential prominence of participants leads to differing viewpoints or construals of the events and states in which they are involved, and these differing viewpoints are reflected in different linguistic codings of the events and states. For example, Tomlin (in press) has shown that attentionally focusing a referent leads to its selection as syntactic subject, giving rise to Active/Passive alternations in English. In a similar vein, Langacker (1986) has pointed out that the semantic difference between *above* and *below* lies in which referent is viewed as more prominent. Previously, I showed that speakers will alternate between an *above* construal and a *below* construal depending on which referent their visual attention was drawn to prior to sentence formulation (Forrest 1992).

We should not assume, however, that speakers act in a knee-jerk fashion to stimuli which enter their consciousness from the outside world or from their memories. Speaking is a goal-oriented action, and people structure their utterances to meet the goals of the discourse in which they are momentarily engaged. Thus, I argue, if the construal of an event or state which enters consciousness at a particular moment in time does not meet the goals of the present discourse, speakers must manipulate their conceptualization of the event until it is brought into line with their discourse goals. Crucially, this manipulation would not come without cost to the speaker; like any other mental operation, it must take time (Posner

---

[1]This project has benefited greatly from discussions with Russ Tomlin, Victor Villa, Bill Staley, Tamara Smith, Bruce McCandliss, and Belinda Young-Davy. Any remaining deficiencies are my own.

1978). Thus, if a reorientation operation occurs prior to the production of a sentence, it can be detected using psychometric techniques. The present study was designed to investigate this hypothesis experimentally.

1. A Model of Sentence Production

In the framework presented here, a speaker describing a scene is assumed to carry out a sequence of groups of mental processes or computations that are, for the most part, serial in nature. Initially, the speaker's mental computations lead to the visual perception of the scene. Of course, this involves many component computations, and these component computations may occur in parallel, but as a group, the visual perception processes are basically completed before those related to formulating an utterance begin. That is, the speaker determines what has been presented before he or she begins to talk about it. If the viewpoint from which the scene is witnessed is sufficient for the speaker's discourse purpose, then sentence preparation processes can be initiated immediately. These sentence preparation processes will lead to appropriate syntactic, morphological, and phonological structures.

If the initial viewpoint on the scene is not one that meets the speaker's discourse goals (for example, because the speaker's visual attention was drawn to a referent that is not important or thematic), then some sort of reconstrual of the scene must take place. Although the reconstrual takes place in the service of linguistic goals, it is hypothesized to take place prior to (rather than during) the sentence preparation processes. Thus, the reconstrual processes "set up" the mental representation of the event so that it will fulfill the goals of the discourse, similar to the notion of "thinking for speaking" (Slobin 1987).

By hypothesizing that the sequence of mental processes occurs in this way, at least two empirically testable predictions can be made. First, speakers should be able to begin speaking sooner when a scene they have witnessed does not need to be reconstrued. Second, since the reconstrual processes are seen as occurring more or less serially between the visual perception processes and the sentence preparation processes, any delay created by the reconstrual should delay all the sentence preparation processes. Thus, if processing were interrupted with a probe at some point in time that was early in the sentence preparation processes when reconstrual has taken place, this same point in time should be late in the sentence preparation processes when reconstrual has not taken place. These two types of predictions were tested in separate experiments described in Section 3. The hypothesized time course of sentence production is diagrammed in Figure 1. The diagram illustrates that utterances which do not require a reconstrual of the visual scene can be produced more quickly than utterances which do.

Also, a probe placed at the same point in time will occur late in the sentence preparation processes for utterances which do not require reconstrual, but early in these same processes when reconstrual is necessary.

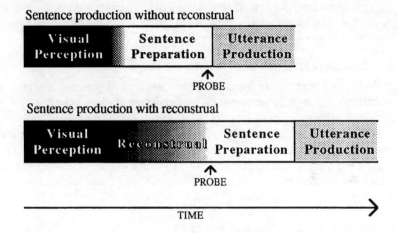

Figure 1. Time Course for Producing a Sentence

2. Manipulating Focus of Attention Experimentally

These experiments depend critically on an understanding of the nature of visual attention and how it can be manipulated. In the last 15 years, psychologists have made a great deal of progress in understanding the psychology and neuropsychology of attention. (See Posner & Petersen 1990 and Kahneman & Treisman 1984 for reviews.) A common metaphor in this literature is "attention as a spotlight." The beam of the "spotlight" may be quite narrow or relatively wide, but objects "within the beam" are perceptually more prominent and are responded to more quickly than objects "outside the beam," i.e., unattended. Furthermore, when a perceiver moves attention from one location to another, the "beam" "sweeps across" the intervening space. The time course of these attentional shifts is well-studied (Posner 1980, Maylor 1985, Posner & Briand 1990), and the experiments described below take advantage of the fact that attention requires a certain amount of time to move to a new location.

Attention can be directed by either exogenous or endogenous control (Posner 1980). Exogenous cues, such as flashes of light or transient motion, are events in the outside world which draw the perceiver's attention to some object or location in space independently of any intention by the perceiver to orient attention to that object or location. Endogenous control of attention originates from within the perceiver and is guided by his or her internally generated plans in carrying out some task. In the following experiments, both techniques for directing attention are used. It is argued that when an exogenously cued object is also an important one in terms of the speaker's internally held discourse goals, speakers do not need to reconstrue their mental representation of a scene which they have witnessed to order to report what they saw.

3.   The Experiments and Results

In both experiments, the speaker's main task was to produce a sentence describing the spatial relationship between two figures presented on a computer screen.[2] Speakers were prompted to take a particular "point of view" on this simple event by using an exogenous cue, a small bright cross, which appeared on the screen just prior to the two figures. The figures were presented so that one figure always occurred at the location where the cue had been. The timing between the cue and the figures (150 ms) was such that a speaker's visual attention should arrive at the cued location just as the figures were presented; thus, the figure that was presented at the cued location would be visually attended. The figures remained on the screen just long enough to be seen by the speaker (117 ms), and then they were masked. The rapid presentation assured that the speaker's visual focus of attention remained on a single figure only throughout the presentation. The time course of these events is shown in Figure 2.

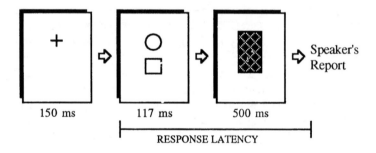

Figure 2.   Time Course of a Trial

Speakers were encouraged to regard one referent is more important to the discourse task by using the nonlinguistic cue of color. In every pair of figures, one figure was yellow and the other white. (They were presented on

---

[2]Both vertical and horizontal relations were presented; however, since many speakers report difficulties with 'right of' and 'left of', only data from vertical trials was analyzed.

a dark blue background.) The speakers were asked to report "where the yellow figure is in relation to the white figure." By setting up the speaker's task this way, the yellow figure is always the one whose position is being predicated; it will always be the Figure in Talmy's (1983) framework or the trajector in Langacker's Cognitive Grammar framework. In order to do this task appropriately, the speaker's response would have the form, "The *[name of yellow figure]* is *[spatial relation]* the *[name of white figure]* ," i.e., with the yellow figure as the syntactic subject and the white object in a prepositional phrase. For example, if speakers saw a white heart above and a yellow bird below, they should report "the bird is below the heart."[3]

Speakers' visual attention was cued to either the yellow figure or to the white. When visual attention was cued to the yellow figure , the viewpoint which was presented to the sensory system was <u>Congruent</u> with the discourse goal of "talking about" the yellow figure's relationship to some landmark figure. On the other hand, when visual attention was drawn to the white figure, the viewpoint which was presented to the sensory system was <u>Noncongruent</u> with the discourse goal, and speakers should need to mentally reconstrue the event before giving a verbal report of it.

This basic experimental task was used to test the predictions made by the sentence production model discussed in Section 1. In the first experiment, the latency of onset of utterance was compared in the Congruent and Noncongruent conditions. The second experiment uses a probe to interrupt the sentence preparation process and measure the activation of the two nouns under these same conditions.

3.1 A Test of Response Latency during Sentence Production (Experiment 1)

Speakers should be quicker to begin utterances when their visual attention has been cued to the discourse-important (yellow) referent, i.e., in the

---

[3]Clark & Chase (1972) showed that speakers prefer visual elements that are good figures (such as stars) as syntactic subjects and elements that are good grounds (such as lines) as locatives when these two types of elements are presented together. Talmy (1983), Osgood & Bock (1977), MacWhinney (1977), Flores d'Arcais (1987), and others have discussed perceptual factors which lead to the preferential selection of some elements as Figures. However, in many situations, no such bias is present, as in Huddleston's (1970) well-known example concerning whether the bank is by the post office or the post office by the bank. In the latter situation, I argue, the choice depends only on the speaker's mental construal of the scene in a particular discourse situation. It is this case which this study seeks to duplicate in the laboratory. To that end, all visual elements are relatively good figures (stars, birds, hearts, etc.) that should not lead to obvious preferences for one particular description. Furthermore, these figures are randomly paired and are presented in both orientations. Thus, any preferences speakers might have for one orientation should be counterbalanced in this data, and any statistical results should be due solely to the experimental manipulation.

Congruent condition. In the Noncongruent condition, speaker's visual attention is drawn to the unimportant (white) figure which will appear in the locative phrase of the utterance. According to the model of sentence production presented in Section 1, speakers' utterances will be delayed in this condition because they need to reconstrue the event they witnessed. This hypothesis was tested in the first experiment.

The trials were constructed using MacroMind Director software running on a Macintosh IIcx. There were 60 trials in the entire film, of which 32 were vertical trials of interest here. The trials were designed so that all combinations of cueing and color were counterbalanced over the experiment. Nineteen native speakers of English participated. They were given a short warm-up session of 21 trials, and then their responses were tape recorded. A 100 ms tone, inaudible to the speaker, was recorded on the tape at the beginning of the presentation of each pair of figures. Sound file editing software was used to measure the latency from the reference tone to the beginning of the first phoneme of the speakers response.

The means for each speaker in each experimental condition were used in the data analysis. The overall mean for the Congruent condition was approximately 87 ms faster than that for the Noncongruent condition. These are shown in Table 1 and graphed in Figure 3.

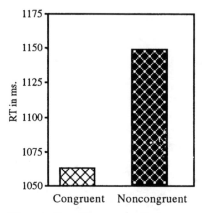

Figure 3. Response Latency for Sentence Production

Table 1. Means and Standard Deviations of Response Latencies for Sentence Production

CONDITION	M	SD
Congruent	1063.4	238.1
Noncongruent	1150.0	252.1

RT in ms.

A repeated measures analysis of variance with one fixed within-subjects factor, Congruency, with two levels (Congruent, Noncongruent) was performed; the Congruency factor was significant ($p < .025$,

F' (1,21) = 7.41).[4] Thus as predicted, speakers were quicker to begin their utterances when their visual focus of attention was directed to the discourse-important yellow object. This suggests that when speaker's attention was not drawn to the referent they needed to talk about, they required extra time to shift attention before formulating the utterance. This amounts to shifting their construal of the relationship of the two figures from, for example, an *above* construal to a *below* construal.

3.2 Assessing the Activation of Nouns During Sentence Preparation (Experiment 2)

According to the sentence production model discussed in Section 1, if the viewpoint that is presented to the visual system is not the viewpoint that will meet the speaker's discourse needs, then some set of reconstrual computations must take place prior to the initiation of sentence preparation processes. These reconstrual computations will delay all components of the sentence preparation process, including the activation of word forms in the speaker's mental lexicon. Suppose the activation of the names of the referents in the utterance were measured at some specified point in time. If this point in time were late in the sentence preparation processes in the Congruent condition, the names of the referents to be used in the sentence should be highly activated in the speaker's mental lexicon. However, if reconstrual had delayed the beginning of the sentence preparation processes, as in the Noncongruent condition, then these same words should be less activated at this same point in time.

This hypothesis was tested using the same production task as Experiment 1, but occasionally interrupting it with a lexical decision task. A lexical decision task requires the subject to decide as quickly as possible whether a string of characters is a real word or not. When a word is already mentally activated, subjects can made positive decisions more quickly. In Experiment 2, the probe words were the name of one of the figures in the sentence that the speaker was trying to utter. These were presented between the stimulus pictures and the beginning of the utterance, as the speaker was formulating the utterance. A probe early in the speaker's preparation of the sentence should show that the names of figures are less activated than the same words later in the preparation period. (See Figure 1 for the approximate location of the probe during the time course of sentence production.)

In Experiment 2, speakers watched a film similar to the one in Experiment 1. As before, they were asked to tell where the yellow figure

---

[4]Both Figures and Speakers were treated as random factors and an F' statistic computed, as recommended by Clark (1973).

was in relation to the white one, and either figure could be visually cued. On 28 percent of the trials, the sentence production task was interrupted with an unexpected lexical decision task. A word or a pronounceable nonword was flashed on the center of the screen just as the two figures were masked, approximately 117 ms into the sentence production process. Speakers were asked to discontinue the sentence production task and press a mouse button as quickly as possible whenever they saw a real English word; they were asked to ignore any nonwords. On two-thirds of real word trials, the word was the name of a referent in the sentence the speaker was attempting to produce; on the other one-third of trials, the word was the name of an object not used in the experiment, but similar to experimental words in familiarity, frequency, and length.

The responses of interest here are those involving the names of referents in the sentence being produced. These were presented in a Latin square design such that each speaker saw some words in every experimental condition, and each probe word appeared in every experimental condition for some speakers, but each speaker saw each probe word only once during the experiment. For example, each speaker saw the probe word *sun* in one of four situations: In the Congruent condition, the sun figure could be either visually cued and the subject of the sentence being formulated (i.e., the yellow object) or not visually cued and the locative of the sentence (i.e. the white object). In the Noncongruent condition, the sun figure could be either not visually cued and the sentence subject (yellow) or visually cued and the sentence locative (white). These conditions are shown in Figure 4.

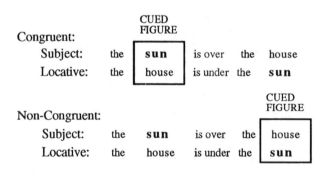

Figure 4. Response Conditions for the Word "sun"

The means for each speaker in each experimental condition were submitted to a repeated measures analysis of variance. There were two fixed within-subjects factors, Congruency with two levels (Congruent and

Noncongruent) and Grammar with two levels (Subject and Locative). The Congruency factor is the factor relevant to the present hypothesis. The Grammar factor refers to whether the probe word would be the subject or locative in the sentence being formulated. It is critical that there be no interaction between the Congruency factor and the Grammar factor. If the reconstrual computations are seen as occurring more or less serially between the visual perception processes and the sentence preparation processes, any delay created by reconstrual computations should delay the activation of <u>both</u> nouns in a sentence being produced, irrespective of their grammatical relation. An interaction between the Congruency factor and the Grammar factor would suggest that reconstrual does not affect both nouns of the sentence in the same way and that whatever is going on is not serial in nature.

The ANOVA results showed significant main effects for both the Congruency and Grammar factors, but importantly, there was no significant interaction between them (Congruency, $p < .001$, $F (1,35) = 12.83$; Grammar $p > .0012$, $F (1,35) = 12.49$; Congruency x Grammar $p < .1807$, $F (1,35) = 1.87$).[5] The means are shown in Table 2 and graphed in Figure 4.

Table 2. Means and Standard Deviations of Reaction Times to Probe Words in the Lexical Decision Task

CUE TYPE	M	SD
Congruent		
Subject word (yellow object)	768.0	121.6
Locative word (white object)	827.1	114.5
Noncongruent		
Subject word (yellow object)	818.0	112.0
Locative word (white object)	850.2	130.2

RT in ms.

---

[5]This analysis uses Subjects as the random factor. An analysis with Items as the random factor gives similar results.

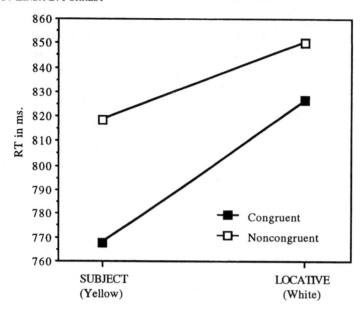

Figure 5. Reaction Times to Probe Words in the Lexical Decision Task

The results show that when the visual focus of attention was cued to the discourse-important figure (the Congruent condition), response time to <u>both</u> nouns in the sentence was faster overall. When visual attention was cued to the unimportant figure, response to these same nouns was slower. This delay affected both nouns in the Noncongruent sentences equally, suggesting that it resulted from extra processing which took place prior to the activation of word forms in the speaker's mental lexicon. Thus, these results support the hypothesis that some set of reconstrual computations takes place prior to sentence preparation processes when the viewpoint presented to the visual system is not the viewpoint that will meet the speaker's discourse needs.[6]

4.   Conclusion

The results presented above suggest that speakers do actively manipulate their mental construal of an event or state to bring it in line with some internally conceived discourse goal, rather than simply responding to stimuli

---

[6]It is also the case that the Grammar factor was significant, indicating that subject nouns were responded to more quickly than locative nouns. Although interesting, this effect is independent of and thus has no bearing on the issue of re-construal processes.

as presented to them by the external world. This manipulation appears to be carried out by basic cognitive processes, such as attention, which allow the speaker to "set up" a mental representation for the purpose of speaking about it. These manipulations of mental representations do, however, require extra mental processing prior to producing the utterance, and the traces of this added processing can be detected experimentally.

References

Allport, Alan. 1989. Visual Attention. In Michael I. Posner, ed., *Foundations of Cognitive Science*, 631–682. Cambridge, Mass.: MIT Press.

Bock, J. Kathryn. 1982. Toward a Cognitive Psychology of Syntax: Information Processing Contribution to Sentence Formulation. *Psychological Reviews*, 89:1–47.

Bock, J. Kathryn, and Richard K. Warren. 1985. Conceptual Accessibility and Syntactic Structure in Sentence Formulation. *Cognition*, 21:47–67.

Chafe, Wallace L. 1976. Givenness, Contrastiveness, Definiteness, Subjects, Topics, and Points of View. In Charles N. Li, ed., *Subject and Topic*, 27–55. New York: Academic Press.

Clark, Herbert H. 1973. The Language-as-fixed-effect Fallacy: A Critique of Language Statistics in Psychological Research. *Journal of Verbal Learning and Verbal Behavior*, 12:335–359.

Clark, Herbert H., and W. G. Chase. 1972. Perceptual Coding Strategies in the Formation and Verification of Descriptions. *Memory & Cognition*, 2:101–111.

Flores d'Arcais, Giovanni B. 1987. Perceptual Factors and Word Order in Event Descriptions. In Gerard Kempen, ed., *Natural Language Generation: New Results in Artificial Intelligence, Psychology, and Linguistics*, 441–451.. Dordrecht: Martinus Nijhoff.

Forrest, Linda B. 1992. *How Grammar Codes Cognition: Syntactic Subject and Focus of Attention*. M.A. Thesis, University of Oregon.

Kahneman, Daniel, and Anne Treisman. 1984. Changing Views of Attention Automaticity. In Raja Parasuraman & D. R. Davies, eds., *Varieties of Attention*, 29–61. New York: Academic Press.

Huddleston, Rodney. 1970. Some Remarks on Case Grammar. *Journal of Linguistics*, 1:501–510.

Langacker, Ronald W. 1986. Settings, Participants, and Grammatical Relations. In *Proceedings of the Second Annual Meeting of the Pacific Linguistics Conference*, 1–31. Eugene, Ore.:University of Oregon, Linguistics Dept.

Levelt, Willem J. M., Herbert Schriefers, Antje S. Meyer, Thomas Pechmann, Dirk Vorberg, and Jaap Havinga. 1991. The Time Course of Lexical Access in Speech Production: A Study of Picture Naming. *Psychological Review,* 98:122–142.

MacWhinney, Brian. 1977. Starting Points. *Language,* 53:152–168.

Maylor, Elizabeth A. 1985. Facilitory and Inhibitory Components of Orienting in Visual Space. In Michael I. Posner and Oscar Marin, eds., *Attention and Performance XI,* 189–204. Hillsdale, N.J.: Erlbaum.

Osgood, Charles E., and J. Kathryn Bock. 1977. Salience and Sentencing: Some Production Principles. In Sheldon Rosenberg, ed., *Sentence Production: Developments in Research and Theory,* 89–140. Hillsdale, N.J.: Erlbaum.

Posner, Michael I. 1978. *Chronometric Explorations of Mind.* New York: Oxford University Press.

Posner, Michael I. 1980. Orienting of Attention. *Quarterly Journal of Experimental Psychology,* 32:3–25.

Posner, Michael I., and Kevin A. Briand. 1990. *Attention.* Tech. Rep. No. 90-2. Eugene, Ore.: University of Oregon, Institute of Cognitive and Decision Sciences.

Posner, Michael I., Peter G. Grossenbacher, and Paul E. Compton. In press. Visual Attention. In M. Farah and G. Ratcliff, eds., *The Neuropsychology of High-level Vision: Collected Tutorial Essays.* Hillsdale, N.J.: Erlbaum.

Posner, Michael I., and Steven E. Petersen. 1990. The Attention System of the Human Brain. *Annual Review of Neuroscience,* 13:25–42.

Slobin, D. 1987. Thinking for Speaking. In Jon Aske, Natasha Beery, Laura Michaelis, Hana Filip, eds., *Proceedings of the Thirteenth Annual Meeting of the Berkeley Linguistics Society,* 435-445. Berkeley, Cal.: University of California at Berkeley.

Talmy, Leonard. 1983. How Language Structures Space. In Herbert L. Pick, Jr. and Linda P. Acredolo, eds., *Spatial Orientation: Theory, Research, and Application,* 225–282. New York: Plenum Press.

Tomlin, Russell S. 1983. On the Interaction of Syntactic Subject, Thematic Information, and Agent in English. *Journal of Pragmatics,* 7:411–432.

Tomlin, Russell S. In press. Focal Attention, Voice, and Word Order: An Experimental, Cross-linguistic Study. In Michael Noonan and Pamela Downing, eds., *Word Order and Discourse.* Amsterdam: J. Benjamins.

Winer, B. J. 1971. *Statistical Principles in Experimental Design,* 2nd ed. New York: McGraw-Hill.

Biographical Information

Linda Forrest is pursuing a Ph.D. at the University of Oregon. She is interested in the relationship between cognitive processes, such as attention, and the linguistic devices which encode them.

Salish Lexical Suffixes: A Case of Decategorialization

DONNA B. GERDTS & MERCEDES Q. HINKSON

Simon Fraser University

1. Introduction

Salish languages, and other languages of northwestern North American languages, are well-known for their lexical suffixes. These are substantival suffixes that bear little or no resemblance to free-standing nominals with the same or similar meaning. Some lexical suffixes and corresponding free nouns in Halkomelem are given in (1):[1]

(1) -*cəs*   *céləš*   'hand'
     -*šən*   *sx̌én'ə*   'foot'
     -*'éx̌ən* *t̓élu*   'arm, wing'
     -*wil*   *lə́wəx̌*   'rib'

Most Salish languages have approximately 100 lexical suffixes denoting

Thanks go to Wayne Suttles and Charles Ulrich for comments and suggestions on the data and analyses presented here. We would like to thank members of the audiences at the Salish Syntax workshop in Victoria and the CSDL for their questions and comments. Any remaining inadequacies are our own responsibility. This research was supported by a SSHRC grant.

[1]Data that are unlabelled or simply referred to as Halkomelem are from Gerdts' fieldnotes on Halkomelem as spoken by the late Arnold Guerin, a speaker of the Island dialect. Her research on Halkomelem was supported by the Jacobs and Phillips research funds. The abbreviations used in glossing the data are: ADV = advancement, ASP = aspect, AUX = auxiliary, BEN = benefactive, CN = connective, DET = determiner, ERG = ergative, INT = interrogative, INTR = intransitive, LCTR = limited control transitive, OBL = oblique, PL = plural, POS = possessive, REFL = reflexive, SUB = subject, TR = transitive, 1 = first person, 2 = second person, 3 = third person.

body parts (*hand, foot, heart, nose*), basic physical/environmental concepts (*earth, fire, water, wind, tree, rock, berry*), cultural items (*canoe, net, house, clothing, language*), and human/relational terms (*people, spouse, offspring*).

In this paper, we present a survey of some of the properties of Salish lexical suffixes. Data are drawn from two languages, Halkomelem, a Coast Salish language, and Lillooet, an Interior Salish language. The Halkomelem data are from Suttles's (in prep.) grammar of the Musqueam dialect and from Gerdts' fieldnotes on Island dialects. The Lillooet data are from van Eijk's (1985) grammar. Taking the forms with lexical suffixes given in the Musqueam and Lillooet grammars, we created a database consisting of 445 Musqueam words with 48 different lexical suffixes and 712 Lillooet words with 68 different suffixes.[2]

Lexical suffixes are used in several types of constructions. One common use is as the head of the theme in a complex predicate, as the Halkomelem data in (2) and (3) illustrate:

(2) *ni   cən   yə́qʷ-əlʔ-cəp.*
     AUX   1SUB   burn-CN-firewood
     'I made a fire.' (lit. 'I burned wood.')

(3) *ni   cən   k̓ʷə́s-cəs.*
     AUX   1SUB   burn-hand
     'I burned my hand.'

Such examples, of course, are reminiscent of noun incorporation found in other languages of the Americas and thus raise the question: Should lexical suffixes be regarded as incorporated nouns? Sapir (1911, 251–252) says no. He claims: "... As long, however, as they are lexically distinct from noun stems proper, they must be looked upon as grammatical elements pure and simple, however concrete their signification may seem." If we accept Sapir's viewpoint, then we are nevertheless left with a problem: What is a grammatical element? Furthermore, how are the properties of lexical suffixes accounted for within a theory of grammatical elements?

In this paper, we propose that lexical suffixes are the final stage of a

---

[2]Words with different derivational endings were given separate entries, but words that differed only in inflection were grouped under the same entry. Lexical suffixes that had similar form and meaning were grouped under a single "mega-gloss". For example, Suttles cites the various forms $-aʔθ/-áʔθ/-θən/-á\cdot y-θən/-áyəθə/-əyə-θín/-θ/-áθən$ with meanings such as 'mouth', 'edge', 'border', 'lip', and 'margin'. We treated this as a single suffix in our counts.

process whereby a free noun becomes increasingly fused to an element with which it is compounded until it emerges as a bound form. Other functionally similar processes—noun stripping (Miner 1986) and noun incorporation (Mithun 1984)—can be considered stages in this process:

(4) The noun to suffix cline:
   free noun > stripped noun > incorporated noun > bound form

Viewed from this perspective, the functional similarities between incorporated nouns and lexical suffixes are not accidental. Given the cline in (4), we expect some overlap in behavior between a lexical suffix and an incorporated noun.

Here we examine lexical suffixes in four constructions: noun compounds, compounding incorporation, classifying incorporation, and applicatives. We show that in the first two uses the lexical suffix contributes the categorial feature *noun* to the compound form. In the other two uses, however, the lexical suffix behaves acategorially. This lack of nouniness is what we expect if the lexical suffix is a grammatical element rather than an incorporated noun, as Sapir claims.

How can we reconcile these conflicting results? The four uses of lexical suffixes can be treated as showing different degrees of grammaticalization. We see an increasing abstraction of meaning concomitant with a gradual decategorialization. This is exactly as expected under theories of grammaticalization (e.g. Heine et al. 1991, Hopper and Traugott 1993), given our claim that lexical suffixes originated from nouns.

2. Lexical Suffixes in Compounds

First, some recent comparative work has shown that Salish lexical suffixes developed from free-standing nominals. Egesdal (1981), Mattina (1987), and Carlson (1989) have argued that lexical suffixes developed from nominal roots used as the right member of a compound. We will not repeat their evidence here. However, we briefly note that compounding is very frequent in Salish languages. The data in (5) illustrate some typical Halkomelem compounds.

(5)   *θi qáʔ*   'big' + 'water' > 'ocean'
        čikmən šéɫ   'steel' + 'road' > 'railroad'
        cìcəɫ támǝxʷ   'up above' + 'land' > 'heaven'
        sx̌ə̀x̌ə-ɫ-nét   'sacred' + CN + 'night' > 'Sunday'

Note that they are right-headed, that some of them take connective morphology, and that some are best analyzed as single words on phonological grounds. The historical picture in Salish is that the second element in compounds like these was phonologically shortened and eventually became a bound form.[3] Subsequently, new, longer, free-standing forms have been invented.

The claim, then, is that the second elements in right-headed compounds developed into lexical suffixes. This kind of right-headed structure, see (6), is still the most frequent use of lexical suffixes.

(6)

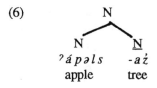

```
         N
        /\
      N    N
  ʔápəls  -aź
  apple   tree
```

Examples are given in (7).

(7)   N + lexical suffix = N
        Lillooet:

ʔápəls-aź	'apple tree'	'apple' + 'plant'
pṣúṣ-aź	'bitter cherry'	'bitter cherry' + 'plant'
pankʷúp-amx	'Vancouverite'	'Vancouver' + 'person'
kʷuṣuh-áɫċaʔ	'pork'	'pig' + 'flesh'
sil-álc	'tent'	'cloth' + 'dwelling'
lam-áwtəxʷ	'liquor store'	'rum' + 'house'

        Musqueam:

sàlaʔac-éwtxʷ	'house mat house'	'house mat' + 'house'
ɫqʷə́m-əɫp	'thimbleberry bush'	'thimbleberry' + 'plant'
wi·l-éʔɫ	'tule mat'	'tule' + flexible 'material'
səṁsəṁyə-élə	'hornets' nest'	'hornet' + 'container'
qáʔ-liʔc	'water box'	'water' + 'container'
tə́x̌ʷac-əɫp	'yew tree'	'bow' + 'plant'

Our claim that the lexical suffix serves as the head of the compound in the above examples is based largely on semantic considerations. However, note that lexical suffixes can be combined not only with noun stems, as illustrated above, but also with verb stems:

[3]We can see the process at work by examining one form sqáx̌aʔ, as in the Lillooet example in (i).

(i)   kʷan-sqáx̌aʔ   'get one's horse'   'get' + 'domestic animal'

This exists only as a bound form in Interior Salish languages. In some Coast Salish languages, it is a free-standing noun, however.

(8)   V + lexical suffix = N
      Lillooet:

ʕʷuy̓t-íc̓aʔ	'pajamas, nightie'	'sleep' + 'hide'
qʷəcp-úlməxʷ	'earthquake'	'shake (ASP)' + 'land'
ṗaṅt-átqʷaʔ	'back eddy'	'return' + 'water'
wáw-əlckzaʔ	'poplar'	'shout' + 'leaf'
zél-kʷaʔ	'whirlpool'	'go around, twist' + 'water'
say̓sz̓-átxʷ	'gym'	'play' + 'hub/locus'

      Musqueam:

qʷáʔ-cəp	'spark'	'get through' + 'firewood'
qəq̓-əyás	'barrel'	'bind it' + 'face/circle'
xiləx̌-áwəɬ	'battleship'	'make war' + 'vessel'
z̓ím-eIeʔc	'berry basket'	'pick berries' + 'container'
ɬìwəyəɬ-éwtxʷ	'church'	'worship' + 'house'
qiq̓-éwtxʷ	'jail'	'be bound' + 'house'

When such compounding results in a word of the category N, as represented in (9), we can see that the lexical suffix, which we take to be the head, determines the category of the word.

(9)

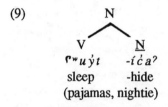

```
          N
         / \
        V   N
      ʕʷuy̓t  -íc̓aʔ
      sleep  -hide
      (pajamas, nightie)
```

This is an extremely common pattern in Salish. For example, of the 712 words in the Lillooet corpus, 440 are Ns while 214 are Vs. We discuss compounds of the latter type in the next section. Of the 440 Ns, 108 were based on N stems while 121 were based on V stems. Other forms are adjectival or indeterminate without further data. Thus we see that using lexical suffixation to create a N from a V stem is very common.

The above data show that the lexical suffix carries the categorial feature N which determines the feature of the compound.[4] Given the possibility of zero derivation, this evidence may not seem convincing. However, we can point out cases of stems that cannot appear as nouns without nominal

---

[4]Despite the bad press given the noun/verb distinction in Salish, it is easy to distinguish these categories on formal and functional grounds (van Eijk and Hess 1986, Suttles in prep.). The forms that we take to be Ns have the typical distributional properties associated with this category.

morphology, for example the forms with the *s-* prefix in (10), which nevertheless form N compounds without the need for further nominalization:

(10) Musqueam:

s-qéwθ	'potato'	qewθ-éwtxʷ	'potato cellar'
s-máq̓ʷaʔ	'blue heron'	məq̓ʷaʔ-én	'heron feather'
s-íθám̓	'bone'	íθám̓-əcən	'bracelet'
s-lí·m	'sandhill crane'	lí·m-əs 'a	'month name'

Lillooet:

s-q̓əl-t	'mud'	q̓əl-t-úl̓-wił	'earthenware pot, crock'

This fact suggests that the noun-hood of the lexical suffix itself is sufficient to determine the category of the compound.

What we have shown so far is that lexical suffixes appear as heads in right-headed compounds. They are suffixed to noun or verb stems and the resulting compound is a N. Our claim then is that the lexical suffix, which developed historically from a free-standing N, continues to function as a N in nominal compounds. All of the lexical suffixes in our database appear in compounds of this sort. As far as we know, all lexical suffixes attach to either N or V stems. Thus we see that compounding of this type is a pervasive and general process.

3. Lexical Suffixation Paralleling Noun Incorporation

Next, we turn to a second major use of lexical suffixation. As noted above, lexical suffixes also commonly appear in complex predicates. That is, they are attached to a verb stem, and the resulting compound functions syntactically as the main predicate of a clause. Examples are given in (11) and (12):[5]

(11) V + lexical suffix = V
lexical suffix = theme
Lillooet:

ník̓-łća?	'cut meat'	'cut' + 'flesh'
líʕʷ-alc	'tear down a house'	'tear down' + 'dwelling'
łúkʷ-wił	'bail out a canoe'	'bail out' + 'vessel'
kʷułn-áwł	'borrow a car, canoe'	'borrow' + 'vessel'
məc-úl-wił	'paint a canoe'	'paint' + 'vessel'
məys-áwł	'repair a car, boat'	'fix, repair' + 'vessel'

---

[5] These forms act inflectionally and derivationally as verbs.

Musqueam:

$pá\cdot-ĺcəp$	'blow on a fire'	'blow on' + 'firewood'
$q̓ʷə́m-əw̓s$	'pluck a bird'	'pull out' + 'body'
$θék̓ʷ-əlyən$	'pull a net'	'pull ' + 'basket/net'
$məx̌'-é·lže?$	'return wealth'	'return' + 'hide'
$səw̓q̓-íw̓s$	'search for a lost person'	'seek' + 'body'
$łəc̓-álqən$	'shear wool'	'cut' + 'head'

(12)   V + lexical suffix = V
       lexical suffix = adjunct
       Lillooet:

$zəx̌-láp$	'crawl on the floor'	'move' + 'ground'
$zənm-ús$	'go around the top'	'go around' + 'face'
$x̌ax̌am̓-ús$	'go up a hill'	'go up' + 'face'
$k̓ʷus̓?-ál̓nup$	'wet one's bed' (of man)	'urinate' (man) + 'flat surface'
$cíxʷ-al̓-us$	'be able to see'	'reach over there' + 'eye'

Musqueam:

$sxʷ-nə-xín̓$	'walk'	'be there' + 'foot'
$q̓ət-á-θən$	'walk along'(shore, etc.)	'go along' + 'mouth'
$k̓ʷc-áləs$	'see with one's own eyes'	'see' + 'eye'
$xʷ-q̓ə-wíl-t$	'go with him on a canoe'	'accompany' + 'vessel'
$xʷ-?ə́w̓-cəs-t$	'show him with the hand'	'show, guide' + 'hand'
$xʷ-k̓ʷən-wíl-t$	'transfer it from one craft to another'	'transfer' + 'vessel'

When lexical suffixation is used to form complex predicates, the process directly parallels noun incorporation as found in other languages of the world. Whether noun incorporation is treated as a syntactic rule of head-movement (Baker 1988) or as a lexical rule (Rosen 1989) the result is the same: a piece of a complex predicate (namely, the incorporated noun) is in a nominal relationship to the verb stem. Lexical suffixes also function in this fashion.

Two core properties of noun incorporation can also be seen in lexical suffixation. First, in typical cases of noun incorporation, the noun functions as the object of the predicate or as a locative or instrumental adjunct.[6] The

---

[6]As with incorporated nouns, lexical suffixes do not refer to subjects of transitives or unergatives, nor to indirect objects or benefactives.

data in (11) and (12) above show that lexical suffixes in complex predicates have these functions as well. Second, it is typical of noun incorporation that when the head of the object nominal is incorporated, object properties can be transferred to other nominals in the clause, for example to a possessor, benefactive, or locative. This happens as well in lexical suffixation:[7]

(13) lexical suffix = head
    Musqueam:

$\theta \partial y$-$é$$?$$\dot{l}$-$t$	'make his bed'	'fix it' + 'flexible material'
x^{w}-$?$$\partial m q$-$\dot{l}$$é\cdot l$-$t$	'take food to them'	'take it to him' + 'throat'
$k^{w}\acute{\partial} x$-$n \partial c$-t	'name its price'	'name' + 'end'
$?$$\acute{\partial} m$-$n \partial c$-$t$	'put money down on it'	'give' + 'end'

3.1. Lexical Suffixation Paralleling Compounding Noun Incorporation

We see then that lexical suffixation parallels noun incorporation in two key respects. This raises a further issue. Research on noun incorporation has revealed that there are two basic types. Following Rosen (1989), we will refer to these as compounding and classifying noun incorporation. In compounding NI, the incorporation of the notional object results in surface intransitivity. No external modifiers or doubling of the incorporated N with a free-standing form are possible. In classifying NI, on the other hand, the clause remains transitive even when the object is incorporated, and external modification and doubling is possible.

In Salish, complex predicates formed from lexical suffixation generally mirror compounding NI. First, we can see that when the lexical suffix refers to the object, the form is intransitive, since the subject in a clause like (14) determines absolutive rather than ergative agreement (Gerdts 1988).

(14) ni $y\acute{\partial} q$^{w}-$\partial l$$?$-$c \partial p$(*-$\partial s$).
    AUX burn-CN-firewood(-*3ERG)
    'He made a fire.'

Furthermore, external modification is usually not possible:

---

[7]One of the most common uses of lexical suffixes is to represent body parts. The possessor of the body part always takes the argument position. We see a case of a possessor as subject in (3) above and as object in (15) below. Inalienable possession is not a requirement for transference, however, as the first example in (13) shows.

(15) *ni   lək^w-əl-wíl-t-əs*   ((*k^wθə) *łíx̌^w) k^wθə   John
AUX   break-CN-rib-TR-3ERG   DET   three   DET   John
'He broke (*three of) John's ribs.'

(16) *ni   lə́k^w-šə-n-əm*   *ʔə-ẋ̣*   John
AUX   break-foot-LCTR-INTR   OBL-DET   John
*(*k^wθə sʔiyáləm̓-šanʔ-s) lə stɛ́niʔ*
DET   right-foot-3POS   DET woman
'John broke the woman's (*right) foot.'

Finally, the lexical suffix usually cannot be doubled with a free-standing noun of the same or more specific meaning as (17) and (18) show:

(17) *q^ws-íẏən*   *(*tə-n̓   swɔ́ltən)*
go.into.water-net   DET-your   net
'Set your net.'

(18) *ni   tší-ʔq^w-t-əs*   (*k^wθə sx̌áləməs-s)*
AUX   comb-head-TR-3ERG   DET   white hair-3POS
łə   stálʔəs-s
DET   spouse-3POS
'He combed his wife's (*white hair) hair.'

The above data show that lexical suffixation generally parallels compounding noun incorporation. We see that lexical suffixes, just like incorporated nouns, have the syntactic characteristics of a nominal in an argument or adjunct position in the clause. And while we have no direct evidence that the lexical suffix should be assigned the categorial status of N, we note that it does block a free-standing N of the same or more specific meaning from occurring in the clause.

3.2. Lexical Suffixation Paralleling Classificatory Noun Incorporation

We turn now to a third use of lexical suffixation. A small subset of lexical suffixes in each Salish language can serve as numeral classifiers. The thirteen found in Halkomelem are: *-as* 'round or spherical object' (used for counting dollars, months), *-aq^w* 'head' (cabbage, animals, derogatorily of people), *-e·łp* 'tree, plant', *-emət^θ* 'long object' (boards, logs, poles), *-ew̓tx^w* 'building'. *-aleʔc* 'bundle' (blankets), *-iẇs* 'body' (birds), *-eł* 'time', *-qen* 'container', *-ela* 'person', *-mat* 'stuff' (clothing, flexible material), *-wil/-wəł/-x^wəł* 'vessel' (canoes, conveyances), and *-winx^w/-e·nx^w* 'season' (years, fish runs). The classifier constructions are used for counting.[8] Only a few, very common objects have classifiers.

Other nominals are simply referred to periphrastically with a cardinal number and the nominal.

This type of lexical suffixation parallels classificatory noun incorporation. In the case of numerals, the classifier is usually doubled with an elaborating nominal:

(19) łíxʷ-əqən   lisék
     three-containers   sack
     'three sacks'

(20) teʔcs-élə   kʷθə   nə   mémənə
     eight-people   DET   1POS   children
     'I have eight children.'

In addition, we have found a handful of examples where the classificatory suffixes attached to a lexical verb can double with a free-standing nominal. Examples are given in (21), (22), and (23).

(21) źs-əléʔc-t   tə   nə́wəkʷaʔ
     nail-container-TR   DET   coffin
     'nail up the coffin' (Musqueam: Wayne Suttles p.c.)

(22) wə-nə́y kʷs   źəx̌-wíl-t   ct   tə   lepát
     only   DET   wash-vessel-TR 1PL.SUB DET   pot
     ʔi   tə   lá̓ʔθən
     and DET   dish
     'We only wash pots and plates.' (Musqueam: Wayne Suttles p.c.)

---

[8]We also find that numeral classifiers are used instead of free-standing Ns in connected speech. For example, the response to a question like (a) could be formed as a plain numeral, but a response like (b), where the lexical suffix refers anaphorically to the nominal in (a), is considered better style.

(i) (a) ʔi   ʔə ʔápen kʷən?   sənníxʷəł ʔə́ləp
         AUX   INT ten   DET+2POS canoe   PL
         'Do you all have 10 canoes?'

    (b) ʔə́wə   ʔu   θémə-xʷəł   ʔalʔ
        no   just two-vessel   just
        'No, just two.'

(23)   lexical suffix = classifier
       Lillooet:

     záw-aĺk-an̓   'scoop smt. off'   'scoop' +
                       (cream off milk)   'flexible material'

     Musqueam:

     q p̓-áleʔc-t   'tie them up in a bundle'   'tie it' + 'container'
     yəx̌ʷ-áleʔc-t   'untie it' (a bundle)   'untie it' + 'container'
     ƛ̓əx̌ʷ-wíl-t   'wash them' (dishes)   'wash it' + 'vessel'

What we see in these cases is that the lexical suffix does not saturate the object position. The free-standing nominal behaves as the grammatical object. The lexical suffixes do not behave like full-fledged Ns in these cases. Rather they are grammatical elements reminiscent of pronominal agreement. They sketch in the general properties of the entity which can then be identified through context or by elaboration.

4.   Lexical Suffixes as Applicatives

Finally, we would like to make some speculative comments about some grammatical affixes in Salish languages. These languages are fairly polysynthetic; a great number of affixes referencing nominals appear in the verb complex. These include agreement markers, transitive suffixes, reflexives, reciprocals, and applicative suffixes. The applicatives are particularly relevant to this paper since the three applicative suffixes in Halkomelem, ADV(ancement suffix) A, B, and C (Gerdts 1988, p. 25f.) are suspiciously similar to lexical suffixes. The dative suffix appears to be the suffix for 'face', the benefactive appears to be 'belly', the seat of emotions in Salish, and the causal appears to be the instrumental suffix.[9]

(24)   ADV A: *-əs* dative (aka redirective) (< *-as* 'face')

     ʔéʔəm   'give'   *ʔá·m-əs-t*   'give it to him/her'
     xʷáyəm   'sell'   *xʷáyem-əs-t*   'sell it to him/her'
     ʔíw̓-   'instruct'   *ʔíw-əs-t*   'show it to him.her'
     yáθ   'tell'   *yáθ-əs-t*   'tell him/her about it'
     k̓ʷál   'spill'   *k̓ʷl-ás-t*   'throw liquid on him'

---

[9]The use of the instrumental suffix as an applicative seems to occur widely in Salish languages, but the use of 'face' and 'belly' as applicatives seem to be Halkomelem innovations.

ADV B: -ałc benefactive (<-ałcə 'belly' ?)

q̓ʷə́l	'bake'	q̓ʷə́l-ałc-ət	'bake it for him/her'
θə́y-t	'fix it'	θə́y-ałc-ət	'fix it for him/her'
x̌ə́lʔ-t	'write it'	x̌ə́lʔ-ałc-ət	'write it for/to him/her'

ADV C: -meʔ stimulus, causal (< -mən 'instrument/residue' ?)

łcíws	'tired'	łciws-méʔ-t	'tired of him/her'
q̓élʔ	'believe'	q̓elʔ-méʔ-t	'believe him/her'
síʔsiʔ	'afraid'	sìʔsiʔ-méʔ-t	'afraid of him/her'
x̌íʔx̌iʔ	'embarrassed'	x̌íʔx̌iʔ-méʔ-t	'embarrassed by him/her'

The hypothesis that the applicative markers are actually lexical suffixes is supported by phonological and morphological evidence. We can tell that the dative applicative is underlying -as since it appears like this under stress, as in the form for 'throw a liquid on him'. Furthermore, as Suttles (in prep.) notes, like the lexical suffix for 'face', the dative applicative triggers vowel harmony in the root vowel. For example, the form ʔéʔəm 'give' harmonizes to ʔá·m- before the applicative suffix. It is also obvious that the applicatives occupy the same post-stem position as lexical suffixes. Compare the forms in (24) with those in (23), for example. Finally, it can be noted that applicative suffixes share some distributional properties with lexical suffixes. Transitive clauses form reflexives with the suffix -θət, but clauses with lexical suffixes use a middle form, based on the general intransitive suffix instead, as (25) shows.

(25) ni   ʔəx̌-ay-θín-əm   /   *ni   ʔəx̌-ay-θín-θət
     AUX   scrape-CN-mouth-INTR   AUX   scrape-CN-mouth-REFL
     'He shaved.'

The same fact holds for applicatives:

(26) ni   cən   q̓ʷə́l-ałc-əm   /   *ni   cən   q̓ʷə́l-ałc-θət
     AUX   1SUB   bake-BEN-INTR   AUX   1SUB   bake-BEN-REFL
     'I cooked it for myself.'

Finally, it should be noted that forms for 'face' have developed into grammatical markers in other languages. Brugman (to appear) shows that the Mixtec form for 'face' is used in locative and dative applicatives, and MacLaury (1989) shows that the Zapotec form for 'face' is used in applicatives based on verbs of speaking.

Thus, while our comments concerning applicatives are necessarily speculative, the identification of these suffixes as grammaticized forms of lexical suffixes is a reasonable hypothesis.

5. Conclusion

Hopper and Traugott (1993, 105) state: "When a form undergoes grammaticalization from a lexical to a grammatical form, ... it tends to lose the morphological and syntactic properties that would identify it as a full member of a major grammatical category such as noun or verb." This is what we claim has happened to Salish lexical suffixes.

However, the four uses of lexical suffixes show different degrees of decategorialization and grammaticalization. Lexical suffixes in N compounds act like N heads and have nominal semantics. Lexical suffixes in incorporation-like structures have the semantics and the argument structure of Ns. Lexical suffixes used as classifiers carry the semantic weight of Ns but do not behave like Ns syntactically. Applicative morphemes behave as pure grammatical elements, contributing only grammatical meaning to the construction.

Thus we conclude that Sapir is right in assigning lexical suffixes the status of grammatical elements since they have lost the crucial property of being able to stand as independent words. However, our discussion has shown that there is nothing "pure" or "simple" about grammatical elements. The different properties associated with a major category can exist in different degrees in the minor categories that arise from them.

References

Baker, Mark C. 1988. *Incorporation: A Theory of Grammatical Function Changing.* Chicago: University of Chicago Press.

Brugman, Claudia M. To appear. Metaphor in the Elaboration of Grammatical Categories in Mixtec.

Carlson, Barry F. 1989. Compounding and Lexical Affixation in Spokane. *Anthropological Linguistics* 31:69–82.

Egesdal, Steven M. 1981. Some Ideas on the Origin of Salish Lexical Suffixes. *University of Hawaii Working Papers in Linguistics* 13.2:3–19.

Gerdts, Donna B. 1988. *Object and Absolutive in Halkomelem Salish.* New York: Garland.

Heine, Bernd, Ulrike Claudi, and Friederike Hünnemeyer. 1991. *Grammaticalization: a Conceptual Framework.* Chicago: University of Chicago Press.

Hopper, Paul, and Elizabeth Traugott. 1993. *Grammaticalization.* Cambridge: Cambridge University Press.

MacLaury, Robert E. 1989. Zapotec Body-Part Locatives: Prototypes and Metaphoric Extensions. *International Journal of American Linguistics* 55:119–154.

Mattina, Anthony. 1987. On the Origin of Salish Lexical Affixes. Paper presented at the 26th Conference on American Indian Languages, AAA, Chicago.

Miner, Kenneth L. 1986. Noun Stripping and Loose Incorporation in Zuni. *International Journal of American Linguistics* 52:242–54.

Mithun, Marianne. 1984. The Evolution of Noun Incorporation. *Language* 60:847–94.

Rosen, Sara Thompson. 1989. Two Types of Noun Incorporation: A Lexical Analysis. *Language* 65:294–317.

Sapir, Edward. 1911. The Problem of Noun Incorporation in American Languages. *American Anthropologist* 13:250–82.

Suttles, Wayne. In preparation. *A Reference Grammar of the Musqueam Dialect of Halkomelem.*

van Eijk, Jan P. 1985. *The Lillooet Language.* Doctoral dissertation: Universiteit van Amsterdam.

van Eijk, Jan P., and Thom Hess. 1986. Noun and Verb in Salish. *Lingua* 69:319–331.

Primitive and Compound Metaphors

JOE GRADY, SARAH TAUB & PAMELA MORGAN
University of California, Berkeley

1. Introduction: Difficulties for Metaphorical Mappings

Recent research on the cognitive and linguistic phenomenon of metaphor—in particular, work which follows the principles outlined in *Metaphors We Live By* (MWLB, Lakoff & Johnson, 1980)—defines metaphors as systematic correspondences, or "mappings," between one conceptual domain and another. Such mappings motivate not only the use of particular language from the "source domain," but also inferences and other cognitive structure which are applied to the "target domain" in various, principled ways. All conceptual metaphors are said to arise from bodily experience, in some broad sense, and this "experientialism" is a feature which distinguishes this theory from other theories of language and thought characterized by more formal and abstract structure.

This paper concerns a number of difficulties which arise from trying to reconcile the theory, as it has been elaborated and applied in the literature, with particular metaphorical cases. The problems are of various types—for instance, some concern data while others concern metatheoretical questions about the relationships between metaphors—but all are addressed by an account which treats complex metaphors as "compounds" decomposable into "primitives." After outlining the problems which motivate the analysis, we describe the proposal itself, and finally turn to a number of implications of the analysis for metaphor theory and for other areas of cognitive and linguistic study.

1.1 Poverty of Mappings

In many metaphors which have been discussed in the literature, important aspects of the source domain fail to map to the target domain. Given that metaphor theory takes seriously the commitment to offering explanations and analyses with a plausible experiential or bodily basis, it cannot be a trivial matter that many of the most salient experiential aspects of certain source domains play no role in the metaphors in which those domains participate.

A good example of this problem is the THEORIES ARE BUILDINGS metaphor, which was discussed in *MWLB* and has been cited since as a prime example of a conceptual metaphor. This metaphor is robustly supported, by examples such as the following:

(1) a. You have failed to *buttress* your arguments with sufficient facts.
b. Recent discoveries have *shaken* the theory to its *foundations*.
c. Their theory *collapsed/caved in* under the weight of scrutiny.

On the other hand, there are crucial experiential elements of buildings which are not conventionally mapped onto theories. Consider the following sentences, which are less than felicitous (at least in the absence of context[1]):

    d. ?This theory has no *windows*.
    e. ?The *tenants* of her theory are behind in their *rent*.

Among the important aspects of buildings which fail to map are *parts* like floors, walls, ceiling; any potential human *occupants* of the building; and the *functions* of buildings—as shelters, homes, workplaces, or even locations. Instead the metaphor is clearly concerned only with certain basic structures and structural properties of buildings.

Note that there is one mechanism which exists in current theory for barring elements of a source domain from being mapped (to use a force-dynamic metaphor for the operation of metaphor itself). This mechanism, "target-domain override," is invoked in cases where there is a clear contradiction between the source and target domains such that the mapping of a particular element or entailment would clash with our established conceptualization of the target domain (see Lakoff 92). A good example of this phenomenon is the observation that if I "give" you an idea, I continue to "have" it as well (leaving aside for the moment the details of how "having" is understood with respect to the target domain of ideas). The fact that physical instances of giving entail that the giver is no longer in possession of the transferred object fails to map onto this metaphorical instance of giving. The "target domain override" mechanism, however, is not applicable to the THEORIES ARE BUILDINGS case, since there is no logical contradiction in claiming that theories have windows; the conventional mapping simply gives us no meaningful way to interpret the statement.

In the absence of any consistent and rigorous mechanism for explaining "gaps" in the data such as those found here, we are left with the problem that a theory which seeks to be experientially accountable proposes a number of metaphors (of which THEORIES ARE BUILDINGS is only one example) where little of the experiential content of the source domains gets mapped.

---

[1] These and other such expressions can, of course, be produced and understood, given the proper context. It is our claim, however, that such expressions are not instances of THEORIES ARE BUILDINGS per se, but are licensed by and interpreted with reference to additional metaphoric structure which is not conventionally associated with this metaphor, but which exists independently and can be invoked in composition with THEORIES ARE BUILDINGS. These issues are addressed further in section 2 below.

1.2 Lack of Experiential Basis

While metaphor theory is distinguished by its insistence that metaphor, like most or all of cognition, is grounded in bodily experience, many metaphors involve pairs of domains for which no plausible correlation can be found.

Unlike the oft-cited example of MORE IS UP—where it is easy to list correlations in experience between having *more* of objects or substances, and seeing the level of those objects or substances *rise*—many metaphors which have been proposed and discussed do not suggest straightforward correlations. Examples include THEORIES ARE BUILDINGS, LOVE IS A JOURNEY (also discussed in *MWLB* and subsequent works), and many others. As stated, the pairs of domains in these metaphors do not seem to have salient experiential correlation, and certainly not the type of direct experiential overlap which underlies MORE IS UP. Actual travel has little to do with the progress of our romantic relationships, and theories certainly do not seem closely tied to the buildings in which we generate, discuss and dismantle them.

It should be noted at this point that to date, discussions of experiential basis have been sketchy: there is no clear or consistent understanding of what counts as experiential basis, nor of what the typology of experiential bases might be.

1.3 Independence of Submappings (Inefficiency of Analysis)

A third problem with the workings of current metaphor theory involves both a type of formal inelegance and, quite possibly, a misleading conception of the relationships between certain sets of metaphorical data, and between certain metaphorical mappings.

Current theory often invokes huge metaphorical complexes in order to account for basic correspondences, and corresponding linguistic evidence, which seem to be explainable more directly on their own terms. This strategy is questionable from a technical perspective in that it makes analyses less efficient than they might be—i.e., a great deal of content is invoked to account for data which might be explained more economically. More importantly, however, it is conceptually problematic if it obscures the cognitive status of and motivation for the more basic correspondences.

Consider the following example in English:

(2)   He's *weighed down* by lots of assignments.

The current analysis is that this use of *weighed down* has the meaning it does because it is an instance of the mapping DIFFICULTIES ARE BURDENS, which is a special case of DIFFICULTIES ARE IMPEDIMENTS TO MOTION, which in turn is a submapping of the ACTION IS SELF-PROPELLED MOTION branch of the EVENT STRUCTURE METAPHOR, the other branch of which maps actions and events onto transfer of objects rather than motion over paths (see Lakoff, 1992).

While such an analysis arises from a very legitimate desire to find the generalizations which bring together broad classes of metaphorical data, one also wonders whether there might be an analysis which requires less structure to account for an expression which, after all, does not even refer to motion. This question becomes a practical issue when one is working on a project to compile a database of cross-linguistic metaphorical data (as a number of U.C. Berkeley linguists have been), and is also a substantive one, since we are concerned with the cognitive reality of our analyses. There are a number of Irish expressions which parallel the English expression cited in (2) and raise the same questions:

(3) a. cíos trom
    rent heavy
    'heavy rent' (difficult rent to pay)

    b. Tá orm   labhairt   leis.
    is on-me speak.VN with-him
    'It is on me to speak to him.' (I must speak to him.)

    c. Tá mála mór air.
    is sack big on-him
    'There is a big sack on him.' (He is holding/carrying a big sack.)

(A) and (b) show that in Irish, as in English, difficulties and obligations are expressed as burdens. (C establishes that "on" may be used with respect to burdens in Irish, though this is not common in English.) Must these Irish expressions be analyzed as deriving from a mapping of action onto self-propelled motion, or might there be a more parsimonious account which also captures a more direct cognitive motivation for such mappings? Certainly these sentences are *compatible* with metaphors for action as motion, but the question is whether they should properly be understood as *instances* of such metaphors.

1.4 Inconsistency of Mappings
Many if not all complex metaphors show multiple, and inconsistent, variations of some of their key correspondences. Current theory treats such cases as versions of the same metaphor, calling them by such names as "branches" and "duals." The theory would also allow for the possibility of treating them as unrelated metaphors, which happen to share much of their structure and content. Neither of these solutions is satisfying, since neither adequately specifies the relationship between metaphors that appear to be very closely related.

A relevant example of this problem is illustrated by some Uighur EVENT STRUCTURE data in which the word for 'stand' has come to have metaphoric uses meaning both 'continue' and 'cease':

(4) a. turkelnɨŋ ʒɨɣɨliʃni turdurdum
Turkel-GEN cry-NOM-ACC stand-CAUS-PAST-1S
'I caused Turkel's crying to stand.' (I made Turkel stop crying.)

b. ʒɨɣɨlɨp turdum.
cry-P stand-PAST-1S
'I stood and cried.' (I continued to cry.)

The difficulty here is that we appear to have two conceptualizations of event structure motivating these different uses of 'stand.' Current theory gives us little guidance in stating the nature of the relationship between these two "versions" of the event structure mapping. Are they best understood as variants of a single metaphor, co-existing but independent metaphors, or perhaps metaphors which are related in a way not treated by the theory in its current form? Additional examples of this uneasy situation are major branches of the EVENT STRUCTURE METAPHOR (STATES ARE LOCATIONS vs. PROPERTIES ARE OBJECTS), and in fact all instances of "duality."

2. Solution: Metaphoric Primitives and Compounds
The analysis which addresses all of the problems outlined above is the following: Many or all complex metaphors are compositional in nature ("compounds"); the simpler submappings of which complex metaphors are composed are "primitives."[2]

2.1 Definitions
(5) a. A primitive is a metaphorical mapping for which there is an independent and direct experiential basis and independent linguistic evidence.
b. A compound is a self-consistent metaphorical complex composed of more than one primitive.

A number of examples of primitives and compounds will be discussed below. The general idea is that primitive metaphors exist independently of any particular complex metaphorical structures into which they may be recruited. Constraints on building compound metaphors arise from issues of

---

[2] Note that the concept of metaphoric primitives under discussion here is quite distinct from the concept of semantic primitives proposed by Wierzbicka (and others).

logical compatibility of the primitive mappings[3]. Figure 1 represents self-contained primitives, which may occur in various compounds.

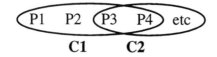

Fig. 1

2.2 Treatment of THEORIES ARE BUILDINGS

As an example of how decomposition of complex metaphors into primitives works, we return to THEORIES ARE BUILDINGS. Consider the following simpler metaphoric statements:

(6) a. LOGICAL STRUCTURE IS PHYSICAL STRUCTURE
    b. PERSISTING IS REMAINING ERECT

When the entities and relations that make up these two metaphorical mappings are lined up in correspondences, the resulting compound—which could be called (VIABLE) LOGICAL STRUCTURES ARE ERECT PHYSICAL STRUCTURES—accounts for all the data that we have called THEORIES ARE BUILDINGS. In fact, although a full exploration of this subject would require more space than can be spared here, the "source" language and concepts of this metaphor are not particular to buildings, but refer to erect physical structures in general.

Significantly, this analysis solves the "poverty of mapping" problem, since references to floors, decor, occupants, and other non-structural aspects of buildings are not expected. No mechanism is needed to explain the "gaps" since the conventional data illustrates the actual mapping quite fully—on this analysis there are no gaps to be accounted for.

Furthermore, this analysis solves the problem concerning the lack of an experiential basis for the metaphor. Both of the primitives in (6) might arise quite naturally from experience (or possibly even neurological structure, a question will have to be neglected here for lack of space). It isn't hard to imagine a plausible experiential correlation between the physical structures we encounter and the abstract principles which allow us to assemble, disassemble and manipulate them. We also have quite a bit of

---

[3] "Combination" here may be understood as referring to a process or mechanism very much like "unification" in unification-based grammatical theories.

experience with things that remain upright while they are functional, viable, and so forth, but fall down when they are not.

Figure 2 represents the combination of these primitives, and also reflects the fact that the primitive metaphor LOGICAL STRUCTURE IS PHYSICAL STRUCTURE need not occur in combination with PERSISTING IS REMAINING ERECT, but may be combined with other primitives instead to yield different compound metaphors for theories and other abstract structures.

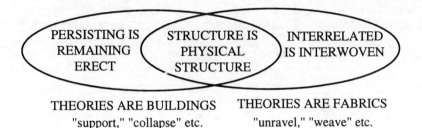

THEORIES ARE BUILDINGS   THEORIES ARE FABRICS
"support," "collapse" etc.   "unravel," "weave" etc.

Fig. 2

2.3 Treatment of Irish OBLIGATIONS ARE BURDENS

As suggested earlier, the current treatment of expressions like "heavy rent" is not only formally cumbersome, but it may be misleading if it diverts attention from the way in which misfortunes and obligations are naturally and directly mapped onto physical weights, such as the sack in (3c) above. This analysis may in fact obscure the mechanisms by which basic metaphorical mappings arise.

We suggest instead that DIFFICULTIES/OBLIGATIONS ARE BURDENS is a metaphoric primitive. Such a mapping has independent motivation: enduring difficulties and discharging obligations require effort, attention, and expenditure of energy, just as supporting heavy weights does, independent of whether the burdened person is trying to move. Furthermore, linguistic contexts in which there is no direct evidence for interpreting heavy weights as impediments to motion are not hard to come by; neither (2) nor (3a, b) refer to motion, for instance. This analysis solves the problems of formal inelegance and improper conceptual focus outlined in section 1.3 above.

2.4 Treatment of Uighur Event Structure

On our analysis the two uses of 'stand' illustrated in (4) instantiate different primitives; the domains of events and spatial configurations are brought together in two distinct ways by the different metaphors:

     a. ACTION IS MOTION: 'stand' :: 'cease'
     b. ACTION IS LOCATION: 'stand' :: 'continue'

The general answer to the "inconsistency" problem is that complex metaphors are related by the primitives they share, and distinguished by the primitives they do not share, as figures 1 and 2 illustrate.

2.5 Additional Examples

The following figures suggest ways in which additional complex metaphors might be decomposed. They represent combinations of primitives into the compound metaphors underlying several different sets of expressions. In figure 3 the primitive mapping of action onto self-propelled motion is combined with two different and orthogonal metaphors related to the target domain of morality. The resulting compounds motivate language such as "crooked" and "devious" vs. "straight and narrow" on the one hand, and "taking the high road" and so forth on the other.

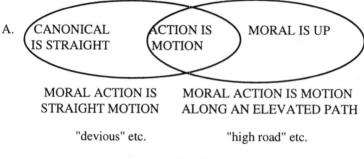

Fig. 3

In figure 4 the conceptualization of a romantic or other relationship as a vehicle (another example from MWLB) is accounted for with reference to a complex of likely primitive metaphors, combined at two levels. Unfortunately, in the present context these analyses must be taken as suggestive rather than proven since a full discussion of them is beyond the scope of this paper.

Note that for all the complex mappings referred to in figures 3 and 4, the various problems enumerated in section 1 would apply to some degree— for instance, there is no plausible experiential basis for correlating moral action and motion along a path at a higher elevation.

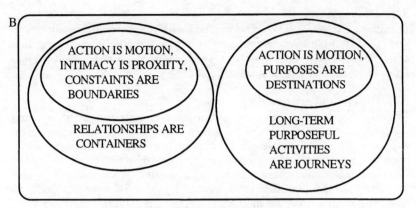

RELATIONSHIPS ARE VEHICLES

Fig. 4

2.6 Summary of the Proposed Analysis

- All metaphors either are, or are composed of, primitives.
- Primitives, by definition, have independent experiential basis, and are instantiated by linguistic evidence independent of any particular compound.
- Coherent metaphors may be unified, resulting in compounds.

3. Implications

The type of analysis discussed in this paper represents a significant refinement of metaphor theory as it currently exists, and a shift of thinking in the direction of close attention to the details of the data and to the experiential motivations which underlie metaphors. In this section we suggest several of the consequences of such an approach for metaphor theory and related fields of study.

3.1 Efficiency of Analysis

Although there are times when parsimony must be rejected in favor of empirical data, efficiency still remains a default goal for any formal analysis. Statement in terms of primitives allows the most parsimonious accounts of the metaphorical basis for linguistic expressions.

3.2 Comparison of Complex Metaphors

Statement in terms of primitives allows the most specific comparison of complex metaphors—either variants within a language, or cross-linguistic examples. Both commonalities and differences among metaphors can be accounted for specifically by reference to the primitives which complex metaphors either do or do not share.

3.3 Universality
Primitives are taken to be the metaphors with the most direct motivation, and the least arbitrary structure, and should therefore be the most common cross-linguistically. This is a claim which can provide direction for future cross-linguistic research, and which can be tested empirically.

3.4 Psychological Reality
Primitive metaphors, which are based most directly on experience, are predicted to be the metaphors for which there is the most psychological evidence. This is perhaps the most important aspect of the present study, since as cognitive linguists we are concerned with investigating the nature of conceptualization, reason, and other cognitive processes, and we are interested in extra-linguistic evidence which can corroborate our findings. The experimental work on this subject remains to be done, but we predict that the psychological reality of primitives—such as INITIMACY IS PROXIMITY—can be established more strongly than that of the compounds—such as RELATIONSHIPS ARE VEHICLES—which they comprise.

3.5 Acquisition
For the same reasons relating to directness of motivation and lack of arbitrary structure cited above, primitives should prove to be the first conceptual metaphors to be acquired—assuming experiments could be devised to test such a hypothesis—and should correlate most strongly with other aspects of child cognition, including Piagetian stages of development, for instance.

There is much more to be said about the exact nature of primitive and compound metaphors—details about how primitives combine, how they arise, how they might relate to grammatical processes and grammaticalization, how compounds become conventional, and so forth. Based on what has been discovered so far we feel that the notions of primitives and compounds presented here will suggest important new directions for research into the mechanisms by which metaphor shapes our cognition.

References:
Grady, Joseph. THEORIES ARE BUILDINGS Revisited. Ms., U.C. Berkeley.
Grady, Joseph. Irish Prepositional Idioms. Ms., U.C. Berkeley.
Lakoff, George and Mark Johnson. 1980. *Metaphors We Live By*. Chicago: University of Chicago Press.
Lakoff, George. 1987. *Women, Fire, and Dangerous Things: What Categories Reveal about the Mind*. Chicago: University of Chicago Press.

Lakoff, George. 1992. The Contemporary Theory of Metaphor. In Ortony, Andrew. *Metaphor and Thought* (2nd edition). Cambridge: Cambridge University Press.

Ó Dónaill, Niall, ed. 1977. *Foclóir Gaeilge-Béarla.* Dublin: Government of Ireland.

Sweetser, Eve. 1990. *From etymology to pragmatics: metaphorical and cultural aspects of semantic structure.* Cambridge: Cambridge University Press.

Taub, Sarah. Uighur Event Structure. Ms., U.C. Berkeley.

What's So Easy about Pie?: The Lexicalization of a Metaphor[1]

CAITLIN HINES

San Francisco State University

There is an ample body of literature demonstrating that metaphors are not "a matter of mere language [but] rather...a means of structuring our conceptual systems," in Lakoff and Johnson's (1980) formulation. This paper, however, is a case study of the convergence of *both* linguistic and conceptual systematicity in one narrowly defined family of metaphorical expressions.

The metaphor to be dissected equates women-as-sex-objects with desserts, as evidenced by the linguistic expressions *crumpet, cupcake, tart,* etc., and as experientially manifested in customs such as women jumping out of cakes. The presence of a virtual bakery of these terms (see appendix) suggests an underlying conceptual metaphor of WOMAN AS DESSERT; shared semantic, syntactic, lexical, and phonetic features of the specific terms used, contrasted with those available but not used, suggest, as Wierzbicka wrote of the grammar of mass nouns, that "the system of formal distinctions and the system of conceptual distinctions are mutually isomorphic" (1988:553-4).

In this paper I use an "ecological" approach, in Rhodes and Lawler's sense of "reject[ing] monocausal explanations" (1981:1), to examine this particular family of rather opaque metaphorical expressions in terms of distinctive features, showing how specific instantiations, comprising a discrete subset of the numerous and varied food/sex terms in the lexicon, are subject to multiple and sometimes overlapping linguistic motivations. Because the semantic fields of eating and sex are highly taboo, especially in the subfields of desserts and women, I have drawn on a variety of sources, some decidedly beyond the academic Pale, for citations of actual use, of metaphor as she is spoke.

---

1 An earlier version of this paper was presented at the Third Berkeley Women and Language conference, April 9, 1994 (Hines, *forthcoming*). Many friends and colleagues indulged me by discussing subsequent revisions. My special thanks to Mary Bucholtz, Steve Greenberg, John Lawler, Margaret Magnus Nizhnikov, Thomas Scovel, Eve Sweetser, Carol Wilder, and Julia von Helga Williams. I also want to thank Sherry Hines, my mother and chief research assistant, in particular for giving me a reprint of Grose's *A Classical Dictionary of the Vulgar Tongue* (1796).

189

1.1 Evolution of the Metaphor

Briefly, the evolution of the WOMAN AS DESSERT metaphor is as follows: it begins with PEOPLE ARE OBJECTS, an example of which would be the special case PEOPLE ARE BUILDINGS, as in *eyes are windows to the soul*. This is then joined with the stereotype "women are sweet" (as in the Mother Goose rhyme "what are little girls made of?/Sugar and spice and everything nice..."), and finally combines with another common metaphor, ACHIEVING A DESIRED OBJECT IS GETTING SOMETHING TO EAT (as in *the taste of victory*): yielding WOMEN ARE SWEET OBJECTS (→in this case, DESSERTS).[2] The metaphor is productive: novel expressions, such as *my little croissant* or *pop tart*, are easily understood. This much is pretty uncontroversial; what I would like to do next is to change the focus from the abstract to the concrete, by examining the lexicalization of the metaphor.

2.1 Synchronic Feature Analysis

My first task was to separate central metaphorical terms from peripheral ones, *cupcakes* from *buttered buns*. I have followed Lehrer (1974) in using the criteria of Berlin and Kay's classic *Basic Color Terms* (1970) as my inspiration in "making the semantic cut." My tests for metaphorical centrality were as follows:

1) Term must be monolexemic
(rules out peripheral *cream puff, jelly roll*)

2) Referent must exist in the real world (and be able to be served for dessert)
(rules out fanciful *honeybun(ches), sweetie*)

3) There must be multiple citations
(rules out nonce terms *croissant, pop tart*)

---

2 Lakoff & Johnson's *Metaphors We Live By* (1980), especially chapter 22, "The Creation of Similarity," provides the scaffolding on which this analysis is built. The present paper was indirectly inspired by a quite different assignment in George Lakoff's Metaphor course at UC Berkeley in Fall 1992; this version was completed in Thomas Scovel's Psycholinguistics seminar at San Francisco State University in Fall 1994.

Applying these three tests to the data collected yields the list of central dessert terms for women shown in Table 1; it was not necessary to specify a fourth stipulation, "used exclusively of women," since the attested gender-ambiguous terms were already disallowed by virtue of being polylexemic (as in *cream puff)* and/or fanciful (as in *sweetie-pie-honey-bun).*[3] The feature [-male], along with the other semantic, syntactic, phonetic, and lexical features detailed below, "falls out" naturally.

TABLE 1. *Central dessert terms for women-as-sex-objects.*

> (piece of) cake, cookie, crumpet [*Brit.*], cupcake,
> pancake *[Brit.],* (a tasty bit of) pastry, (cherry) pie,
> poundcake, pumpkin (pie, tart), punkin, muffin,
> [jam] tart, tartlet/-lette

A methodological point: all of these terms are actual, attested examples, although it is unlikely that any one speaker would use or even accept all of them. In fact, speakers often disagree about whether a term can be used and what, exactly, it means. This inter-speaker variability was the main reason I selected the three tests for centrality described above, since I wanted to define this inherently controversial set as uncontroversially as possible. Having done so, I next analyzed the set on the basis of shared distinctive features, which interact in largely unpredictable ways. Nevertheless, much of what at first appears synchronically to be "crazy" variation (following Givón 1979:237) is in fact systematic when analyzed componentially. Puzzling exceptions inevitably remain; as Keith McCune nicely puts it,

An analysis of [these] patterns cannot account for 100% of the data in an elegant and exhaustive way, because the users of a language often have goals more important than precision (1983:450).

---

3 *Cheesecake,* which in an earlier version of this paper I had intuitively assumed to be central because of its frequency (Hines, *forthcoming),* turned out on closer inspection to be syntactically odd, and thus peripheral. While one may order a piece of cheesecake to eat, an image of scantily-clad women would generally be described simply as "cheesecake," not "a piece of cheesecake"—a functional shift from noun to adjective.

Additionally, the distinctive features described in this paper are postulated only for the set of central *metaphorical* dessert terms. I am not prepared to make a claim as to whether this usage mirrors the centrality of actual dessert terms, although the data certainly suggests such a reading, with *pie, tart,* and *cake* as monomorphemic exemplars.

2.2 Semantic Analysis

Semantically, the terms are isomorphic: firm on the outside, soft or juicy in the middle, and either able to be cut into more than one piece (*cake, (cherry) pie, poundcake),* or conceptualized as one (snatched) serving of an implied batch *(cookie, cupcake, tartlet).* Terms such as **custard, *ice cream cone,* or **mousse* do not occur with this meaning; speakers "know" and adhere to the unstated rules governing well-formed expressions of the metaphor. (Compare the British *she's joined the Pudding Club,* or the American *she has a bun in the oven,* meaning 'be pregnant,' i.e., depicted as being sexually unavailable.)

 Note that all of the central metaphorical terms refer to foods which have been heated, either baked (like a *cake)* or cooked on a griddle (like the chiefly British *crumpet),* as opposed to, say, frozen desserts. This is coherent with the metaphors for lust described by Lakoff: THE OBJECT OF LUST IS FOOD and LUST IS HEAT (1987:409-10). Such cross-domain structural coherence allows the perception of similarity, so that women as heated desserts can be easily seen as the objects of lust.[4]

 There is a further distinction between edible and appetizing, between *buttered bun* and *pumpkin (pie),* as in this suggestive entry in a seventeenth-century book of proverbs:

I love thee like pudding, if thou wert pie I'de eat thee.

-J. Ray, *English Proverbs* (1670)
(in Browning 1982:384)

---

4 This also corresponds nicely with the inescapable conflation in slang between WOMAN AS DESSERT and WOMAN AS PROSTITUTE: as Lehrer notes,

The semantic distinction is that baking refers to the preparation of cakes...and other things which are sold in bakeries and prepared by professional bakers. Cooking refers to the preparation of most other kinds of food (1969:41).

Both kinds of tart can be sold, and both can be prepared by "professionals," in the sense that a pimp or madam grooms his or her girls, thus motivating the metaphoric extensions of *cakeshop [Austr.]* and *tart shop [Brit.]* meaning 'brothel.'

2.3 Syntactic Depersonalization

Syntactically, selectional restrictions suggest promiscuity: a *slice* or *piece* of the mass nouns *pie* or *cake* implies a remainder, and a single serving of a *cupcake* or a *tartlet* implies the batch. Put simply, these desserts are made to be shared. Such syntactic objectification reinforces the semantic depersonalization: one piece of *pie* or one *cookie* is very much like another.

2.4 Lexical Domain Overlap

There is also an overlapping lexicon between the semantic fields of women and of desserts; both a *cupcake* and a woman can be described as *decadent, an indulgence, inviting, luscious, mouth-watering, seductive, sinful, tasty, voluptuous,* and so on, making a straightforward cross-domain mapping of the ontological correspondences of the metaphor formally unsatisfying at this stage. Metaphor and metonymy, which interact in creative ways, must first be teased apart, as in the suggestive slang double entendre *Next time you bake a pie, will you give me a piece?* (defined as 'a male hint to a girl that she should sexually cooperate with him' in Partridge 1986:215). Another example is the somewhat puzzling phrase which gives rise to the title of this paper, *easy as pie*, which has an unexpected secondary meaning, as in this entry for *pie* in a 1981 dictionary of slang (Spears): "a woman considered sexually. From the expression 'as easy as pie,' also reinforced by 'nice piece of pie,' which is euphemistic for 'nice piece of ass.' Cf. *cake, tart.*" Hence, to be *easy as pie* for some speakers is to be sexually available. This image schema recurs in the expression *everybody in town has had a slice of her,* which *Playboy's Book of Forbidden Words* (note distinguished reference!) defines as:

An intrigue with a married woman...the origin is probably the old proverb that "a slice off a cut loaf is not missed." This may explain the odd imagery in piece, piece of ass, piece of tail (Wilson 1972:266.)

2.5 Phonetic Considerations

A striking correspondence which merits further study is the shared phonetic shape of these metaphorical expressions. There is an overwhelming tendency for each of the central terms to begin each stressed syllable with one of the three possible English voiceless stops, /p/, /t/, or /k/ (as in *pumpkin (pie), tart, cookie*); terms such as **gingerbread, *scone,* or **sherbet* do not occur with this meaning, and occurring terms which violate these constraints of apparent sound symbolism either do not catch on (*?angel cake, ?biscuit, ?golden doughnut*) or are of ambiguous gender reference (*baby cakes, jelly roll, sweet-potato-pie*). Even among the peripheral terms, however, there is a striking preponderance of stops and affricates and very few liquids and fricatives. There is also strong pressure to conform to the monolexemic prototype, so that *punkin* appears for *pumpkin pie* and *pastry* for *a tasty bit of pastry*.

Of course, dessert terms for women must be drawn from the preselected lexical set of "all dessert terms,"[5] so it could be argued that these phonetic patterns, if they say anything at all, say more about a linguistically-encoded attitude towards sweet foods than towards women—if there were not other terms available which are *not* used. Consider the phonetically incorrect set { *brownie, *gingerbread, *scone, *shortcake, *waffle}, each of which passes the tests of being monolexemic and having a real-world referent, but for which I have not found a single citation to describe women-as-sex-objects.[6] The obvious question is "why?" In the absence of an established theory, I propose a tentative analysis that syllable-initial voiceless stops in English are often associated with diminutive or trivial things, as in the contrasting end-of-scale pairs /p/*uny* vs. /b/*ig*, /t/*iny* vs. /d/*eep*, /c/*ute* vs. /gr/*eat*. Admittedly, the case is circumstantial, and counterexamples will be easy to find, since what I am suggesting is a tendency rather than an absolute rule. However, as John Lawler wrote of the contrasting assonance pair /br-/ and /pr-/, as in *broad* and *prude*, *bray* and *pray*:

One is tempted to look at this as a sociosemantic version of Grimm's Law, with the devoicing of the stop cluster an iconic representation of "devoicing" of the social connotations of the role stereotypes (1990:37).

The closest thing to a minimal pair in the data to illustrate this point would be the (voiced) male *beefcake* and the (devoiced) female *pancake [Brit.]*; but a more intuitively satisfying contrast for an American audience is suggested by the pair *beefcake* and *cheesecake* (as John Lawler, personal communication, reminded me).[7]

---

5 A point which was painfully obvious to me as soon as Steve Greenberg called it to my attention.

6 An example of this phonetic distinction in popular culture is Jimmy Stewart affectionately calling his little daughter *gingersnap* (not *cookie* or *cupcake)* in the 1946 Frank Capra movie *It's a Wonderful Life*.

7 I am venturing out onto a limb with this hypothesis. Although I have no "proof," nothing I have seen contradicts the spirit of the analysis (see Lawler 1990, Rhodes and Lawler 1981, and especially McCune 1983. I am also deeply grateful to Margaret Magnus Nizhnikov, who generously permitted me access to her unpublished MIT Ph.D. dissertation on sound symbolism (1993), wherein she goes into detail not possible here).

2.6 Interacting Linguistic Levels: Phonosemantics

The most intriguing result of my research is the finding that these phonetic and semantic features are coterminous: there is a subtle but crucial semantic distinction between actual items which could be ordered off a menu, such as *cupcake, pumpkin (pie)*, or *tart*, which almost all follow the phonetic pattern, and mere toothsome objects, such as *cutie pie, honey(bun(ches))*, or *sweetie*, which may or may not. The peer pressure is so strong that the phonetically ill-formed *sweetheart*, originally from a cake in the shape of a heart, and originally somewhat risqué in metaphorical use, has been supplanted over the past hundred years by the phonetically correct *tart* (a back clipping of the presumed rhyming slang *jam tart*), while there has been a corresponding semantic shift; *sweetheart* has undergone amelioration, whereas *tart* has narrowed, at least in American usage, to the specific sense of 'loose woman' or 'prostitute' (Holder 1989:178; Mills 1989:235; *Oxford English Dictionary*, s.v. "sweetheart," "tart"). I have tried to capture some of the interaction of linguistic levels in Figure 1, below: this interplay motivates the use of *cake* but not the equally phonetically plausible **custard*, which fails on semantic grounds; and the use of *pancake* (formerly served as a dessert) but not the morphologically comparable **shortcake* or the semantically parallel **waffle*, neither of which patterns phonetically. The previously-mentioned counter-examples **brownie, *gingerbread*, etc., are also shown, although I hasten to add that a two-dimensional representation is necessarily a gross oversimplification. As Givón cautions, "iconicity is not a monolith, but rather may operate at many different levels; and...occasionally motivations derived from different—equally natural—sources may come into conflict. And the resolution of such conflicts is not always predictable..." (1983:212).

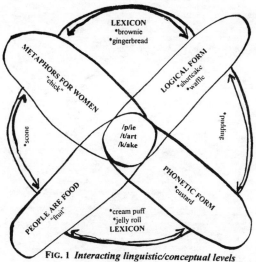

FIG. 1 *Interacting linguistic/conceptual levels*

3.1 Conclusion: Coincidence or Conspiracy?

In this paper, I have presented evidence of multiple motivations for the metaphorical use of specific lexical items. Either this is some peculiar coincidence, or there is a conspiracy of linguistic features at play, challenging the tenet of "the arbitrariness of the sign" and suggesting instead what might be called "the eccentricity of the sign." From this eccentric orbit we can infer the existence of additional variables which may be relevant in metaphor description, some of which have been discussed above, but further research is needed to determine what "counts" as an expression of this metaphor before we can definitively "characterize both the source and the target domains, together with the mapping between them," as Langacker (1990:155) urges us. The present paper is an attempt to provoke such further research, by elucidating some of the complex interdependencies of thought and language, of cognitive linguistics.

References

DICTIONARIES/WORD SOURCES

Browning, D.C., compiler. 1982. *The Everyman Dictionary of Quotation and Proverbs*. London: Chancellor Press.

Davis, John. 1993. *Buzzwords: The Jargon of the 1990s*. New York: Crown Trade Paperback.

Farmer, John S., and W.E. Henley, eds. *Slang and its Analogues*. 7 vols. 1890-1904. Reprint (7 vols. in 3). New York: Kraus Reprint Corp., 1965.

Green, Jonathon. 1986. *The Slang Thesaurus*. London: Penguin.

Grose, Captain Francis, ed. *A Classical Dictionary of the Vulgar Tongue*. 1796. Reprint (edited by Eric Partridge). New York: Dorset Press, 1992.

Holder, R. W. 1989. *The Faber Dictionary of Euphemisms*. Rev. ed. London: Faber and Faber.

Lighter, J.E., ed. 1994. *Random House Historical Dictionary of American Slang, vol. 1 A-G*. New York: Random House.

Major, Clarence. 1994. *Juba to Jive: The Dictionary of African-American Slang*. New York: Penguin.

Mills, Jane. 1989. *Womanwords: A Dictionary of Words about Women*. New York: Henry Holt.

Oxford English Dictionary, 2nd ed.

Partridge, Eric. 1984. *Partridge's Dictionary of Slang and Unconventional English*. Edited by Paul Beale. New York: MacMillan.

Partridge, Eric, ed. 1986. *A Dictionary of Catch Phrases*. New York: Stein and Day.

Rawson, Hugh. 1989. *Wicked Words*. New York: Crown Trade Paperback.

Spears, Richard A. 1981. *Slang and Euphemism*. New York: Jonathan David.

Wentworth, Harold, and Stuart Berg Flexner, eds. 1975. *Dictionary of American Slang*. Second supplemented ed. New York: Thomas Y. Crowell.

Wilson, Robert A., ed. 1972. *Playboy's Book of Forbidden Words*. Chicago: Playboy Press.

GENERAL

Givón, Talmy. 1979. *On Understanding Grammar*. New York: Academic Press.

Givón, Talmy. 1983. Iconicity, Isomorphism, and Non-arbitrary Coding in Syntax. In John Haiman, ed., *Iconicity in Syntax*, 187-220. Amsterdam: John Benjamins.

Hines, Caitlin. Let me call you "Sweetheart": The WOMAN AS DESSERT metaphor. In Mary Bucholtz, Anita C. Liang, Laurel Sutton, and Caitlin Hines, eds., *Communicating in, through, and across Cultures: Proceedings of the Third Berkeley Women and Language Conference*. Berkeley: Berkeley Women and Language Group, *forthcoming*.

Lakoff, George. 1987. *Women, Fire, and Dangerous Things*. Chicago: University of Chicago Press.

Lakoff, George, and Mark Johnson. 1980. *Metaphors We Live By*. Chicago: University of Chicago Press.

Langacker, Ronald W. 1990. *Concept, Image, and Symbol: The Cognitive Basis of Grammar*. Berlin: Mouton de Gruyter.

Lawler, John. 1990. Women, Men, and Bristly Things: The Phonosemantics of the *BR-* Assonance in English. *Michigan Working Papers in Linguistics*, 27-38.

Lehrer, Adrienne. 1969. Semantic Cuisine. *Journal of Linguistics* 5 (April, 1969):39-55.

Lehrer, Adrienne. 1974. *Semantic Fields and Lexical Structure*. Amsterdam:

North-Holland Publishing Co.

McCune, Keith M. 1983. *The Internal Structure of Indonesian Roots.* 2 vols. Doctoral dissertation, University of Michigan.

Nizhnikov, Margaret Magnus. 1993. *What's in a Word?: Evidence for Phonosemantics.* Unpublished doctoral dissertation, MIT.

Rhodes, Richard A., and John Lawler. 1981. Athematic Metaphors. In *Papers from the Seventeenth Regional Meeting, Chicago Linguistic Society.* Chicago: Chicago Linguistic Society.

Wierzbicka, Anna. 1988. *The Semantics of Grammar.* Amsterdam: John Benjamins.

APPENDIX: LEXICAL ITEMS

CENTRAL DESSERT WORDS FOR WOMEN

(piece of) cake
cookie
crumpet [Brit.]
cupcake
pancake [Brit.]
(a tasty bit of) pastry
(cherry) pie
poundcake
pumpkin (pie, tart), punkin
muffin
[jam] tart
tartlet/-lette

PERIPHERAL   WORDS/WOMEN   AS...

a) TOOTHSOME OBJECTS

angel cake
available jelly [roll]
baby cake(s)*
biscuit [= "cookie" [Brit.]]
buttered bun
croissant
cream puff*
cutie pie*
golden doughnut
honeybun(ches)*, honeycakes*,
 honeypie*
jelly roll*
pop tart
sugar doughnut
sugar pie*
sugar-pie-honey-bun
sugar plum
sweetie pie,* sweet-potato-pie*
sweets,* sweetie,* sweetness*
sweetmeat
sweet thing/thang

b) MISCELLANEOUS

bit (on a fork, of jam), bite
cheesecake (adj.)
coffeehouse, coffee-shop
dish*
easy*, easy as pie
morsel
next time you bake a pie, will you
give me a piece?
slice, everybody in town has had
a slice of her
snack, snatch
treat

E X T E N S I O N S

cake eater [= 'ladies' man']
cakeshop [= 'brothel' [Austr.]]
cut the cake [= 'deflower a
virgin']
frosting [= 'makeup']
sugar hill [= 'brothel']
tart shop [= 'brothel' [Brit.]]

*=can also be used of men

Metaphor, Metaphorical Extension, and Grammaticalization: A Study of Mandarin Chinese -*qilai*[1]

CHU-REN HUANG & SHEN-MING CHANG
Academia Sinica & Fu-hsing Junior College

This paper studies the interaction of metaphor and grammar. We first reiterate the position that grammaticalization can be motivated by metaphorical extension (e.g., the Localist Hypothesis, Lyons 1977) and propose a unified account of Mandarin -*qilai* constructions, based roughly on the account of Chang (1994). We then show that metaphorical constraints apply to aspectual -*qilai*. This result contradicts the objectivistic view that linguistic relations are necessarily arbitrary once grammaticalized. It also suggests that Conceptual Structure should not be treated as an autonomous (and thus isolated) module, such as in typical derivational theories. Rather it should be the semantic base that all grammatical components of a language have access to.

---

[1] This paper was presented at the conference on Conceptual Structure, Discourse, and Language at UCSD in November 1994. The authors would like to thank Kathleen Ahrens, Mei-chun Liu, Lily I-wen Su, and an anonymous reviewer of CSLI, Stanford for reading an earlier version of this paper and for their helpful suggestions. We would also like to thank Adele Goldberg, George Lakoff, and other participants of the conference for their comments. Our colleagues at CKIP, Academia Sinica provided gracious help as well as comments on an earlier version of this paper. Research in this paper is partially supported by a grant from the Chiang Ching-Kuo Foundation for International Scholarly Exchanges. Any remaining errors are of course our own.

I. V-*qilai* Constructions and Their Classification

The mono-clausal V-*qilai* construction is identified with at least three meanings in the literature (e.g., Lu et al 1984, and Yeh et al. 1993): directional as in (1), inchoative (cf. Chao 1968) as in (2), and completive as in (3).[2]

(1)a. *ta   tiao-le-qilai*
      S/he jump-PERF-qilai
      "S/he jumped upwards. "

   b. *ta (cong di-shang) jian-qilai yi-ben shu*
      S/he from ground   pick-*qilai* one-CLASS book
      " S/He picked up a book from the ground" .

(2)a. *lichu ku-le-qilai*
      Lichu cry-PERF-*qilai*
      "Lichu began crying" .

   b. *xinkui renzhen-qilai-le*
      Xinkui serious-qilai-PERF
      "Xinkui become serious" .

(3)a. *laoba jishi   duo-qilai*
      Old-Pa in-time hide-*qilai*
      "Old-Pa hid (successively) just in time" .

   b. *..jiang dulun matou baowei-qilai*
      JIANG ferry dock surround-*qilai*
      "...(completely) surrounded the ferry dock" .

        In this section, we will show that these three apparently dissimilar meanings can actually be derived from one identical basic meaning via interaction with the lexical semantics of different classes of verbs.

---

[2] Data cited in this article are extracted from a 20 million character corpus (Huang and Chen 1992, Huang 1994) whenever possible. When the argumentation calls for constructed examples, native speakers in addition to the authors are consulted.

I.1. Directional -*qilai*

First, since the lexical verb *qilai* 'rise-come, to (get) up' denotes upward movement, its directional use and its selection of movement and posture verbs implying upward movement is transparent as observed in Yeh et al. (1993). We also observe that the lexical meaning of -*qilai* denotes a stage, not a state. It is shown in (4) that the construction is compatible with the aspect marking of +Stage imperfective *(zheng4)zai4*, but not with the +State imperfective -*zhe*.[3]

(4)a. *zhangsan zhengzai zhanqilai de shihou ..*
      Zhangsan PROG.   stand-up DE time
      "While Zhangsan was standing up, ..."

  b. **zhangsan zhanqilai-zhe*
     Zhangsan stand-up-DUR.
     (Compare, "Zhangsan was standing (upright)" .)

This is because the affixation of -*qilai* focuses on the upward directionality of the movement. Thus it denotes the manner of a continuing activity, not a state.

I.2. Inchoative -*qilai*

Second, the inchoative construction is so-called because it denotes a situation where a new event begins and continues. This fact can be accounted for by invoking the metaphorical extension of the spatial movement to the temporal PATH (Lakoff 1987, Goldberg 1992, and Goldberg 1995).

---

[3] Note that the general term of 'progressive' has been somewhat confusingly used in the literature to refer to the aspect marked by either -*zhe* (e.g., Chao 1968) or *(zheng4)zai4* (e.g., Chu 1983 and Smith 1991). I adopt Smith's (1991) feature of +Stage and +State to distinguish the two imperfective aspects. I will, however, not adopt her term of 'stative imperfective' to refer to -*zhe* since it is misleading. For instance, -*zhe* marks the most typical active construction of the imperative, as in *zuo4zhe* '(remain) seated'. Chu's (1983) term of 'concomitative' is intuitive but obscure and not defined.

(5)

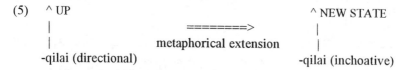

(5) diagrams how the vertical spatial relation denoted by -*qilai* can be metaphorically extended to represent the temporal relation with UP as now standing for a NEW STATE, as in TO START (A NEW STATE) IS TO MOVE UP. We consider this metaphor an elaboration of the prototype metaphor ACTIVATION IS MOTION (Lakoff 1987). We observe that, even though there are instances such as 'What's up?' (as in 'What's new?'), the predicates most commonly used to instantiate this metaphor in English are 'to go' (as in 'He went crazy'). However, it can be shown that *shang4* 'up, to move up' is used in Mandarin Chinese for the TO START IS TO MOVE UP metaphor. For example:

(6) *shang ba*
　　 UP　　PART
　　"Let's go" .

In addition, *shang4* also instantiates the metaphor 'TO START IS TO MOVE UP' when it occurs both as the first and second Verb (V) in a V-V compound, as in (7)-(8).[4]

---

[4] It is interesting to note that *shang4*-V is ambiguous when the complex predicate is ambiguous with both a stage-level and an individual-level reading, such as 'going to school' and 'going to work'. However, even though the complex verbs containing *shang4* are ambiguous, its metaphorical extension remains identical when applied to either the stage-level or the individual-level reading, as in (i). This is further evidence for the linguistic existence of the metaphor of TO START IS TO MOVE UP in Mandarin.

(i)a. *Xiao-Li　meitian　shangxue*
　　 Xiao-Li　everyday　UP-school
　　"Xiao-Li goes to school everyday" .

　 b. *Xiao-Li　shiliusui　　shangxue*
　　 Xiao-Li　sixteen-year　UP-school
　　"Xiao-Li started school at sixteen" .

(7) *shang-yin   de qingshaonian bu   shao*
UP-addiction DE youth-teenager NEG few
" (The number) of the youth and teenagers who became addicted is not small" .

(8) *ta   ai-shang-le   tongban   tongxue*
s/he love-UP-PERF same-class schoolmate
"S/He fell in love with her/his classmate" .

 The use of a distinct morpheme *shang4*, both as an independent word and as a dependent morpheme in a complex predictate, to represent the same metaphoric extension provides independent evidence for the existence of the metaphor TO START IS TO MOVE UP in Mandarin Chinese. Based on the attested existence of this metaphor, we will elaborate below on how a slightly different meaning is assigned when the extension is marked by *-qilai*.
 First, since the lexical item *qilai* marks both the spatial and the metaphoric meaning, this metaphorical extension account correctly predicts the facts that (i) movements verbs, and other verbs compatible with the directional reading, are ambiguous with both readings and can be disambiguated by context, as in (9)-(10); and that (ii) non-movement verbs, such as the activity verb *ku* 'to cry' (2a) and the state verb *renzhen* 'to be serious', are unambiguous and can only have the inchoative reading.[5]

(9) *ta   (cong di-shang) tiao-le-qilai*
S/he from ground-top jump-PERF-qilai
"S/he jumped upwards from the ground" .

(10) *ta   yi-ting   yinyue jiu tiao-le-qilai*
S/he one-hear music JIU jump-PERF-*qilai*
"S/he starts jumping/dancing as soon as s/he hears the music" .

---

[5] Although the orientation of the inchoative aspect is compatible with the orientational metaphor FUTURE IS UP, we feel that the 'up' direction of the future is an inherent nature of our linguistic representation of time instead of the central metaphoric use in this construction. This position is supported by the fact that the inchoative *-qilai* does indeed occur in the past time.
(i) *Zhangsan sange zhongtou qian   chang-le-qilai,*
Zhangsan 3-CLS hour   before sing-LE-*qilai*
    dao xianzai hai mei ting
    till now   yet NEG stop
"Zhangsan started to sing three hours ago and has not stopped yet" .

Second, since the predicate *qilai* denotes upward motion, it is natural for a metaphor-based account to predict that both the directionality (i.e., UP) and the path of the motion (i.e., the upward route) could be mapped. This suggests that the viewpoint focus of *-qilai* could be on the continuation of the situation (i.e., the upward portion of the movement). We have shown that the lexical semantics of directional *-qilai* is not compatible with the +State imperfective aspect *-zhe* even though it can be marked by the +Stage imperfective *(zheng4)zai4*. However, the inchoative *-qilai* does not allow additional marking by the +Stage imperfective *(zheng4)zai4*, as in (11b).

(11) *zhangsan zhengzai tiao-qilai de   shihou ..*
    Zhangsan PROG.   jump-up DE   time
a. "While Zhangsan was jumping up, ..."
b. BUT * "While Zhangsan was beginning jumping ..."

The interpretation of (11) provides further evidence for the fact that the viewpoint focus of the inchoative aspect *-qilai* is on the continuation of the situation. We assume that the V-*qilai* construction does not allow the marking of *(zheng4)zai4* because the lexical semantics of *(zheng4)zai4* conflicts with the lexical semantics of *-qilai*. *(Zheng4)zai4* implies a progress event composed of stages while *-qilai* implies a progress event with a continuing state. In addition, we also predict the fact that inchoative V-*qilai*, as an imperfective predicates does not co-occur with durational adjuncts, but does co-occur with change-of-state adjuncts.[6]

The contrast in (12)-(14) below show that *-qilai* as a marked imperfective aspect has different distributions from either the stative imperfective *-zhe* or the perfective *-le*. The a) sentences contain a durational adjunct *santian*, which is not compatible with imperfective events. The b) sentences contain a durational adjunct *yizhi*, which is not compatible with bounded events. Lastly, the c) sentences contain a change-of-state adjunct *turan*, which is incompatible with un-bounded events. Take note that sentence final *-le* in (14c) is accounted for as marking a new state.

(12)a. *Ta   congming-qilai-le santian*
      S/He clever-*qilai*-PERF three-day

---

[6] Thus *-qilai* marks an imperfective aspect, as argued in Chang (1994) but contrary to Smith's (1991) claim that it is telic by virtue of its start point

b. *Ta   yizhi   congming-qilai-le
   S/He always clever-*qilai*-PERF

c. Ta   turan   congming-qilai-le
   S/He suddenly clever-*qilai*-PERF
   "S/He suddenly became clever" .

(13)a. *Ta   ting-zhe   santian
       S/He listen-DUR three-day

b. Ta   yizhi   ting-zhe
   S/He always listen-DUR
   "S/He has always been listening" .

c. *Ta   turan   ting-zhe
   S/He suddenly listen-DUR
   "S/He suddenly became clever" .

(14)a. Ta   bing-le   santian
       S/He sick-PERF three-day
       "S/He has been sick for three days" .

b. *Ta   yizhi   bing-le
   S/He always sick-PERF

c. Ta   turan   bing-le
   S/He suddenly sick-NEW_STATE
   "S/He suddenly became sick" .

Like other imperfective constructions (13a), V-*qilai* constructions do not take post-predicative durational adjuncts (12a). However unlike typical imperfective predicate (13b), but like a bounded event (14b), it does not co-occur with a durative adjunct (12b). In addition, they co-occur with the change-of-state manner adjunct *tu2ran2*, exemplified by (12c). This is because their event structure has the start point marked, allowing the change-of-state interpretation. This behavior is unlike typical imperfective constructions, and hence our classification of the inchoative -*qilai* as a marked imperfective aspect.

I.3. Completive -*qilai*

Lastly, this grammaticalization account is extended to the recalcitrant completive -*qilai*. Previous literature usually simply lists this use due to the opaqueness of its meaning, especially when the meaning of completive seems to be opposite of that of inchoative (i.e., to start). We first observe that this use is limited to a small class of verbs and that they are in complimentary distribution with verbs occurring with inchoative -*qilai*. We next observe that these verbs all have a locatum argument (subject of *duo* 'to hide' and object of *baowei* 'to surround' as in (3)) and can denote both the activity affecting the locatum and the state/location of that locatum. Further, the implication is that the initiation of the state coincides with the completion of the activity (e.g., the locatum is surrounded only when the activity of encircling is completed, and the locatum is hidden only when the activity of hiding is completed.) In other words, the lexical semantics of these verbs are inherently complex with an event structure that include both activity and state tiers. Verbs with such event structures belong to the traditional classification of accomplishment predicates (cf. Vendler 1967).

We adopt the above two-tier representation of the conflated event structure of the accomplishment predicates selected by completive -*qilai* such that their interaction with the viewpoint focus of the aspects (Smith 1991) can be easily illustrated.[7] When the aspect of -*qilai* (15) is mapped to an event structure , the only possible convergence is (16a). The highlighted double arrow in (16) indicates that the viewpoint focus is on state. (16b) explicates the application of this imperfective viewpoint focus with the verb *bao1wei2*.

(15) Inchoative/completive -*qilai*

                        START
                        |------------------------------------->

Time -->

---

[7] Smith uses 'F' to stand for 'Final' and 'I' to stand for 'Initial'. 'Endpoint' refers to either end of a continuum (i.e., an 'Initial endpoint' (also a start point) and a 'Final endpoint').

(16)a. Event Structure of Verbs selected by Completive *-qilai*

```
activity  ---------------->| F (Endpoint)
                           |
state    (Endpoint) I      |=======================>

Time -------------------------------------------------------->
```

b. Event Structure of *bao1wei2* 'to surround'

```
activity  ---------------->| F (Endpoint)
(AGT to surround)          |
                           |
state    (start point) I   |=====================>
(TH being surrounded)

Time -------------------------------------------------------->
```

With (17a), we show that the progressive aspect marking can focus on the activity tier of the event, while in an unmarked sentence (17b) the aspect tends to be focused on the state tier.

(17)a. Meijun   zhengzai baowei   haidi
        America-army PROG   surround Haiti
        "The U.S. armed forces are encircling Haiti" .

   b. *Meijun   baowei   haidi*
       America-army surround Haiti
       "The U.S. armed forces has surrounded Haiti" .

The interaction of the two tiers can be more vividly highlighted with an unaccusative predicate as in (18) .

(18)a. *xiaotou zhengzai duo (jingcha)*
        thief   PROG   hide police
        "The thief is evading (the police)" .

   b. *xiaotou duo-qilai-le*
       thief   hide-qilai-LE
       "The thief is hiding" .

While the +Stage imperfective aspect *(zheng4)zai4* focuses on the on-going activity without referring to either endpoint, the imperfective *-qilai* focus on the continuation of an event with an (linguistically unmarked) initial endpoint. With the event structure thus stipulated, the aspect *-qilai* can only bring focus on the state tier of these complex predicates. However, since the final endpoint of the activity and the initial endpoint of the state necessarily coincide for an accomplishment verb, the semantic implicature of completion of the activity is inferred and the completive reading derived.

Thus, the completive *-qilai* is not a different construction but only a special case of inchoative *-qilai*. This analysis not only explains the completive meaning, and the fact that completive and inchoative *-qilai* co-occur with complimentary sets of predicates, it also correctly predicts the identical distribution of the two alleged constructions with regard to three types of adjuncts, as demonstrated by (19), in comparison with the inchoative constructions exemplified by (12).

(19)a. *Ta   duo-qilai-le   santian*
       S/He hide-*qilai*-PERF three-day

   b. *Ta   yizhi   duo-qilai-le*
      S/He always hide-*qilai*-LE

   c. *Ta   turan   duo-qilai-le*
      S/He suddenly hide-*qilai*-PERF
      "S/He suddenly hid him/herself" .

II. Grammaticalization and Metaphoric Extension

In this section, we study the interaction of metaphor and grammaticalized metaphorical extension by examining the assumption that grammaticalized elements are semantically bleached. We will show that, in spite of the grammaticalization process, these predicates cannot contradict the metaphor that they are based on. This result has very important implications for the structure of the grammar and gives us interesting insights regarding how metaphorical extensions work in language.

We first observe that the inchoative *-qilai* is seemingly free from the semantic restrictions of other Orientational Metaphors (Lakoff and Johnson 1980). For instance, to cry is sad, and SAD IS DOWN. Nevertheless, *ku-qilai* occurs with the inchoative meaning (1a). The following examples from the CKIP corpus also suggest that grammaticalization motivated by metaphoric extension is not contradicted by semantically contrary non-orientational metaphors.

(20) *youdian   zi-bei-qilai*
     somewhat self+inferior-*qilai*
     "[S/he] started to feel somewhat inferior" .

(21) *ta zhengge ren   dou weishuo-qilai,*
     s/he whole person ALL withdraw-*qilai*
            zhi   xiang suojin   ying-ke-li
            only want shrink-into hard+shell-IN
     "S/he became withdrawn in every respect, and only wanted to shrink
        into a hardshell" .

(22) *yi xiayu, wuzi sizhou de jinguan dunshi   yin-yu-qilai*
     once rain house environs DE scene   suddenly dark+gloomy-*qilai*
     "Once it rains, the surroundings of the house all of a sudden become
        dark and gloomy" .

From (20)-(22), we can see that all three predicates that -*qilai* attaches to seem to involve the orientational metaphor of DOWN or LOW. Hence *zi-bei* involves low self-esteem in (20); *suo-jin* involves shrinking and down-sizing in (21), and *yin-yu* involves becoming gloomy as in (22).

However, it can also be observed that the above three predicates refer to the event that leads to these states, but not the states that the metaphors refer to directly. Thus we have 'to have low self-esteem,' 'to shrink into,' and 'to become dark and gloomy' respectively. Similarly, the inchoative focus for *ku-qilai* is on the activity of crying without direct reference to the state of sadness. Thus these examples only *appear* to contradict the orientational metaphor. Indeed, among the 736 instances of predicates occurring before -*qilai* in the 10 million word CKIP corpus, there is no instance directly involving the contradictory DOWN metaphor.

(23)a. *jian-qilai (subtract-*qilai*)   [MORE IS UP]
    b. *chu-qilai (divide-*qilai*)   [MORE IS UP]
    c. *huai-qilai (bad-*qilai*)   [HEALTH IS UP]
    d. *bing-qilai (ill-*qilai*)   [HEALTH IS UP]

e. *beishang-qilai (sad-qilai)   [HAPPY IS UP]
f. *duoluo-qilai (debase-qilai)   [VIRTUE IS UP]

On the other hand, many instances were found in which -qilai appeared with compatible metaphors. For example:

(24)a. jia-qilai 'to add up'   [MORE IS UP]
   b. cheng-qilai 'to multiply'   [MORE IS UP]
   c. hao-qilai 'to become well, to recover'   [HEALTH IS UP]
   d. jiankang-qilai, 'to become healthy'   [HEALTH IS UP]
   e. gaoxing-qilai 'to become happy,'   [HAPPY IS UP]
   f. shoufa-qilai 'to become law-abiding'   [VIRTUE IS UP]

Even though their semantic counterparts are attested in (24), the constructed unacceptable predicate -qilai sequences in (23) never showed up in our large corpus, and are considered impossible (with regard to the inchoative reading) by the native speakers we consulted as well. Since their semantic counterparts take -qilai, this restriction cannot involve the grammatical selection of the inchoative aspect but the conceptual selection of the metaphors.

The logical explanation is that these verb-aspect constellations, if allowed, would simultaneously contain two contradictory metaphors (UP from -qilai, and DOWN from the predicate), and are therefore semantically anomalous. The above observation can also be extended to the verbs selected by the completive -qilai: *tao-qilai (to escape, DISAPPEARANCE IS DOWN).

A further complication that actually supports the above position is that there is no such restrictions on the metonymic extension of conditional -qilai, as in (25) (Chang 1994, Liu 1994).

(25) ta   bing-qilai dou yao hao ji   ge yue cai   hao
     s/he sick-qilai ALL need good several CL month ONLY well
    "When s/he gets sick, it will always take him/her several months to
       recover" .

Chang (1993) observes that conditional -qilai occurs only in the subordinate clause of a bi-clausal constructions. It is claimed in Liu (1994) that this use can be considered a metonymic extension of the inchoative -qilai. The metonymic extension can be explicated on the basis of our event-structure account of inchoative -*qilai*. In our account, inchoative -*qilai* invokes the metaphor of TO START IS TO MOVE UP. However, in terms of viewpoint aspect, its focus is on the continuity of the event after the startpoint. Thus it could be extended to refer to the duration of that event. Next, the conditional meaning is metonymic with the (concurrent) duration. Adopting this account, the conditional -*qilai* makes no direct reference to an UP metaphor and will not be contradictory with predicates involving a DOWN metaphor.

Lastly, this account underlines the crucial position the lexicon plays in the grammar and will interact with a theory of lexical diffusion (Wang 1969) to accomodate speaker variations with regard to grammatical judgments. When a linguistic item is sufficiently lexicalized, such as when *duo4luo4* (fall-fall) 'to debase' loses its 'falling downwards' meaning for a speaker, then the *duo4luo4-qilai* 'to start to become debased' verbal constellation will no longer be a contradiction for that speaker. Hence it should and does occur for some speakers, as attested by the fact that several speakers we questioned found this construction acceptable though somewhat marked.

III. Concluding Remarks: Conceptual Structure and the Grammar

To sum up, we offer a unified account of the various V-*qilai* constructions based on metaphoric extensions. We show that the inchoative -*qilai* is actually a metaphoric extension of the straightforward directional -*qilai* based on the metaphor TO START IS TO MOVE UP. In addition, the completive -*qilai* is actually a special case of inchoative -*qilai* when the predicate involves a conflated complex event structure. Since the TO START IS TO MOVE UP metaphor can only be applied to the open-ended part of the event structure, it is applied to the STATE portion of the complex event and the completive meaning is derived since the start of STATE denoted by these accomplishment predicates coincides with the completion of an ACTIVITY. In addition, we also suggested that the conditional -*qilai* can be accounted for as a metonymic extension of the inchoative -*qilai*. The extension will be from the viewpoint focus on the continuity of the inchoative to the duration of the conditional. This account offers support of Liu's (1994 & 1995) claim of V-V compounds forming a radial category in Mandarin.

A small but crucial fact observed in this paper is that even though the metaphoric extension of TO START IS TO MOVE UP motivates the grammaticalization of the inchoative aspect -*qilai*, it still interacts with other metaphors. We observe that the grammatical marking of the inchoative aspect with -*qilai* is impossible when the predicate itself represents the contradictory metaphor of DOWN. This is somewhat surprising given the standard formal assumption that grammaticalization is characterized by the loss of extra-grammatical influences. To account for the data involving -*qilai*, we must abandon this assumption and assume instead that conceptual structures interact at all grammatical levels. Thus, this study not only offers support for the position that language and concepts can be physically-grounded through the mapping of metaphorical extension (Lakoff 1987), it also suggests that such metaphorical extensions must be mapped to the same physical background if they are referring to the same event. It is this identical base of the oriental space that allows us to predict that a verb involving a DOWN metaphor cannot co-occur with the -*qilai* aspect containing a UP metaphor.

The above metaphor-based account has important implications for the modular representation of linguistic competence in general and on the position of conceptual structure in particular. The standard assumption of generative theories seems to be that there is a single monotonic mapping from conceptual structure to the lexicon to syntax (e.g., Bresnan and Kanerva (1989) and Jackendoff (1972)). This view predicts that there will be no interaction between conceptual structure and grammaticalized elements. The interaction between metaphors and the selection of the inchoative aspect of -*qilai* suggests otherwise.

Thus, our study suggests that conceptual structure is not autonomous but can be accessible to all lexical and grammatical operations through the lexicon via the mechanisms of metaphorical and metonymic extensions. In addition, we also found that orientational metaphors involved in the same verb constellation are mapped to the same orientational space. This fact provides the conceptual basis of semantic restrictions on the collocation of -*qilai* and verbs as well as additional strong support for metaphor-based conceptual operations across grammatical modules.

References

Bresnan, Joan and Jonni M. Kanerva. 1989. Locative Inversion in Chichewa: A Case Study of Factorization in Grammar. *Linguistic Inquiry.* 20.1.1-50.

Chang, Shen-Min. 1993. V-*qilai* Compounds in Mandarin Chinese. *Proceedings of the First Pacific Asia Conference on Formal and Computational Linguistics.* 62-81.

____, 1994. *V-qi-lai Constructions in Mandarin Chinese: A Study of Their Semantics and Syntax.* Unpublished M.A. Thesis. National Tsing Hua University.

____, and Chu-Ren Huang. 1994. The Semantics of *Qilai* in Mandarin: Directionality and Inchoativity. *[In Chinese] Proceedings of the Fourth International Conference on Teaching Chinese as a Foreign Language.* Volume on Linguistic Analysis. Pp. 147-157. Taipei: World Chinese Association.

Chao, Yuan Ren. 1968. *A Grammar of Spoken Chinese.* Berkeley: University of California Press.

Chu, Chauncey Cheng-hsi. 1983. *A Reference Grammar of Mandarin Chinese for English Speakers.* New York: Peter Lang.

Goldberg, Adele E. 1992. In Support of a Semantic Account of Resultatives. *CSLI Technical Report* 92-163.

____, 1995. *Constructions: A Construction Grammar Approach to Argument Structure.* Chicago: University of Chicago Press.

Huang, Chu-Ren. 1994. Corpus-based Studies of Mandarin Chinese: Foundational Issues and Preliminary Results. In M. Y. Chen and O. J-L. Tzeng. Eds. *In Honor of William S-Y. Wang: Interdisciplniary Studies on Language and Language Change.* Pp. 165-186. Taipei: Pyramid.

____, and Keh-jiann Chen. 1992. A Chinese Corpus for Linguistic Research. In the *Proceedings of the 1992 International Conference on Computational Linguistics* (COLING-92). pp. 1214- 1217. Nantes, France.

Jackendoff, Ray. 1972. *Semantic Interpretation in Generative Grammar.* Cambridge: MIT Press.

Lakoff, George. 1987. *Women, Fire, and Dangerous Things.* Chicago: University of Chicago Press.

____, and Mark Johnson. 1980. *Metaphors We Live By.* Chicago: University of Chicago Press.

Liu, Meichun. 1994. Semantic Schema and Metaphorical Extension: A Study of the Mandarin V-R Compounds as a Radial Category. In the *Proceedings of the Fourth International Symposium on Chinese Languages and Linguistics*. 462-473. Taipei: Academia Sinica.

____, 1995. Conceptual Manipulation and Semantic Distribution: The Case of Mandarin Post-verbal *de*-Complaints. In this Volume.

Lu, Shu Xiang et al. 1984. *Xiandai Hanyu Ba Bai Ci* [Eight Hundred Words in Modern Chinese]. Hong Kong: Shangwu.

Lyons, John. 1977. *Semantics*. Cambridge: Cambridge University Press.

Smith, Carlota. 1991. *The Parameter of Aspect*. Dordrecht: Kluwer.

Vendler, Zeno. 1967. *Linguistics in Philosophy*. Ithaca: Cornell University Press.

Yeh, Mei-li, Zhao-ming Gao, and Chu-Ren Huang. 1993. On the Interpretation of V-*qila*i: A Corpus-based Study. Presented at the Second International Conference on Chinese Linguistics (ICCL-II). Paris. June 23-25.

Wang, Willian S.-Y. 1969. Competing Changes as a Cause of Residue. *Language*. Vol. 45. pp.9-25.

The *Way* Constructions Grow[1]

MICHAEL ISRAEL

University of California, San Diego

This paper examines the history of the Modern English *way*-construction, a construction which has recently been the focus of a number of theoretical works on argument structure constraints in synchronic grammar (Levin & Rapoport 1988, Jackendoff 1990, Marantz 1992, Goldberg, in press). The present work seeks to show the relevance of a diachronic perspective to the general issues of synchronic grammatical representation raised by these studies. It will be shown that the modern construction arose out of three distinct, but related early usages, and that each of these usages developed independently through a process of gradual, analogical extensions. Drawing on a diachronic corpus of 1,211 examples from the OED on CD-ROM, along with 1.047 contemporary examples from the Oxford University Press corpus, I will argue that the evolution of this construction provides strong support for a usage-based model of grammar in which linguistic knowledge is organized around the two complementary principles of (global) schema extraction and (local) analogical extension (cf. Bybee 1988, Langacker 1988, Barlow & Kemmer 1992).

Following Langacker, I assume that the grammar of a language is properly understood as "a structured inventory of conventional linguistic units" (1987: 57), and that the organization of this inventory largely reflects the experience speakers have of actual linguistic usage. This usage-based approach to language is distinguished from traditional generative approaches by being maximalist, non-reductive and bottom-up. The approach is maximalist in that it views language as "a massive, highly redundant inventory" in which conventional units "run the gamut from full generality to complete idiosyncrasy" (1988: 131). It is non-reductive in that it allows for both general rules (or schemas) and specific instances of those rules as part of a speaker's grammatical competence. Finally, it is bottom-up in that the general rules are themselves understood as schematizations over experienced instances, so that the overall structure of the grammar is determined

[1]This paper has benefitted from the comments of Kathleen Ahrens, Michael Barlow, Kathy Carey, Rich Epstein, Gilles Fauconnier, Adele Goldberg, Ron Langacker and Karin Pizer. Special thanks are due to Suzanne Kemmer who first set me on this project and whose influence pervades its results. The foolish things that remain are entirely my own fault.

not by general cognitive principles alone, but also crucially by the probabilistic vagaries of experienced linguistic usage. In what follows, I provide empirical support for this general theoretical view of language.

1. The Modern *Way*-Construction

The modern *way*-construction is illustrated below in (1-3).

(1) Rasselas dug his way out of the Happy Valley.
(2) The wounded soldiers limped their way across the field.
(3) %Convulsed with laughter, she giggled her way up the stairs.

Each of these examples in its own way entails the movement of the subject referent along the path indicated by the prepositional phrase. In (1) the verb codes a means of achieving this motion, i.e. the creation of a path. In (2) the verb elaborates the manner in which this motion is achieved. And in (3) the verb describes an incidental activity of the subject as she moves along the path. These three usages--means, manner, and incidental activity--give a rough sense of the range of the present day construction, though we should note that examples like that in (3) are at best marginal for many speakers. As will be seen, this usage is a late entry in the history of the construction.

A variety of facts justify us in viewing these sentences as instances of a grammatical *construction*, that is, as a conventional pairing of form and meaning (Fillmore, Kay and O'Connor 1988, Fillmore and Kay 1993; for further arguments that the construction is a *construction*, see Jackendoff 1990 and Goldberg 1995, in press). First, the construction assigns an idiomatic interpretation to sentences having the general form [NP$_j$ [V NP$_j$'s *way* OBL]]: in all cases the subject's movement is entailed, whether or not that entailment can be derived from the normal lexical semantics of any part of the sentence. Moreover, the argument structure of these sentences is often not regularly projected from the meaning of the verb: in (2) the normally intransitive *limp* takes a direct object; in (3) *giggle* acts like a motion verb with both a direct object and a directional PP. Finally, despite this idiomatic interpretation and unusual argument structure, the construction is used productively with a diverse array of predicates.

These facts are amply illustrated by modern attested examples in which we find, among other things, a woman crunching her way across a glass-strewn room, a gadget that bleeps and snoops its way into answering machines, a man who knits his way across the Atlantic, a film with Glenn Gould brooding his way across a frozen lake, and some unfortunate people who snorted and injected their way to oblivion. Such diverse examples show that we are dealing here with a very productive pattern. One way or another, the construction must be listed as a conventional part of English grammar.

Still the question remains, how should the construction be represented? The most economical way would be to posit a single schematic entry that captures all and only the range of possible usages. Such is the strategy advocated by Jackendoff, who proposes the correspondence rule reproduced in figure 1 (1990: 221):

$$[_{VP} V_h [_{NP} NP_j \text{'s} \quad \text{way}] PP_k] \text{ may correspond to}$$

$$\begin{bmatrix} \text{GO} \; ([\alpha]_j, \; [\text{Path}]_k) \\ \text{AFF} \; ([\;\;]_i^\alpha, \;\;) \\ [\text{WITH/BY} \quad \begin{bmatrix} \text{AFF} \; ([\alpha], \;\;) \\ \text{- BOUNDED} \end{bmatrix}_h] \\ \text{EVENT} \end{bmatrix}$$

<u>Figure 1</u>

Abstracting from the formal details, Jackendoff presents the construction as a conventional correspondence between a syntactic form and a conceptual structure. As he notes, the representation is much like that of a simple lexical entry, differing only in that instead of specifying the syntactic head and leaving the complements open, it specifies a complement (NP's *way*) and leaves the head open (1990: 222).

But there is reason to think that the head is perhaps not quite so open. As noted above, not all verbs are equally felicitous in the construction, the incidental activity usage in (3) being for many speakers marginal or worse. For this reason, Goldberg (in press) suggests that minimally the construction should be viewed as a simple polysemy network, with the incidental activity interpretation counting as an extension from a more basic means sense[2]. This minimal enrichment effectively splits the representation in two, thus capturing the construction's variable interpretation (note the WITH/BY split in Jackendoff's conceptual structure) and according a different status to each of the two interpretations. The split has the further advantage of allowing us to associate different semantic

---

[2]My terminology differs from that of Goldberg, who uses *manner* for what I term *incidental activity* and handles examples like 1 and 2 both as instances of a means usage.

constraints with each interpretation. As Goldberg notes, while the means interpretation is generally limited to coding motion achieved despite some obstacle or difficulty, no such constraint appears to hold for the incidental activity usage.

Still, there is reason to think that the simple polysemy hypothesis does not go far enough. As Goldberg herself points out, a survey of attested examples reveals that usage tends to cluster around certain narrowly defined semantic verb classes. Thus we commonly find examples with verbs of winding motion (*pick, thread, wind, wend, worm, snake, serpent, weave*) and laborious motion (*plod, crawl, grind, slog, stumble*); with fighting verbs (*fight, force, claw, elbow, knee, push*) and cutting verbs (*cut, hack, plow, dig, tunnel, eat, chew*); and with noisy verbs (*crash, crunch, clang, warble, sob, snarl*), among others. As Goldberg has argued for the English ditransitive construction, clusterings of this sort suggest that speakers are aware, not only of general syntactic patterns, but also of the particular ways those patterns tend to be instantiated in use (1995: 133-136).

In what follows, I argue that speakers are indeed aware of both the general patterns and their specific instances, and further that the specific instances play an important role in the grammar. The *way*-construction will thus be viewed as a massive and highly redundant network of related usages represented at multiple levels of schematicity. At the most fine-grained level, the representation includes information about specific verbs and their frequency of occurrence in the construction. Moving up a level of schematicity, verbs are clustered into types along a variety of semantic parameters. Because these types more or less fill up all of semantic space (or that portion covered by unbounded activity verbs) they provide ample motivation for higher order representations schematizing over prominent subsets of usages, and ultimately for Jackendoff's maximally schematic entry specifying only that the verb should mark an unbounded activity. These schematic categories may then serve as the basis for novel usages of the construction, and thus can be seen to play an important and complementary role to that of the specific instantiations.

2. Growth and History of the Construction

The modern *way*-construction can be traced back to three early usages in which a possessed *way* appeared in direct object position with verbs of motion, path creation and possession. All three of these proto-usages were independently motivated by the lexical semantics of *way*, and each formed the basis for an independent thread of analogical extensions. In this section I briefly trace the development of two of these analogical threads from the fourteenth century to the present, confining my attention, for the most part, to the verbs which characterize them. The manner thread started with simple verbs of motion and gradually evolved to include a wide range of very colorful predicates coding a manner of motion. The means thread began with verbs of path clearing and creation and evolved to include predicates coding almost any means of achieving motion[3]. Not until the nineteenth century, when both threads were already quite richly elaborated, did they begin to tangle into a single category and so to obscure their original, independent motivations.

2.1. The Manner Thread. The manner thread has its roots in a much more general ME construction, the *go-your-path*-construction, in which a motion verb took an optional possessed path argument: as (4-5) suggest, any noun meaning something like "way" appears to have worked in this construction.

(4)   To madian lond, wente he his ride. (c. 1250. *Genesis & Exodus*, 3950)
(5)   Tho wente he his strete, tho flewe I doun. (1481. Caxton, *Reynard (Arb)*, 55)

Examples with *way* constitute a special case of this more general construction and are common from at least 1350 on. Early instances tend to feature high-frequency motion verbs like *go, ride, run, pursue, wend* and *pass.*

(6)   He lape one horse and passit his way. (1375. Barbour, *The Bruce* xxxiii)
(7)   The kyng took a laghtre, and wente his way. (1412. Hoccleve, *De Reg. Princ.*, 3400)
(8)   Now wyl I go wende my way With sore syeng and wel away. (1450. *Coventry Mysteries*, "Cain & Abel" 193)
(9)   I ran my way and let hym syt Smoke and shitten arse together. (1557. *Welth & Helth*)

Up to 1700 only sixteen distinct verb types are attested in this thread, and most of these are common, basic-level words. The construction gradually expands, as verbs coding path shape, rate, and manner of motion find their way into usage by analogy with the

---

[3]The third thread, which I omit for lack of space, involved usages with verbs like *keep, hold, take, snatch* and *find* coding the acquisition or maintenance of possession of a path. These usages were very common in early stages of the construction. But unlike the other two threads, this usage shrank rather than expanded over time, so that now only *find* (still one of the most of the common predicates in the modern construction) and a few other verbs remain to represent it.

more basic motion verbs already established in the construction. In addition to those shown in (10-12), these novel verbs include *sweep, wale, creep, plod, pick* and *wheel*, among others.

(10) From Samos have I wing'd my way. (1667. Congreve, *Semele* ii. i. 2)
(11) He windes his oblique way Amongst innumerable Stars. (1667. Milton, *P.L,* iii. 563)
(12) The moving legions speed their headlong way. (1715-20. Pope, *Iliad*, ii.)

By the early nineteenth century, the construction had become fairly productive, and between 1826 and 1875 we find as many as 38 distinct verbs of motion occurring in the construction. By now the role of analogy as a guiding force in the construction's evolution is apparent, as new forms entering the construction tend to cluster around certain well-defined semantic prototypes. In particular, we find a large number of verbs coding difficult or laborious motion--*plod, totter, shamble, scramble, churn, sap, grope and grabble, grind, flounder* and *fumble*--as well as a good number of verbs coding winding, tortuous paths--*wend, wind, thread, corkscrew, worm, serpentine* and *insinuate*. The examples in (13-16) give some small sense of the construction's range at this point.

(13) She started up, and fumbled her way down the dark stairs. (1801. *Gabrielli's Mysterious Husband*, III. 80)
(14) The poor Dominie..weariedly plodded his way towards Woodbourne. (1815. Scott, *Guy M.* xxviii)
(15) Mr. Bantam corkscrewed his way through the crowd. (1837, Dickens, *Pickwick Papers* xxxv)
(16) He was merely serpentining his way to the part of the details. (1837. T. Hook, *Jack Brag* viii)

Finally, by the end of the nineteenth century we begin to find verbs like *crunch, crash, sing, toot* and *pipe*--encoding not motion per se, but rather the noise that inevitably accompanies certain forms of motion. While this extension begins with a few isolated instances (examples with *ring* (1836) and *crunch* (1851) lead the way), a well-defined usage quickly emerges as novel verbs are added by analogy with these innovating leaders.

(17) There is a full stream that tumbles into the sea..after singing its way down from the heights of Burrule. (1890. Hall, *Caine Bondman*, ii. iii)

(18) Such a paltry collection of commonplace tunes..as jingle-jangles and drums its way through the piece. (1899. *Westminster Gazette*, 13 Feb 3/1)

(19) The cars that buzzed and clanged their way past Wayne were filled to the running-boards. (1917. Mathewson, *Second Base Sloan*, 248)

The remarkable thing about this long evolution is the consistency of usage over the centuries. In every period certain predicates--*go, make, work, pursue, wing*--tend to recur and predominate in usage. And as new usages modestly build on the range of established of predicates, the construction gradually increases in productivity. Long strings of analogical extensions lead to discrete clusters of usage, which then license the extraction of more abstract schemas for the construction. These basic observations turn out to hold equally for the means thread.

2.2. The Means Thread. The created path usage which forms the basis for the means thread comes in fairly late at the end of the sixteenth century. By 1650, examples include verbs like *pave* and *smooth* from the domain of road building, verbs of path clearing like *cut, furrow out, poke out* and *eat out*, as well as the more general *force out* coding the general physical exertion required to make one's way.

(20) Like as a fearefull Dove, which through the raine Of the wide ayre her way does cut amaine. (1590. Spenser, *F. Q.* i. v. 28)

(21) Arminius paved his way first by aspersing and sugillating the fame and authority of Calvin. (1647. Trapp, *Com. Acts* xxi. 28)

(22) Bacon was one of those that smoothed his way to a full ripeness by liquorish and pleasing passages. (1653. A. Wilson, *Jas.* I, 37)

Over the next hundred years many of these predicates recur and many similar ones enter into usage. By 1750 we find several more examples from the domain of road building--*bridge, chalk out*--and many more coding some notion of clearing or cutting--*hew out, sheer, shave out, corrode, plough, dig, clear, free*. Note that usages like these necessarily imply that the motion is not easy (otherwise, why build a path?), and so lay the basis for Goldberg's constraint that motion be achieved despite some obstacle.

The "cutting" category remains the main attractor of new predicates for some time, but extensions do gradually emerge. The "fighting" usage, illustrated in (23) and (24), is a particularly prominent example, entering into usage around 1770 and rapidly becoming entrenched as a new source of analogical extensions.

(23) Every step that he takes he must battle his way. (1794. Southey,

Bot. Bay. Eclog. iii)

(24) Fighting his way to a chair of rhetoric. (1816. Scott, *Antiquities,* xxxi)

The usage here is presumably motivated by the common use of *force* in the construction and, perhaps, by a frequent occurrence of the cutting usage for battle scenes. By 1875 examples include uses with *push, struggle, jostle, elbow, shoulder, knee, beat* and *shoot.*

In the nineteenth century, as the manner thread experiences a rapid expansion, the means thread begins to allow verbs encoding increasingly indirect ways of reaching a goal. In (25-28) the verbs do not depict any physical exertion but rather mark various social and psychological sorts of activity which enable (literal or metaphorical) motion. In (29-30), where the overtly coded action only incidentally enables motion, the causal link is even more indirect. Cattermole may get to oblivion by means of his bad painting, but there is no sense in which this activity necessarily leads to this end, nor even that Cattermole was ever trying to get there.

(25) Sad deeds bewailing of the prowling fox; How in the roost the thief had knav'd his way. (1821. John Clare, *The Village Minstrel* I. 18)

(26) He...smirked his way to a pedagogal desk. (1823. New Monthly *Magazine* VII. 386)

(27) Not one man in five hundred could have spelled his way through a psalm. (1849. Macaulay, *History of England* iii. I. 405)

(28) The passionate absorbedness with which..intellect has plumbed its way forward in search of God. (1881. Robertson, in *Sunday Mag.,* April, 245)

(29) Cattermole...now prostitutes his talent...and blots his way to emolument and oblivion. (1844. John Ruskin, *Modern Painters* Pref. 67)

(30) Addison wrote his way with his Whig pamphlets to a secretaryship of state. (1890. T. F. Tout, *History of England,* 111)

By the time examples of this sort appear in the construction, the cutting and fighting usages were well entrenched, and these, along with the well established manner uses, allowed for the extraction of increasingly abstract schemas which could generalize over the range of established usages. Such schemas naturally supply a solid basis for increasingly far-flung extensions. The farthest-flung are cases in which the verb codes neither a means nor a manner of motion, but rather some incidental activity that happens to accompany motion. As noted in section 1, usages of this sort are still unacceptable for many speakers; however, they have been around since at least 1866.

(31) He..whistled his way to the main front-door. (1866. Blackmore, *Cradock Nowell* xvi)

(32) He ahs and ers, and hums and hawes his way through an incredibly fatuous pronouncement. (1931. *Time & Tide* 12 Sept. 1057)

Note that this extension appears to be equally well-motivated as stemming from either the means or the manner thread. Until well into the twentieth century instances of this sort consistently involve sounds produced in the process of moving, and as such they appear to be extensions from examples like (17-19) in which the verb encodes a noisy manner of motion. On the other hand, it is equally plausible to think of these as extensions from the means thread, since the notion of an incidental activity that accompanies motion is really but one small step away from cases like (29-30) coding activities that incidentally enable motion.

Really, there is no reason we should have to choose. By the time such usages begin to emerge, the two threads are already so entangled that it is often difficult to decide for a particular novel extension whether it should count as means or manner. The growth of the two threads had inevitably led to areas of overlap between them, and the extreme range of established usages naturally led speakers to reanalyze the categories that underlay them. Doubtless, the reanalysis was not sudden, for there is no discernible break in the long chain of analogical extensions that clearly precipitated it. Still, speakers must have gradually reorganized the links that mediated this increasingly vast network of usages, uniting them into what then became the modern construction[4].

3. Generalizations and Discussion

The basic developments that characterize the growth of the *way*-construction appear to be remarkably straightforward. Early predicates associated with the construction tended to be less unusual and more schematic, while later predicates include nonce forms (e.g. in 32), onomatopoetic noisy verbs, and generally a variety of unusual and highly specific subordinate-level words. As usage began to include increasingly recherché sorts of verbs, the construction's conceptual range gradually expanded: in early stages the construction was limited to verbs which were somehow directly related to motion or path creation; in later stages, the construction

---

[4]For similar developments in which diachronic pressures led to the reconceptualization of a complex category see Geeraerts (1990), Melis (1990) and Winters (1989).

allows verbs which are only marginally or incidentally related to the actual expressed motion.

It is useful, in this light, to consider the construction, in the terminology of Fauconnier and Turner (1994, this volume), as an example of a syntactic blend--that is, as a specialized grammatical pattern serving to combine disparate conceptual contents in a single, compact linguistic form. Essentially, the modern construction provides a way to blend the conceptual content of an activity verb with the basic idea of motion along a path. The trend toward verbs coding activities which are increasingly marginal to the achievement of motion thus reflects the construction's gradually increasing power to blend different types of events into a single conceptual package.

Crucially, the construction did not acquire this power over night. The transition from the early simple uses to the later more elaborate ones involved a long process of local extensions, with each successive phase of usage building on the established patterns of earlier generations. While this paper has emphasized the conceptual side of these extensions, it is important to note that the construction's emergence has a formal side to it as well, and that this formal development was also very gradual in nature.

Note that several of the diachronic examples (6-10, 12) lack an overtly expressed oblique argument, despite the fact that in modern usage the oblique is essentially obligatory in the construction. In coding the corpus, my strategy was to accept as an instance of the construction any sentence which: (1) includes a non-oblique possessed *way* argument; (2) has the possessive coindexed with the subject; and (3) entails, or at least allows the implicature, that motion was achieved. The result is that many examples without overt obliques are included in the corpus; interestingly, however, their distribution is hardly random.

Table 1

	Total Tokens	# No Obl.	% No Obl.
1374-1587	40	24	60%
1588-1650	64	35	55%
1651-1700	72	28	39%
1701-1800	107	31	29%
1801-1825	77	19	25%
1826-1850	138	21	15%
1851-1875	190	34	18%
1876-1900	210	24	11%
1901-1945	169	18	11%
1946-1960	74	4	05%

Table 1 lists the total number of tokens occurring at each stage in the history of the construction, and shows in the rightmost columns the number and percentage of tokens occurring without an overt oblique. As can be seen, while such instances were common in early stages of the construction, originally including more than half of the attested examples, their frequency gradually declined over several centuries. Indeed, by the twentieth century what few examples remain tend to occur in specialized, idiomatic instances of the construction, as in the expression *I went my own way*. The gradual disappearance of such examples follows a linear function. It thus appears that, just as the construction's general productivity emerged from a long series of analogical extensions and increasingly abstract constructional schemas, so did the construction's modern form slowly emerge as general statistical tendencies became strengthened into rigid, categorial constraints.

4. Conclusions

The *way*-construction emerged gradually over the course of several centuries. There is no single moment we can point to and say, "This is where the construction entered the grammar." Rather, a long process of local analogical extensions led a variety of idiomatic usages to gradually gain in productive strength even as they settled into a rigid syntax. As the range of predicates spread, increasingly abstract schemas could be extracted from them and this in turn drove the process of increasing productivity.

Trivially, any synchronic model of grammatical organization must be reconcilable with the observed facts of linguistic change. Since the growth of the *way*-construction only makes sense if speakers somehow kept track of which verbs were used in it and how frequently they were used, it follows that such information must be available to speakers as part of their knowledge of a language. The evidence from the *way*-construction suggests that while speakers surely do rely on abstract grammatical knowledge, the role of actual linguistic usage in organizing that knowledge may be much greater than is generally supposed.

I should emphasize that these conclusions are not just special facts about unusual idioms like the *way*-construction. One clear result from work on grammaticalization is that change tends to occur in local contexts (Hopper and Traugott 1993:2). Recent work by Carey (1994, this volume) demonstrates that the shift from resultativity to the coding of perfect aspect in English started with narrowly defined usages involving verbs of mental state, perception and communication, and only gradually expanded to uses with other verbs. Similarly, Hare and Elman (in press) provide a connectionist model showing how the growth of English strong and weak verb classes was driven by analogical extensions within narrowly defined verb classes (cf. Tabor 1993 for similar work on the degree modifiers *kinda* and *sorta*). More generally, the work reported here reflects a tendency in theoretical work towards viewing the organization of grammar as driven by and arising from the demands of actual linguistic processing and usage (Barlow and Kemmer 1992, Bates and MacWhinney 1987, Bybee 1988, Kemmer and Israel 1994, Langacker 1987, 1988).

By way of conclusion, I would like to suggest two very general principles that might be invoked to explain the sorts of phenomena discussed in this paper.

1. The Production Principle (Analogical Usage):

Utterances should sound like things the speaker has heard before.

2. The Comprehension Principle (Schema Abstraction):

Representations should capture similarities across experienced usages.

These principles are intended to capture the complementary roles of schema extraction and analogical extension in the organization of grammatical knowledge. The production principle represents a tendency toward conservatism and reflects the fact that people tend to talk like the people they identify with. The comprehension principle, on the other hand, is a force for innovation and reflects the fact that, in general, people will seek to accommodate and make sense of even the most unexpected novel utterances. Of course, individuals may be expected to show considerable variation both in their commitment to these principles and in their ability to execute them (not everyone is a perfect mimic, and not everyone will extract the same generalizations). Still, I would suggest that the two principles together do provide a useful basis to begin thinking about the complementary roles of innovation and imitation in mediating between abstract linguistic abilities (i.e. competence) and actual linguistic usage (i.e. performance).

References

Barlow, Michael & Suzanne Kemmer. 1992. "A Schema-Based Approach to Grammatical Description." Paper delivered at the 21st Annual Linguistics Symposium, "The Reality of Linguistic Rules," University of Wisconsin, Milwaukee.

Bates, Elizabeth, & Brian MacWhinney. 1987. "Competition, Variation, and Language Learning." In B. MacWhinney, ed., *Mechanisms of Language Acquisition*, 157-193. Hillsdale, NJ: Erlbaum.

Bybee, Joan. 1988. "Morphology as Lexical Organization." In Michael Hammond and Michael Noonan, eds., *Theoretical Morphology*, 119-141. San Diego: Academic Press.

Carey, Kathleen. 1994. *Pragmatics, Subjectivity and the Grammaticalization of the English Perfect*. PhD dissertation, UC San Diego.

Fauconnier, Gilles and Mark Turner. 1994. "Conceptual Projection and Middle Spaces." Technical Report 9401. Dept. of Cognitive Science, UCSD.

Fillmore, Charles J., and Paul Kay. 1993. *Construction Grammar*. Ms., U.C. Berkeley.

Fillmore, Charles J., Paul Kay, & Mary Catherine O'Connor. 1988. "Regularity and Idiomaticity in Grammatical Constructions: The Case of *Let Alone*." *Language* 64: 501-38.

Geeraerts, Dirk. 1990. "Homonymy, Iconicity, and Prototypicality." *Belgian Journal of Linguistics* 5, 219-231.

Goldberg, Adele. 1995. *Constructions: A Construction Grammar Approach to Argument Structure*. Chicago and London: The University of Chicago Press.

———. In press "Making One's Way through the Data." In Alex Alsina, Joan Bresnan & Peter Sells, eds., *Complex Predicates*, Stanford: CSLI.

Hare, Mary, & Jeff Elman. In press. "Learning and Morphological Change." In *Cognition*.

Hopper, Paul & Elizabeth Traugott. 1993. *Grammaticalization*. Cambridge: Cambridged Univ. Press.

Jackendoff, Ray. 1990. *Semantic Structures*. Cambridge, Mass: MIT Press.

Kemmer, Suzanne & Michael Israel. 1994. "Variation and the Usage-Based Model." In *Papers from the Parasession on Variation and Linguistic Theory*. Chicago: CLS.

Langacker, Ronald W. 1987. *Foundations of Cognitive Grammar. Vol. I: Theoretical Prerequisites*. Stanford: Stanford University Press.

———. 1988. "A Usage-Based Model." In Brygida Rudzka-Ostyn, ed., *Topics in Cognitive Linguistics*, 127-161. Amsterdam: John Benjamins.

Levin, Beth & T. Rapoport. 1988. "Lexical Subordination." *CLS 24*.

Marantz, Alec. 1992. "The *way*-Construction and the Semantics of Direct Arguments in English: A Reply to Jackendoff." In *Syntax and Semantics Vol. 26: Syntax and the Lexicon.* New York: Academic Press.

Melis, Ludo. 1990. "Pronominal verbs in Old and and Modern French, or How prototypes can be restructured on the basis of permanent meaning effects. *Belgian Journal of Linguistics* 5: 87-108.

Tabor, Whitney. 1993. "The Gradual Development of Degree Modifier *Sort of* and *Kind of*: A Corpus Proximity Model." to appear in *CLS* 29. Chicago: CLS.

Winters, Margaret. 1989. "Diachronic Prototype Theory: on the evolution of the French subjunctive." *Linguistics* 27: 703-730.

Emphatic *-Self* in Discourse

SUZANNE KEMMER & MICHAEL BARLOW
Rice University

It is well known that English *-self* has two basic functions, emphatic and reflexive, illustrated in (1) and (2) respectively.

(1) Aristotle <u>himself</u> believed that the arts and sciences have been discovered many times and then lost again.

(2) The old horse heaves <u>himself</u> out of the mud and jumps it cleanly. (LOB corpus)

Reflexive *-self* is the subject of an extensive literature, but emphatic *-self* is a much less studied element. Our aim in this paper is to look at a fair amount of usage data for emphatic *-self*, to see what recurrent uses there are and how these can best be described. Our assumption is that the analysis of any linguistic phenomenon should be based on an empirically rich database; and that emphatic *-self* in particular, whose distribution is largely governed by discourse considerations, should be studied with reference to its discourse functions.

We identify three major semantic/pragmatic usage patterns for emphatic *-self*, each of which is associated with particular formal characteristics. The three types are referred to as schemas (cf. Barlow and Kemmer 1994) or as constructions, following traditional grammar and more recent constructional approaches to syntax (Fillmore et al. 1988, Lakoff 1987, Goldberg 1995).[1] These constructions have been described to a certain extent by linguists cited below. We propose to go beyond existing descriptions by considering the functions of *-self* as observed in actual usage events in discourse. Doing so allows us to give both a characterization of the lexeme *-self* that holds across several emphatic constructions, and a more complete explication of the specific constructions containing emphatic *-self* than previously proposed.[2]

---

[1]Schemas and constructions are equivalent to 'constructional schemas,' (Langacker 1987 inter alia). Barlow and Kemmer 1994 describe the basic ideas of schema-based grammatical theories in contrast to rule-based theories.

[2]The relation of emphatic to reflexive *-self* in English is not treated here; see Kemmer 1995.

We used data from two online text corpora of ca. one million words each of British English: Corpus Collections A and B published by Oxford University Press, containing newspaper articles and academic prose, respectively. We did not have available a spoken language corpus of a sufficient size, but we did examine emphatic -self in a small spoken corpus (400,000 words), and the results suggested no major differences between -self in spoken and written discourse.

1. Headed Emphatics

The syntactic structure associated with emphatic -self that is most markedly different from the reflexive is that in which -self is a kind of adjunct to a lexical or pronominal head, as in (1) above. We use the term **headed emphatic** for this type, since this is the only one of three main use types to have such a head.[3]

The [head + Pron-self] complex can serve any grammatical function in a clause, and the head can either be a lexical element or a pronoun. In this paper we focus mainly on the forms *himself* and *itself*, which show far and away the largest numbers of tokens in the database. Most of the generalizations observable in the data refer to these forms, and they provide a useful contrast between animate and inanimate which will turn out to be relevant.

As argued in Kemmer 1995, to arrive at a reasonably comprehensive characterization of the meaning of emphatic -self, it is necessary to make reference to a cluster of four properties.

One is the notion of contrast, familiar from the characterization of emphatic -self in traditional grammar, as well as from more recent descriptions such as found in Erteschik-Shir 1973, 1981. We can formulate this notion using the base/profile distinction in Cognitive Grammar (Langacker 1987). -Self evokes a base, or background conceptualization, of a set of explicit or implicit referents. These comprise an ad-hoc pragmatic set, inferable by the hearer from contextual cues.[4] Thus, in (1), Aristotle is implicitly contrasted with other potential referents. From the larger context it is

---

[3]This construction is perhaps a unique type of configuration among noun phrases, and the syntactic status of the two elements may be amenable to different analyses (cf. Bickerton 1987). Our description in no way depends on a particular syntactic analysis; we use the terms 'head' and 'adjunct' for convenience.

[4]In one extension of this basic function, instead of a simple set, we have an ordered pragmatic scale. The head NP refers to an entity high on that scale, such that -self means something like 'even' in *The king himself was there* (cf. König 1991).

clear that the relevant contrast set is the set of Greek philosophers.

Also part of the base is the fact that one or more of the entities in this set are seen as more likely to be referred to *instead* of the -*self*-marked entity. In other words, there is a pragmatic expectation arising in the local context regarding which referent is going to be chosen to be next referred to. The role of expectation in the meaning of -*self* was argued for in Edmonson and Plank 1978 and (also for German *selbst*) Plank 1979.

The profile of emphatic -*self*, that is, what it designates, is the referent picked out of the contrast set as the one unexpectedly referred to. Thus, -*self* has the function of excluding all other potential referents in the set in favor of one particular antecedent. The three notions of **contrast set**, **unexpected reference**, and **exclusion** of other referents combine in a single integrated conceptualization, or cognitive model (Lakoff 1987).

The fourth characteristic of emphatic -*self* is **accessibility** of the -*self*-marked referent, in the sense of Ariel 1988, 1990. Accessibility is a psychological notion referring to the degree of ease of retrieval of mental entities, including referents. Chafe 1987, 1994 uses the term to refer to the degree of psychological activation of referents, where activation refers to bringing to consciousness the conception of a particular entity.[5] Both definitions get at essentially the same psychological notion of heightened or focused attention on a particular piece of information.

Based on psycholinguistic and discourse data, Ariel arrived at a ranking of types of referring expressions on a scale of accessibility: from least to most accessible. A similar accessibility hierarchy was independently posited by Givón 1983 and elsewhere in his work on topic continuity.

Ariel, analyzing reflexive -*self* , locates it towards the high end of the accessibility hierarchy (cf. also Kemmer 1995). Emphatic -*self*, we claim, is associated with high accessibility as well. First, in the headed emphatic, -*self* redundantly points to a referent just mentioned in the NP head, and hence is accessible by virtue of recency. Second, the whole [NP + Pron-*self*] complex is associated with relatively high accessibility of the referent it

---

[5]Chafe (1994) refers to a three-way contrast: "An active concept is one that is currently lit up, a concept in a person's focus of consciousness. A semi-active concept is one that is in a person's peripheral consciousness, a concept of which a person has a background awareness, but which is not being directly focused on. An inactive concept is one that is currently in a person's long term memory."

accesses. We can use (1) again to illustrate this point. It is given in its larger context in (3):

(3) Consequently, it is not surprising that in this period the main philosophical schools tended to reject the idea of progress and to hold cyclical views concerning the nature of time. Aristotle himself believed that the arts and sciences have been discovered many times...

Several sentences earlier in the passage, Plato and Aristotle and their views were mentioned. Then follows a switch away from those referents to views generally accepted by philosophers of the time regarding progress. It is at that point the discourse goes back to Aristotle.

We can paraphrase the instructions given by the headed -self construction as follows: Reactivate a referent that is prominent and easily accessible in the context, namely the one mentioned in the head; exclude the other potential referents that have just been mentioned, which by virtue of having been made new local topics had considerable likelihood to have been continued with; and make it clear that although these others are candidates, it is the referent of the head noun instead which is to be attended to.

This return-to-topic pattern, in fact, crops up quite consistently with animate referents. It can also occur with inanimates, as in (4) (where the 'national government', a coalition government in post-World War I Britain, has been discussed throughout the discourse).

(4) ...among Conservatives, the motives for an election were clear: for those left out of the government... a desire to reunite the party, and simple self-preservation. It was, however, Geoffrey Dawson, editor of The Times, who, in an editorial on 16 September, was the first to suggest that the National Government itself, and not the parties separately, should make an appeal to the country 'on a broad programme of reconstruction which will include a tariff'.

Inanimate referents, however, are far less likely to be topics (even in 4, the referent is a social unit and hence not strictly inanimate). Inanimate referents of emphatic -self are most typically not topics, but are for other reasons highly accessible. (5) illustrates such a case:

(5) A running engine must produce heat, and the accumulated heat fatigues the machinery <u>itself</u>. (LOB corpus)

   In the text up to this point, machinery has not been mentioned. However, machinery is part of an overall conceptualization of an engine, in fact the most salient part of that conceptualization, given that an engine is structurally and functionally constituted by machinery. Numerous cases of such 'implicit referent' uses of -*self* are found with inanimates in the database.[6]
   The generalization that linking the two uses of -*self*, for topics and for non-topical, implicit referents, is that the headed emphatic designates a highly prominent and hence easily accessible participant—but not necessarily the most immediately accessible one, which is most often the referent just mentioned.
   Table 1 presents some numerical information on emphatic -*self* which bear on these points. Let us focus on the top third of the table, summarizing usages of headed emphatic -*self*.

Table 1.

	himself	*itself*	*myself*	*yourself*
Headed emphatics				
Lexical	139	268	0	0
Pronominal	15	0	1	0
Total	154	268	1	0
Coord/Compar.	13	50	0	0
Argument emphatics				
Reflexive	42	20	3	5
Non-refl	15	3	23	0
Total	57	23	26	5
Coord/Comp.	47	9	24	2
Predicate emphatics				
Total	54	91	10	3
Coord/Compar.	0	1	0	1
Ethical Dative	1	0	5	0
Total	265	382	42	8

---

   [6]This use of *self* to refer to a salient essential aspect of an inanimate referent is most likely an extension of its animate use. The noun *self* refers most basically to the essence of a person. Emphatic particles cross-linguistically have as their lexical source words referring to selfhood, such as 'soul', 'mind', 'body' or 'head', all metonymic ways of referring to the essence of a person.

We can see first of all that the heads in this construction are far more likely to be lexical rather than pronominal. This distribution is expected from a construction whose prototypical use is to activate referents that are accessible, yet not immediately so. As shown by both Givón 1983 and Ariel 1988, pronouns are used to refer to the most accessible referents, while lexical nouns activate less accessible entities. This general property is reflected in this specific construction, in which the head is giving the most information about which entity is being picked out by the construction as a whole, and the -*self* part is redundantly pointing to the same referent.

To be sure, it is possible to use this construction with referents that are at the very high end of the accessibility scale. Pronouns represent the special case where a referent is extremely high in topicality, yet for some context-specific reason, another referent is more likely in a particular role. Such cases are not the norm, since very high topicality normally correlates with *high* likelihood of next mention, rather than unexpected mention of a less likely referent. But cases where these two factors are at odds do occur. Hence, pronoun heads are not categorically absent from the distribution of the construction; they simply represent a relatively small number of cases.

Table 1 also gives information on how often the headed emphatic occurs within comparative and coordinate constructions. An example in a comparative construction is exemplified in (6):

(6) Many were amazed that the war against Bolshevism was already more or less over, but no less a person than the Führer <u>himself</u> had again lent support to such notions with his proclamation to the soldiers on the eastern front...

As Table 1 shows, among headed emphatics such structures are not found very often with *himself*, but there are a significant number with inanimate *itself*. The latter, however, still comprise only about 20% of cases of emphatic *itself*.

The difference between animate and inanimate here, we suggest, is due to the difference in topicality between animate and inanimate referents. This difference, as indicated earlier, results in a difference of distribution of animates and inanimates in the return-to-topic pattern. This pattern most often does *not* occur with coordinate or comparative structures, as we might expect given its function of reactivating a global topic and excluding recently-mentioned entities. In the typical inanimate pattern, on the other hand, *-self* marks a salient aspect of a referent, as in (5). Contrast with other aspects of the entity may be implicit, but it may also be made explicit in a coordinate or comparative structure. Example (7) shows a typical case of this type, in which there is a contrast between the sport of soccer, the global topic, and an associated, more peripheral entity (integrity of its players).

(7) The older code, which put the integrity of players and the game <u>itself</u> above money, had been abandoned.

We might add regarding animacy that *himself* most often appears on NPs which are subjects in their clause (about 70% of the time), while *itself* appears on subjects only about 33% of the time. This distribution too reflects the difference in typical discourse functions of animate and inanimate *-self*, which in turn follows from the general discourse distribution of animate vs. inanimate referents. Subjects are likely to be topics and hence subject position is a natural locus for animate *-self* referents, which are also most likely to be topics. Likewise, the large number of inanimate referents which are non-subjects allows many more possible occurrences for *itself* in non-subject role than for *himself* in that role.

We return in the next section to the significance of comparative and coordinate structures in relation to emphatic *-self*.

2. Argument Emphatics
The second type of emphatic *-self* construction is what we term **argument emphatics**. These have no separate NP head, but by themselves function as an NP argument in the clause.[7] In (8), for instance, *himself* is an oblique participant in the clause, playing a role distinct from that of its antecedent referent Mr de Klerk.

(8) It will be interesting to see whether Mr de Klerk has the courage to lift the state of emergency, unban the ANC and unleash against <u>himself</u> and his government the full might of the Sisulu family.

For third person instances, the antecedent is very often the clausal subject, in which case we are dealing with a reflexive, as

---

[7]'Argument' here simply means participant filling some NP slot in the clause distinct from that of its antecedent, regardless of whether the participant is selected for by the verb.

well as emphatic use, as in (8). Since our focus is on emphatic reflexives, we excluded from the database all cases of reflexives that
were not obviously also emphatic.[8]

In Table 1, argument emphatics are subclassified into reflexive
and non-reflexive cases. This distinction is difficult to make categorically; in part, it hinges on whether "reflexive" is taken to
include coreference of any participant NP with a subject, or just
those NPs selected for by the verb, a notoriously slippery distinction when dealing with actual examples. (It should be noted also
that different analysts define 'reflexive' with different degrees of
inclusiveness; see for example definitions used in Reinhart and
Reuland 1993 and references cited therein). We took as reflexive all
cases of emphatics in which an NP argument is coreferential with
the subject of its clause or a long-distance subject, including
examples like (9).

(9) An individual's genes are not unique to <u>itself;</u> they occur also in
    animals to which it is genetically related through genealogical
    descent.

An example of a non-reflexive argument emphatic is given in
(10).[9] The most frequent instances of this type were found in the
first person, in expressions like *John and myself* which occur in all
argument roles.

(10) Only 18 months ago, it was little more than a dream, the
     brainchild of <u>himself</u> and a few radical economists...

The distinction between reflexive and non-reflexive argument
emphatics, as it happens, turns out not to tell us much, other than
that non-reflexive cases are much rarer than reflexive ones. A more
interesting and significant result comes from observing the relation
of argument emphatics to coordinate and comparative structures.
Such structures have often been noted as a locus of emphatic *-self;*

---

[8]The obligatory presence of some degree of stress on the *-self* form is a
good diagnostic of an emphatic (cf. Kemmer 1993, 1995 for the difference
between reflexive and emphatic); thus we eliminated all examples that could
be produced with unstressed *-self*.

[9]Cases of argument *-self* with non-subject antecedents have attracted
notice because they violate Chomsky's binding conditions. Such cases have
been shown to involve the discourse notion of point of view. For analyses of
point of view uses of *-self*, which has some special properties, see Kuno 1987,
Zribi-Hertz 1989, Deane 1992, van Hoek 1992, and Kemmer 1995.

for example, in Erteschik-Shir's discussion of what are here called argument emphatics, she attempts to define emphatic function in terms of a notion called "dominance". Dominance is in turn defined in terms of "focus": Dominant NPs either bear sentence focus (the primary sentence stress), or else are one focused element in a multiple focus construction.[10] Multiple focus constructions include comparative structures, conjunctive or disjunctive listing, or implicit membership in a closed set. These cases serve to show us that argument emphatics, like headed emphatics, have as part of their characterization the notion of a contrast set.

We can go beyond Erteschik-Shir's characterization if we compare the occurrence of comparative and conjunctive/disjunctive (which we call coordinate) structures with headed emphatics vs. argument emphatics. The percentage of argument emphatics found in such structures is considerably larger than found in headed emphatics. For third person animate headed emphatics, only 8% occurred in these overt contrast structures. This jumps to 82% for third person animate argument emphatics. With inanimate *itself*, the percentages go from under 19% for the headed emphatics, to almost 40% for the argument emphatics. Although argument emphatics are a good deal less frequent in general than headed emphatics, these differences in distribution are nonetheless striking.

We suggest an account for this distribution based on a major difference in discourse function between the headed emphatics and the argument emphatics. We propose that emphatic -*self* does have contrast as a part of its semantics, across the board. With headed -*self*, however, the locus of the contrast is generally to be found in the larger discourse context, where there may be any number of competing referents that could potentially occur in the relevant slot (cf. Givón 1992). Such referents come from larger discourse frames that are being developed as the discourse unfolds.[11] In such a situation it is of course possible to have more local contrast structures, such as coordinate constructions; but the occur-

---

[10]We assume that focus is essentially a psychological notion, an attentional phenomenon part of whose characterization involves activation. We also assume that the notion applies more generally than simply to emphatic constructions.

[11]We use the term "frame" here after Fillmore 1976. Such frames can also be understood as Idealized Cognitive Models in the sense of Lakoff 1987. The type of frame under discussion here is not simply a typical scenario, but the highly contextualized understanding and integration of information in an ongoing discourse.

rence of such structures is not particularly tied to the function of -*self* in the headed emphatic construction.

In the case of argument emphatics, on the other hand, we maintain that the construction itself is being used as a signal of explicit contrast within the clause. The discourse scope in this case is much smaller; it is in most cases quite easy to determine what the contrast set is when the sentence is taken out of context, exactly because the set is so locally specified. We suggest also that the function of contrast with other potential referents in the clause is especially useful for animates, just because animates are intrinsically more topical and thus we might expect there to be a greater number of competing potential referents.

3. Predicate Emphatics

Let us now turn to a third type of emphatic construction, which is rather different from the other two both formally and functionally. This third type, which we will refer to as the **predicate emphatic,** is the most complex case and we can scarcely begin to do it justice here.

Consider the example in (11).

(11) Some 169 Washington babies died before their first birthday ... bringing the capital's infant mortality rate to 32.3 deaths for every thousand live births. ... This is more than triple the national average, <u>itself</u> one of the worst in the developed world.

Here, the -*self* form does not serve as a pro-form filling an NP participant role, as in the previous type. In fact, there *is* no separate participant role for -*self*. Unlike with argument emphatics, it is possible to simply omit the -*self* form without affecting acceptability. Nor is there an NP head to the construction—it is possible to identify an NP antecedent in the clause, but it does not form a constituent with the -*self* form. Yet predicate emphatics do resemble the headed emphatics in terms of function, as we will see; it is as though the -*self* form is displaced from its expected position next to an antecedent head. This resemblance shows up distributionally. We can see in Table 1 that the role of comparative and coordinate structures is minimal in this construction; it is more similar in this regard to the headed, rather than the argument emphatic.

We analyze the function of the -*self* form in this construction as follows: it serves to pick up a highly accessible referent and reiterate it, specifically in order to indicate its unexpected relationship to a particular predicate. Let us observe (11) more closely. *Itself* repeats the reference to "the national average"; the rest of the sentence then predicates a property of that referent, in a kind of predicative appositive structure. The *itself* marks a switch to that referent as topic from the most immediately recent topic (the capital's infant mortality rate), and a predication is made about the new topic.

The effect of this use is something like "in turn." The passage began with a grim statistic about the magnitude of the Washington infant mortality rate. A similar predication is made about the second mortality figure introduced, specifically that this figure, the national average, compares dreadfully with mortality rates in the developed world in general. The result is the information that Washington's rate is even worse than we might have imagined from the first statistic alone.

The basic function here is to set up a contrast so that a similar, or even the same, predication can be made about another referent.

It is possible, in fact, to construct a minimal pair with two readings of a predicative emphatic, one with a "same predication" effect, and the other making a contrasting predication. Consider (12):

(12) I'm a Harvard man, <u>myself</u>.

This sentence, spoken to a new acquaintance, can be a declaration that you have something in common with your interlocutor. On the other hand, uttered with a different intonation contour (strong stress on Harvard, an intonation break after *man* and low pitch and falling contour on *myself*), the same words might be said in response to someone who has just asked you for a donation to Yale. The inference is that you will be making your contributions elsewhere, since you do not share his alma mater.

The difference between the two readings turns on the predicate made reference to by -*self*. In the first case the predicate is the same for both referents, and the contrast is between the referents. In the second case, the predicates are similar (they share the superordinate 'college') yet they contrast at a lower level. The reason the predicate emphatic construction is so fascinating is that it seems to be able to pick out predicates at different degrees of inclusiveness as a basis for contrast.

Along similar lines, Moravcsik 1972 observed that this type shows different scope effects with VP ellipsis as compared with sentences identical except for the placement of -*self* --in other words, headed emphatics.

(13) John <u>himself</u> washed his car but his boss didn't.

(14) John washed his car <u>himself</u>, but his boss didn't.

In neither case did the boss wash his car. However, in the case of the headed emphatic in (13), the most normal inference is that the boss's car did not get washed at all. In (14), on the other hand, we understand that the boss's car was washed, but not by the boss personally. In other words, in the first case, the -*self* is not in the scope of the elliptic VP (*wash his car*); but in the second case it is in the VP's scope (*wash his car himself*).

Moravcsik made the basic observation that in this construction, the function of -*self* is more adverbial than pronominal. She drew parallels between this use, in which -*self* Kemmerseems to float loose of the head it referentially belongs with, and floating quantifiers, which are also focus elements that operate at the predicate level. It appears that the predicate emphatic allows for very rich sets of context-dependent inferences to arise about exactly what is being contrasted and what is held constant.

We will not attempt further analysis of the predicate emphatic, whose apparently less noun-like grammatical and functional status is certainly deserving of an investigation on its own. We will move instead to a semantic characterization of the various constructions we have discussed.

4. The Semantics of Emphatic -*Self* and its Associated Constructions
We find it reasonable to think of the three uses of -*self* described above as constructions which share some commonalities that are due to the lexical meaning of the forms of emphatic -*self*, which is best characterized in terms of properties making direct reference to discourse.[12] This lexical meaning we represent as in Figure 1:

---

[12]It is plausible to posit in addition a more general lexical representation for -*self* incorporating its reflexive use, since speakers most likely consider -*self*, whether emphatic or reflexive, to be the same word. Reflexive -*self* can be described as referring to coreference with a maximally

Figure 1.

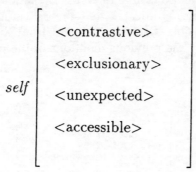

$$self \begin{bmatrix} <\text{contrastive}> \\ <\text{exclusionary}> \\ <\text{unexpected}> \\ <\text{accessible}> \end{bmatrix}$$

This discourse representation can be slotted into the three constructions we have identified for emphatic *-self*, utilizing a representation for discourse linking as described in Barlow 1992. We will exemplify with the headed emphatic and the argument emphatic, leaving the predicative emphatic and its complexities for another work.

The headed emphatic construction is a form-meaning pair described as follows. The form [NP + Pron-*self*] is linked to a discourse structure containing information contributed by *-self* and the pronoun it is attached to. This complex is then integrated with the head. Figures 2 and 3 represent these two levels of integration for the noun phrase *Aristotle himself*, which is an instantiation of this construction.

In Figure 2, the properties associated with the pronoun, male third person referent, are integrated with those for *-self*, yielding the representation for *himself* on the righthand side of the figure. The bracketed element on the left is the instantiation of the discourse representation of the NP element, *Aristotle*. In Figure 3, the discourse specifications for this referent are unified with the information structure for *himself*, yielding a single, complex referent. This referent has the semantic/pragmatic properties of being contrastive, exclusionary, unexpected as a referent in the position it

---

accessible entity, related by a verbal predication (Ariel 1990, van Hoek 1992). Kemmer 1993, 1995 refines this characterization with the notion of unexpectedness of coreference. The more schematic supersense thus includes the notions "unexpected" and "accessible"; but the characterization of each subsense is semantically richer and associated with more specific formal properties as well. (See also Barlow forthcoming for a corpus-based study of reflexive *-self*.)

occurs, and of activating an accessible referent. The latter property, abbreviated as "accessible," indicates that the NP must still be integrated with an accessible discourse referent from the context (provided, in this case, by the previous mentions of the prominent participant Aristotle).

Figure 2

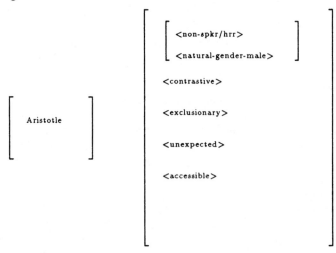

Figure 3

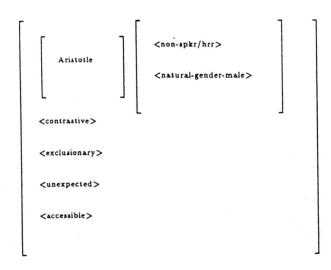

The argument emphatic -*self* construction is one in which the linking between the antecedent and the -*self* form occurs within a single event frame (cf. Barlow 1992). The formal part of the form-discourse mapping is a schema of the form s[...NP-arg ... Pron-*self*...]. This form is linked to a discourse representation in which there is some discourse referent corresponding to an NP which is formally an argument in a sentence S; and there is another discourse element, formally expressed as a pronominal -*self* form, which is specified as linking up with a highly accessible yet unexpected referent. We can represent the relevant elements of such a structure with an illustration from (8). This is shown in Figure 4, in which a number of discourse referents are given ('de Klerk', 'courage', and others unspecified), followed by the discourse structure for the element *Pronoun-self* , which is specified as an argument of the sentence (the person, number and gender specifications are abbreviated with three dots). In Figure 5, the integrated structure is shown, in which the referent 'de Klerk' is identified as the referent of the -*self* argument in the clause.

Figure 4

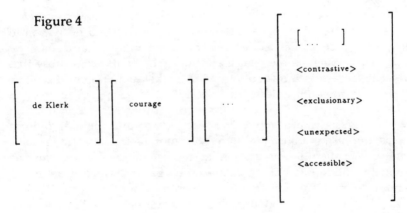

In the process of integration, the referent is accessed and the structure is locally complete. No other accessible referent need be searched out for further integration, unlike in the case of the headed emphatic; hence, the specification "accessible" is no longer present in the representation. The referent of *himself* is understood by the speaker, and a single, integrated discourse structure is the result.

To conclude, we see all of the three uses of -*self* described above fundamentally as discourse elements, and therefore best described

Figure 5

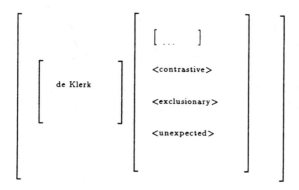

as discourse constructions, or mappings of forms and associated schematic discourse representations. Further, we find no reason to segregate *-self* constructions referring to a more local domain of application such as the clause and its participants from those that refer to larger discourse structures. We take the notion of discourse linking to be applicable to all three types. In each case there is an on-line construction of discourse/conceptual representations in which referents are activated, reactivated, and linked to form richer representations. We therefore require representational tools that reflect such linking and online representational assembly. The model of discourse linking proposed by Barlow 1992 for anaphora and agreement satisfies the requirements for such a representation, as it allows for the modeling of the integration of on-line information structures found in human discourse. We have presented just a brief sketch of the workings of this model, but we believe its basic mechanisms will be useful for representing discourse with explicitness. In regard to the analysis as a whole, we believe that by building on a number of disparate accounts of various aspects of *-self*, and enriching the analysis with discourse data, we have made considerable progress in terms of descriptive coverage, generality and semantic/pragmatic detail.

References

Ariel, Mira. 1988. Referring and Accessibility. *Journal of Linguistics* 24:65-87.

Ariel, Mira. 1990. *Accessing Noun-phrase Antecedents*. London: Routledge.

Barlow, Michael. 1992. *A Situated Theory of Agreement*. (Garland Outstanding Dissertations in Linguistics.) New York: Garland.

Barlow, Michael. Forthcoming. Corpora for Theory and Practice. In Carol Chapelle and Robert Hart, eds., *Computer-Assisted Language Learning as a Context for Second Language Acquisition*.

Barlow, Michael and Suzanne Kemmer. 1994. A Schema-based Approach to Grammatical Description. In Roberta Corrigan, Gregory Iverson and Susan Lima, eds., *The Reality of Linguistic Rules*, 19-42. Amsterdam: Benjamins.

Bickerton, Derek. 1987. *He Himself:* Anaphor, Pronoun, or ... ? *Linguistic Inquiry* 18:345-348.

Chafe, Wallace. 1987. Cognitive Constraints on Information Flow. In Russell Tomlin, ed., *Coherence and Grounding in Discourse*, 21-52. Amsterdam: Benjamins.

Chafe, Wallace. 1994. *Discourse, Consciousness, and Time: The Flow and Displacement of Conscious Experience in Speaking and Writing*. Chicago: University of Chicago Press.

Deane, Paul. 1992. *Grammar in mind and brain: Explorations in cognitive syntax*. Berlin: Mouton de Gruyter.

Edmondson, Jerrold, and Frans Plank. 1978. Great Expectations: An Intensive Self Analysis. *Linguistics and Philosophy* 2:373-413.

Erteschik-Shir, Nomi. 1973. *On the Nature of Island Constraints*. Doctoral dissertation, Massachusetts Institute of Technology.

Erteschik-Shir, Nomi. 1981. On Extraction from Noun Phrases (Picture Noun Phrases). In*Theory of Markedness in Generative Grammar. Proceedings of the 1979 GLOW conference*, 147-169. Pisa: Scuola Normale Superiore.

Fillmore, Charles. 1976. Frame Semantics and the Nature of Language. In S. Harnad et al., eds., *Origins and Evolution of Language and Speech*. New York: New York Academy of Sciences.

Fillmore, Charles, Paul Kay, and Mary Catherine O'Connor. 1988. Regularity and Idiomaticity in Grammatical Constructions: The Case of Let Alone. *Language* 64:501-538.

Givón, T. (ed.). 1983. *Topic Continuity in Discourse: A Quantitative Cross-language Study*. Amsterdam: Benjamins.

Givón, T. 1992. The Grammar of Referential Coherence as Mental Processing Instructions. *Linguistics* 30:5-55.

Goldberg, Adele. 1995. *A Construction Grammar Approach to Argument Structure* . Chicago: University of Chicago Press.

Kemmer, Suzanne. 1993. *The Middle Voice*. (Typological Studies in Language 23.) Amsterdam: John Benjamins.

Kemmer, Suzanne. 1995. Emphatic and Reflexive *-Self:* Expectations, Viewpoint, and Subjectivity. In Susan Wright and Dieter Stein, eds., *Subjectivity and Subjectivization in Language*. Cambridge: Cambridge University Press.

König, Ekkehard. 1991. *The Meaning of Focus Particles: A Comparative Perspective*. London: Routledge.

Kuno, Susumo. 1987. *Functional Syntax: Anaphora, Discourse and Empathy*. Chicago: University of Chicago Press.

Lakoff, George. 1987. *Women, Fire and Dangerous Things*. Chicago: Univ. of Chicago Press.

Langacker, Ronald. 1987, 1991. *Foundations of Cognitive Grammar*, Vols. I and II. Stanford: Stanford University Press.

Moravcsik, Edith. 1972. Some Cross-linguistic Generalizations about Intensifier Constructions. In Paul Peranteau et al., eds., *CLS 8: Papers from the Eighth Regional Meeting of the Chicago Linguistic Society*. Chicago: CLS.

Plank, Frans. 1979. Exclusivierung, Reflexivierung, Identifizierung, Relationale Auszeichnung: Variationen zu einem Semantisch-pragmatischen Thema. In Inger Rosengren, ed., *Sprache und Pragmatik*, 330-354. Lund: CWK Gleerup.

Reinhart, Tanya, and Eric Reuland. 1993. Reflexivity. *Linguistic Inquiry* 24:657-720.

van Hoek, Karen. 1992. *Paths through Conceptual Structure: Constraints on Pronominal Anaphora*. Doctoral dissertation, University of California, San Diego.

Zribi-Hertz, Anne. 1989. Anaphor Binding and Narrative Point of View: English Reflexive Pronouns in Sentence and Discourse. *Language* 65:695-727.

The Metaphor System for Morality

GEORGE LAKOFF
University of California, Berkeley

The metaphorical language of morality and immorality is puzzling at first glance. Here are some examples to give you a sense of the difficulty:

She's on the *straight and narrow* path.
His record is *spotless.*
He's an *upright* man.
He's *black*-hearted.
He's committed a crime and now he has to *pay* for it.
You have to develop *moral fibre.*
There is an *epidemic* of immorality.
Who are the *white* hats in this story?
He's a *bastard!*
That was a *noble* deed.
He has transgressed all moral *boundaries.*
He doesn't *care about* anyone.
She's *pure as the driven snow.*
A good beating will *straighten* him out.
It's not easy to *stand up* to evil.
He's always been *square* with me.

Language is, however, the least of it. These expressions come with inference patterns. For example, if you don't have moral fibre, then you cannot stand up to evil. The people in the white hats are the ones who do noble deeds. If you're pure as the driven snow, you haven't trangressed any moral boundaries.

Part of our job as linguists is to find what systematicities there are in our metaphorical language and metaphorical inferences. We have to answer such questions as "Why can you *pay* someone back for kindesses?" or "Why can you speak of immoral behavior as an *epidemic* that can *spread*?" A deeper part of our job is to figure out why all of the above expressions are about morality, rather than, say, about causation. This paper is a contribution to an understanding of such fundamental linguistic questions. It represents an early stage in research on our moral system.

The Experiential Basis of Morality

Morality around the world has its basis in the promotion of the material well-being of others and the avoidance and prevention of material harm to others. In the basic physical sense, "well-being" is constrained as follows: Other things being equal, you are better off if you are

healthy rather than sick,
rich rather than poor,
strong rather than weak,
safe rather than in danger,
cared for rather than uncared for,
cared about rather than ignored,
happy rather than sad, disgusted or in pain,
whole rather than lacking,
beautiful rather than ugly,
if you are experiencing *beauty* rather than ugliness,
if you are functioning in the *light* rather than the dark, and
if you can stand *upright* so that you don't fall down.

These are among our basic experiential forms of well-being. Their opposites are forms of harm. Immoral action is action that causes harm, that is, action that deprives someone of one or more of these -- of health, wealth, happiness, strength, freedom, safety, beauty, and so on.

These are, of course, norms and the qualification "other things being equal" is necessary, since one can think of special cases where these may not be true. A wealthy child may not get the necessary attention of its parents, someone beautiful may be the target of envy, you need to be in the dark in order to sleep, excessive freedom can sometimes be harmful, sadness and pain may be necessary to appreciate happiness, and so on. But, on the whole, these conditions on material well-being hold.

But morality goes far beyond such material matters, such aspects of direct experience. As we shall see, there is an abstract as well as an experiential morality. Indeed, there are two forms of abstract morality, both based on metaphors that derive from experiential morality.

The Moral Metaphor System

There is a much more important and profound form of abstract morality that arises through metaphor and is grounded in experiential morality. It resides in an extensive system of conceptual metaphors for what morality is, metaphors used to characterize our very forms of abstract moral reasoning.

The dimensions of material well-being -- strength, health, happiness, wealth, freedom, safety, protection, nurturance, empathy, cleanliness, beauty, uprightness, and light -- provide the basis for metaphors for morality. In each metaphor, morality is conceptualized in terms of one of these dimensions of well-being, and immorality is conceptualized as the opposite of morality. For example, we both think and speak of moral strength, moral uprightness, moral purity, moral danger, and moral bankruptcy. We conceptualize good as light and evil as dark. As we explore the metaphorical dimensions of morality, we shall see that they are extensive, and anything but arbitrary. Every form of metaphorical morality has its source in experiential morality. Consequently we shall speak of abstract morality as being "grounded" in experiential morality, that is, in the promotion of experiential well-being.

Abstract (that is, metaphorical) moral schemes provide the rational skeletons for moral reasoning. They define moral ground rules. They give structure to abstract moral thought. Each metaphorical moral scheme has its own logic. There is a logic of moral strength and uprightness, of moral fibre and standing up to evil and keeping oneself from falling. There is a different logic of moral debts, moral credit, and moral bankruptcy. And a still different logic of moral purity and filth and disease. The logics come from "source domains" -- from what we know about strength and uprightness, about debits and credits, about filth and disease.

Each metaphorical moral scheme not only comes with a logic, but with a language. Consider expressions like "You'll *pay* for that," or "We don't want our children *exposed* to such *filth*," or "You've got to *stand on your own two feet*." These are linguistic reflections of metaphorical modes of moral thought. Much of our moral discourse is metaphorically structured in two respects: metaphorical moral schemes provide both the logic of abstract moral discourse and much of its language.

But metaphorical moral schemes provide even more than just logic and language. They are also the source of many moral stereotypes. Conceptualizing morality as uprightness invites the stereotype of a moral person as standing tall and straight and upright. Conceptualizing morality as beauty invites the stereotype of the handsome hero and the ugly and deformed villian. Seeing good as light and bad as dark invites the stereotype of black people as immoral. Technically, this phenomenon is called "metaphorical stereotyping," where the source domain of the metaphor, say uprightness, becomes the stereotype of what it is a metaphor for -- morality. Such stereotypes can be overridden if one is thoughtful, but they do exist and they have a powerful cultural effect.

My goal is to characterize our system of abstract moral schemes, name them, reveal their logic, demarcate their language, point out their stereotypes, and study their workings.

The Basic Metaphorical Conceptions of Morality

Moral Accounting

We all conceptualize Well-being as Wealth. We understand an increase in well-being as a "gain" and a decrease of well-being as a "loss" or a "cost." This is combined with a very general metaphor for causal action in which causation is seen as giving an effect to an affected party (as in "The noise *gave* me a headache"). When two people interact causally with each other, they are commonly conceptualized as engaging in a transaction, each transferring an effect to the other. An effect that helps is conceptualized as a gain; one that harms, as a loss. Thus moral action is conceptualized in terms of financial transaction. Just as literal bookkeeping is vital to economic functioning, so moral bookkeeping is vital to social functioning. And just as it is important that the financial books be balanced, so it is important that the moral books be balanced.

Of course, the source domain of the metaphor, the domain of financial transaction, itself has a morality: It is moral to pay your debts and immoral not to. When moral action is understood metaphorically in terms of financial transaction, financial morality is carried over to morality in general: There is a moral imperative not only to pay one's financial debts, but also one's moral debts.

Moral Accounting

The general metaphor of Moral Accounting is realized in a small number of basic moral schemes: Reciprocation, Retribution, Restitution, Revenge, Altruism, etc. Each of these moral schemes is defined using the metaphor of Moral Accounting, but the schemes differ as how they use this metaphor, that is, they differ as to their inherent logics. Here are the basic schemes.

Reciprocation

If you do something good for me, then I "owe" you something, I am "in your debt." If I do something equally good for you, then I have "repaid" you and we are even. The books are balanced.

From the perspective of cognitive science, there is much here to be explained. Why are financial words like "owe," "debt," and "repay" used to speak of morality? And why is the logic of gain and loss, debt and repayment used to *think* about morality?

The answer given here is that we use conceptual metaphor to think about aspects of morality and that among the general conceptual metaphors used to think and talk about morality are Well-Being is Wealth, and Moral Action is Financial Transaction. But the discovery of these conceptual metaphors (Taub, 1990; Klingebiel, 1990; Johnson, 1993) raises still another question. Why should well-being be conceptualized as wealth? The answer is the one given above. Our metaphors for morality rest on our notions of basic material well-being. Wealth forms one basis for a metaphor for morality, and as we shall see, health, strength, and other forms of well-being lead to other metaphors for morality.

But let us return to the moral scheme of reciprocation, where your doing something good for me places me in your "debt," and I can repay what I "owe" by doing something equally good for you.

Even in this simple case, there are two principles of moral action.

The First Principle: Moral action is giving something of positive value; immoral action is giving something of negative value.

The Second Principle: There is a moral imperative to pay one's moral debts; the failure to pay one's moral debts is immoral.

Thus, when you did something good for me, you engaged in the first form of moral action. When I did something equally good for you, I engaged in *both* forms of moral action. I did something good for you *and* I paid my debts. Here the two principles act in concert.

Retribution

Moral transactions get complicated in the case of negative action. The complications arise because moral accounting is governed by a moral version of the arithmetic of keeping accounts, in which gaining a credit is equivalent to losing a debit and gaining a debit is equivalent to losing a credit.

Suppose I do something to harm you. Then, by Well-Being is Wealth, I have given you something of negative value. You owe me something of equal (negative) value. By moral arithmetic, giving something negative is equivalent to taking something positive. By harming you, I have taken something of value from you. Are you going to "let me get away with it?"

By harming you, I have placed you in a potential moral dilemma with respect to the first and second principles of moral accounting. Here are the horns of dilemma:

The First Horn: If you now do something equally harmful to me, you have done something with two moral interpretations. By the first principle, you have acted immorally since you did something harmful to me. ("Two wrongs don't make a right.") By the second principle, you have acted morally, since you have paid your moral debts.

The Second Horn: Had you done nothing to punish me for harming you, you would have acted morally by the first principle, since you would have avoided doing harm. But you would have acted immorally by the second principle: in "letting me get away with it" you would not have done your moral duty, which is to make "make me pay " for what I have done.

No matter what you do, you violate one of the two principles. You have to make a choice. You have to give priority to one of the principles. Such a choice gives two different versions of moral accounting: The Morality of Absolute Goodness puts the first principle first. The Morality of Retribution puts the second principle first. As might be expected, different people and different subcultures have different solutions to this dilemma, some preferring retribution, others preferring absolute goodness.

In debates over the death penalty, liberals rank Absolute Goodness over Retribution, and conservatives tend to prefer Retribution: a life for a life.

Suppose again that you do something to harm me, which is metaphorically to give me something of negative value. Moral arithmetic presents another form of retribution. By moral arithmetic, you have taken something of positive value from me by harming me. If I take something of equal positive value back from you, I have taken "revenge." Revenge is a form of retribution, another way of balancing the moral books.

Restitution

If I do something harmful to you, then I have given something of negative value and, by moral arithmetic, taken something of positive value. I then owe you something of equal positive value. I can therefore make restitution -- make up for what I have done -- by paying you back with something of equal positive value. Of course, in many cases, full restitution is impossible, but partial restitution may be possible.

An interesting advantage of restitution is that it does not place you in a moral dilemma with respect to the first and second principles. You do not have to do any harm, nor is there any moral debt for you to pay, since full restitution, where possible, cancels all debts.

Altruism

If I do something good for you, then by moral accounting I have given you something of positive value. You are then in my debt. In altruism, I cancel the debt, since I don't want anything in return. I nonetheless build up moral credit.

Morality as Fairness

Children learn very early what is and isn't fair. Fairness is when the cookies are divided equally; when everybody gets a chance to play; when following the rules of the game allows for an equal chance at winning; when everybody does his job; and when you get what you earn or what you agree to. Unfairness is not getting as many cookies as Jimmy; not getting a chance to play; cheating, or bending the rules of the game to increase your chances of winning; not doing your job and therefore making others do it for you; or not getting what you earn or what is agreed upon.

In short, fairness is about the equitable distribution of objects of value (either positive or negative value) according to some accepted standard. What is distributed may be material objects -- say cookies or money -- or metaphorical objects, such as chances to participate, opportunities to win, tasks to be done, punishments or commendations, the ability to state one's case.

Fairness necessarily involves a form of moral accounting, the keeping of a set of moral books. To guarantee fairness, somebody has to keep track of who gets what. If you adopt the conception of Morality-as-Fairness, it is moral to be fair and immoral to be unfair.

Morality as Nurturance

Nurturance presupposes empathy. A child is helpless, it cannot care for itself. It requires someone to care for it, and to care *for* a child adequately, you have to care *about* a child. You have to project your capacity for feeling onto a child accurately enough to have a sense of what that child needs. Nurturance also requires self-nurutrance, that is, taking care of yourself. If you don't take care of yourself, you can't care for others. It also requires the nurturance of social ties, both within the family and the community, so that help will be there when you need it. And finally, fully adequate nurturance requires happiness, for two reasons. First, since people tend no to want others to be happier than they are, they are more like to empathize with others if they are happy themselves. Second, happiness is a gift; it something postive that you give to others. People tend to "get something" important be being around happy people.

The conception of morality as nurturance can be stated as the following conceptual metaphor:
•Moral agents are Nurturing parents
•People needing help are Children needing care
•Morality is Nurturance

Since nurturance entails empathy, self-nurturance, the nurturance of social ties and happiness, conceptualizating Morality as Nurturance entails a collection of related metaphors, namely, Morality as Empathy, Morality as Self-Nurturance, Morality as the Nurturance of Social Ties, and Morality as Happiness. (See Lakoff, 1996, Chap. 6)

Moral Self-Interest

Morality concerns the promotion of the well-being of others and the avoidance or prevention of harm to others. Thus, it might seem that the pursuit of one's self interest would hardly be seen as a form of moral action. Indeed the term "moral self-interest" might seem to be a contradiction in terms. Yet there is a pair of metaphors that turns the pursuit of self-interest into moral action.

The first is an economic metaphor: Adam Smith's metaphor of the Invisible Hand. Smith proposed that, in a free market, if everyone pursues his own profit, then an Invisible Hand will guarantee that the wealth of all will be maximized.

The second is a familiar metaphor: Well-being is Wealth, whereby an increase in well-being is a gain and a decrease in well-being is a loss. When combined with Well-being-is-Wealth, Smith's economic metaphor becomes a metaphor for morality: Morality is the Pursuit of Self-Interest.

This metaphor presupposes the metaphor of Moral Fairness. In an economic market, there is competition for profit. Smith's Invisible Hand works only if the competition is fair -- if there is a "level playing field." Giving some a competitive advantage over others is immoral by this metaphor. It is, first, a form of unfairness, which is in itself immoral. Second, it is a restraint on free markets, which, according to Smith's metaphor, reduces overall profit. By the metaphor of Well-Being is Wealth, a reduction in overall profit is a reduction in over well-being. By Moral Accounting, anything that reduces overall well-being is immoral. Hence, restraints on the pursuit of self-interest are seen as immoral, given the metaphor of Moral Self-Interest.

•Morality is the Pursuit of Self-Interest
•Immorality is a Restraint on the Pursuit of Self-Interest

For those who believe in the Morality of Self-Interest, it can never be a moral criticism that one is trying to maximize one's self-interest, as long as one is not interfering with anyone else's self-interest.

The Morality of Self-Interest fits very well with the Enlightenment view of human nature, in which people are seen as rational animals and rationality is seen as means-end rationality -- rationality that maximizes self-interest. Indeed, the Morality of Self-Interest comes out of such a view of what a human being is.

Moral Bounds

It is common to conceptualize action as a form of self-propelled motion and purposes as destinations that we are trying to reach. Moral action is seen as bounded movement -- movement in permissible areas and along permissible paths. Given this, immoral action is seen as motion outside of the permissible range, as straying from a prescribed path or transgressing prescribed boundaries. To characterize morally permissible actions is to lay out paths and areas of where one can move freely. To characterize immoral action is to limit one's range of movement. In this metaphor, immoral behavior is "deviant" behavior -- a form of metaphorical motion that moves in unsanctioned areas and toward unsanctioned destinations.

Because human purposes are conceptualized in terms of destinations, this metaphor has considerable consequences. Since action is self-propelled motion in this metaphor, and such motion is always under the control of the whoever is moving, it follows that any destination is a freely chosen destination, rejecting the destinations chosen by others. Someone who moves off of sanctioned paths or out of sanctioned territory is doing more than merely acting immorally. He is rejecting the purposes, the goals, the very mode of life of the society he is in. In doing so, he is calling into question the purposes that govern most people's everyday lives. Such "deviation" from social norms goes beyond mere immorality. Actions characterized metaphorically as "deviant" threaten the very identity of normal people, calling their most common and therefore most sacred values into question.

Part of the logic of this metaphor, has to do with the effect of deviant behavior on other people. When people are moving through an area or along a road, it is common for other people to follow them unthinkingly. Those who transgress boundaries or deviate from a prescribed path may "lead others astray." And so, according to this metaphor, people who are immoral, or even act differently than others, may lead others to act immorally, and hence present a danger to the community that goes beyond their actual behavior since they may lure others into immoral behavior. "Moral deviants" are thus doubly threatening: they call into question the values of everyday life and lure even more into immorality, which in turn calls values and the very identity of normal people even more into question.

That is why people who are seen as "deviant," who act outside of the norms of society, arouse such anger. "Deviants" -- people who "go too far" -- threaten the moral fabric and the very identity of normal people. For the protection of the community, they need to be isolated from the community at large -- made outcasts.

Moral Authority

A moral authority has the ability to set moral bounds. The very idea of moral authority is based on parental authority (hence, the term "paternalism"). Young children need to be told what will hurt them and when they are hurting others. They need to learn what's safe and what's harmful, what's right and what's wrong, or they are likely to get hurt or hurt others. Parents have the responsibility of protecting and nurturing their children, teaching them how to protect and care for themselves, and how to act morally toward others.

The metaphor that characterizes moral authority in terms of parental authority is as follows:
- Moral Authority is Parental Authority
- An Authority Figure is a Parent
- A Moral Agent is a Child
- Morality is Obedience

Knowledge mapping:
- Your parents have your best interests at heart and know what is best for you; therefore you should obey them.
- A moral authority has your best interests at heart and knows what is best for you; therefore you should obey him.

There are many kinds of moral authorities -- the gods, prophets, and saints of various religions; people (e.g., spiritual leaders, dedicted public servants, people with a special wisdom); texts (e.g., the Bible, the Koran, the Tao Te Ching); institutions with a moral purpose (e.g., churches, environmental groups). What counts as a moral authority to a given person will depend on that person's moral and spiritual beliefs as well as his understanding of parental authority.

Moral Strength

One can *know* what is moral and immoral and still not have the ability to *do* what is moral. An essential condition for moral action is strength of will. Without sufficient moral strength, one will not be able to act on one's moral knowledge. That is, one will be not be able to implement whichever of the above moral schemes one gives priority to.

The metaphor of moral strength is rather complex. Let us begin our discussion of it with a very general metaphor that Moral Strength makes use of:
- Good is Up
- Bad is Down.

We see this in expressions like: "Things are looking *up*." "Things went *downhill* after the election."

When applied to people, this metaphor yields a metaphor for morality:
- Being Good is Being Upright
- Being Bad is Being Low

Examples include: He's an *upstanding* citizen. He's on the *up and up*. That was a *low* thing to do. He's *underhanded*. He's a *snake* in the grass.

Doing evil is therefore moving from a position of morality (uprightness) to a position of immorality (being low). Hence,
•Doing Evil is Falling
The most famous example, of course, is the *fall* from grace.

A major part of the Moral Strength metaphor has to do with the conception of immorality, or evil. Evil is reified as a force, either internal or external, that can make you fall, that is, commit immoral acts.
•Evil is a Force (either Internal or External)
Thus, to remain upright, one must be strong enough to "stand up to evil." Hence, morality is conceptualized as strength, as having the "moral fibre" or "backbone" to resist evil.
•Morality is Strength
But people are not simply born strong. Moral strength must be built. Just as in building physical strength, where self-discipline and self-denial ("no pain, no gain") are crucial, so moral strength is also built through self-discipline and self-denial, in two ways:
1. Through sufficient self-discipline to meet one's responsibilities and face existing hardships;
2. Actively through self-denial and further self-discipline.

One consequence of this metaphor is that punishment is good for you, since going through hardships builds moral strength. Hence, the homily "Spare the rod and spoil the child."

By the logic of the metaphor, moral weakness is in itself a form of immorality. The reasoning goes like this: A morally weak person is likely to fall, to give in to evil, to perform immoral acts, and thus to become part of the forces of evil. Moral weakness is thus nascent immorality -- immorality waiting to happen.

There are two forms of moral strength, depending on whether the evil to be faced is external or internal. *Courage* is the strength to stand up to *external* evils and to overcome fear and hardship.

Much of the metaphor of moral strength is concerned with *internal* evils, cases where the issue of "self-control" arises. What has to be strengthened is one's will. One must develop will power in order to exercise control over the body, which seen as the seat of passion and desire. Desires -- typically for money, sex, food, comfort, glory, and things other people have -- are seen in this metaphor as "temptations," evils that threaten to overcome one's self-control.

Anger is seen as another internal evil to be overcome, since it too is a threat to self-control. The opposite of self-control is "self-indulgence" -- a concept that only makes sense if one accepts the metaphor of moral strength. Self-indulgence is seen in this metaphor as a vice, while frugality and self-denial are virtues. The seven deadly sins is a catalogue of internal evils to be overcome: greed, lust, gluttony, sloth, pride, envy, and anger. It is the metaphor of moral strength that makes them "sins." The corresponding virtues are charity, sexual restraint, temperance, industry, modesty, satisfaction with one's lot, and calmness. It is the metaphor of moral strength that makes these "virtues."

Moral Essence

Physical objects are made of substances, and how they behave depends on the what they are made of. Wood burns and stone doesn't. Hence, objects made of wood will burn and objects made of stone will not.

We commonly understand people metaphorically as if they were objects made of substances that determine how they will behave. It is thus common to conceive of a person as if he had an essence or a collection of essences that determined his behavior. This is called the Metaphor of Essence.

• A person is an Object.
• His Essence is the Substance the Object is Made of.

Imagine judging someone to be inherently stubborn or reliable. To do so is to assign that person an inherent trait -- an essential property that determines how he will act in certain situations. If the trait is a moral trait, then we have a special case of the Metaphor of Essence -- the metaphor of Moral Essence. In the field of social psychology, there is an expert version of this metaphor called the "trait theory of personality." We are discussing the folk version here.

According to the metaphor of essence, people are born with, or develop in early life, essential moral properties that stay with them for life. Such properties are called "virtues" if they are moral properties, and "vices" if they are immoral properties. The collection of virtues and vices attributed to a person is called that person's "character." When people say "She has a *heart of gold*" or "He doesn't have *a mean bone in his body*" or "He's *rotten to the core*," they are making use of the metaphor of Moral Essence. That is, they are saying that the person in question has certain essential moral qualities that determine certain kinds of moral or immoral behavior.

Moral virtues are defined relative to particular moral schemes. The metaphorical schemes of moral empathy, moral nurturance, and the nurturance of social ties define virtues like care, compassion, responsibility, charity, tact and flexibility and vices like self-centeredness, insensitivity, irresponsibility, stinginess, tactlessness, and inflexibility. The metaphor of moral strength defines virtues like self-discipline, courage, temperance, sobriety, industry, and perseverance and vices like self-indugence, cowardliness, lust, drunkeness, sloth, and faintheartedness. Virtues and vices don't simply exist objectively. They depend upon the moral schemes that one accepts.

The metaphor of Moral Essence has three important entailments:
• If you know how a person has acted, you know what his character is.
• If you know what a person's character is, you know how he will act.
• A person's basic character is formed by adulthood (or perhaps somewhat earlier).
These entailments form the basis for certain currently debated matters of social policy.

Take for example, the "Three strikes and you're out law" now gaining popularity in the United States. The premise is that repeated past violations of the law indicate a character defect -- an inherent propensity to illegal behavior that will lead to future crimes. Since the felon's basic character is formed by adulthood, he is "rotten to the core" and cannot change or be rehabilitated. He therefore will keep performing crimes of the same kind if he is allowed to go free. To protect the public from his future crimes, he must be locked up for life.

Moral Purity

Immorality is commonly metaphorically conceptualized as something disgusting, dirty, and impure, while morality is thought and spoken about in terms of purity and cleanliness. Language makes this clear: That was a *disgusting* thing to do. He's a *dirty* old man. We've to to protect our children from such *filth*. She's *pure* as the driven snow. We're going to *clean up* this town.

The metaphor can be stated as:
• Morality is purity

•Immorality is impurity

Moral Purity is often paired with Moral Essence. Something that has been "corrupted" is something that has been made impure and hence unusable-- such as corrupted blood samples or corrupted databases. Metaphorically, someone who is "corrupt" has an impure essence, which, by Moral Purity and Moral Essence, makes him inherently immoral.

Moral Health

In this culture, impurities are seen as causes of illness. This link between impurity and has led to a further metaphor in which morality is conceptualized as health and immorality as disease.

•Morality is Health

•Immorality is Disease

This leads us to speak of immoral people as "sick" or having "a diseased mind."

The logic of this metaphor is extremely important: Since diseases can spread through contact, it follows from the metaphor that immorality can spread through contact. Hence, immoral people must be kept away from moral people, lest they become immoral too. This is part of the logic behind urban flight, segregated neighborhoods, and strong sentencing guidelines even for nonviolent offenders. The same logic lies behind guilt-by-association arguments.

Moral Light

Immorality is commonly conceptualized as dark and morality as light. This is coherent with morality being clean and immorality being dirty.

•Morality is Light

•Immorality is Dark

Hence, we speak of immoral people as "black-hearted," immoral deeds as "dark deeds." A nonharmful lie is a "white lie." The existence of this metaphor is why it makes sense to speak of the "light of goodness." And, of course, there is the tradition of heroes wearing white hats and villians wearing black hats.

Moral Beauty

Morality is commonly conceptualized as beauty and immorality as ugliness.

•Morality is Beauty (" a beautiful thing to do")
•Immorality is Ugliness ("Things are getting ugly.)

A moral deed can be spoken of as "a beautiful thing to do." When people start acting immorally in a situation, we can say "Things are getting ugly." Similarly, we can refer to an extremely immoral act as "monstrous" and a person who commits such acts as a "monster."

Since regularity of form is commonly associated with beauty and irregularity with ugliness, morality can also be characterized in terms of regularity of form and immorality in terms of irregularity of form.

•Moral is Regular ("He's a straight arrow; a square.")
•Immoral is Irregular ("He's crooked.)

Thus, we can speak of a moral person as "a straight arrow." A reformed felon can be said to "go straight." If someone does something mildly immoral, his punishment can be seen as "straightening him out." If someone is moral to the extreme, he is called a "square." Correspondingly, a corrupt person is called "crooked".

Morality is Wholeness

We speak of a "degenerate" person, moral "decay," the "erosion" of moral standards, the "rupture" or "tearing" of our moral fabric, the the "chipping away" at, and "crumbling" of, moral foundations. All of these are cases where morality is seen as wholeness and immorality as a departure from that state. Wholeness here is abstract and may apply to any kind of entity: a building can crumble, a hillside erode, an organism decay, a fabric tear, a stone can be chipped away at, and so on. It is the wholeness that is at issue, not whether the entity is a building or a hillside or an organism. The kind of entity that is whole or not doesn't matter. Builings and hillsides are mere special cases of entities that can be whole or not. The general metaphor is:

•Morality is Wholeness
•Immorality is Degenertion

Wholeness entails a homogeneity -- things made of radically different substances may not hold together. Wholeness also entails an overall unity of form that makes an entity strong, and resistent to pressures. Homogeneity and unity of form also make an entity stable and predictable in the way it functions. An object with physical integrity can be trusted to function the way it is supposed to function. Wholeness also entails naturalness -- something that has the form that it is supposed to have.

When an object that is whole starts to crumble, tear, or rot, it in danger of not holding together and therefore not being able to function physically.

Moral Wholeness combines with Moral Essence to yield the virtue of integrity -- the virtue of being morally whole. Someone who has integrity has moral wholeness -- the moral equivalent of phsyicall wholeness. A person with integrity has consistent moral principles -- the moral equivalent of physical homogenity and parts the form a unified whole. The overall unity of moral principle makes someone with integrity strong -- not able to be easily swayed by social or political pressures or fashions. A person with integrity acts predictably, in a way consistent with his moral principles, and can be trusted to act in the way he is morally supposed to act. A person with integrity also acts according to his nature -- there is nothing artificial or contrived about him.

When the Society-as-Person metaphor is combined with the metaphors of Moral Wholeness and Moral Essence, an inherently good society is seen as a person with moral integrity. But if that moral integrity starts to erode, crumble, tear, decay, etc., then the society is in danger of losing its integrity and being unable to function in its natural moral way. The logic is clear: it is important to constantly be on the lookout for signs of moral decay and erosion and to stop them immediately, because once rot sets in or the foundation crumbles, repair may be impossible and immorality will become rampant.

Immorality is Sexual Degradation

Finally, treating someone immorally can be understood as sexually degrading them. Hence, someone who has been treated immorally can say "I've been fucked" or "I've been screwed." By moral accounting, someone who treats another immorally deserves the same immoral treatment in return. Hence, people will commonly say to someone who they feel has acted immorally toward them "Fuck you!" , "Screw you!", "Up your ass!" and so on.

This metaphor lies behind the use of the word "bastard" to indicate an immoral person. The "logic" is this: The bastard's mother, who gave birth out of wedlock, was sexually degraded. The metaphor that Immorality is Sexual Degradation gives rise to a metaphorical stereotype of sexually degraded people as being immoral. Hence, the bastard's mother is immoral, and by the folk theory that people inherit their parent's characteristics, the son is also immoral. That is why "bastard" means an immoral person.

This has been an abbreviated presentation, and because of length limits, an important distortion has been introduced. It may appear that our systems of moral metaphors are just unstructured lists. They are not. For a discussion of the structure of the system, see Lakoff, 1996.

References

Taub, Sarah. 1990. Moral Accounting. UC Berkeley, unpublished ms.

Klingebiel, Chris. 1990. Moral Arithmetic. UCBerkeley, unpublished ms.

Johnson, Mark L. 1993. *Moral Imagination*. Chicago: U. of Chicago Press.

Lakoff, George. 1996. *Moral Politics: What Conservatives Know That Liberals Don't*. Chicago: U. of Chicago Press.

On the Formal and Functional Relationship between Topics and Vocatives. Evidence from French*

KNUD LAMBRECHT

University of Texas, Austin

1. Introduction. Little attention has been paid in traditional and in generative grammar to the syntax and semantics of vocatives.[1] The reason for this general neglect has to do, I believe, with the inherently deictic nature of vocatives and with their grammatical status as non-arguments. Elements which can be omitted from a sentence without influencing its syntactic well-formedness have traditionally been considered less worthy of syntactic theorizing than constituents whose presence is obligatory.

It is precisely this 'marginal' status of vocative phrases as non-arguments, or adjuncts, that I am concerned with in this paper. What interests me is the nature of the relationship between these adjuncts and the sentences to which they are adjoined, and the correlation between their syntactic status and their pragmatic function in discourse. However, it is not so much the grammar of vocatives per se that I want to explore here but certain striking similarities between the grammatical and pragmatic behavior of vocative NPs and that of certain TOPIC expressions. The data I will analyze are from French, especially from the spoken language, but the conclusions I will draw on the basis of the French data have important cross-linguistic implications.

Let me first define the object of analysis. By 'vocative' I do not mean a morphological case form but a kind of sentence constituent. The constituents *garçon* and *Madame* in (1) (a) and (b) are vocative expressions of the kind I have in mind:

(1) a. *Garçon, il y a une mouche dans ma soupe!*
         'Waiter, there's a fly in my soup!'
     b. Que *désirez-vous, Madame*?
         'May I help you, ma'am?'

Vocatives serve to call the attention of an addressee in order to establish or maintain a relationship between this addressee and some proposition. They differ functionally (and often formally) from EPITHETS and INTERJECTIONS, with which they are sometimes confused. While vocatives are used to REFER, the primary function of epithets and interjections is to PREDICATE.

---

* I would like to thank Laura Michaelis and Masha Polinsky for many helpful comments on this paper.

[1] Notable early exceptions in generative grammar are Downing 1969 and Zwicky 1974.

EPITHETS express a speaker's subjective judgment about an addressee or a third person, as shown in (2):

(2)   (Man seeing a street musician:)
       Saleté de guitaristes! 'Goddamm guitarists'

Further examples of (more or less coarse) French epithets are *salaud!* 'bastard', *imbécile!* 'idiot', *espèce de con!* 'you jerk', *le veinard!* 'lucky you/him', etc. INTERJECTIONS express a speaker's subjective judgment about a state of affairs. A sample of French interjections, with approximate glosses, is given in (3):

(3)   *merde!* 'shit' - *zut alors!* 'oh bother' - *mon pauvre ami!* 'oh boy' - *putain de chaleur!* 'fucking heat', etc.

The peculiar use of the definite article in an expression like *le veinard* or of the preposition *de* in expressions like *espèce de con* or *putain de chaleur* suggests the existence of a special grammar of epithets and interjections, which would be well worth exploring. However such exploration is not the purpose of the present paper.[2]

The starting point for this paper is the observation, which to my knowledge has not been made before, that the grammar of vocatives resembles in interesting ways that of TOPIC NPs in LEFT-DETACHED and RIGHT-DETACHED position.[3] The syntactic parallelism between the two expression types is shown in the juxtaposition of (4) and (5). Using terminology which I adopted in earlier work, I will label left-detached and right-detached topic constituents TOP (topic) and A-TOP (antitopic) constituents, respectively. Analogously, I will use the terms VOC and A-VOC (antivocative) to refer to vocatives in left-detached and right-detached position. Regarding the structures in (5), I should stress that they are extremely common in spoken French (see e.g., Lambrecht 1981, 1987, Barnes 1985, Ashby 1988), unlike English, where NP detachments are considered somewhat marginal:

(4)   VOCATIVE NP:

    a. $[Chérie_i]$ *je t_i'ai dit que j'étais malade.*   VOC
        'Darling, I told you I was sick.'
    b.   *Je t_i'ai dit que j'étais malade* $[chérie_i]$.   A-VOC
        'I told you I was sick, darling.'

---

[2] For generative analyses of the syntax and semantics of epithets in French see Milner (1978: chs. V and VI) and Ruwet (1982).

[3] The analysis of detached NPs as topics is justified in Lambrecht 1981 and 1986.

(5)   TOPIC NP:

    a.   [*Jean$_i$*] *il$_i$ m'a dit qu'il était malade.*   TOP
       'Jean (he) told me he was sick.'

    b.   *Il$_i$ m'a dit qu'il était malade* [*Jean$_i$*].   A-TOP
       'He told me he was sick, Jean.'

Both in (4) and in (5) an NP appears to the left or to the right of a complete sentence containing a pronoun which corefers with this NP. The main difference between the two sets is that the pronoun is in the second person in (4), but in the third person in (5). As expected from the discourse function of each category, the pronoun is deictic in (4), but anaphoric (or cataphoric) in (5). As we will see later on, the pronominal anaphor is in fact syntactically speaking optional in most cases.

On the basis of formal similarities such as those between (4) and (5) I will argue that vocatives and topics belong to the same grammatical construction type in French. A few construction-internal differences, especially between A-VOC and A-TOP constituents, can be explained as predictable consequences of the different pragmatic functions of the two types. I will refer to the two constructions illustrated in (4) and (5) as the TOP CONSTRUCTION and the A-TOP CONSTRUCTION, respectively, regardless of whether the phrase occurring in the TOP or the A-TOP position functions as a topic or as a vocative. I will argue that the formal parallel between vocatives and topics is the manifestation of a deep functional relationship between the two categories. Both serve to establish a RELEVANCE relation between a DISCOURSE REFERENT and a PROPOSITION.[4] In both cases, a nominal constituent which is not an argument of the predicate and whose referent is pragmatically recoverable from the discourse context is semantically associated with a clause which expresses information that is in one way or another relevant to this referent.

The form of the TOP and the A-TOP construction is motivated by a general cognitive principle, which I refer to as the PRINCIPLE OF THE SEPARATION OF REFERENCE AND RELATION (Lambrecht 1994, Chapter 4). According to this principle, which is manifested particularly in spoken language, the referential information necessary to establish a topical referent in a discourse is best coded independently of the proposition which contains the relevant information concerning this referent. The two constructions under analysis allow speakers to conform to this principle by marking

---

    [4] As so many other little-known facts, the functional relationship between vocatives and topics was noticed by the great Charles Bally: "Destiné à attirer l'attention de l'entendeur sur l'énonciation qui va lui être communiquée, le vocatif fonctionne comme un *thème général sur lequel repose l'énoncé proprement dit dans sa totalité*" (1950: 63; emphasis mine).

vocative and topic NPs as REFERENCE-RELATED rather than ROLE-RELATED constituents.

2. Formal and Functional Similarities between Vocative and Topic NPs.
In this and the next section I will describe the most important formal properties of topic and vocative constructions. In each case, I will show how the given formal property correlates directly with the pragmatic function of the construction in discourse.

2.1 Internal and External Syntax of Vocative and Topic Constituents.
The constituent structure and phrasal category of vocative and topic phrases is of minor concern here and I will content myself with some cursory remarks. The internal syntax of vocative constituents differs from that of topic constituents in interesting yet expectable ways. While topic constituents have the syntax of ordinary argument expressions (noun and prepositional phrases, complement clauses, bare or marked infinitival verb phrases, etc.), the syntax of vocative constituents is highly idiosyncratic.[5]

Given their isolated distribution in the sentence, the phrasal category of vocatives is difficult to ascertain. Since nothing in the present paper hinges on their category membership I will assume, for simplicity's sake, that vocatives are NPs. As for their INTERNAL SYNTAX, vocative NPs appear mainly under the following forms:

(6) a. N (common N: *garçon* 'waiter'; proper N: *Jacqueline*)
     b. Adj. + N (*petit poisson* 'little fish', *cher collègue* 'dear colleague')
     c. def. Det. + N (*Silence, les enfants!* 'silence, children!')
     d. poss. Det. + N (*mon ami* 'my friend', *mon général* 'general')
     e. poss. Det. + Adj. + N (*mon cher ami* 'my dear friend')
     f. strong Pro (*toi , vous* 'you')
     g. strong Pro + PP (*vous là-bas!* 'you over there!')
     h. title (*Madame, Monseigneur, Docteur*)
     i. title + proper N (*Maître Jacques, Professeur Chomsky*)
     j. title + appositional NP (*Monsieur le Président* 'Mister President')

Among the many peculiar features of the internal syntax of these vocative NPs, the most revealing is perhaps the fact that they may be BARE nouns (see e.g., *garçon* in (1a) or *chérie* in (4)). While the use of bare Ns is not unique to vocatives--they occur e.g., as predicate nominals (cf. *Elle est médécin* 'She's a doctor')--it is only in the vocative construction that they may function referentially. Unlike bare predicate nouns, vocative Ns may

---

[5] For an account of the strikingly idiosyncratic synax of vocative phrases in English see Zwicky 1974.

also be modified (compare *cher médécin* 'dear doctor' with **Il est médécin cher* 'He's an expensive doctor'). In a sense, then, bare-N vocatives can be said to have a kind of 'vocative case marking'.

This unique syntactic feature of vocative NPs is clearly motivated by their function in discourse. Given the type of communicative situation in which vocatives are used, the referents of vocative NPs are necessarily assumed to be uniquely identifiable: one does not address someone without assuming that the addressee is able to identify herself as the person addressed. The presence of a definite determiner, whose purpose is to make a referent uniquely identifiable, is therefore functionally speaking unnecessary.[6]

2.2 Semantic Role. By their very nature, VOCATIVE NPs lack a semantic case role (or theta role) in the sentence. This semantic feature prompted early grammarians to exclude the vocative case from the list of cases proper (see the entry for *vocatif* in Marouzeau 1961). Interestingly, this feature also holds of TOPIC NPs. With one minor exception (see Section 3.2.6), it is not possible to predict from the form and position of a TOP or A-TOP phrase what role its referent plays in the proposition, hence what grammatical relation it will be associated with in the sentence. This is in sharp contrast to the behavior of intraclausal argument NPs.

Consider the sentences in (7), (8) and (9). Here and in the following examples, the presence of two or more subscripts on a noun indicates that the NP may be construed either as a topic or as a vocative; the subscript 'x' indicates that the NP is not linked to an anaphor in the clause. EXP stands for the experiencer role associated with the predicate *aimer* 'to love' and CONT for the role of the content of the experience:

(7)   a.   *Nicole* (EXP-SUBJ) *n'aime pas Marie* (CONT-OBJ).
          'Nicole doesn't like Marie.'
      b.   *Marie* (EXP-SUBJ) *n'aime pas Nicole* (CONT-OBJ).
          'Marie doesn't like Nicole.'

(8)   a.   *Nicole*$_{i,j,x}$, *Marie*$_{i,j,x}$ [*elle*$_i$ *ne l*$_j$'*aime pas*].
      b.   [*Elle*$_i$ *ne l*$_j$'*aime pas*] *Nicole*$_{i,j,x}$, *Marie*$_{i,j,x}$.

(9)   a.   *Nicole*$_{i,j}$, *Marie*$_{i,j}$ [*tu*$_i$ *la*$_j$ *connais*]?
          'Nicole, Marie do you know her?'
      b.   [*Tu*$_i$ *la*$_j$ *connais*] *Nicole*$_{i,j}$, *Marie*$_{i,j}$?

---

[6] Again, Bally's observations are right on target: "Le vocatif est actualisé du fait qu'il est un nom propre de la parole. *Maître! Patron!* sont sur le même pied que *Monsieur Dupont!*, etc. (...) L'absence d'article devant le vocatif n'est pas plus étonnante que l'absence du pronom-sujet devant l'impératif: Viens! = "Je veux que tu viennes". En outre, le vocatif est en marge de la phrase, comme un titre est en marge du texte. (1950:294)

As predicted by case grammar, in the canonical SVO sentences in (7) the experiencer role is necessarily linked to the preverbal grammatical subject and the content role to the postverbal grammatical object. In other words, (7a) cannot mean the same thing as (7b). In contrast, the semantic roles of the two left-detached or right-detached NPs in the sentences in (8) and (9) cannot be determined on formal grounds. Thus (8a/b) can have the meaning of either (7a) or (7b). Moreover, since one of the NPs in (8) may be a vocative, these sentences systematically have one more reading than those in (7), resulting in multiple ambiguity.[7] One obvious difference between (8) and (9) is that in (9) one of the NPs must be linked to the subject *tu* and that this NP must be a vocative, while in (8) both NPs may be topics.

This freedom of semantic linking between topic/vocative NPs and intra-clausal arguments is consistent with the reference-oriented nature of these expressions. Their referential function takes precedence over the need to express a semantic relation between the referent and the proposition. As we will see in Section 3, there often is in fact no available theta role for the NP in the sentence, in which case the relation between the referent and the proposition is pragmatically construed on the basis of relevance alone.

2.3 Adjunct Status. The reference-related rather than role-related function of vocative and topic expressions also accounts for the fact that they are always syntactically speaking OPTIONAL. Both vocatives and topics are adjuncts, in the sense that they do not partake in the predicate-argument structure of the sentence. However, they differ from most adjunct phrases (time, place, or manner adverbials and other circumstancial complements) in that they may be anaphorically linked to an argument within the clause, as in (4) and (5).

The difference between vocatives or topics and regular adjunct phrases is manifested in the restriction on the PRAGMATIC RELATION they may enter with a proposition. While regular adjuncts may have either a topic or a focus relation to a proposition, vocatives and topics are necessarily non-focal (focal denotata are by definition not omissible; see Lambrecht 1994, Chapter 5). Consider the set of synonymous sentences in (10):

(10) a.   [*Il*$_i$ *a vendu sa maison HIER*] *Jean*$_{i,x}$.
           'He sold his house yesterday, Jean.'
      b.   [*Il*$_i$ *a vendu sa MAISON*] *hier, Jean*$_{i,x}$.
      c.   *[*Il*$_i$ *a vendu sa maison hier JEAN*$_{i,x}$]
      d.   *[*Il*$_i$ *a vendu sa maison JEAN*$_{i,x}$] *hier*.

---

[7] I'm ignoring here the possibility of the two NPs in (8a/b) being juxtaposed vocatives, as when the speaker adresses himself to Nicole and Marie at the same time.

In (10a), the adverb is focal and the topic/vocative NP non-focal. In (10b), both the adverb and the NP are non-focal. But in (c) and (d), the NP occupies clause-final focus position, resulting in ungrammaticality of the sentence. Topic or vocative status and focus relation exclude each other.

2.4 Clause-external Position. As we saw in (4), (5), (8), and (9), vocatives and topics appear either in PRE-SENTENTIAL or in POST-CLAUSAL position. This positional feature is further illustrated in (11) and (12):

(11) a. *Jean$_{i,x}$ il$_i$ m'a dit qu'il me rendrait mon ARGENT.*
          'Jean (he) told me that he would give me my money back.'
    b. *Monsieur$_i$, vous$_i$ m'avez dit que vous me rendriez mon ARGENT.*
          'Sir,you told me that you would give me my money back.'

(12) a. *Il$_i$ m'a dit qu'il me rendrait mon ARGENT, Jean$_{i,x}$*
    b. *Vous$_i$ m'avez dit que vous me rendriez mon ARGENT Monsieur$_i$.*

Given that vocative and topic NPs occupy the same positions, they are also BANNED from the same positions in the sentence. One position which they may not occupy is the clause-final slot, as we saw in examples (10) (c) and (d). Another position is that between the verb and its object, as shown in the following examples:

(13) a. *Elle$_i$ ne m'a pas rendu mon ARGENT, Nicole$_{i,x}$.*
          'Nicole (she) didn't give me my money back'
    b. *Elle ne m'a pas rendu, Nicole, mon ARGENT.

(14) a. *Tu$_i$ ne m'as pas rendu mon ARGENT, Nicole$_i$.*
          'You didn't give me my money back, Nicole.'
    b. *Tu ne m'as pas rendu, Nicole, mon ARGENT.

(15) a. *Il$_i$ a vendu sa maison à PROFIT, Jean$_{i,x}$.*
          'Jean (he) sold his house at a profit'
    b. *Il a vendu sa maison, Jean, à PROFIT.

Notice that the positional constraint shown here holds independently of whether the complement of the verb is direct, as in (13) and (14), or oblique, as in (15).[8] Further positional constraints on vocative and topic NPs will be discussed in Section 3.2.

---

[8] In the case of vocatives, the positional constraint shown in (13) through (15) is sometimes violated in formulaic or poetic language. Sentence (i) is a letter-closing formula, (ii) is a verse from LaFontaine's fable "Les animaux malades de la peste", and (iii) is a radio announcement:
    (i) *Veuillez agréer, Monsieur, l'expression de mes sentiments distingués.*
    (ii) *Vous leur fîtes, Seigneur, en les croquant beaucoup d'honneur.*
        'You did them, Sir, by eating them, much honor'

Thus vocative and topic NPs occupy the same positions in the sentence, and these positions are OUTSIDE the clause with which they are semantically associated. Using Bally's felicitous formulation (see footnote 6), we can say that vocatives and topics occur 'at the margins' of the sentence or clause. Since the right clause boundary is prosodically marked in French by the focus accent, A-VOC and A-TOP constituents may also be characterized as POST-FOCAL.

The positional characteristics illustrated here correlate directly with the function of vocative and topic NPs as reference-related rather than role-related categories. Since the function of such NPs is not to carry a semantic role in a proposition but merely to NAME a referent with respect to which a given proposition is to be construed as relevant, it makes sense that they should occur INDEPENDENTLY of the clause coding this information, i.e., either before or after it, as stipulated by the Principle of the Separation of Reference and Relation.

It is necessary to mention one clear exception to the positional rule stated above for antivocative and antitopic NPs. While these NPS are disallowed before nominal objects, they may appear before CLAUSAL COMPLEMENTS. Thus, in addition to the A-VOC and A-TOP versions in our paradigm examples (4b) and (5b), we also find the versions in (16):

(16)　a.　*Je t$_i$'ai dit [chérie$_i$] que j'étais malade.*
　　　　　'I told you, darling, that I was sick.'
　　　b.　*Il$_i$ m'a dit [Jean$_{i,x}$] qu'il était malade.*
　　　　　'He told me, Jean, that he was sick.'

And instead of (12a) and (12b), we could also find the versions in (17):

(17)　a.　*Il$_i$ m'a dit, Jean$_{i,x}$, qu'il me rendrait mon ARGENT.*
　　　b.　*Vous$_i$ m'avez dit, Monsieur$_i$, que vous me rendriez mon ARGENT.*

In (16) and (17), the NP appears between the verb and a *que*-marked complement clause. This exception to the rule that antitopics and antivocatives must appear in postclausal position is no doubt related to the cross-linguistically observed adjacency difference between nominal and clausal complements.[9]

(iii)　*Vous allez écouter, chers auditeurs, la symphony en re majeur de ...*
　　　'You are going to listen, dear hearers, to the symphony in d major
　　　　by ...' (Weinrich 1982:288)
In these examples, a vocative NP intervenes between a verb and its direct object. All three sentences have a distinctively archaic or 'written' flavor.

[9] As pointed out to me by Steve Matthews, the phenomenon in (16) and (17) may have to with the processing factor which Hawkins (1995) calls

2.5 Free Ordering of Constituents in TOP and A-TOP Position. Unlike clause-internal argument positions, the topic/vocative slots may be occupied by more than one (non-conjoined) constituent. And when two or more constituents occur, they may be ordered freely with respect to each other, again in sharp contrast to clause-internal argument constituents. This positional freedom within the TOP and A-TOP slots is illustrated in (19), which contrasts with (18). Notice that (18a) and the various sentences in (19) are synonymous or not, depending on whether the NP *Nicole* in (19) is construed as a vocative or a topic:

(18) a. *Nicole* (SUBJ) *donne l'argent* (DO) *au flic* (IO).
          'Nicole gives the money to the cop.'
      b. **L'argent donne Nicole au flic.*
      c. **Nicole donne au flic l'argent.*
      d. *etc.

(19) a. *Nicole$_{i,x}$, l'argent$_j$ [elle$_i$ le$_j$ lui$_k$ donne] au flic$_k$.*
      b. *L'argent, Nicole [elle le lui donne] au flic.*
      c. *Le flic, Nicole [elle le lui donne] l'argent.*
      d. *L'argent [elle le lui donne] au flic, Nicole.*
      e. *L'argent [elle le lui donne] Nicole, au flic.*
      f. *[Elle le lui donne] Nicole, l'argent, au flic.*
      g. etc.

(The different forms of the phrase containing the noun *flic* in TOP and A-TOP position will be discussed in Section 3.2.) While the position of the clause-internal arguments in (18) is fixed, that of the topic and vocative NPs in (19) is syntactically speaking entirely free, whether they appear to the left or to the right of the clause. The choice of position for a given topic or vocative phrase is made by the speaker on pragmatic grounds (see Section 3.1 below).

'syntactic weight' and which explains, e.g., why the extraposed version in (i) below is clearly preferable to the canonical version in (ii):

   (i)   I find it a pity [that nobody is interested in this].
   (ii) I find [that nobody is interested in this] a pity.

In the same vein, the relative weight of the complement clauses in (16) and (17) might make it easier to process the sentence if the topic/vocative NP appears first, explaining the well-formedness of these sentences.

   In the Government-and-Binding theory the contrast between (13b)-(14b) and (16)-(17) follows from the fact that the former but not the latter sentences violate adjacency (see e.g. Sells 1985:54). However, this explanation does not account for the fact that vocatives and topics may not precede PPs either, as shown in (15b). Since in GB PPs are not case-marked by the verb, the adjacency constraint does not apply. Nevertheless the sentences are bad.

To understand the syntactic behavior of topic and vocative constituents as illustrated in (19) it may be useful to think of the TOP and A-TOP slots as 'containers' for 'names' of discourse referents, rather than as positions for the coding of syntactic or semantic relations. The container metaphor accords well with the fact that these positions can be occupied by more than one constituent and that the constituents occupying them may be scrambled. The function of the TOP and A-TOP containers is to host constituents which pragmatically pose referents in a discourse without assigning them roles in a proposition. Since the position of the constituent is not linked to a semantic or syntactic role, the respective order of the constituents within the container is functionally irrelevant. Hence the positional freedom illustrated in (19).

2.6 Definiteness and pragmatic accessibility. As I mentioned earlier, the inherently deictic character of vocatives entails that the referents of vocative NPs must be assumed to be IDENTIFIABLE for the addressee, or 'hearer-old', to use Prince's (1992) term. One cannot call someone without knowing who one calls, and one cannot know that one is being called without knowing who one is oneself. Hence the necessary DEFINITENESS of vocative NPs, which makes sentences like (20) (a) or (b) unacceptable:[10]

(20) a. *Quelqu'un là-bas, venez par ici un instant!*
          'Someone over there, come over here for a minute!'
      b. *Venez par ici un instant, une femme avec un chandail rouge!*
          'Come over here for a minute, a woman in a red sweater!'

The situation is essentially the same for TOPIC NPs, as predicted by the definition of 'topic' in Lambrecht 1994 (Chapter 4). One cannot effectively process information ABOUT a referent if one isn't sure what the referent is.[11] As a result, TOP or A-TOP NPs cannot be INDEFINITE, as shown in (21) (a) and (b), unless the indefinite NP codes a generic referent, as in (21c):

(21) a. *Quelqu'un là-bas il est venu par ici.*
          'Someone over there he came here.'

---

[10] As pointed out to me by George Lakoff, English permits such sentences as *Somebody help me!*, in apparent contradiction to the pragmatic principle invoked here. Similarly, as Gilles Fauconnier (p.c.) has reminded me, French permits sentences such as *Eh quelqu'un, ma chemise est en feu!* 'Hey somebody, my shirt's on fire!' The use of such sentences is severely constrained, as (20a) shows. It would seem that *somebody/quelqu'un* can be used with vocative force only if the unidentifiable referent is not linked to an argument in the clause.

[11] In Michaelis & Lambrecht (1994) this constraint on the cognitive state of topic referents is stated as a pragmatic constraint on property attribution.

    b. *Elle s'est approchée de moi une femme avec un chandail vert.
       'She approached me, a woman in a green sweater.'
    c. Un bébé ça fait du bruit.
       'A baby makes noise.'

Notice that for a vocative NP to be used appropriately, it is not sufficient that its referent be identifiable. The referent must also have a degree of pragmatic ACCESSIBILITY in the text-external world. In order to call someone, one must not only know who one is calling but this person must also be able to hear you. In fact, vocative referents are often fully 'given' or ACTIVE (Chafe 1987) in the discourse, as demonstrated by the fact that vocative NPs can be second-person pronouns.

This pragmatic accessibility requirement, which is obvious in the case of vocatives, also applies to TOPICS, though perhaps in a less obvious way. As argued in Lambrecht 1994 (Chapter 4), for a denotatum to be construable as the topic of a proposition it must be taken to be a center of present concern in the discourse and its occurrence in the sentence must in some sense be expectable for the addressee at the time of utterance. And to be expectable in this way, the denotatum must have a degree of pragmatic accessibility in the discourse. In Prince's (1992) terms, a topic referent must be not only 'hearer-old' but 'discourse-old', i.e., it must have been in one way or another evoked in prior discourse. The empirical validity of this claim can be demonstrated only on the basis of extensive text analyses, which I cannot provide here. The reader is referred to the analyses in Lambrecht 1981 and 1987.

In spite of the striking parallel between vocatives and topics with respect to the discourse requirements of identifiablity and accessibility, it would be incorrect to characterize the two categories as cognitively and pragmatically identical. In the case of vocatives, but not topics, the accessible referent and the addressee are necessarily the same individual. Therefore, the cognitive parameter of accessibility, which crucially involves the speaker's assumptions concerning the mental state of the addressee, do not strictly speaking apply to vocatives. For an addressee to be able to identify herself as the individual designated with a vocative NP, the speaker's assumptions about her state of mind are irrelevant.

In this section I have presented evidence that vocatives and topics belong to the same grammatical category and I have shown that their grammatical similarity is motivated by a fundamental similarity in function. In both constructions, a constituent coding a referent which is accessible from the speech setting or from the linguistic context is associated with a sentence via a pragmatic link of RELEVANCE. As cooperative speakers, we call an addressee's attention only when we think that what we have to say is of relevance to that person. Similarly, we establish a topic referent in a discourse only when we want to communicate some relevant information about this referent to our addressee. The main difference between the topic and the vocative situation is that in the former the relevance relation between the proposition and the referent is communicated TO the addressee while in the latter the relevance relation holds between the proposition and the addressee herself. In the vocative case, referent and addressee coincide; in the topic case, they are distinct. From the point of view of grammar, however, this difference is irrelevant. What counts is the overriding function which the two categories have in common: the relating of a referential expression to a proposition on the basis of relevance.

3. The TOP Construction and the A-TOP Construction

3.1 An Iconic Ordering Principle. Having· established that vocatives and topics belong to one superordinate grammatical and functional category, we must now address the question of why this category occurs in two different environments: the TOP construction and the A-TOP construction. I propose that the functional difference between the left-hand and the right-hand position is determined by a fundamental ICONIC ORDERING PRINCIPLE. According to this principle, the position of a topical constituent in the sentence correlates with the activation status of the representation of its referent in the mind of the hearer at the time of utterance. While PRECLAUSAL occurrence signals the ANNOUNCEMENT of a relation between the referent and the proposition, POSTCLAUSAL occurrence signals the CONTINUATION of an ALREADY ESTABLISHED relation.

In the case of vocatives, I take the validity of this iconic principle to be a matter of common sense. When we call the attention of an addressee who was not previously part of the conversation it is necessary that the calling act PRECEDE the act whereby we inform the called person of some state of affairs. But once an addressee is part of the conversation, the act performed to secure the continued attention of the addressee may FOLLOW the informing act, whose communicative importance at this point prevails in our mind. The correlation between the two types of communicative situation and the two positions in which vocatives may appear has been acknowledged by Schegloff (1968), who refers to left-hand vocatives as 'summonses' and to right-hand vocatives as 'terms of address'. In a similar vein, Zwicky (1974) speaks of 'calls' for the former and of 'addresses' for the latter.

I will argue that the same iconic principle which determines the occurrence of vocative constituents in either the TOP or the A-TOP position also applies to topic constituents. And I will show that the cognitive difference between the two positions correlates in turn with a number of syntactic and prosodic differences between the TOP and the A-TOP construction. Since in the case of vocatives the workings of the principle seem relatively straightforward, the discussion will be somewhat biased in favor of the syntax and pragmatics of topic expressions.

3.2 Differences between TOP/VOC and A-TOP/A-VOC Constituents.

3.2.1 Prosody. The validity of the ordering principle postulated in 3.1 is supported by the PROSODIC difference between the two positions. VOC and TOP constituents necessarily receive a PITCH ACCENT of greater or lesser intensity; in contrast, A-VOC and A-TOP constituents are marked by the ABSENCE OF PITCH PROMINENCE. The intonation drop from the clause-final focus to the adjacent antitopic is often misinterpreted as a pause, hence the common use of a comma before the A-TOP constituent; in my examples, I have preserved any commas found in the source.

As various researchers have shown, absence of pitch prominence on a referential constituent signals assumed ACTIVENESS (or givenness) of the referent of the constituent in the mind of the addressee (see e.g., Selkirk 1984, Chapter 5, Chafe 1987, Lambrecht 1994, Chapter 5). The presence of pitch prominence, on the other hand, regularly (though not necessarily) indicates that the referent is NOT discourse-active. We can express the basic cognitive difference between left-hand and right-hand coding of referents in the form of a general principle: LOW ACTIVATION LEFT, HIGH ACTIVATION RIGHT.

I would like to emphasize that the absence of prosodic prominence on A-VOC NPs is not a self-evident feature. Given the intuitive notion of vocatives as 'calling' expressions, as manifested in the etymology of the term 'vocative' (i.e., 'calling form'), and given the intuitive association between calling and loudness, we would expect all vocative expressions to be prosodically prominent. The fact that antivocative expressions are NOT prominent constitutes strong evidence for the validity of the proposed principle. Since antitopics share this striking prosodic property with antivocatives, the facts of prosody corroborate the fundamental relationship between the vocative and the topic categories.

3.2.2 Constraints on Embedding. The TOP construction is an instance of what has been referred to in the generative literature as a 'main clause phenomenon'. TOP and VOC constituents cannot freely occur in embedded clauses. As I have shown in earlier work (Lambrecht 1981, 1986), the degree to which embedding is tolerated correlates with the degree to which the propositional content of the embedded clause is pragmatically ASSERTED rather than PRESUPPOSED. Thus the varying degrees of acceptability in the examples in (22) correlate with the different presuppositional structures of the different types of subordinate clauses. As before, the subscript x indicates a possible vocative reading of the NP:

(22)   a.   *Pierre$_{i,x}$ je lui$_i$ ai rendu son bouquin hier.*   (main clause)
             'Pierre I gave him his book back yesterday.'
       b. ? *Il me semble que Pierre$_{i,x}$ je lui$_i$ ai rendu son bouquin hier.*
          (complement clause)
          'It seems to me that I gave P. his book back yesterday.'

c. *??QuandPierre*$_{i,x}$ *je lui*$_i$ *ai rendu son bouquin il*$_i$ *était content.*
(adverbial clause)
'When P. I gave him his book back he was happy.'

d. **Le bouquin*$_j$ *que Pierre*$_{i,x}$ *je lui*$_i$ *ai rendu c*$_i$*'était la Bible.*
(relative clause)
'The book that I gave back to P. was the Bible.'

As (22) (c) and (d) show, the constraints against TOP/VOC embedding are strongest in the case of subordinate clauses whose propositions are pragmatically presupposed, in particular in the case of relative-clause 'islands'.

No similar constraints are found in the case of the A-TOP construction, as the corresponding sentences in (23) show:

(23) a. *Je lui*$_i$ *ai rendu son bouquin hier, à Pierre*$_i$. (main clause)
      b. *Il me semble que je lui*$_i$ *ai rendu son bouquin hier, à Pierre*$_i$.
          (compl. clause)
      c. *Quand je lui*$_i$ *ai rendu son bouquin, à Pierre*$_i$, *il était content.*
          (adverbial clause)
      d. *Le bouquin que je lui*$_i$ *ai rendu, à Pierre*$_i$, *c'était la Bible.*
          (relative clause)

(Note that in (23) no vocative reading is available because the A-TOP constituent is a prepositional phrase; see the section on case marking below.) The examples in (23) show that A-TOP constituents can be freely embedded. Unlike the TOP construction, the A-TOP construction is not a main clause phenomenon.

This difference between the two construction types with respect to the possibility of embedding finds a straightforward explanation in terms of our iconic ordering principle. Since the function of the TOP construction is to announce a referent, association of a TOP/VOC constituent with a clause whose proposition is pragmatically presupposed results in a clash between two conflicting presuppositional structures. Indeed, inasmuch as the proposition expressed in the subordinate clause is assumed to be already known to the addressee, its topic is necessarily known too, hence there is no need to announce it. In the case of the A-TOP construction, no such clash arises. Since the A-TOP referent is formally marked as being already established in the discourse, its association with a presupposed proposition is pragmatically felicitous.

3.2.3 Locality. TOP NPs (and, a fortiori, VOC NPs) may appear at an INDEFINITE REMOVE from the clause containing the anaphor, and this clause may be at an ARBITRARY LEVEL OF EMBEDDING. Two examples are given in (24):

(24) a. *Pierre$_{i,j}$, c'est simple, si tu$_j$ t'en va, il$_i$ va devenir fou.*
      'Pierre, it's very simple, if you leave, he's going to go crazy.'
   b. *Pierre$_{i,x}$, les films qui le$_i$ passionnent, c'est tous des pornos.*
      'The movies that interest Pierre are all x-rated.'

In contrast, the antitopic construction is subject to a strict locality constraint: the A-TOP phrase must be SISTER-ADJOINED to the S containing the anaphor. To use Ross' felicitous term, the A-TOP constituent is subject to the 'Right Roof Constraint', i.e., it cannot be dominated by a higher S node to the right.[12] Consider the examples in (25) and (26):

(25) a. *Les films qui le$_i$ passionnent, Pierre$_{i,x}$, c'est tous des pornos.*
   b. **Les films qui le$_i$ passionnent, c'est tous des pornos, Pierre$_i$.*
   c. *Les films qui le$_i$ passionnent, c'est tous des pornos, Pierre$_x$.*

(26) a. *De les$_i$ discipliner, ces enfants$_i$, c'est impossible.*
      'To discipline these children is impossible.'
   b. **De les$_i$ discipliner, c'est impossible, ces enfants$_i$.*
   c. *De les$_i$ discipliner, c'est impossible, les enfants$_x$.*
      'To discipline them is impossible, guys.'

As the comparison of the (a) examples with the (b) examples in (25) and (26) reveals, the A-TOP phrase must occur immediately after the boundary of the clause to which it is anaphorically linked. Predictably, the locality constraint illustrated in these examples does not apply to vocatives in A-VOC position, as the (c) examples in (25) and (26) show. Since vocatives are not necessarily anaphorically linked to an intra-clausal argument their pragmatic 'scope' can be construed as including any preceding clausal domain. Thus sentence (25b) becomes acceptable if *Pierre* is interpreted as a vocative, as in (25c). Similarly, the ill-formed (26b) contrasts with the grammatical (26c) (recall that the NP *les enfants* can be used as a vocative; see item (6c) above).

The locality difference between the constituent in TOP and in A-TOP position is motivated by the same fundamental principle governing left-hand vs. right-hand position in the sentence, although this may be less obvious in the present case. The function of the TOP/VOC constituent is to announce the referent with respect to which the communication of a given state of affairs is relevant. Once the referent is announced, the hearer can be expected to keep it in mind until the clause containing the relevant piece of information is uttered. The situation is different in the A-TOP case. Once the clause containing the piece of information is uttered, mention of the

---

[12] The constraint illustrated in (26) and (27) is discussed for English in Ross 1983 (pp. 257ff).

referent with respect to which it is to be construed as relevant cannot be delayed. As stated earlier, one cannot assess the relevance of a piece of information until one can identify the referent with respect to which it is meant to be relevant. Hence the locality constraint on A-TOP constituents.

3.2.4 Unlinked Topic Constructions. One of the most interesting syntactic parallels between vocatives and topics in spoken French is found in a construction which I call the 'unlinked topic construction' (see Lambrecht 1994, Ch.4). In this construction, which occurs also in spoken English, the TOP position is occupied by an NP which is not anaphorically linked to any argument. The semantic relation between the topic referent and the proposition is pragmatically construed on the basis of relevance alone. Attested examples of the unlinked topic construction are listed in (27); in (b), an unlinked TOP NP cooccurs with a linked one. (28) shows analogous vocative structures:

(27) a. *La mer*$_X$, *tu vois de l'eau.* (François corpus)
          'The ocean, you see water.'
      b. *Le français*$_X$, *l'Amérique*$_i$ *c*$_i$'*est le paradis.* (Ashby)
          'The French, America is paradise.'
(28) a. *Monsieur*$_X$, *je vois de l'eau.*
          'Monsieur, I see water.'
      b. *Madame*$_X$, *l'Amérique*$_i$ *c*$_i$'*est le paradis.*
          'Ma'am, America is paradise.'

As the parallel between (27) and (28) reveals, the unlinked topic construction is formally identical to the ordinary vocative construction.

   Parallel to the unlinked TOP construction in (27) there is no unlinked A-TOP construction. An A-TOP phrase must be anaphorically linked to an argument inside the preceding clause, witness the ungrammaticality of (29) (a) and (b). As (29c) shows, this constraint does not hold for antivocatives:

(29) a. **Tu vois de l'eau, !a mer.*
          'You see water, the ocean.'
      b. **C'est le paradis, le français, l'Amérique.*
          'It's paradise, the French, America.'
      c. *Je vois de l'eau, Monsieur.*
          'I see water, Monsieur.'

   The functional motivation for the difference between (27) and (29) is related to the one that accounts for the locality constraint above. From a cognitive point of view, it is relatively easy to process one or more TOP NPs whose referents are already identifiable and subsequently to construe a loose relevance relation between these referents and a proposition. It is also relatively easy to process a clause containing pronominal arguments and to keep the referents of these arguments 'on hold' until the immediately following A-TOP phrase is reached which provides the missing referential information. But it is difficult to first process a proposition whose predicate-argument structure is complete and whose topic-comment articulation is understood and subsequently to establish a relevance relation between this already processed proposition and an additional referent which is not represented in the argument structure of the clause. I believe this processing difficulty accounts for the ill-formedness of (29) (a) and (b). The reason this constraint does not apply to vocatives in A-TOP position, as shown in (29c), has to do with the deictic nature of vocative NPs. The identity and presence of an addressee is always taken for granted, therefore its coding in A-TOP position causes no processing difficulties.[13]

3.2.5 'Double-Topic' Constructions.

Spoken French has a particular subtype of unlinked topic construction (which also is attested in spoken English), in which two NPs are juxtaposed in TOP position, the first establishing a semantic frame within which the second is located. Often, the first NP is construed as having the role of possessor with respect to the second. This construction is illustrated in (30):

(30) a. *Jean$_{i,x}$ sa$_i$ soeur$_j$ je la$_j$ déteste.*
          'Jean, his sister I hate her.'
      b. *Marie-Paule$_{i,x}$, sa$_i$ voiture$_j$ elle$_j$ est complètement foutue.*
          'Marie-Paule, her car is a complete wreck.'

Again, no double-topic occurrence is possible in the antitopic construction:

(31) **Je la déteste, Jean, sa soeur.*
       'I hate her, Jean, his sister

Since one of the two constituents in the double-topic construction is unlinked, the functional explanation for the constraint illustrated in (31) is the same as in the case of the previously discussed unlinked-topic construction.

3.2.6 Case Marking.

The constraint manifested in (29) and (31), which requires that an A-TOP constituent must be linked to an overt

---

[13] Predictably, the constraint illustrated in (29) (a) and (b) holds for the unlinked topic construction in English too. Example (i,a) was uttered by a linguistics professor in a discussion about verb phrases; (i,b) occurred in a conversation about gardening:

(i) a. Cause *the languages I work with*, there aren't any.
     b. *Tulips*, you have to plant new bulbs every year?
(ii) a. *Cause there aren't any, *the languages I work with*.
     b. *You have to plant new bulbs every year, *tulips*?

argument in the preceding clause, also accounts for the different behavior of TOP and A-TOP constituents with respect to prepositional CASE MARKING We noticed this difference in passing in examples (19) and (23). A-TOP constituents must be marked by a preposition if their anaphor is neither a subject nor an object. TOP (and of course VOC) constituents, however, do not receive such marking. Consider the sentences in (32) and (33):

(32) a. *Il faut aller à la plage quand il fait chaud.*
         'You should go to the beach when it's hot.'
     b. **Il faut aller la plage quand il fait chaud.*

(33) a. *La plage_i il faut y_i aller quand il fait chaud.*
     b. *Il faut y aller quand il fait chaud, à la plage.*
     c. **Il faut y aller quand il fait chaud, la plage.*

The contrast between (33b) and (33c) shows that the A-TOP constituent must agree in case with the pronominal anaphor *y* 'there', i.e., that it must have the same marking as the argument in the canonical version in (32a). The TOP constituent, however, goes unmarked, as shown in (33a).

The explanation for this case-marking difference is essentially the same as in the two preceding cases. Since in the A-TOP construction the predicate-argument structure of the proposition is already established by the time the A-TOP constituent is reached, it is impossible to construe the role of the A-TOP referent without reference to its case-marked pronominal cataphor. In the TOP construction, however, the semantic role of the TOP referent is not yet determined, hence the lack of case marking on the NP. The syntactic generalization covering this and the two preceding cases is that an A-TOP constituent must always be linked to a cataphor and that it must appear in the syntactic form it would have if it occurred in canonical argument position.

3.2.7 Freestanding NP. Since both VOC and TOP phrases can occur without any overt semantic link to an associated clause, it is natural that they may occur also in total syntactic isolation from verbal context. In the case of vocatives, this phenomenon is well-known. We often call people just to attract their attention and leave it at that. For example, in (34) we can imagine the individual named 'Marie-Claude' being called by her mother with or without the sentence following the vocative expression:

(34) *Marie-Claude! (viens manger!)*
     'Marie-Claude! (come to dinner!)'

The same phenomenon occurs with TOP NPs, although much less frequently so. A natural example is the utterance in (35), which we have to imagine in a situation in which the speaker's disgust with linguists is evident from the context:

(35)   *Les linguistes... (je vous jure!)*   'Linguists... (I swear!)'

In fact, it is not difficult to imagine conversational contexts in which the various unlinked TOP (or VOC) phrases in the earlier-mentioned examples could occur in this freestanding form.

Such freestanding NPs are unimaginable in A-TOP position, even though this is a little hard to demonstrate. Thus uttering (36) or (37) would be absurd, since we cannot imagine a referent standing in an already established topic relation with a non-existing proposition:

(36)   * ... *Marie-Claude.*

(37)   * (*Je vous jure!*) ... *les linguistes.*   '(I swear!) ... linguists.'

The absurdity of these sentences correlates with the impossibility of making an independent utterance which totally lacks prosodic prominence, as required for all A-TOP constituents. The functional explanation for the phenomenon of freestanding topic or vocative NPs is of course the same as that given for the unlinked topic construction.

3.2.8 Null Anaphora/Cataphora of subjects. We saw earlier that TOP expressions are like vocatives in that they may occur without an anaphoric link to a subsequent clause. However, in those cases in which the TOP expression is linked to the subject argument, the anaphor must be OVERTLY EXPRESSED. In contrast, in the case of A-TOP constituents, which are always linked to a cataphoric argument, the subject argument may be NULL-INSTANTIATED (see Fillmore & Kay 1992).[14] This interesting syntactic phenomenon is shown in the attested examples in (38) and (39):

(38)   Father looking at misbehaving guest at dinner table:
   a. ϕ_i *Mérite des baffes, ce petit con_i.* (Reiser)
        'Deserves a slap in the face, this little jerk.'
   b.   ?? *Ce petit con_i, ϕ_i mérite des baffes.*

---

[14] The case of null-instantiated subjects discussed here is to be distinguished from that of null-instantiated DIRECT OBJECTS, which is very common in spoken French (see Lemoine 1992 and Lambrecht & Lemoine, forthcoming):
   (i)   (*Les haricots verts,*) *j'ϕ'aime pas beaucoup.*
        'Green beans, I don't like a lot.'
   (ii) *J'ϕ'aime pas beaucoup* (*,les haricots verts*).
        'I don't like a lot, green beans.'
Both the TOP and the A-TOP construction are compatible with null instantiation of direct objects. Notice that (i) is not an instance of Topicalization since the detached NP is optional.

286 / KNUD LAMBRECHT

(39) Man sitting at bistrot table, knocking on table surface:
    a. ø$_i$ *Sont en plastique maintenant, les tables de bistrot*$_i$? (Reiser)
       '(Are) made of plastic nowadays, bistrot tables?'
    b. ?? *Les tables de bistrot*$_i$, ø$_i$ *sont en plastique maintenant?*

(Of course (38b) and (39b) are ill-formed only in the TOP reading, not in the reading where the initial NP occupies canonical subject position.) In fact, in the A-TOP construction, both the subject pronoun and the copula may be null-instantiated, while this is impossible in the case of the TOP construction. Consider (40):

(40) a. ø$_i$ ø *Bizarre, ce truc*$_i$. (= *Il est bizarre, ce truc.*)
       'Strange, that thing'
    b. **Ce truc*$_i$, ø$_i$ ø *bizarre.*

A nice example is the following street sign put up by the Département de l'Intérieur in Paris:

(41) *Couché, le bruit.*   '(Lie) down, noise.'

(41) is particularly appropriate to the present analysis because it happens to play on the formal ambiguity between topics and vocatives. In the topic reading, the sentence is construed on the model of *Fini, la comédie* 'Enough of this comedy'; in the vocative reading it is construed like an order given to a dog.[15]
    I believe that the difference between the TOP and the A-TOP construction with respect to the possibility of subject null-instantiation can be accounted for in terms of our general iconic ordering principle. Since the A-TOP construction is conventionally associated with discourse situations in which the relation between the topic referent and the proposition is assumed to be already established at the time of utterance and in which the topic referent is pragmatically highly salient, it is natural that this referent should not always have to be coded twice in the same sentence. The situation is crucially different in the case of the TOP construction. Since the relation between the topic referent and the proposition is not assumed to be recoverable at the time of speech and since the TOP referent has not yet been activated, the topic referent is not salient enough in the discourse for the anaphoric pronoun to be null-instantiated.

4. Conclusion. In this paper, I have compared two apparently heterogeneous semantic and pragmatic categories, vocatives and topics, and I have demonstrated that they belong to the same formal type. Minor

---

[15] I am grateful to David Birdsong for bringing this example to my attention.

differences in the internal and external syntax of vocative and topic phrases follow from their different pragmatic function. Both occur either in sentence-initial or in post-clausal position, instantiating two superordinate templates: the TOP construction (or Left-detachment) and the A-TOP construction (or Right-detachment). The striking formal parallel between vocatives and topics correlates with a fundamental functional similarity. In both cases, a pragmatically accessible discourse referent is associated with a proposition via a relevance link without being directly involved in the predicate-argument structure of the proposition.

The form of the TOP and the A-TOP construction is motivated by a general cognitive principle, which I have called the Principle of the Separation of Reference and Relation. This principle requires that the linguistic act of establishing a topical referent in the discourse and that of expressing information about this referent be as much as possible carried out separately. Due to this principle, speakers favor syntactic structures in which the constituent which codes the topical referent occurs outside the clause expressing the proposition which is relevant with respect to this referent.

The TOP construction and the A-TOP construction are used in different discourse contexts, depending on the assumed activation status of the referent of the detached constituent. The difference in use is determined by an iconic ordering principle whereby sentence-initial position signals the announcement of a relation between the referent and the associated proposition while post-clausal position signals the continuation of an already established relation. The phenomena analyzed in this paper support a view of grammar in which formal structure and information structure interact directly to give rise to form-function pairings which code specific communicative functions.

References

Ashby, William J. 1988. The Syntax, Pragmatics, and Sociolinguistics of Left- and Right-Dislocations in French. Lingua 75. 203-229.

Barnes, Betsy. 1985. *The Pagmatics of Left Detachment in Spoken Standard French.* Amsterdam: John Benjamins.

Bally, Charles. 1950. *Linguistique Générale et Linguistique Française.* (3rd edition) Bern: A. Francke.

Chafe, Wallace. 1987. Cognitive Constraints on Information Flow. In Russell Tomlin (ed), *Coherence and Grounding in Discourse.* Amsterdam: John Benjamins. 21-52.

Downing, Bruce T. 1969. Vocatives and Third-Person Imperatives in English. Papers in Linguistics 1.3. 570-92.

Fillmore, Charles J. & Paul Kay. 1992. *Construction Gammar Coursebook.* University of California, Berkeley.

Hawkins, John. 1995. *A Performance Theory of Word Order and Constituency.* Cambridge: Cambridge University Press.

Lambrecht, Knud. 1981. *Topic, Antitopic, and Verb Agreement in Non-Standard French*. Amsterdam: John Benjamins.

----- 1986. *Topic, Focus, and the Grammar of Spoken French*. Unpublished PhD dissertation, University of California, Berkeley.

----- 1987. On the Status of SVO Sentences in French Discourse. In R. Tomlin (ed). *Coherence and Grounding in Discourse*. Amsterdam: Benjamins. 217-262.

----- 1994. *Information* structure and sentence form. A *Theory of Topic, Focus, and the Mental Representations of Discourse Referents*. Cambridge: Cambridge University Press.

----- & Kevin Lemoine. forthcoming. Vers une Grammaire des Compléments d'Objet Zéro en Français Parlé. To appear in Travaux Linguistiques du CerLiCO. Rennes: Presses Universitaires de Rennes.

Lemoine, Kevin. 1992. *Definite Null Complementation in Spoken French*. Unpublished M.A. thesis, UT Austin, Dept. of French & Italian.

Marouzeau, Jean. 1961. *Lexique de la Terminologie Linguistique*. Paris: Geuthner.

Michaelis, Laura & Knud Lambrecht. 1994. On Nominal Extraposition: A Constructional Analysis. In S. Gahl et al. (eds), Proceedings of the Twentieth Annual Meeting of the Berkeley Linguistics Society. 262-73

Milner, Jean-Claude. 1978. *De la Syntaxe à L'interprétation*. Paris: Editions du Seuil.

Prince, Ellen F. 1992. The ZPG Letter: Subjects, Definiteness, and Information-Status. In William C. Mann & Sandra A. Thompson (eds), *Discourse Description. Diverse Linguistic Analyses of a Fund-Raising Text*. Amsterdam: John Benjamins. 295-325.

Ross, John R. 1983. *Infinite Syntax!* Norwood, New Jersey: Ablex Publishing Corporation.

Ruwet, Nicolas. 1982. Grammaire des Insultes. In *Grammaire des Insultes et Autres Études*. Paris: Editions du Seuil. 239-314.

Schegloff, Emmanuel A. 1968. Sequencing in Conversational Openings. American Anthropologist 70, 6. 1075-95.

Selkirk, Elisabeth O. 1984. *Phonology and Syntax: The Relation between Sound and Structure*. Cambridge, Mass.: MIT Press.

Sells, Peter. 1985. *Lectures on Contemporary Syntactic Theories*. Stanford: CSLI.

Weinrich, Harald. 1982. *Textgrammatik der Französischen Sprache*. Stuttgart: Ernst Klett Verlag.

Zwicky, Arnold M. 1974. Hey, Whatsyourname! In Michael W. La Galy, et al. (eds), Papers from the Tenth Regional Meeting, Chicago Linguistic Society. Chicago, Illinois. 787-801.

A Constraint on Progressive Generics

RONALD W. LANGACKER
University of California, San Diego

It is well known that generic sentences can assume a variety of forms, some of which are exemplified in (1).

(1) a. *Cats stalk birds.*
   b. *A cat stalks a bird.*
   c. *Every cat stalks birds.*

One of my objectives is to reconcile the overt forms of these expressions with their meanings. I suggest that they have different meanings, even when each is used to make a generic statement of universal validity. Another objective is to explain a rather striking difference in their grammatical behavior. With a plural generic, it is possible to use the progressive to signal that the generic property holds for only a limited span of time, as specified by the adverb *these days* in (2)a. A progressive with this import is not however possible with singular generics, as seen in (2)b. Such expressions are also bad with *every*, though not to the same degree.

(2) a. *Cats are being born with extra toes these days.*
   b. **A cat is being born with extra toes these days.*
   c. *?*Every cat is being born with extra toes these days.*

As background, I need to introduce a few basic notions and analyses of cognitive grammar (Langacker 1987a, 1991). There is first the familiar distinction between "active" and "stative" verbs (e.g. *learn* vs. *know*), distinguished by whether they take the progressive and whether they occur in the simple, "true" present tense:

(3) a. *He is {learning/*knowing} the poem.*
   b. *He {*learns/knows} the poem right now.*

I describe the two aspectual classes as *perfective* and *imperfective* to highlight the role of *bounding* in their characterization. A perfective verb *profiles* (i.e. designates) a relationship conceived as being bounded in time, an imperfective verb one that is not intrinsically bounded. Abbreviatory notations for these classes are given in Figure 1(a)-(b). Heavy lines indicate profiling.

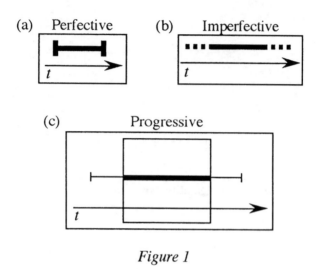

Figure 1

The progressive construction *be...-ing* only occurs with perfectives. As shown in Figure 1(c), it derives an imperfective by restricting the profiled relationship to an arbitrary internal portion of the overall event, which is unbounded within the limited "viewing frame" thus imposed (Langacker 1987b). Since the progressive in English requires a perfective, it indicates that the overall process on which it takes an internal perspective is conceived as being bounded. Thus the genericity marked progressive in (2)a must be construed as bounded, hence temporary rather than of open-ended duration.

An expression profiles either a *thing* or a *relationship*, each term being understood in an abstract technical sense (Langacker 1987b). Abbreviatory notations are given in Figure 2. Especially important here is our manifest ability to conceive of *higher-order* things and relationships. Clearly, we are able to construe a number of component things as collectively constituting a higher-order thing that functions as a unitary entity for linguistic purposes; such an entity functions, for example, as the profiled referent of terms like *group*, *stack*, *pile*, etc. Likewise, we are able to conceive of a number of component relationships (events, states, etc.) as collectively constituting a higher-order relationship; e.g., *Three boys ran up the hill* profiles a higher-order event comprising three component events.

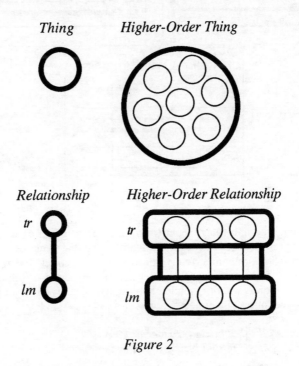

Figure 2

The participants in a relational expression are accorded varying degrees of prominence. One participant is singled out as the *trajector (tr)*, i.e., as the *primary figure* in the profiled relationship. At the clausal level, the trajector is manifested by the subject. Often another participant is accorded a lesser degree of focal prominence. This is called a *landmark (lm)*, i.e. the *secondary figure* in a profiled relationship. A clausal object manifests the landmark at that level. Importantly, the trajector (or the landmark) of a higher-order relationship is the higher-order thing comprising the trajectors (or the landmarks) of the component relationships, as shown in Figure 2.

Higher-order relationships can also be either perfective or imperfective. If perfective, they can take the progressive, which imposes an "internal perspective" on the overall, bounded higher-order relation. These notions are sketched in Figure 3. (Observe that the format used in Figures 1 and 3 represents aspectual properties of a verb or clause, whereas the format of Figure 2 represents participants. A fuller representation would have to include both kinds of information.)

(a) Higher-Order Perfective (b) Higher-Order Imperfective

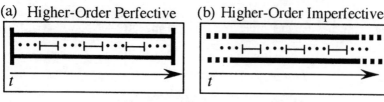

(c) Higher-Order Progressive

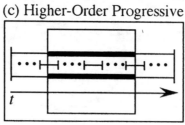

Figure 3

I analyze habituals, repetitives, and plural generics as profiling higher-order relationships. We have already noted that generics can profile either a perfective or an imperfective process, as respectively exemplified in (2)a and (1)a. Habituals as well can either be perfective or imperfective, indicating temporary vs. open-ended habituality. If perfective, they require the progressive for present-time reference:

(4) a. *My cat stalks that bird every morning.*
    b. *My cat is stalking that bird every morning again.*

By contrast, a repetitive is always construed as bounded. For present-time reference, the progressive is therefore necessary:

(5) a. *At this very moment, Jane is repeatedly ringing the doorbell.*
    b. **At this very moment, Jane repeatedly rings the doorbell.*

For a variety of reasons (discussed more fully in Langacker *to appear*), generics and habituals can be grouped as *general validity predications*. The situation they describe may hold for either a bounded or an unbounded span of time, i.e. their validity has a temporal *scope*. An indefinite, potentially open-ended set of instances of the basic event type can occur within that scope. General validity predications do not however profile these instances, but rather the higher-order relationship (of genericity/habituality) that they constitute or manifest.

This initial characterization needs to be refined and clarified. In particular, since repetitives also profile higher-order relationships, we need to specify what distinguishes them from generics and habituals. Crucial here is a distinction argued for by Goldsmith and Woisetschlaeger (1982:80): "...Use of the progressive marks a distinction which we shall call the 'structural/phenomenal' distinction, and which corresponds to two rather different types of knowledge about the world...One may describe the world in either of two ways: by describing what things happen in the world, or by describing how the world is made that such things may happen in it." They claimed that one value of the progressive is to express *phenomenal* (as opposed to *structural*) knowledge:

(6) a. Phenomenal: *This engine isn't smoking anymore.*
        [actual or temporarily structural]
   b. Structural: *This engine doesn't smoke anymore.*
        [structural (indefinite scope)]

They are making basically the right distinction, but I believe they are wrong in attributing it to the progressive per se. Note that (6)a can in fact be either phenomenal or structural, i.e., an actual ongoing occurrence or a temporary habitual. Thus, my own descriptions of the examples are given below in brackets. I will use the word *actual* in lieu of "phenomenal".

On my account, the progressive is merely symptomatic of perfectivity (bounding), rather than directly coding the actual/non-actual (or phenomenal/structural) contrast. That contrast is not specifically marked in English by any morphological element. The notion of non-actuality ("structural knowledge") reflects an idealized cognitive model to be called the *structured world model*: the notion that the world has a stable structure providing a kind of framework for the occurrence of actual events. One obvious manifestation of this ICM is in science. The western scientific tradition is based on the notion that the world works in a certain way, that there is such a thing as scientific truth, that some claims about the world are false, and that valid experimental results can be replicated.

For representational purposes, I will distinguish between the *actual plane* and the *structural plane*. Instances of a given event type can be found on either plane. The actual plane comprises event instances that are conceived as actually occurring. Crucially, however, the requisite notion of actuality is independent of time and modal status: an actual event's occurrence may be a matter of either past reality or future potentiality, it may be asserted or denied, etc. On the other hand, the structural plane comprises event instances with no status in actuality. These instances are conceived merely for purposes of characterizing "how the world is made". They have no existence outside the structural plane, which can be thought of metaphorically as "blueprints" for the world's structure.

Event instances in the structural plane will be described as *arbitrary*. An arbitrary instance of a type is one "conjured up" just for some local purpose, with no status outside the *mental space* (in the sense of Fauconnier 1985) thus created. Arbitrary instances figure in numerous linguistic phenomena (see Langacker 1991). Consider (7), for example.

(7) *Zelda wants to buy a fur coat.*

On the non-specific interpretation, there is no particular coat that Zelda wants to buy. The instance referred to is an arbitrary one, an instance "conjured up" just for purposes of characterizing the nature of Zelda's desire. It has no existence or status outside the mental space representing her desire. Similarly, events in the structural plane represent arbitrary instances conjured up just for purposes of characterizing the world's structure.

We are now able to characterize the similarities and differences among the sentence types in (8):

(8) a. Repetitive: *My cat repeatedly stalked that bird.*
    b. Habitual: *My cat stalks that bird every morning.*
    c. Plural generic: *Cats stalk birds.*

A *repetitive* profiles a higher-order event residing in the actual plane, whereas habituals and plural generics — grouped as general validity predications — profile higher-order events in the structural plane. The basic structure of a repetitive, like (8)a, is diagrammed in Figure 4.

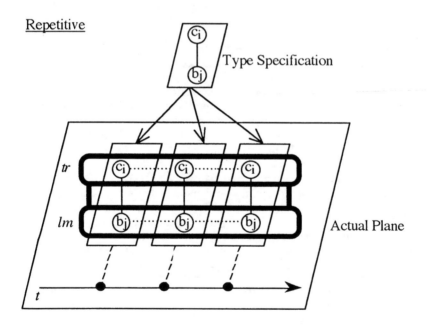

Figure 4

The sentence profiles a higher-order event comprising multiple instances of the same event type, namely *my cat stalk that bird*. Observe that the common type specification of these event instances refers to specific individuals: a particular cat (c_i) and a particular bird (b_j). Dotted correspondence lines indicate that the same individual functions as the trajector of each component event instance, and the same individual as the landmark of each such instance. Because these event instances belong to the actual plane, they are anchored to particular points in time. It is however the higher-order event that is profiled; (8)a does not designate a single, atomic instance of bird-stalking, but a complex event consisting of multiple component instances.

The basic structure of habitual expressions like (8)b is sketched in Figure 5. Once again the event type specifies an interaction between particular individuals, so the same individuals figure in each component event instance. And it is once more the higher-order relationship that is profiled. The contrast with repetitives lies in the fact that this profiled relationship occupies the structural rather than the actual plane. Hence the component events are not anchored to any particular points in time. It is merely specified that the occurrence of multiple instances of the type *my cat stalk that bird* is characteristic of the world's structure.

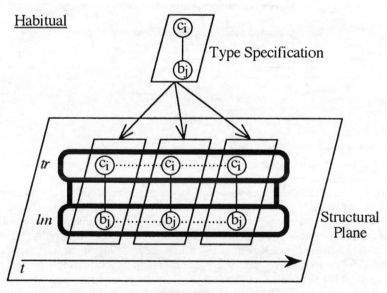

Figure 5

Lastly, a plural generic like (8)c has the structure shown in Figure 6. Here the type specification does not refer to particular individuals, but only to the thing types *cat* (c) and *bird* (b). There are no correspondence lines because there is no supposition that any two event instances have the same trajector or the same landmark. Otherwise a plural generic is analogous to a habitual, profiling a higher-order relationship in the structural plane. That is, one facet of the world's structure is the occurrence of multiple instances of the event type *cat stalk bird*.

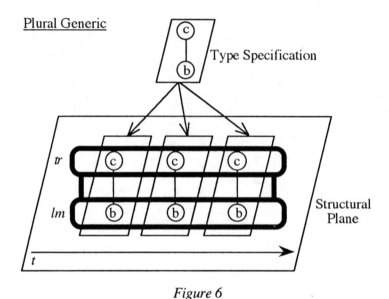

Figure 6

Observe that, in regard to number, the forms of these sentences fall out from their semantic characterizations. The singular subjects and objects in (8)a-b reflect the incorporation in the type specification of reference to specific individuals. Because the trajectors and landmarks of the component events thus collapse to a single cat and a single bird, respectively, the higher-order trajector and landmark each consist of just a single individual. This is not so with a plural generic, where different individuals presumably participate in each event instance. In that case the higher-order trajector consists of multiple cats, and the higher-order landmark of multiple birds.

What then can we say about the fact that generic statements assume a variety of forms, as in (1)? I presume that these differences in form correspond to subtle differences in meaning, even though all three kinds of sentences make universal statements about the members of a class. These kinds of generics impose different *construals*, i.e., they use different strategies for indicating that the ascription of a property has general validity for the class in question. While all of them evoke the structured world model, they differ in what they choose for their profile and focal participants. I will try to show that the differential ability of generic constructions to take the progressive (for indicating temporary genericity) falls out from the semantic characterization suggested by the contrasting grammatical forms.

The examples in (2) actually represent only part of a broader pattern. Plural generics with a zero determiner belong to a paradigm with those taking the quantifiers *all, most*, and *some*. As seen in (9), these pattern alike in allowing both open-ended generics and temporary generics signaled by the progressive:

(9) a. *{All/most/some/Ø} cats die before the age of 15.*
    b. *{All/most/some/Ø} cats are dying before the age of 15 these days.*

By contrast, singular generics with the indefinite article belong to a paradigm with those taking the quantifiers *every* and *any*. From (10), we see that these only allow open-ended generics; temporary generics in the progressive are precluded.

(10) a. *{Every/any/a} cat dies before the age of 15.*
    b. *{?*Every/*any/*a} cat is dying before the age of 15 these days.*

Why *every* works better in this construction than *any* or *a* can also be explained in terms of the proposed description.

The description hinges on a proper conceptual analysis of the semantics of these quantifiers (Langacker 1991:ch. 3). *All, most, some*, and *Ø* are *proportional quantifiers*. They profile a set of entities (P) characterized as some proportion of the *reference mass* (R_T), i.e., the set of all instances of the nominal category. In the case of *all*, P coincides with R_T. With *most*, the boundaries of P approximate those of R_T. *Some* indicates that P is non-empty. *Ø* is neutral in regard to proportion, allowing a universal construal ($P = R_T$) as a special case.

These notions are sketched in Figure 7, taking *most* as a specific example. The two conceived masses P and R_T each consist of instances of the thing type T. *Most* indicates that P comes close to exhausting R_T but does not quite match its full extension.

most

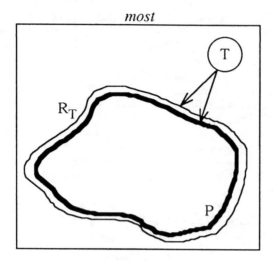

Figure 7

On the other hand, *every, any,* and *a* are *representative-instance quantifiers.* That is, they profile a single, arbitrary instance of the category, but one which is somehow guaranteed to be representative of it. Universal coverage is achieved indirectly, via this notion of representativeness, even though just one member of the class is actually mentioned. *Any* implies random selection from the reference mass (if an instance from R_T is chosen at random, it will exhibit the property in question). *Every* specifically construes the profiled instance against the background of a set of equivalent instances conceived as exhausting R_T. *A* is more neutral but allows the construal of representativeness as a special case.

A representative-instance quantifier is diagrammed in Figure 8, with *every* chosen for illustration. The box on the left is taken as specifying a type of relationship, and the circle on the right (T), a type of thing. Only one instance of that thing type is actually profiled by *every* (or by a nominal such as *every cat*), but that instance is specifically conceived against the background of other instances construed as being exhaustive of R_T. Besides instantiating the same thing type, they are equivalent in the sense that each participates in an instance of the same type of relationship. In this way the arbitrary instance of T singled out for profiling achieves the representativeness responsible for the quantifier's universality.

every

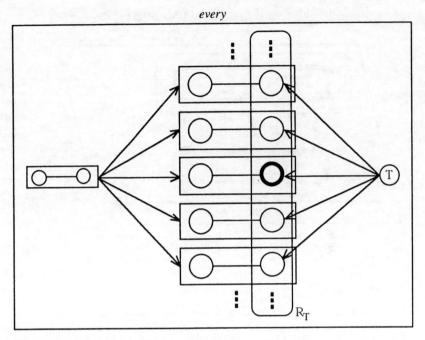

Figure 8

The crucial point is that proportional quantifiers profile a set of entities, whereas representative-instance quantifiers profile a single, albeit representative instance. Directly reflecting this difference is the plural vs. singular contrast in the nouns they quantify. Their use in generics, where they quantify the subject of a clause, is respectively diagrammed in Figures 9 and 10. Figure 9 corresponds to sentences like those in (9), where the profiled higher-order process can either be bounded or open-ended (hence the heavy dashed lines). Note that the trajector is characterized as a proportion of the reference mass, the specific proportion depending on the quantifier chosen. The point to observe is that the profiled relationship is the higher-order, collective process, and that this process may—as one option—be bounded (perfective), yielding a temporary generic. Under this option the progressive appears with the present tense, as in (9)b, in accordance with regular patterns of English.

Generic Construction: Proportional Quantifier

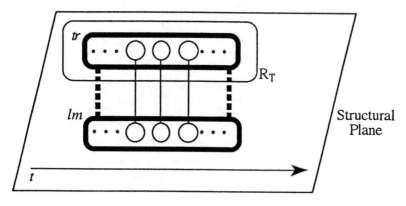

Figure 9

On the other hand, Figure 10 exemplifies the generic use of representative-instance quantifiers, with *every* chosen once more for specific illustration. A sentence like *Every cat dies before the age of 15* profiles a single, arbitrary instance of dying in the structural plane (on the part of a single, arbitrary cat), but portrays this event (and this cat) as being representative. The expressions in (10)a are therefore possible as full generics. However, the configuration in Figure 10 does not support the progressive, which takes an internal perspective on a profiled perfective process. Here only a single instance of the basic event type is profiled; the notion of a higher-order process remains implicit and unprofiled. Because the progressive cannot impose its internal perspective on the higher-order process constituting a bounded episode of genericity, expressions like (10)b are not available as temporary generics.

Why does *every* work better than *any* or *a*, as indicated in (10)b? The reason is that *every* makes salient reference to multiple event instances, implying a higher-order event, even though only one component event is in profile. Strictly speaking, the progressive requires a profiled perfective process on which to impose its limited "viewing frame", but at least with *every* a higher-order relationship is present, since the profiled event is specifically construed in relation to others of the same type. By contrast, *any* (involving the notion of random selection) and *a* (intrinsically singular) focus exclusively on just one event instance. Their representativeness implies the possibility of other instances, but any notion of a higher-order event comprising multiple instances remains latent or at least farther in the background.

Generic Construction: Representative-Instance Quantifier

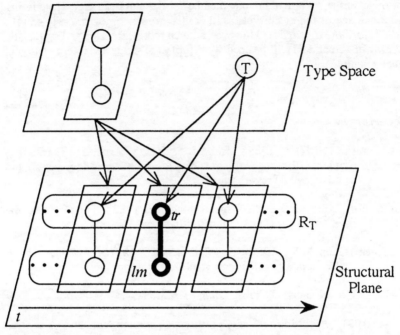

Figure 10

Observe that singular generics in the progressive improve when the object is made plural:

(11) a. *?Every cat is stalking birds these days.*
   b. *??Any cat is stalking birds these days.*
   c. *?*A cat is stalking birds these days.*

The reason, I think, is that a generic statement usually implies habituality on the part of any given individual. In saying that cats stalk birds, it is contemplated that a single cat does so habitually. Hence there are multiple instances of bird-stalking on the part of a single cat, distributed through time, and collectively these instances can be construed as constituting a higher-order event of the sort required for the progressive. With a plural object, this latent higher-order event is brought to the fore, since the plurality reflects multiple instances of the event type. In other words, the progressive in (11) may pertain in some fashion to the habituality ascribable to each member of the set of cats, rather than to the genericity per se. The judgments are clearest when this possibility is eliminated, when the nature of the event is such that any one member of the class can participate in just one instance of the event type, as in (2) [*be born with extra toes*] and (10) [*die before the age of 15*]. However, a much more extensive and systematic survey of actual data will be needed to clarify the status and interpretation of such examples.

References

Fauconnier, Gilles. 1985. *Mental Spaces: Aspects of Meaning Construction in Natural Language*. Cambridge, Mass. and London: MIT Press/Bradford.

Goldsmith, John, and Erich Woisetschlaeger. 1982. The Logic of the English Progressive. *Linguistic Inquiry* 13:79-89.

Langacker, Ronald W. 1987a. *Foundations of Cognitive Grammar*, vol. 1, *Theoretical Prerequisites*. Stanford: Stanford University Press.

-----. 1987b. Nouns and Verbs. *Language* 63:53-94.

-----. 1991. *Foundations of Cognitive Grammar*, vol. 2, *Descriptive Application*. Stanford: Stanford University Press.

-----. To appear. Generics and Habituals.

Conversational Use and Basic Meaning of Finnish Demonstratives[1]

RITVA LAURY
California State University, Fresno

This paper concerns the use of demonstrative pronouns in Finnish conversation. I will show that speakers of Finnish use demonstratives in a dynamic fashion to negotiate their mutual access to referents and to express their stance toward them in the interactional context of ongoing talk. I will argue that, contrary to what has been previously proposed, the use of the Finnish demonstratives in conversation is not primarily based on concrete distance, but that demonstratives reflect and create social meanings. Further, it is these social meanings, and not meanings based on concrete distance, which are the source of the extended or grammaticized uses of the demonstratives.

1. Data

The data for this study come from eight multi-party face-to-face conversations audiotaped in Finland. Seven of them are spontaneous conversations between friends and family members; one is a recording of a meeting of eight teachers of Finnish.

2. The basic meaning of demonstratives

Traditionally, the meanings of demonstratives have been thought to be based on concrete spatial circumstances. Although many studies have carefully noted the non-concrete uses of demonstratives, they have generally, either implicitly or explicitly, taken the use of demonstratives to indicate actual spatial proximity or distality as basic, and the uses which

---

[1] I would like to thank Auli Hakulinen, Eeva-Leena Seppänen, Marja-Leena Sorjonen, Hongyin Tao, Sandy Thompson, and Graham Thurgood for their many valuable suggestions on various drafts of this paper. All the mistakes and omissions are my own.
Financial support for the fieldwork on which this study is based was provided by a grant from the American-Scandinavian Foundation.

are not based on actual distance as derived from these meanings (Fillmore 1971:8, 1982:48; Lakoff 1974; Lyons 1977b:95, 1982:121; Anderson and Keenan 1985:278, among others).

The assumption that the non-concrete uses of demonstratives must have developed from concrete spatial uses is seductive because it is so well in keeping with the general tendency for concrete meanings to precede social meanings[2] in semantic development in general and in grammaticization processes in particular (for example, Traugott 1982, 1989; Sweetser 1990).

However, from the observation that in semantic development and grammaticization the direction is generally from concrete to abstract, it does not follow that such development can never have social meanings as a starting point (see Romaine 1988:146-157; Hakulinen and Seppänen 1992). Neither does it follow that the basic meanings of all grammatical morphemes, such as demonstratives, must be, or at one point must have been, concrete in nature. As Herring (1991:254) has pointed out, this line of argumentation ultimately leads to the awkward conclusion that "at some remote earlier stage [interpersonal] meanings were not expressed, or were expressed with a far lower frequency."

The idea that in the diachronic development of demonstratives, spatial meanings must have preceded the social meanings is an a priori notion. If we take seriously Lyons' observation that "the grammaticalization and lexicalization of deixis is best understood in relation to what may be termed the canonical situation of utterance (1977a:637)," that is, face-to-face conversation, then comparable diachronic data which would ascertain that concrete meanings did indeed precede the social meanings is in principle impossible to obtain. I am unaware of any studies describing the development of social meanings from spatial meanings in demonstrative reference based on diachronic data[3]. In fact, several scholars have noted

---

[2] In fact, it could reasonably be argued that there is no reason to assume that spatial notions such as 'near' and 'far', which demonstratives are thought to encode, are in principle any more concrete or less subjective than socially based participant roles encoded by speech act pronouns such as 'you' and 'I'.

[3] In the studies describing the development of articles from demonstratives, for example, the assumption that the source morpheme expresses spatial distance has always, to my knowledge, been made a priori; see, for example, Greenberg 1985:271; Traugott 1982:252.

the difficulties inherent in accounting for how exactly the social meanings might have developed from the spatial meanings (Lakoff 1974:355; Lyons 1977a:671; Klein 1983:291).

In the absence of diachronic data on the use of demonstratives in face-to-face conversation, we might look to child language acquisition to see whether the spatial meanings are indeed basic[4]. Experimental studies have shown that children learn the contrastive meaning of *this* and *that* as well as *here* and *there* before they learn the contrastrastive meaning of *near* and *far*, (Tanz 1980:87), but after the *my* and *your* contrast (1980:89-90). Similarly, the results obtained in the study by de Villiers and de Villiers (1974) suggest that it is the first/second person contrast which is the elementary deictic contrast, on which additional deictic contrast then build. In other words, the socially and interactionally based speaker/hearer contrast is more likely to be the basis for the acquisition of deictics than is spatial distality.

Further light on this issue could be shed by studies of actual use of demonstratives in discourse. While those accounts of demonstratives which have suggested that the basic meanings are spatial in nature have generally been based on introspective data and illustrated with invented or elicited examples, studies based on naturally occurring data have come to somewhat different conclusions. Thus Sacks ([1966] 1992) noted that even in uses where 'here' is used ostensibly to refer to the current location of the speaker, it is not just a place term; and Mithun (1987) pointed out that a major function of demonstratives in discourse is to focus attention on important referents and to establish orientation. Further, numerous accounts of the use of demonstratives in several typologically unrelated languages have directly disputed the distance-based accounts. Kirsner (1979), Strauss (1993) and Tao (1994) all insist that proximity and distality do not explain actual uses of demonstratives in, respectively, Dutch, English, and Mandarin; and Hanks (1990), whose extensive account of Mayan deixis is entirely based on actual use in context, notes that "the standard assumption that space is always foundational in deixis is an inconvenient fiction not borne out comparatively (1992:52)." In

---

[4] It does seem quite clear that deictic or 'situational' functions precede anaphoric or 'textual' functions of determiners in child language acquisition (see, for example, Karmiloff-Smith 1979). I thank Lisa Dasinger for pointing out this fact to me. What I am concerned with here is, of course, whether spatial or social/interactive uses are basic in deictic use.

addition, Strauss (1993), based on a rather extensive data base of spoken English, points out that exophoric use of demonstratives (uses pointing to referents outside the text) is not even the most frequent use; of the 823 uses of *this* and *that* in her data base, only 89, or 11%, were used exophorically. So that uses where demonstratives even could refer to actual distance could not be the most frequent ones. If frequency of use has anything to do with basicness of meaning, Strauss' study strongly suggests that concrete meanings are not basic.

Those studies of the demonstratives which claim that the social and interactive meanings are derived from spatial meanings can be taken as examples of what Silverstein (1976:18) has called the "semantico-referential" style of linguistic analysis. Silverstein points out (1976:13) that it is presumptuous to assume that social meanings of linguistic items are residual and derived from referential functions. I have argued here that neither diachrony nor ontogeny provide support for the claim that the meanings of demonstratives are primarily based on spatial distinctions, and use in discourse provides very clear counterevidence for such a claim.

3. The use of Finnish demonstratives in conversation

The Finnish demonstratives are *tämä* 'this', *tuo* 'that' and *se* 'that; it; the'. They have been traditionally considered to form a system based on actual distance from the speech act participants (Setälä 1891; Penttilä 1963; Karlsson 1983; Larjavaara 1985; 1990). *Tämä* has generally been thought to be a proximal demonstrative, but there has been some disagreement about the relative position of *tuo* and *se* on the proximal-distal scale. Thus, while some scholars have claimed that *tuo* is more distal than *se*, others have claimed that *se* is the more distal one (see Larjavaara 1985:28ff for a discussion). *Se* is generally said to be less demonstrative than *tämä* and *tuo*, and to refer to something that has already been mentioned; *se* has an important anaphoric use (Hakulinen 1985:340).

A different view has been proposed by Itkonen (1966; 1979) who claims that the Finnish demonstratives do not express concrete distance. He describes the demonstratives in terms of what he calls perceptual spheres (havaintopiiri); according to Itkonen, *tämä* refers to something in the speaker's perceptual sphere, *se* to something in the addressee's perceptual sphere, and *tuo* to something in the speech participants' mutual sphere. Larjavaara (1985; 1990) combines Itkonen's speech role based account with the traditional distance-based accounts.

It is important to note that all these earlier studies of the Finnish demonstratives have also been based on constructed examples. None of them has offered a discussion of the use of demonstratives in actual use in discourse. The assumption that demonstratives primarily express actual, concrete circumstances is made, paradoxically, without examining actual, concrete uses.

My claim here is that the use of the Finnish demonstratives in conversational discourse is not based on, and cannot be explained with reference to concrete physical proximity or distality, but that they are used by speakers in a dynamic fashion to express their orientation and stance toward referents. Demonstratives function to draw the attention of the addressee to a referent and to express who the speaker considers the referent to be accessible to. In their most basic use, the Finnish demonstratives include or exclude the referent in question in the speech participants' (speaker's or addressee's) current, socially defined sphere.

Thus, in my view, *tämä* presents[5] a referent or referents which the speaker includes within his or her current sphere, while *tuo* points to referents which the speaker considers to be outside his or her current sphere. *Se* is used for referents which the speaker considers to be within the addressee's current sphere.

The spheres are specifically social rather than spatial entities. The demonstratives express social and cognitive accessibility, and not concrete accessibility such as the ability to reach and manipulate something, although such ability may of course coincide, and often does, with social and cognitive accessibility[6]. My approach is thus close to Itkonen's (1979), although I do not consider the speech participants' spheres to be given in advance by what the participants can perceive or touch, but rather

---

[5] By using the term 'present' I am not implying that the referent of *tämä* is new to the discourse. In fact, as can be seen from examples in this paper, referents of *tämä* may have already been mentioned in the discourse. -- The suggestion that *tämä* presents a referent, while *tuo* points one out was originally made by Grönros (1980), as quoted in Hakulinen (1985:339). This is a particularly apt characterization of the function of these morphemes, and also quite compatible with my analysis.

[6] Thus I would not deny the obvious fact that in relative terms, the referent of *tämä* will often be close to the speaker, while the referent of *tuo* will be far from the speaker. However, I do claim that in such cases the nearness and farness are ultimately socially determined.

constituted by the use of demonstratives and at all times subject to modification. What matters is not what each of the speech participants is able to perceive, but rather how the situation is construed by the speakers.

In what follows, I will first discuss the exophoric use of demonstratives for referents present in the situation (both objects and people). I will then briefly discuss endophoric use of demonstratives, and finally I will discuss how the meanings of demonstratives are reflected in grammaticized uses.

4. The use of demonstratives for referents present in the situation

Even when demonstratives are used for concrete objects which are present in the speech situation, their use does not depend on actual distance. For example, as shown in example (1) below, a speaker may refer to a location adjacent to her own body with *tuo*, which is traditionally considered a distal demonstrative.

(1)
E: .. *ku se oli* ^*ihan* ***tossa*** *'korvan vieressä*.
    as 3SG be-PST quite TUO-INE ear-GEN side-INE
    when it was right there by [my] ear.

Examples like this can not be explicated in terms of spatial distance. There is even more convincing evidence that the use of demonstratives does not depend on the actual distance. In the course of interaction, speakers may also switch between different demonstratives even though the objects referred to remain stationary. Below is an example of such a use. This is an example taken from a dinner-table conversation. O, the host, is directing the attention of his son, S, to the empty glasses of some of the guests.

(2)
11 O: *'Simo ku sä olet* ***siel*** *se* ^*snapsin vartija,*
      Simo as 2SG be-2SG SE.LOC-ADE SE schnapps-GEN guard
      Simo, since you are the schnapps guard over there,

12 *ni* ***tääl*** *on* ***'näitä%*** --
      so TÄMÄ.LOC-ADE is TÄMÄ-PL-PART
      here are some of these --

13   ... ^laseja   *[<X tyhjinä X>].*
       glass-PL-PART empty-PL-ESS
       empty glasses.

14 S: *[Näitä]* ...   *<X hörppä X>*.
           TÄMÄ-PL-PART   gulp
           These gulp (ones).

15 O   **Siel**   *on*   .. *^Martti ja on- --*
           SE.LOC-ADE is   Martti and is
           Martti is over there and --

16   .. *^Martilla*   *ei*   *o [enää]*   *eikä,*
        Martti-ADE NEG be any.more NEG-and
        Martti doesn't have any more and neither,

17 S   *['Mhm,]*

18 O   .. *^Eilalla.*
        Eila-ADE
        (does) Eila.

O's first use of *siel* 'over there' in line 11, a local-adverbial form of *se*, points to S's location. In line 12 O uses *tämä* 'this' twice. The first use of *tämä* stands for the location of the glasses and indicates that O considers the glasses to be in his own sphere. The other use of *tämä*, in line 12 is a determiner of the noun *laseja* 'glasses' in line 13. This use also indicates that O considers the glasses to be in his current sphere. In line 14, S uses *tämä* for the glasses. His response constitutes an acceptance of the glasses into his sphere. And in line 15, O uses *siel* 'there', the same demonstrative he has used in line 11 to point to S's location, to refer to the location of the guests whose glasses need refilling, although in line 12 he has used *tääl* 'here' for the location of the glasses. Thus O has shifted his use of demonstratives to refer to the location of concrete objects present in the situation although there has been no actual movement of the objects in question. The function of this shift was to allocate the glasses from O to S; this was accomplished through the use of demonstratives, which effected a realignment of S's and O's spheres in such a way that S's sphere, for the purpose of this exchange, now includes the glasses that need refilling. Example (2) shows that demonstratives can be used to hand objects over from one person to another through purely linguistic means; the objects themselves do not need to move. The transfer is effected entirely through the use of demonstratives.

Analyses of demonstratives which are based on concrete distance would not easily account for examples such as (2) where there is a shift in demonstratives used but no actual movement of objects. However, a socially based analysis can account for both these uses as well as uses where the objects referred to do move. One context where speakers shift from one demonstrative to another is when they hand something over to someone else. What I would like to claim is that in such uses, the demonstratives are also doing the job of announcing, and thereby in fact accomplishing, a shift in spheres. In example (3), two sisters, S and V, are playing with small dolls and their equipment which S has just received as a present. Each girl has picked out a doll to play with and S is dividing the equipment between the two girls. In the excerpt below, she is handing something over to V.

(3)
155 S: ... ^*Hye=i=*.
       hey
       Hey.

156   ... '*Sille*   '*vielä* ^*tällä'ne*.
       SE-ALLAT still TÄMÄ-ADJ
       Another [one of] this kind for that [one].

157 V: ... <XP *Ootaha* PX>.
       wait.IMP-PRTCL
       Wait a minute.

158 S: ... ^*Tossa*.
       TUO-INESS
       There.

159   ... ^*Laita* *s- se* --
       put.IMP SE
       Put it --

This example shows how a speaker shifts from *tämä* to *tuo* and finally to *se* as she hands an object over to her addressee and its location changes from being inside the speaker's sphere, to being outside the speaker's sphere, and finally inside the addressee's sphere. In line 156, S calls V's attention to a piece of equipment that belongs to V's doll. *Sille* "for it", an allative form of se, refers to V's doll. The choice of demonstrative here indicates that the doll that *sille* refers to is in V's, the addressee's current sphere. *Tällänen* 'one of this kind' designates an object that S most likely is showing to V; the choice of demonstrative indicates that that object is in S's sphere. And the allative case on *sille*, the form referring to V's doll, shows that the object referred to with *tällänen* is meant for V's doll.

V's turn in 157 shows that she has interpreted S's turn to mean that S is about to hand her something - or at least that she expects S to do something that involves her. She is asking S to hold on a minute.

In S's next turn in line 158 she uses a form of *tuo* to point to the current location of the object she is handing to V. This use indicates that the object is now outside her current sphere.
And in line 159 she refers to the object she has now handed to V with *se*, indicating that she considers the object to be in V's sphere.

I would like to stress that even in cases where the demonstrative uses could be explained on the basis of concrete distance, a socially based analysis is in fact even more plausible. In handing-over behaviours, the use of demonstratives reflects the transfer of an object from one person's sphere to another person's sphere, and not primarily the degree of proximity to the speaker[7]. A socially based analysis is therefore more powerful because it can explain, in reference to objects concretely present, both those uses where the objects in question move, as well as those uses where the objects do not move. And in uses of demonstratives where the referents are not even present in the speech situation, distance-based meanings are obviously not relevant.

I have argued here that the basic meanings of demonstratives are social in nature. In the next two sections, I will argue that social meanings are also basic to the extended uses of demonstratives in endophoric reference and in grammaticized uses where demonstratives do not do referential work.

---

[7] Interestingly, a longitudinal study of the semantic development of one child (Carter 1975, as reported in Tanz 1980:102) found that the English demonstrative adverbs *here* and *there* were first invariably associated with handing-over behaviours and with completion of actions, and used without spatial significance.

5. The endophoric use of demonstratives

One problem for those approaches which consider actual distality or proximity to be basic to the meaning of demonstratives has been accounting for how their non-concrete uses are related to or develop from these purportedly basic meanings, as Lakoff (1974:355) and Klein (1983:291) have noted.

One suggestion has been that in endophoric uses, demonstratives index the actual distance of the previous mention through an iconic mapping of perceptual space into discourse time (Greenberg 1985; Lyons 1977b). However, as Lyons has pointed out, due to limitations of human memory, "referents can not be indexed solely, or even primarily, in terms of recency of mention or relative order of previous mention (1977b:100)." Further, iconic mappings of distance criteria are of course only possible if demonstratives really do express concrete distance, which I have contested here.

Although the endophoric use of demonstratives is a complex topic which I will not be able to fully account for here, I would suggest that much of the use of demonstratives for textual entities is based on what could be called "social addresses" of information. In using demonstratives for discourse entities, speakers express the accessibility of information to the different speech participants as well as their stance toward what is being said. I will illustrate this point with example (6) below.

This example comes from a discussion between several teachers of Finnish considering the use of literature in schools. At the point that the turn below was taken, there had been some trouble in the conversation. One of the speakers, PY, has been discussing what he considers a poor selection of literature at school libraries. Another speaker, KM, has been interrupting, overlapping and questioning him several times during his previous turn. PY then turns to a point where he disagrees with KM.

(4)
1 PY .. *mut ^täs   on 'juuri muuten%,*
      but TÄMÄ-INE is just otherwise
      'but here we have however,
2   %=

3   *tom--*

4 .. *tohon* ^*sun* .. '*juttuus*,
   TUO-ILL 2SG-GEN story-ILL-2SGPOSS
   about that thing of yours,

5 *ni tähän* ^*peruskoulun* *tuloon*,
   so TÄMÄ-ILL basic-school-GEN coming
   about this arrival of the comprehensive school,

6 *ni* ^*meillä* *esimes on käyny*
   so 1PL-ADE example is go-PST.PPLE
   with us for example it has worked out

   näitten ^*kirjahankintojen* *suhteen*,
   TÄMÄ-PL-GEN book-procurement-PL-GEN with.respect.to
   with these book purchases,

7 *jos* ^*palataan* *viel niihin* .. ^*hankintoihi.*
   if return-PASS-PERS still SE.PL-ILL procurement-PL-ILL
   if we get back to the purchases.

Earlier in the discussion, KM has indicated that the arrival of the comprehensive school has improved the selection of books at school libraries. PY disagrees. In line 4, he uses *tuo* as a determiner of the noun phrase referring to KM's earlier discussion, thus dissociating himself from that point of hers (cf. Hakulinen 1985:342). The use of *tuo* puts KM's turn outside PY's sphere - here, it expresses that he does not accept KM's view. PY then goes on to "appropriate" the topic - in lines 5 and 6 he modifies with *tämä* the noun phrases referring to the arrival of the comprehensive school and the book purchases to indicate that these topics (which were earlier discussed by KM) are now in his sphere, and he intends to discuss them. And in line 7 he makes appeal to his addressees' memory of the earlier discussion of the book purchases by using the addressee-centered *se* as a determiner of the noun phrase referring to the purchases.

In example (6) above, all three Finnish demonstratives are being used in reference to KM's previous turn and the topics she discussed. Therefore, it is not plausible to suggest that endophoric demonstrative use is based on criteria having to do with referential distance. Instead, PY uses the demonstratives to express his stance (in this case, disagreement) and to show whose knowledge of the referents is currently relevant.

6. Grammaticized uses of demonstratives

Further, it seems fairly clear that when demonstratives become grammaticized, it is the social meanings that form the basis of the grammaticization process, and concrete distance is not a factor. Consider the separate paths of development that two Finnish demonstratives, *se* and *tuo* are taking. Their grammaticizing uses are based on the social meanings I have discussed above. I will argue that the grammaticized uses of *se* as a developing definite article and as a response token are addressee-relevant, while the use of *tuo* as a hesitation marker and as a marker of evidentiality are speaker-relevant.

The demonstrative pronoun *se* is currently undergoing the process of being grammaticized as a definite article in spoken Finnish (L. Hakulinen 1979:510; A. Hakulinen 1985:342; Chesterman 1991:176ff.; Vilkuna 1991:135; Juvonen To appear; and others). What is involved in this development (Laury 1991; 1993) is that from being used referentially for objects which are considered by the speaker to be in the addressee's sphere, the use of *se* as an article has originated from uses where the speaker focuses the attention of the addressee on important referents which are cognitively accessible to the addressee (in the sense of Chafe 1987; 1994). Since information which is accessible to the addressee is always identifiable, *se* has developed into a marker of information which the addressee can identify.

Another grammaticized use which is based on the addressee-centered meaning of *se* is the use of *niin* (the plural instructive form of *se*) as a response token. According to Sorjonen (In progress), one basic use of *niin* is its use as an affirmative answer to a subclass of yes/no questions and statements of B-events. *Niin* is also used as a response when the previous speaker's turn is incomplete syntactically, semantically or interactionally. In these cases, a *niin*-response treats the prior turn as one that has not provided a point yet, and invites the previous speaker to continue. A third use type is one where *niin* offers a claim of agreement with an assessment by a coparticipant (Sorjonen p.c.). What these uses of *niin* have in common is that they all make appeal to the information offered by or available to the addressee.

The addressee-relevant uses of *se* as a definite article and as a response token contrast with the use of *tuo* as a hesitation marker and with certain uses of *tuo* observed in certain eastern Finnish dialects.

Tota, the partitive form of the demonstrative *tuo*, is commonly used as a marker of hesitation or word search in spoken Finnish. By using a token of *tota*, the speaker may indicate that he or she is searching for a word or an expression; simultaneously, the use of *tota* may count as an attempt to hold the floor. This use can be seen as an extension of the referential uses of *tuo*. As I have shown above, in its use for referents concretely present in the situation, *tuo* is used to indicate that its referent is outside the speaker's current sphere. The use of *tota* as an index of hesitation or a word search can, in my view, be traced back to this basic meaning of *tuo*. Its use is quite different from the use of *niin* as a discourse particle in that *tota* is a reflection of the speaker's internal process of hesitation or search, and also an attempt to hold the floor; these uses are speaker-relevant. In contrast, typical uses of *niin*, as discussed above, are ones where the speaker either requests more information from the addressee or agrees with what the addressee has said.

Another use of *tuo* is an epistemic use observed in certain eastern Finnish dialects. Forsberg (1993a; 1993b) found that in her spoken corpus, speakers frequently used the pronoun *tuo* in clauses which were in the potential mood. What is interesting for our purposes here is that the more formal markers of uncertainty that showed up in the clauses in Forsberg's corpus, the more likely it was that *tuo* would occur. Thus Forsberg found *tuo* in one fourth of those potential clauses which were questions, and a full half of those potential clauses in her corpus which were negative questions contained the pronoun *tuo*. Forsberg notes that these uses of *tuo* can not be traced back to a meaning of distality, but rather to the fact that *tuo* indexes the speaker's subjective stance toward some situation or some information. While many of the uses of *tuo* discussed by Forsberg were referential pronouns, she points out that in many other cases a form of *tuo* was functioning as a particle and was not referential. This may be an indication that the use of *tuo* in the dialects studied by Forsberg may be grammaticizing as a non-referential index of a speaker's epistemic stance.

What seems to be happening when demonstratives become grammaticized is that they cease to refer independently, and retain only their indexical features (cf. Laitinen 1992, esp. 272-278). And in each case discussed above, the speech role based, social meanings are the meanings which form the basis of the grammaticized uses. These are the meanings that are retained when pronouns become grammaticized and cease to refer.

Interestingly, Forsberg suggests that the use of *tuo* contrasts with the use of *se* in her corpus in such a way that they index whether the matter at hand is being viewed from the speaker's or the addressee's perspective. She identifies this variation as an example of the crystallization of the basic speech roles of speaker and addressee in the semantic structure of the language. I could not agree more.

7. Conclusion

I have argued that the meanings of Finnish demonstratives are not based on concrete distality or proximity of referents, but that instead, speakers use them to negotiate their mutual access to referents in the context of ongoing talk. I have also argued that the extended and grammaticized meanings of demonstratives are based on their social meanings.

References

Anderson, Stephen R. and Edward L. Keenan. 1985. Deixis. In Shopen, Timothy (Ed.). *Language typology and syntactic description* v. III. Grammatical categories and the lexicon. Cambridge: Cambridge University Press

Chafe, Wallace. 1987. Cognitive Constraints on Information Flow. In Russell S. Tomlin, Ed. *Coherence and grounding in discourse*. Amsterdam: John Benjamins.

Chafe, Wallace. 1994. *Discourse, consciousness and time: The flow and displacement of conscious experience in speaking and writing*. Chicago: University of Chicago Press.

Chesterman, Andrew. 1991. *On definiteness: A study with special reference to English and Finnish*. Cambridge: Cambridge University Press.

Carter, Anne. 1975. The Transformation of Sensorimotor Morphemes into Words: A Case Study of the Development of *here* and *there*. Paper presented at the Stanford Child Language Forum.

De Villiers, Paul and Jill de Villiers. 1974. On This, That, and the Other: Nonegocentrism in Very Young Children. *Journal of Experimental Child Psychology* 18:438-47.

Fillmore, Charles. 1971. Toward a Theory of Deixis. In the *PCCLLU Papers*. Vol. 3, No. 4. Hawaii: University of Hawaii Department of Linguistics.

Fillmore, Charles J. 1982. Towards a Descriptive Framework for Spatial Deixis. In R. J. Jarvella and W. Klein, Eds. *Speech, Place and Action: Studies in Deixis and Related Topics*. New York: John Wiley and Sons.

Forsberg, Hannele. 1993a. *Suomen murteiden potentiaali*. Licentiate thesis in Finnish. University of Joensuu.

Forsberg, Hannele. 1993b. Pragmaattinen tuo suomen murteissa. Paper given at the XX Kielitieteen päivät in Turku, Finland.

Greenberg. Joseph H. 1985. Some Iconic Relationships among Place, Time, and Discourse Deixis. In John Haiman (Ed.) *Iconicity in Syntax*. Amsterdam: John Benjamins.

Hakulinen, Auli. 1985. On Cohesive Devices in Finnish. In Emil Sözer, Ed. *Text Connexity, Text Coherence: Aspects, Methods, Results*. Papers in Text Linguistics v. 49. Hamburg: Helmut Buske Verlag.

Hakulinen, Auli and Eeva-Leena Seppänen. 1992. Finnish kato: From verb to particle. *Journal of Pragmatics* 18:527-549.

Hakulinen, Lauri. 1979. *Suomen kielen rakenne ja kehitys*. Helsinki: Otava.

Hanks, William F. 1990. *Referential Practice: Language and Lived Space Among the Maya*. Chicago: The University of Chicago Press.

Heine, Bernd, Ulrike Claudi and Friederike Hünnemeyer. 1991. *Grammaticalization: A conceptual framework*. Chicago and London: University of Chicago Press.

Herring, Susan C. 1991. The Grammaticalization of Rhetorical Questions in Tamil. In Traugott, Elizabeth Closs and Bernd Heine (Eds.). *Approaches to Grammaticalization*. Vol I. Focus on Theoretical and Methodological Issues. Amsterdam/Philadelphia: John Benjamins.

Itkonen, Terho. 1966. Tutkimus suomen asyndetonista. *Virittäjä* 70:402-423

Itkonen, Terho. 1979. Zur Semantik und Pragmatik der Finnischen Demonstrativa. In *Festschrift für Wolfgang Schlachter zum 70. Geburtstag*. Veröffentlichungen der Societas Uralo-Altaica 12. Wiesbaden: Societas Uralo-Altaica.

Juvonen, Päivi. To appear. Se: On the Path to Becoming a Definite Article in Finnish? In Ingrid Almqvist, Per Cederholm and Jarmo Lainio (Eds.). *Stockholm Studies in Finnish Language and Literature*. Vol. 11

Karlsson, Fred. 1975. Suomen kielen tulevaisuus. *Sananjalka* 17:51-66.

Kirsner, Robert. 1979. Deixis in Discourse: An Exploratory Quantitative Study of the Modern Dutch Demonstrative Adjectives. In Talmy Givon, Ed. *Discourse and Syntax*. (Syntax and Semantics 12) New York: Academic Press.

Klein, Wolfgang. 1983. Deixis and Spatial Orientation in Route Directions. In Pick, Herbert L. and Linda P. Acredolo (Eds.) *Spatial Orientation: Theory, Research and Application*. New York: Plenum Press.

Laitinen, Lea. 1992. *Välttämättömyys ja persoona: suomen murteiden nesessiivisten rakenteiden semantiikkaa ja kielioppia*. Helsinki: Suomalaisen Kirjallisuuden Seura.

Lakoff, Robin. 1974. Remarks on This and That. In *Proceedings of the Tenth Regional Meeting of the Chicago Linguistic Society*. 345-56.

Larjavaara, Matti. 1985. Suomen demonstratiivisysteemin rakenne. *Sananjalka* 27:15-31.

Larjavaara, Matti. 1990. *Suomen deiksis*. Helsinki: Suomalaisen Kirjallisuuden Seura.

Laury, Ritva. 1991. On the Development of the Definite Article se in spoken Finnish. In

SKY 1991. Helsinki: Suomen kieli-tieteellinen yhdistys.

Laury, Ritva. 1995. Grammammaticization of the Definite Article *se* in Spoken Finnish. In Andersen, Henning (Ed.) *Historical Linguistics 1993*. Selected papers from the ICHL XI, Los Angeles, 16-20 August 1993. Amsterdam: Benjamins.

Lyons, John. 1977a. *Semantics*. Vol. 2. Cambridge: Cambridge University Press.

Lyons, John. 1977b. *Deixis and anaphora*. In T. Myers, Ed. The Development of Conversation and Discourse. Edinburgh: Edinburgh University Press.

Lyons, John. 1982. Deixis and Subjectivity: Loquor, ergo sum? In R. J. Jarvella and W. Klein, Eds. *Speech, Place and Action: Studies in Deixis and Related Topics*. New York: John Wiley and Sons.

Mithun, Marianne. 1987. The Grammatical Nature and Discourse Power of Demonstratives. In *Proceedings of the 13th Annual Meeting of the Berkeley Linguistics Society*, 184-194. Berkeley: Berkeley Linguistics Society.

Penttilä, Aarni. 1963. *Suomen kielioppi*. Porvoo: WSOY.

Romaine, Suzanne. 1988. *Pidgin and Creole languages*. London: Longman

Sacks, Harvey. 1992. *Lectures on Conversation*. Vol I. Ed. by Gail Jefferson. Oxford: Basil Blackwell. (Lecture 29, Spring 1966).

Setälä, Emil Nestor. 1891. *Suomen kielen lauseoppi*. Helsinki: Otava.

Silverstein, Michael. 1976. Shifters, Linguistic Categories, and Cultural Description. In Keith H. Basso and Henry A. Shelby, Eds. *Meaning in Anthropology*. Albuquerque: University of New Mexico Press.

Sorjonen, Marja-Leena. In progress. *On discourse particles in Finnish*. Ph.D. dissertation, Dept. of Applied Linguistics, UCLA.

Strauss, Susan. 1993. Why 'this' and 'that' are not complete without 'it'. In *Papers from the 29th Regional Meeting, Chicago Linguistics Society*, 403-417. Chicago Linguistics Society, University of Chicago.

Sweetser, Eve. 1990. *From Etymology to Pragmatics: Metaphorical and Cultural Aspects of Semantic Structure*. Cambridge:Cambridge University Press.

Tanz, Christine. 1980. *Studies in the acquisition of deictic terms*. Cambridge: Cambridge University Press.

Tao, Hongyin. 1994. Demonstratives and the Speaker's Point of View in Mandarin Conversational Discourse. Paper given at the 6th North American Conference on Chinese Linguistics, USC, May 13-15, 1994.

Traugott, Elizabeth Closs. 1982. From Propositional to Textual and Expressive Meanings;

Some Semantic-Pragmatic Aspects of Grammaticalization. In Winfred P. Lehmann and Yakov Malkiel (Eds.). *Perspectives on Historical Linguistics*. Amsterdam/Philadelphia: John Benjamins.

Traugott, Elizabeth Closs. 1989. On the Rise of Epistemic Meanings in English: An Example of Subjectification in Semantic Change. *Language* 65.1:31-55

Vilkuna, Maria. 1991. *Referenssi ja määräisyys suomenkielisten tekstien tulkinnassa*. Helsinki: Suomalaisen Kirjallisuuden Seura.

Rigid Syntax and Flexible Meaning: The Case of the English Ditransitive

FREDERIKE VAN DER LEEK

University of Amsterdam

1 Introduction

In languages like English, one and the same verb form more often than not fits into more than one syntactic argument structure, and appears to adapt its meaning, chameleon-like, to its syntactic context. At the same time, verbs differ as to their 'alternation' possibilities; thus, certain verbs can 'dativize', i.e. alternate between a prepositional complement structure, [--- NP$_i$ *to/for* NP$_j$], and a ditransitive one, [--- NP$_j$ NP$_i$], while others can only select the former type. On the face of it, it seems as if participation in an alternation depends on the verb being a member of a certain globally definable semantic class, but closer examination reveals that not all the members can actually alternate. Thus, a rough approximation for dativization would be membership of a class that is cognitively compatible with the notion of transfer of possession; given a constraint along those lines, alternation from the prepositional to the ditransitive variant is correctly predicted to be licensed for e.g., *throw* but not *drive*. However, a verb like *push*, which seems cognitively close to *throw*, is not allowed in the ditransitive construction. At the more fine-grained level, then, verbs appear to be arbitrarily choosy as to their alternation possibilities. At the same time language users exhibit partially productive behaviour (thus, they dativize novel verbs such as *fax, e-mail* etc.); since they cannot be assumed to benefit from 'negative evidence', there is, it seems, a paradox ('Baker's paradox', cf. Pinker 1989:7). The question is, then, what sort of knowledge enables a language user to judge whether a particular verb can participate in a particular alternation or not.There are currently two detailed proposals as to how this question should be dealt with, Pinker 1989 and Goldberg 1992 (henceforth Pinker and Goldberg). The former proposes a lexical account, while the latter offers a constructional alternative instead. In what follows I will, restricting myself to dativization, discuss the two proposals and, since I assume Baker's paradox to be fallacious, formulate an account of my own.

2 A lexical account

"Semantic structures", Pinker argues, "constitute an autonomous level of linguistic representation, not reducible to syntax or cognition" (p. 357) and lin-

321

guistic rules are blind to those meaning aspects of verbs that are merely cognitive in nature; therefore verb meanings are represented schematically, their semantic structures only being composed of 'grammatically relevant' primitive semantic components which are drawn from a small set evolved by language in the course of time. Now the essence of alternation, in Pinker's view, is that the verbs that participate, can instantiate two thematic cores that are distinct and partially alike at the same time. A thematic core is a semantic structure that constitutes a "schematization of a type of event...that lies at the core of the meanings of a class of possible verbs" (p. 73) and that via (near) universal linking rules, projects onto a given argument structure. The existence of a particular alternation in a given language shows, then, that that language has evolved a means of relating two thematic cores, in the form of a lexical rule that has one thematic core as input and another as output. Verbs with the right semantic structure (one that satisfies the input of the lexical rule) can therefore adopt the new meaning characterized by the rule's output; it follows that only such verbs can ultimately be linked to the two corresponding syntactic alternatives. In this view, then, syntax is, as pointed out by Goldberg (p. 18), no more than a projection of lexical requirements.

Lexical rules, Pinker furthermore argues, must be of two types: broad- and narrow-range; the former characterizes the broad semantic class of verbs that are potential candidates for alternation. However, language turns out to be more restrictive in that the grammar does not simply allow all the cognitively eligible verbs to participate in the alternation. Instead, it makes an essentially arbitrary selection of subclasses, each a variant of the broad semantic class and only members of such subclasses can actually alternate (the reason being that language users are lexically conservative). Pinker therefore postulates a number of narrow-range lexical rules that together define, by their various inputs, which subclasses can actually participate in the alternation. For English there is, thus, a broad-range rule accounting for dativization in abstracto; it takes as input a thematic core roughly of the form [*x acts-on y*] *effecting that* [*y goes to z*], its output being a new but related thematic core signifying a change of possession, [*x acts-on z*] *effecting that* [*z has y*]. The essential difference is that the Patient role (second argument of ACT-ON) is allotted to the transferred entity in the one case and to the person receiving this entity in the other. Now THROW-type verbs, i.e., verbs of "instantaneous causation of ballistic motion" dativize, whereas PUSH-type verbs, i.e., verbs of "continuous causation of accompanied motion in some manner" (e.g., *push*) do not (Gropen et al. 1989:243-4), this despite what, according to Pinker, can be seen as "their cognitive similarities" (p. 212). Pinker therefore posits a particular narrow-range lexical rule for English, one that includes the former class in dativization but not the latter; this makes it possible to account for the following data (pp. 110-1):

(1)   Lafleur throws/tosses/flips/slaps... him the puck; he shoots, he scores!
(2)   *I carried/pulled/pushed/schlepped/lifted/lowered/hauled John the box.
Following Gropen et al. (1989), Pinker posits seven narrow-range lexical
rules for the grammar of English, each a subvariant of the above broad-range
rule. To account for *for*-dativization, Pinker postulates a somewhat different
broad-range rule; the input thematic core is, roughly, [*x acts-on y*] *for* [*y to
have z*], which changes into [*x acts-on z*] *for* [*y to have z*] *by means of* [*x
acting-on y*], *for/to* signalling both that the preposition involved is *for* and
that the transfer is prospective rather than actual. Two narrow-range rules are
then posited to limit alternation to the two subclasses fitting into this pattern.
    The above brief account makes two things clear about Pinker's system.
Firstly, the grammar is given the task of explicitly spelling out, at the narrow-
range level, the semantic similarities and differences between alternation variants in just as much detail as is necessary to make the system work, so that all
the verbs that can participate, are indeed accounted for; the semantic structures involved being multidimensional in nature, they can accommodate as
many substructures as it takes to distinguish one subclass from another so that
the system is virtually unfalsifiable. Secondly, Pinker's narrow-range rules are
purely stipulative, verbs being "choosy [in that they cannot] appear in all sentences, even when the combination makes perfect sense" (p. 3); other than
lexical conservatism, there is no explanation why certain subclasses of verbs
enter into an alternation to the exclusion of others. As a consequence, the
grammar alone determines, for any individual verb, its range of (linguistic)
meanings (and consequently its range of argument structures), without the
language user's non-linguistic cognitive knowledge being allotted any role in
the process whatsoever. The sole explanatory purpose that the narrow-range
rules serve is that their existence resolves Baker's paradox, local productivity
being perfectly feasible within any of the verbal subclasses participating in
the alternation. Notice, however, that if it can be shown that alternation behaviour is, after all, not based on arbitrary criteria, Baker's paradox ceases to
exist. This is what I intend to show, but before doing so I will first briefly
discuss Goldberg's theory.

3 A constructional account

Goldberg's central thesis is that verb-argument structures form *constructions*, i.e. "form-meaning correspondences that are not strictly predictable
from knowledge of the rest of the grammar" (p. 2). Such 'simple clause constructions' pair (independently of how they are lexicalized) skeletal syntactic
structures with schematic semantic structures of their own, specifying for
each of their semantic roles which syntactic roles (subject/object/oblique)
they link with and profiling those semantic arguments that pair up with a sub-

ject or object (these being the grammatically prominent roles). The fundamental idea behind this approach to simple clause constructions is that the constructional senses involved "reflect scenes basic to human experience" (p. 4), and that language has evolved argument structures to encode such basic scenes. Thus the English ditransitive, which prototypically construes a scene as involving some object's 'successful transfer' from one party to another, has as its central sense the semantic structure [*cause to receive* <Agent, Recipient, Patient>], and the *to*-prepositional variant fits in with the independently existing CAUSED-MOTION construction, characterized as [*cause to move* <Cause, Theme, Goal>]. Verbs, in this view, can 'alternate' between two constructions provided their meaning can be integrated with each of the two constructional senses (without there being a grammatical rule relating the two uses). Each verb has, that is, typically one basic meaning that remains constant across constructions. This meaning gets represented in rich frame-semantic terms, which means that usage of a verb evokes in the language user's mind a 'scene' or complex knowledge frame that stands for "a coherent schematization of experience" (Fillmore 1985:223). The verb's individual frame portrays the scene in terms of verb-specific participant roles, profiling the salient, i.e. normally obligatory, roles; this frame is in turn embedded in a more general frame schematizing the background against which the verb is prototypically used and which one needs to have knowledge of to properly understand the meaning of the verb. As should be clear from this, Goldberg employs both 'macro' and 'micro' roles, i.e., roles operating at constructional and individual verb level respectively, and the question whether verb X fits into construction Y depends, in her view, on the question whether the macro and micro roles in question can 'fuse'. Such fusion results in the creation of a new composite predicate and is conditioned in two ways: (i) only semantically compatible roles can fuse and (ii) all of the verb's profiled micro roles must, with one exception not relevant here, fuse with profiled macro roles of the construction. Since, however, there is no condition dictating that all of the macro roles need to fuse with a micro role, constructions can supply a role of their own to the newly created predicate. This, in fact, constitutes a highly attractive feature of Goldberg's theory, since it obviates the need for stipulating roles for verbs that do not seem to be a natural part of their meaning. Thus there is no need to claim, the way Pinker does, that when a verb like *make* is used in the ditransitive (cf. *Bob made Sue a cake*), it supplies three semantic roles of its own; instead, it comes only with a 'maker' and a 'made' role, the ditransitive construction itself supplying the Recipient role. Notice that we cannot interpret the newly created predicate in the *make* example along the lines of 'causing to receive by making', since the sentence simply does not entail Sue's actual reception of the cake. The reason that *make* can nevertheless dativize is, Goldberg argues, due to the fact that constructions are, like words, polysemous; this means that the ditransitive does not only have the above 'successful transfer' sense. The latter is in fact the construction's central sense, and the grammar lists the verb classes that fit in with this sense, such as GIVE- and THROW-type verbs. Next to this central sense, Goldberg postulates five extended senses, which present the transfer as (i) merely implied by the verb's satisfaction conditions (*promise*), (ii) merely made possible (*permit*), (iii) caused not to take place (*refuse*), (iv) intended (*bake*) and (v) guaranteed in the future (*bequeath*). The claim is, in short, that Baker's paradox can be solved in terms of a set of constructional senses, productivity being limited to verbs that fit into one of the constructional senses that are conventionally determined to be grammatical.

Goldberg's account manages to avoid a number of drawbacks that she notes about Pinker's proposal. Thus, it precludes the need for a multiplicity of "implausible verb senses" (p. 11). Moreover, it avoids the charge of circularity facing any theory that treats syntax as a projection of lexical requirements; that is, in such a theory, cf. the above ditransitive example with *make*, "a verb is an *n*-ary predicate and "therefore" has *n* complements when and only when it has *n* complements" (p. 19). A further advantage of Goldberg's theory is that it allows all we know about a verb's basic meaning to play a role when we face the task of judging which argument structures a verb can fuse with. Thus Goldberg's example of the novel but perfectly acceptable usage of *sneeze* in the CAUSED-MOTION construction, cf. *Sam sneezed the napkin off the table*, is a type of example that is left unexplained in Pinker's framework; that is, our understanding here obviously hinges on our awareness of the 'forceful expulsion of air' aspect in *sneeze*, a purely cognitive meaning aspect that can, by definition, not be appealed to in Pinker's account. Since examples of this type are quite ubiquitous, Pinker's claim that cognition plays no role, seems quite untenable. At the same time, Goldberg's theory faces problems of its own. For one thing, the extended senses that she postulates seem - the *intend to cause to receive* sense excepted - to derive the distinctive part of their meaning from the verbs that they are set up to account for; it is for instance hard to see how the ditransitive construction itself contributes the negative element in *cause not to receive* rather than the verbs slotting into it (*refuse, deny*). Furthermore, certain verbs that can occur in the ditransitive are *by definition* unaccountable and can only be treated as exceptions (e.g., *bet, cost, envy, forgive*). The reason is that, with polysemous constructions, "Each of the extensions constitutes a minimally different construction, motivated by the central sense" (Goldberg :86), so that, in the case of the ditransitive, no extended sense is possible unless it involves transfer of some kind, which is not the case with regard to the above verbs. Unlike Pinker's, the system is not flexible enough. Nor is the polysemy account powerful enough to solve

Baker's paradox completely: Goldberg has to resort to lexical conservatism to explain why e.g., PUSH-type verbs do not dativize (readily), whereas THROW-type verbs do. Lastly, not all the verbs that Goldberg ranges under the central sense (e.g., *throw* etc.) do actually guarantee successful transfer.

Goldberg's account is an important step forward in that it is not, like Pinker's, an immune system and allows interdependent forces (grammar and cognition) to determine a verb's range of argument structures. In view of the above problems, I will propose an alternative of my own, however, one that is inspired by her constructional approach but does not accept the general wisdom that the ditransitive comes with a concrete sense such as *cause to receive*. For reasons to become duly clear, I will talk of 'syntactic frame' rather than 'argument structure' in what follows.

4 An alternative constructional account

Below I am going to argue, mainly using the English ditransitive to support my claim, (i) that the 'objective' event that gets identified by a verb imposes rigid constraints on the verb's meaning potential, (ii) that the way syntactic frames constrain subject and complement roles is fully predictable from these roles' general characterization by the grammar and (iii) that the interaction of these two types of constraints determines the verb's range of syntactic frames, ungrammaticality 'falling out' when the various constraints conflict somehow.

Let me start by pointing out what I consider to be a general constraint on verbs' selecting syntactic frames. The basic cognitive process determining which syntactic frames a verb can fit into, seems to be one of semantic negotiation between what, conceptually speaking, the syntactic frame and the verb's own semantic frame bring in; thus, *give* can select a *to-* but not an *into-* phrase because the notion of goal (*to*) will, but that of container (*into*) will not, 'unify' with the recipient role brought in by *give*. What I see as curbing the unification process, is that a verb root has a "conceptually autonomous core" (Langacker (1991:291), here to be referred to as its skeletal meaning. That is, a verb root uniquely identifies an "individual event" (Croft 1991:165) and the 'objective' properties of this event impose constraints that must (at least in literal usage) be obeyed or else the verb root as such cannot be relied on to make the correct identification. A straightforward example consists in the verb *break* (to use a non-dative example). An event cannot be identified as a BREAKING event unless something separates into parts ('goes kaput'). If we use the verb intransitively, that is all the verb expresses. It can, of course, also select a transitive frame; in that case the construction describes a more elaborate event, which includes the external force responsible for the breaking, while leaving the skeletal meaning of *break* intact. A verb root, it is my claim, may only select syntactic frames that leave its skeletal meaning intact in the sense that they do not coerce the verb root itself into contributing a meaning that differs from its skeletal semantics (since otherwise the verb root itself would have to pair up with an event subtly different from the one it is designated to identify). In van der Leek (1995) I show that this condition explains why *break* cannot be used in the conative. That is, if one tried to interpret the meaning of the verb in **Sam broke at the bread* the way *kick* is used in *Sam kicked at the table* (which leaves it open whether or not Sam 'contacts' the table), this is impossible because (possible) lack of contact entails that there may be no breakage, contrary to what *break's* skeletal meaning requires. Nor is it possible to interpret *break* in the above sentence along the lines of *nibble* in *Sam nibbled at his sandwich*, where Sam is understood to direct himself at his sandwich in a bit-by-bit manner (one natural with *nibble*); to fit into this type of interpretation, *break* would have to be seen as signalling a bit-by-bit process, which it does not. Either way, then, usage of *break* in the conative coerces the verb root itself into contributing a meaning that it does not have of its own accord; the condition that the skeletal meaning should be left intact is, in other words, violated.

My second claim is that syntactic frames impose, independently of the way they are lexicalized, constraints of their own, constraints, that is, that are not individually stipulated but follow from general grammatical principles. Let me begin by looking at the monotransitive frame; this constrains our interpretation in a fixed, schematic way, without resorting to any 'prefab' semantic roles. Firstly, that is, the two roles are by definition complementary, in that they are conceptualized as together 'acting out' the whole of the event their verbal predicate identifies. Secondly, the subject is seen as, relatively speaking, 'in control', with the object playing the 'non-control' role; the rationale is that we need a general way of determining, across verbal predicates, how subjects and objects divide labour, there being no formal clues as to their respective semantic roles in the form of a preposition or semantic Case (cf. Langacker 1991:324 and Croft 1991:219 for similar characterisations of subject-object pairs). There is, then, a fixed subdivison of labour for each subject-object pair but it depends on the nature of the verbal predicate itself into what actual micro roles that subdivision of labour translates. Provided, then, that we know, through the frame-semantic meaning of a verb (its individual frame minimally portraying its skeletal meaning), what event it identifies, we can determine the exact roles of the subject and the object in terms of their hierarchically fixed relationship.

Before looking at syntactic frames involving more than one complement, I first have to mention a third claim that I propose to make, i.e., that there is an essential difference between the function of an NP ARGUMENT (both subjects and objects) and an NP in an OBLIQUE COMPLEMENT. The semantic role of the latter is, in my view, determined in terms of its preposition, and not, as is generally assumed, in terms of the verbal predicate, and the oblique complement as a whole does not function as an argument of the verb but as a subpredicate that pins down the verbal meaning more specifically. In what follows I will, therefore, reserve the term ARGUMENT for subject and object NPs only, while using, for convenience, the term COMPLEMENT as a cover term for both objects and obliques. In the case of a verb taking two NP arguments (a subject and an object) and a PP complement (a verbal subpredicate), we conceptualize the verb and the PP (despite their non-adjacency) as a complex two-place predicate, which thus provides slots for an NP object and an NP subject. The object and subject roles are, then, compositional, i.e., determined in terms of the complex V + PP predicate. In other words, *X gives Y to Z* instantiates a monotransitive frame, be it that its verbal predicate is complex rather than simple. That means we interpret X and Y as playing the complementary roles of 'entity giving to Z' and 'entity given to Z'. Notice, and this is crucial, that these role specifications themselves entail that Y moves to Z. That is, given the language user's knowledge of the (frame semantic) meaning of *give* and the preposition *to* and of the workings of the syntax, there is no need for the grammar to additionally stipulate *X causes Y to move to Z*. The same story holds, mutatis mutandis, for *X bakes Y for Z*; X and Y being interpreted as 'entity baking for Z' and 'entity baked for Z' respectively, there is no way that Y cannot be meant for Z. As for the ditransitive construction, this involves, clearly, three arguments, which, as a threesome, must act out the event identified by the verb, and each of the three roles will have to obey a fixed hierarchy if they are to be identifiable without recourse to abstract predicate argument structures stipulated by the grammar. Moreover, it is crucial, in view of the general system underlying subject-object relations proposed above, that both objects, each in their own way, can be seen as having a complementary role relative to the subject. The way I see this as achieved is as follows. The second object relates to the subject through the simple verb, its role being interpreted as described for monotransitive frames. As for the first object, I assume the second object and the simple verb to form a complex predicate (as sketched above for a simple verb and its oblique complement) and the first object relates to the subject through this complex verbal predicate. In other words, we interpret X, Y, and Z in *X gives/bakes Y Z* as 'entity giving/baking Z', 'entity given/baked Z' and 'entity given/baked' respectively.

In order to see what the above system is able to account for, two questions have to be tackled. Firstly, what enables us to get the interpretation of especially the first object role in the ditransitive right if we get no help from the grammar in the form of some schematic predicate argument structure? Secondly, what determines which verbs can occur in both a *to/for* frame and the ditransitive, only in the former or only in the latter? The two questions are, not surprisingly perhaps, interrelated. My answer to the second question, as already intimated before, is, that the possible range of syntactic frames depends on the skeletal meaning of the verb (and sometimes also on the contents of the arguments that are selected). To begin with the prototypical case, *give* (or *hand, pass* etc.),[1] this verb's semantic frame identifies a scene minimally involving three entities X, Y and Z, where X 'has' Y to start with but makes Z 'take' Y. This scene is compatible with a construal highlighting Y's being moved from (and by) X to Z, while backgrounding the 'taker' role of Z; the *to*-syntactic frame explicates this construal. The above scene is also compatible with a construal highlighting X's making Z take Y, backgrounding the motional aspect; the ditransitive frame codes this construal. Notice that neither syntactic frame coerces the verb into a meaning that it does not have to start with. Alternation is, in short, possible because the skeletal meaning of *give* is flexible enough to fit in with both construals, *give* alone coding a sense involving three arguments, while the *combination* of *give-to* codes the motional sense. Now consider ENVY-type verbs, which are essentially verbs of not-getting/giving (*envy, begrudge, spare* etc.), and which occur in the ditransitive but not in the *to*-variant (more about verbs that only occur in the *to*-variant, e.g., *donate*, later). Let *envy* serve as example. This verb evokes a scene that has no less than three entities X, Y and Z, Y having Z and X wanting to have Z. The ditransitive provides Z, Y and X with the roles of 'entity envied', 'entity envied Z' and 'entity envying /wanting to have Z'. The above frame clearly implies no motion from X to Y (if anything, the opposite), hence the *to*-variant construal is totally incompatible with the skeletal meaning of *envy*. Let me now look at verbs that, unlike GIVE-type verbs, "can result in a change of possession but do not necessarily do so" (Pinker:110), i.e., THROW-type verbs, and compare them with PUSH-type verbs; I will concentrate on *throw* and *push* themselves. These two verbs differ in that the former codes a definite change of position (due to laws of ballistic motion), whereas the latter implies "only an INDEFINITE change of position" (Dowty 1991:568). It is this difference which is responsible for *throw* being freely allowed to dativize (with one proviso, to be discussed later), and for *push* being only fully

---

[1] I also count *promise* as a variant of *give*, in that it simply expresses X giving Y a promise of Z, with Y playing the role of 'entity promised Z'. That Y will get Z if the promise is fulfilled, follows from the meaning of this verb, not from the role Y plays in the ditransitive. The same goes for *refuse, bequeath, permit* etc.

natural in the *to*-frame.[2] That is, in the ditransitive frame relevant to the verb types under discussion, the first object must, through its 'position', be able to identify where the second object moves to (or is located, in the case of non-motion verbs like *envy*); since the skeletal meaning of *push* does not include a definite position, usage of *push* in the ditransitive coerces this verb into expressing a definite change of position and as such violates the principle that skeletal meanings must be allowed to remain intact. Essentially the same story goes for alternation between the ditransitive and the *for*-variant, though here judgments seem to depend rather heavily on the choice of direct object (i.e. at the level where the semantic frames of the verb and the object 'merge', the combination having a skeletal meaning of its own, be it one that is more pragmatic than semantic in nature); thus, *bake a cake* is a complex predicate that of its own accord evokes the thought of a benefactive, whereas *create a work of art* definitely makes one think of an activity done for its own sake. This, it seems to me, explains why *Sam baked Sue a cake* is perfectly acceptable, while speakers reject *Sam created Sue a sculpture*.

To return to the first question asked above, it should be clear that in my view the first object in the ditransitive by definition expresses either a definite goal or a benefactive. However, that can be only part of the answer, since this does not explain why the ditransitive signals what I will call 'internal causation' and 'cooperation' on the part of the subject and first object respectively, whereas the prepositional variant is not subject to such constraints. It is my contention that these differences are a consequence of the syntactic differences between the two constructions, be it that the way they manifest themselves also depends on the lexical contents of ditransitive sentences. To realise what principles are at play, consider first a seemingly unrelated case of two other constructions that partly overlap in meaning while being subtly different as well, cf. *Celia's cheeks reddened* vs *Celia's cheeks became red*. As no doubt has been observed elsewhere, we can use the compound expression when the redness is due to some external cause (say, someone painting

---

[2]Green (1974:119) observes that, with respect to push-type verbs, "Class membership appears to vary from speaker to speaker". This observation should not, it seems to me, be seen as pointing to dialect differences (Pinker's conclusion), but simply to the fact that speakers, when judgments are asked for, are easily swayed towards accepting what they can make sense of even if the effect feels slightly forced. Speakers' intuitions appear, moreover, to be the only evidence. That is, it is an empirical fact that English as a language resists dativization of push-type verbs, as is clear from dictionary evidence, from factual non-occurrence of existing verbs of this type in the ditransitive and from there being no sign of productive ditransitive extension to novel verbs either.

Celia's cheeks red), whereas the simple verb *redden* is only appropriate if the cause is internal to Celia (the blood rising to her cheeks). For want of a better term, I will say that a subject is the internal cause for whatever event 'its' verb itself expresses, not necessarily for other elements that combine with this verb into a more complex predicate. When we apply this notion to e.g., *Sam threw the ball to Sue*, it follows that Sam is the internal cause for the throwing, but he need not have picked Sue as his goal; that is, the throwing may have gone wrong, the wind may have interfered etc. However, in *Sam threw Sue the ball*, each of the three arguments is directly involved in the throwing event. As a consequence, Sam is not only the internal cause for the ball getting thrown, but he must also have intended Sue to be the goal of the throwing. This, then, is a semantic consequence of the ditransitive syntax. Now notice that if a speaker chooses the ditransitive to communicate the above event, the implication is that he assumes Sam to have a reason for selecting Sue as the goal of his throwing the ball, i.e., that she does something with it (most likely that she catches it; hence the ungrammaticality of *Sam threw the tree the ball*). The cooperative constraint is, in other words, pragmatically implied by the 'internal cause' constraint, which itself is due to the ditransitive syntax. The cooperative constraint also explains why *donate* does not dativize; this verb expresses an act of charity, its goal by definition being some kind of institution, which, by its very nature, cannot cooperate. As far as *contribute* and *distribute* are concerned, these verbs presuppose multiple givers and multiple takers/recipients respectively, and this is essentially why these verbs can only select the prepositional frame: the ditransitive requires the roles of subject and first object to be complementary, but that is for both these verbs impossible because the 'multiple' aspect is only part of the subject role (*contribute*) or the first object role (*distribute*). In other words, the above three verbs are, in my view, not exceptional in their behaviour. The only verbs that are semantically exceptional, are the verbs *explain* and *say*; however, there is positive evidence for their exceptional status, cf. e.g., *Sam explained/said *(to) Sue what she should do* vs *Sam told (*to) Sue what she should do*. Data like these, then, will tell a language learner that these verbs do not dativize.

5 Conclusion

What I have argued in the above, is that the selection of the ditransitive and/or *to/for* frame by a verb (class) is not done on an arbitrary, but on a cognitively-principled basis. Pinker very strongly argues against this view when he states that "the *semantic* distinctions [playing a role in the selection] can be so specific to the speaker's particular language or dialect, and so poorly motivated by independent principles of cognitive organization, that equating linguistic semantic representations with the conceptual categories underlying non-linguistic thought is tantamount to a very strong and implausible Whorfian claim" (p. 357). I have, in fact, proposed such "independent principles of cognitive organization". In addition I have pointed out in note 2 that the argument of dialect differences does not have much of an empirical leg to stand on. I have furthermore given evidence that certain exceptions (e.g., *explain*) can be learned on the basis of positive evidence. That leaves me with Pinker's argument of language differences. Pinker is right in saying that it is untenable to claim full equation of semantic and conceptual categories: to a certain (though marginal) extent, individual languages make conventional choices. To give one example (Carla van Kampen, p.c.), the Dutch verb *telefoneren* 'telephone' does not dativize, whereas its English congener does. The reason is that Dutch gives a slightly different interpretation to this verb, which is evident from the fact that it only combines with the preposition *naar*, a preposition that expresses goal but purely in a spatial sense, contrary to *aan* (the Dutch 'dative' goal-preposition). English *to* covers both Dutch prepositions. There is, then, positive evidence in Dutch that *telefoneren* identifies a slightly different event than its English counterpart *telephone*. My conclusion is, then, that verb (classes) are choosy for cognitively-principled rather than arbitrary reasons. Baker's paradox, it seems to me, is based on a fallacy.

References

Croft, William. 1991. *Syntactic Categories and Grammatical Relations*. Chicago, The University of Chicago Press.

Dowty, David. 1991. Thematic Proto-roles and Argument Selection. *Language* 67:547-619.

Fillmore, Charles. 1985. Frames and the Semantics of Understanding. *Quaderni di Semantica* 6:222-253.

Goldberg, Adele. 1992. *Constructions: A Construction Grammar Approach to Argument Structure*. Doctoral dissertation, University of California at Berkeley.

Green, Georgia. 1974. *Semantics and Syntactic Regularity*. Bloomington, Indiana University Press.

Gropen, Jess et al. 1989. The Learnability and Acquisition of the Dative Alternation in English. *Language* 65:203-257.

Langacker, Ronald. *Foundations of Cognitive Grammar II*. Stanford, Stanford University Press.

van der Leek, Frederike. Conative Alternation in English. Ms., University of Amsterdam.

Pinker, Steven. 1989. *Learnability and Cognition. The Acquisition of Argument Structure*. Cambridge, Mass., The MIT Press.

Conceptual Manipulation and Semantic Distinction: The Case of Mandarin Postverbal *'De'*-Complements[1]

MEI-CHUN LIU
National Chiao Tung University

1. Introduction

Recent advances in cognitive semantics have made a central issue the conceptual organization of language (cf. Lakoff 1987; Langacker 1987,1991; Talmy 1991; Tsohatzidis 1990). It is shown that the way language is used interacts with the way human cognitive system works. And the diversity of linguistic coding often reflects the flexibility of conceptualization. Thus, the links between linguistic patterning and conceptual transfer is rather prevalent, as evidenced in a wealth of studies involving 'metaphor' (cf. Lakoff and Johnson 1981, Sweetser 1987, Claudi and Heine 1986, Goldberg 1992 Ch.3, Liu 1994, Huang 1994, etc.). While the important role of conceptualization has been established with regard to lexical-semantic changes and constructional associations, this paper attempts to present a case where manipulation of conceptual schema is the key to resolve semantic ambiguity.

In this paper, I examine the conceptual basis of one particular construction in Mandarin, the complex construction with a postverbal *de*-complement. It aims to characterize the conceptual distinctions among different uses of postverbal *de*-complement and their implication on interpretational constraints. By proposing distinct schemas and associating them with different verb-complement relations, this paper suggests that conceptual manipulation of event views (cf. Croft 1990) is the key to interpretational variation. It also draws inferences on the coding of discourse vs. semantic distinction in grammar.

[1] This paper has undergone several phases of reversion before it takes the final shape. I would like to thank Chu-ren Huang, Le-ning Liu, Adele Goldberg, and Susanna Cumming for their encouraging comments and helpful suggestions in the course of revision.

1.2   The Problem: Interpretational Variation

Mandarin complex constructions with a postverbal *de*-complement pose interesting problems for semantic representation. Though sharing the same grammatical marker *de*, the postverbal complements vary in their interpretation. They may describe three different 'aspects' of an event: the 'resulting state' of the event (a 'Resultative' use)[2], as shown in (1a), or the way the event is carried out (a 'Descriptive' use), as exemplified in (1b), or a 'degree evaluation' of the event (a 'Degree' use), as in (1c):

(1) Three distinct uses of postverbal *de*-complement

    a. Resultative:
    Laoshi ba ta nuer da de   [quan-tui-zi-hei].
    teacher BA 3p daughter beat DE whole-leg-purple-black
    'The teacher beat her daughter black and blue all over the legs.'

    b. Descriptive:
    Wang Siting ru jijei ban da de   [you-qiang-you-zhun].
    NAME like machine alike play DE also-strong-also-accurate
    'Like a machine, Wang Siting played (tennis) powerfully and
     accurately.'

    c. Degree:
    lei de   [bu-de-liao].
    tired DE seriously
    '(He's) extremely tired.'

While the above are clear cases for the specified reading, there are cases where more than one reading could be present, as illustrated in (2):

(2) Interpretational flexibility:

    a. Resultative or Descriptive:
    ta ba buxiugang caizhi de jimu wan de [chu-shen-ru-hua].
    3p BA stainless material NOM blocks play DE out-spirit-in-excellence

---

[2] Mandarin has another morphosyntactic category of resultatives, the Verb-Resultative Compounds, whose conceptual basis and categorial structure are studied in Liu to appear, 1994.

'He played stainless blocks super-skillfully.'
'He played stainless blocks to the point of being super-skillful.'

b. Descriptive or Degree
*gongzuo jinxing **de [xiangdang-shunli]***.
work proceed DE quite-smooth
'The work went pretty smoothly.'
'The progress of the work was good.'

c. Resultative or Degree
*ba shenghuo anpai **de [gen-hao]***.
BA living arrange DE   better
'to arrange life to make it better'
'to arrange life in better ways'

d. Resultative, Descriptive, or Degree
*mei tian   mang **de [yun-tou-zhuan-xiang]***.
everyday busy   DE   dizzy-head-turning-direction
'busy to the point of getting dizzy.'
'busy with a dizzy head.'
'extremely busy.'

The multiple uses and the potential ambiguity of the same surface form, as exemplified above, raises several theoretically interesting questions: what is the key to the interpretational variation? structural constraints? lexical distinctions? or discourse-pragmatic factors? Should the different interpretations be treated as deriving from different structures or maybe separate form-meaning pairs in the sense of constructional grammar (cf. Fillmore, Kay, and O'Connor 1990)? Or should they be considered a case of lexically-derived ambiguity? What are the crucial cues speakers of Mandarin rely on in differentiating these possible meanings?

1.3 The data

Hundreds of occurrences of the target constructions were extracted from a large corpus of written Mandarin which is developed by the CKIP group at Academia Sinica in Taiwan. This corpus contains mainly newspaper articles and has over 20 million Chinese characters. The analysis is mainly based on these 'actually occurring' examples.

1.4 The Proposal

The semantic distinction of postverbal *de*-complements has been studied quite extensively in the literature. In their attempt to distinguish the different readings, most previous work (cf. Huang 1988, 1991; Tang 1992a & b; Chang 1993) took a formal approach and focused on syntactic properties, such as the grammatical status of the V's (Which is the main verb?), clausal structure (coordinate or subordinate?), and the grammatical role of the arguments. Also frequently studied are lexical semantic restrictions on the main verb and the complement (Tang 1992a & b; Chang 1993). Little attention has been paid to the fundamentals of the semantic ambiguity that often arises when interpreting these constructions.

As will be clear below, many of the proposed lexical restrictions do not hold when tested against the large corpus. A pure lexical solution would be too costly if it involves adding specifications to the head of the complement just to match its use in the postverbal de-construction.

The ambiguity also poses a challenge to the theory of *constructional grammar* (Fillmore 1990; Goldberg 1992, 1995). All the examples in (2) demonstrate that the same surface 'form' with the same lexical instantiations may be associated with different 'meanings'. Are there three 'constructions' defined as a *form-meaning pair* or just one? While the problem is potentially solvable within the current constructional framework[3], I would like to direct attention to an alternative approach.

In view of the relatively free distribution of lexical types in either the V or post-V positions (see 3.1) and the absence of observable differences in form, this paper proposes that an intermediate level of conceptual representation be allowed with regard to the relation between the V and the complement. The three readings are to be viewed as deriving from three distinct conceptual schemas, each with its own defining features/constraints. As long as a verb and its complement may be conceptualized into a specific

---

[3] Chu-ren Huang has suggested that since 'construction' stands for the mapping between form and meaning. A strong version of CG could allow different meanings to be mapped with the same form.

schema, they are then taking the corresponding reading.   This paper maintains that the interpretational ambiguity is neither structural nor lexical, but pertaining to conceptual configuration of the semantic relation between the V and the complement.

2.   Conceptual Distinction of Postverbal Complementation

In this section, I will characterize the different readings with a representation of their conceptual structures and defining features, which in term provide explanation for the potential interpretational ambiguity.

2.1 Schematic Representation

The different uses of the postverbal complement essentially highlight three unique semantic relations between the V and the Complement, which can be schematically represented as follows:

(4) Conceptual schemas associated with different readings

a. Resultative:
   Schema A: The Complement expresses a resulting state R and the V
   takes temporal precedence over R.

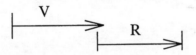

(cf. Goldberg 1992, S.M. Chang 1993)

b. Descriptive:
   Schema B: The Complement expresses a simultaneous characterizing
   Feature that applies (ideally) to every point of the V-Path.

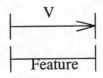

c. Degree

Schema C:The Complement expresses a **scalarly construable** value, as a measure of the particular instance of the V:

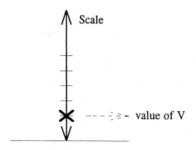

Schema A is a representation of the Resultative reading. It specifies that the beginning of the action coded by the V has to be temporally prior to the beginning of the resulting state (R) coded by the Complement.   Schema B represents the Descriptive relation, where the Complement expresses a simultaneous characterizing feature that applies (ideally) to every point of the V-path.   Schema C represents the Degree use, where the Complement expresses a value on a given scale, implicated by the semantics of the Complement itself, against which the particular instance of the V is measured.

2.2 Defining characteristics

The three schemas are distinguished mainly in terms of two factors: the temporal alignment between the V and the Complement and the inferential character of the Complement.

The key to the distinction between the first two schemas (Resultative vs. Descriptive) is a temporal one. In the resultative schema (A), the complement follows the occurrence of the V, while in the descriptive schema

(B), the complement extends simultaneously along the course of the V.   On the other hand, the degree schema (C) differs from A and B in that while the first two both specify a temporal relation, C describes a non-temporal or atemporal relation.

Another defining factor of the three schemas is the inferential function of the Complement.   No matter what the lexical specification of the Complement may be, a Resultative Complement is considered to be stative or eventive; a Descriptive Complement has to be attributive of verbs; and a degree complement has to be scalar.   The distinctions are summarized below:

(5) Conceptual features of the three schemas:

	Resultative	Descriptive	Degree
Timing Relation bet. V and C	mutually excluded	simultaneous	N/A
Inferential Function of C	eventive/ stative	attributive of V	scalar

3. Implications of the Schematic Distinction

The proposed analysis of the conceptual distinction among different uses of postverbal *de*-complements bear significant implications on several issues, as discussed respectively in the following subsections.

3.1 Conceptual Manipulation vs. Lexical Semantic Constraints

As mentioned before, previous studies tend to associate the interpretational distinction with lexical selection of the V and the complement.   For example, Tang (1992a:38) indicates that descriptive reading is limited to actional dynamic verbs, and Chang (1993:54) observes that stative adjectives taking adjectival complement have a descriptive reading, while actional verbs and mental adjectives taking event complement have a resultative reading.   However, these observations do not hold when tested against the corpus data.   As the above proposed analysis suggests, the interpretational distinction resides mainly on the conceptual schema with different relational frames of the V and Complement.   This analysis will ensure that as long as a V and its complement can be conceptualized into a particular schematic relation, it may take the represented reading.   As a consequence, conceptual manipulation of the relational frame may override, to a significant extent, lexical specification and selectional preferences of the V and the Complement. And this is indeed confirmed by the corpus data: V's of various semantic types may all take the three readings, as illustrated below:

(6) Active V :   *chi* 'to eat'
    a. Resultative: *chi de   [du-man-chang-fei].*
                         eat DE belly-full-intestine-fat
                         'eat to the point of getting a big belly.'
    b. Descriptive: *chi de [jinjin-you-wei]*
                         eatDE saliva-have-taste
                         'eat with relish'
    c. Degree: *chi de [zui-anjing]*
                         eat DE most-quiet
                         'eat most quietly

(7) Stative V: *mang*   'be busy'
    a. Resultative: *mang de [bing-dao] le.*
                         busy DE sick-fall LE
                         'busy to the point of getting sick'
    b. Descriptive: *mang de [hu-li-hu-tu].*
                         busy DE muddleheaded
                         'mindlessly busy'
    c. Degree: *mang de [bu-de-liao].*
                         busy DE seriously
                         'extremely busy.'

(8)   Perceptual V: *ting*   'to listen'
    a. Resultative: *ting de [yi-lian-tie-qing].*
                         listen DE one-face-iron-green
                         'listened to the point of turning livid'
    b. Descriptive: *ting de [ju-jing-hui-shen]*
                         listen DE assemble-energy-gather-vigor
                         'listened attentively'
    c. Degree: *ting de [zui- renzhen].*
                       listen DE most-serious
                         'listened most carefully'

(9) Attributive V: *pang* 'be fat'
    a. Resultative: *pang de [zou-bu-dong].*
                        fat DE walk-NEG-move
                        'fat to the point of not being able to walk'
    b. Descriptive: *pang de [xiang zhu].*
                        fat DE like-pig
                        'fat like a big'
    c. Degree: *pang de [li-pu].*
                        fat de away-manual
                        'unbelievably fat'

With regard to the selection of the Complement, it is also found that the inherent meaning of the complement has little effect on their post-verbal use, except for satisfying the inferential requirement of each schema. As shown in (6)-(9) above, contrary to previous claims, resultative complements may not all be eventive: e.g., in (8a), the non-eventive *yi-lian-tie-qing* 'red on face' marks a result. And descriptive complements may not all be adjectival: e.g., in (8b), the eventive *ju-jing-hui-shen* 'to concentrate one's attention' marks a descriptive feature. What is crucial here is not the inherent meaning of the complement as specified in the lexicon, but the flexible conceptual manipulation of the complement in terms of its inferential function in the schema. As a further illustration, in the example below, the complement *yita-hutu* is lexically stative ('a complete mess or awful state), but is taken as denoting a scalar value of the predicate, due to the imposing of the degree schema and metaphorical transfer of a state to a scalar value:

    (10)   *ta **ziqian** de [**yita-hutu**].*
              3p inexperienced DE a-complete-mess
              'He was extremely young and inexperienced.'

3.2 Source of Interpretational Ambiguity

Potential ambiguity arises when a V + '*de*'-Complement can be conceptualized into more than one schema. For instance, when a Complement, be it lexically eventive or stative, can be perceived as either following or co-occurring with the V-event, it may then be ambiguous between resultative and descriptive reading. The following table summarizes the grounds for possible interpretational ambiguities:

(11) Ambiguity and Conceptual Flexibility

Ambiguity: Possible interpretation	Condition: Complement may be viewed as:
Resultative or Descriptive	Either following or accompanying the occurrence of V
Resultative or Degree	Either eventive/stative or scalar
Descriptive or Degree	Either attributive or scalar
Res., Des., or Deg.	Eventive/stative, attributive or scalar

To the extent that a Complement may fit in all three schemas, capable of denoting an event,   an attribute of V, or a scalar value,   the surface form is potentially three-way ambiguous.

3.3 Co-occurrence Pattern with Resultative

Constructions with a disposal coverb -*ba* and a postverbal *de*-complement have predominantly a resultative reading: only 2 out of   242 instances from the CKIP corpus have a descriptive-manner complement. This observation confirms Cheng (1988)'s analysis that -*ba* only occurs with a *delimited* event (i.e., with a definite temporal endpoint), which complies exactly with the schematic representation of a resultative relation (R as temporal endpoint).

By proposing conceptual schemas as the grounds for interpretational variation, this study allows a unified account of potential ambiguity as well as co-occurrence restrictions.

4.   Discourse Function, Surface Paradigm and Semantic Distinction

The above analysis might lead to a puzzling question: why is it that all three semantically-distinct postverbal complements are coded with the same marker *de* in Mandarin?   The Mandarin grammar seems to be insensitive to the three types of complementation. Nevertheless, such semantic differences are   grammatically differentiated in other languages such as Cantonese and Taiwanese.   In these two languages, the   resultative use is set apart from the other two uses.   The Resultative Complement is introduced by a different marker, *dou* in Cantonese, *ka*   in Taiwanese.   And both markers derive from a verb of spatial motion 'to arrive/go to'. This reveals that in Taiwanese and Cantonese, the postverbal resultative signaling 'a change of state' is compared to a caused-motion signaling 'a change of location' (Goldberg 1992, 1995). In view of the conceptual features proposed, the Resultative Complement, schematically a temporal ending state, is overtly compared to a spatial endpoint, and formally differentiated from the Descriptive and Degree relations, which might be deemed incompatible with spatial-motional conceptualization[4].

The fact that in Mandarin postverbal complementation is uniformly marked by *de*, a completely grammaticalized element, seems to suggest two things:

First, in terms of the correlation between grammar and discourse, all three types of complements may be said to serve the same discourse function, namely, to report an additional 'aspect' to view the event (denoted by V). And it appear to be this level of functioning that the Mandarin grammar is sensitive to, as also suggested in other studies that Mandarin is discourse oriented (Huang 1984), or observing general pragmatic principles (Tai 1985, 1989).

Secondly, in terms of 'competing motivations' (Du Bois 1985), when discourse patterning and semantic differentiation do not go hand in hand in Mandarin, the pressure of discourse forces seems to win over that of semantics-to-grammar differentiation in shaping the surface paradigm.

5. Conclusion

Adopting a different approach from structural and lexical oriented work, this paper provides clear cognitive-semantic criteria for differentiating the resultative, descriptive, and degree readings of the postverbal de-Complement . It points out the crucial, conceptually-based distinction regarding the relation between the V and the Complement, and shows that manipulation of the conceptual schemas is the key to interpretational

---

[4] It is conceivable that the Descriptive and Degree Complements are cognitively more related, as stative modifers can in most cases implicate a scalar value. This may be why they share the same marker even in Taiwanese and Cantonese.

variation. It ultimately argues that semantic interpretation has to do with conceptualization pertaining to event views.

References

Amores-Carredano, Gabriel. 1994. Resultative and Depictive Constructions in English: an LFG-based approach for machine translation. Unpublished network-circulating paper.

Chang, Claire Hsun-huei. 1993. Complex Stative Construction: Resultative or Descriptive. In *Proceedings of the 1st Pacific Asia Conference on Formal & Computational Linguistics* (PACfoCoL I), 50-61. The Computational Linguistics Society of ROC.

Chang, Shen Min. 1993. V+Qi(-Lai) Compounds in Mandarin Chinese. In *Proceedings of the 1st Pacific Asia Conference on Formal & Computational Linguistics*, 62-80. The Computational Linguistics Society of ROC.

Cheng, Lisa L-S. 1988. Aspects of the *Ba*-Construction. In Carol Tenny, ed., *Studies in Generative Approaches to Aspect*, MIT Lexical Project Working Paper 24. Cambridge: MIT Press.

Claudi, Ulrike, and Bernd Heine. 1986. On the Metaphorical Base of Grammar. *Studies in Language* 10:297-35.

Croft, William. 1990. Possible Verbs and the Structure of Events. In S. Tsohatzidis, ed., *Meanings and Prototypes: Studies in Linguistic Categorization*. London/New York: Routledge.

Du Bois, John W. 1985. Competing Motivations. In John Haiman, ed., Iconicity in Syntax, 343-365. Amsterdam: John Benjamins.

Fillmore, Charles J., Paul Kay, and Catherine O'Connor. 1988. Regularity and Idiomaticity in Grammatical Constructions: The Case of Let Alone. *Language* 64:501-538.

Goldberg, Adele. 1992. *Argument Structure Construction*. UC Berkeley Dissertation.

------. 1995. *Constructions: A Construction Grammar Appraoch to Argument Structure*. Chicago: The University of Chicago Press.

Grimshaw, Jane. 1990. *Argument Structure*. Cambridge: The MIT Press.

Huang, Chu-ren. 1994. Metaphor, Metaphorical Extension, and Grammaticalization: A Study of Mandarin Chinese -Qilai. Paper presented at the Conference on Conceptual Structure, Discourse, and Language, UCSD (Also included in this Volume).

Huang, James. 1984. On the Distribution and Reference of Empty Pronouns. *Linguistic Inquiry* 15: 531-574.

------. 1988. 'Wo pao de kuai' in Chinese Phrase Structure. *Language* 64:273-311.

------. 1991. Complex Predicate in Control. In Larson and Higginbotham, eds., *Control Theory*. Dordrecht: Kluwer Academic.

Lakoff, George. 1987. *Woman, Fire, and Dangerous Things: What Categories Reveal about the Mind*. Chicago: Univ. of Chicago Press.

Langacker, R. 1987. *Foundations of Cognitive Grammar*, vol. 1. Stanford: Stanford U Press.

------. 1991. *Foundations of Cognitive Grammar*, Vol. 2. Stanford: Stanford University Press.

Levin, Beth. 1993. *Verb Classes and Alternation*. Chicago: U of Chicago Press.

Li, Charles, and Sandra Thompson. 1981. *Mandarin Chinese: a Functional Reference Grammar*. Berkeley: Univ. of California Press.

Liu, Mei-chun. To appear. Conceptual Basis and Categorial Structure: A Study of Mandarin V-R Compounds as a Radial Category. *Chinese Languages and Linguistics 4*.

------. 1994. Semantic Schema and Metaphorical Extension: A study of the Mandarin V-R Compounds as a Radial Category. In *Proceedings of the 4th International Symposium on Chinese Languages and*

Linguistics, 462-473. Taipei: Academia Sinica.

Sweetser, Eve Eliot. 1987. Metaphorical Models of Thought and Speech: a Comparison of Historical Directions and Metaphorical Mappings in the two Domains. *Berkeley Linguistics Society* 13: 446-459.

Tai, James H-Y. 1985. Temporal Sequence and Chinese Word Order. In John Haiman, ed., *Iconicity in Syntax*, 49-72. Amsterdam: Benjamins.

------. 1989. *Functionalism and Chinese Grammar.* Chinese Language Teachers Association, Monograph Series No. 1.

Talmy, Leonard. 1991. Path to Realization: a Typology of Event Conflation. *Berkeley Linguistics Society* 17: 480-519.

Tang, Ting-Chi. 1992a. Hanyu dongcizu buyu de yufa jiegou yu yuyi gongneng: Beijing hua yu Minnan hua de bijiao fenxi [The Syntax and Semantics of VP Complements in Chinese: a Comparative Study of Mandarin and Southern Min]. In Tang Ting-Chi ed., *Studies on Chinese Morphology and Syntax 4*, 1-93. Taipei: Student Book Co., Ltd.

------. 1992b. The syntax and semantics of resultative complements in Chinese. In Tang Ting-Chi ed., *Studies on Chinese Morphology and Syntax 4*, 165-204. Taipei: Student Book Co., Ltd.

Tsohatzidis, Savas L. ed. 1990. *Meaning and Prototypes: Studies in Linguistic Categorization.* London/New York: Routledge.

Schematic Representations of Discourse Structure

JUNE LUCHJENBROERS
Hong Kong Polytechnic University

1   Introduction

This paper is about cognitive structures and linguistic phenomena that enable inference generation and mappings of on-line information with earlier discourse, whether that information be stated or inferred. The approach taken is grounded in a cognitive approach to information processing, of which linguistic information is considered a subpart. In particular, *Schema Theory* (e.g., Mandler 1985)[1] and *Mental Space Theory* (Fauconnier 1985) are the theoretical perspectives embraced in this research, which makes use of natural discourse - albeit produced in a specific discourse situation. The data are the official transcripts of a six-day Supreme Court murder trial held in Melbourne Australia, encompassing 33 witness testimonies.

A number of assumptions are brought to this study. In particular I presume an interplay between hearers searching for speaker-intended inferences, and speakers structuring the speech-stream to facilitate that search. This then places the responsibility for communicative success on both (all) discourse participants, and presumes that speakers can evaluate what kinds of information are needed for hearer-comprehension, to be able to structure their output accordingly. For this I turn to the (somewhat less than popular) theoretical construct, *mutual ground* (Clark & Carlson 1982). The global process of mutual ground construction is seen as a conceptual process that involves building a schematic representation of the crime narrative being unfolded to the Jury. Such an approach is essential if theorists are to account for the Jurors' task of assimilating all the information presented to them across an entire trial.

Hence, the objects of investigation are the linguistic cues that speakers give hearers about how and where to attach on-line information into the hearer's expected conceptual structure of the body of discourse information. In this paper I will discuss the distribution of Given vs. New information,

---

[1] See also *Prototype* theory -- Rosch 1973, 1977.

347

and the '*x* prep *y*' (head+postmodifier) pattern that serves to both focus new or noteworthy information and anchor that information to the crime narrative being unfolded to the Jury. Ultimately it is argued that specific linguistic patterns function as explicit instructions to hearers about how to integrate on-line information with their presumed existing knowledge representations of discourse information.

2   Mutual Ground / Schema Theory

Mutual ground has been dealt with by a number of discourse and pragmatic theories; although, not always favourably. It has also been formulated as *mutual knowledge, mutual beliefs*, and the somewhat less strong form of *common ground* (cf. Clark & Carlson 1982; Clark & Schaeffer 1987; and refuted in Sperber & Wilson 1982, 1986). Various researchers have grappled with this notion because explanations of the flow of discourse need some concession to those assumptions speakers must be making about the knowledge hearers bring to discourse.

For example, the communication process in a courtroom rests decidedly on assumptions made about what others are expected to know, or not know. As Jurors are the ones who derive the verdict, it is important that they receive a maximally coherent portrayal of the events of the crime they are to decide over. Hence, each subsequent barrister' contribution systematically adds to a mental representation of the trial Jurors are expected to be creating (cf. Luchjenbroers 1990, 1993). In effect, Jurors start with no knowledge of the crime narrative they are to construct during the trial, and come closest to a 'blank-slate' onset which makes this data ideal for observing the process of mutual ground construction.[2]

I take the perspective that narrative construction involves the formation of some kind of *schema* (or *Mental Model* - cf. Johnson-Laird 1980), to accommodate incoming information into a coherent single representation of the crime narrative. Like Schema Theory, which holds that people generalize across similar events to derive a single generalized (or schematized) representation of those events, Jurors would generalize across similar inputs to construct a single template of narrated events (to the best of their abilities).[3]   This schematic approach does not require that all Jurors have exactly the same representations of the discourse information before them; only that they have the same kinds of information within their individual representations (derived from the input). In effect, this approach focuses on what is similar across individuals' conceptual representations, instead of focusing on how they may differ (which could be endless).

---

[2] It may also be argued that courtroom talk is a highly atypical form of discourse, and it therefore remains to be seen to what extent the findings from this setting also hold across other discourse types (Chafe, p.c.).

[3] It remains to be established how good Jurors actually are at performing this task.

The issue then to be addressed is how barristers might exercise some control over the process of information integration that takes place in the hearers' cognitive space, which is arguably the object of the proceedings. In order to establish how barristers might direct Jurors in the formulation of their schematic representations of the crime narrative put before them, I have analyzed barrister contributions in terms of a set of functional characteristics, including (i) the degree of given or newness of information in sentential units, and (ii) spatial characteristics. In this paper I will discuss the former.[4]

3   Degrees of Given and Newness

In the analyses performed on this data, each phrasal unit of each main clause was coded according to the categories given in (1), as a measure of the degree of givenness of information contained in that phrase. As the data-set includes an entire trial, information could be reliably categorized into the following categories, on the basis of whether information had been previously mentioned, or how recently that information had been mentioned.

Discourse in this setting takes place between a series of two persons who have been through most (if not all) the issues before, for the benefit of a third party (the Jury); hence, the notions of *new* and *accessible* information are somewhat fuzzy. Therefore, the category *new Information* includes the first mention of information to the Jury (the real hearers); while *new&given information* includes that which is new to a barrister-witness interaction but not to the Jury - i.e., information previously presented during an earlier testimony. *Given information* is information that is repeated across consecutive contributions; while *accessible information* includes information stated earlier during a single barrister-witness interaction, but is further removed than the previous barrister contribution. *Inferable information* is semantically related to information previously offered during a single barrister-witness testimony. The five categories are intended to reflect increasing degrees of givenness, from 1 to 5.

(1) *New information* = new information to the Jury (i.e., first mention during the trial)

New & Given Info. = (i) a phrase/ clause that contains a new element in addition to already stated information; or
      (ii) information that is new to the current testimony (but not new to the Jury)

Inferable info. = semantically related to reviously stated information.
Accessible info. = previously stated information (a single testimony)
Given information = information stated in the previous contribution.

---

[4] The term *contribution* is used somewhat specifically here, and is not synonymous with either *turn* or *sentence*; instead these are most closely related to main clauses - e.g., *And now I want to ask you, What was his name?* would constitute two contributions: the first is an instruction, *and now I want to ask you*, and the second, *What was his name*, is a wh-question.

The data-set for this study encompasses a total of 11,167 phrases. The categorization of phrasal units includes the syntact categories: Subject, Verb Phrase (Predicate), Object, and Adjunct. As only main clauses were broken down into phrasal units, subordinate clauses were treated as phrasal units - e.g., (2) is broken down into 4 phrasal elements. The inclusion of *predicate* as a syntactic category is to accommodate those verb phrases that are not verbal (i.e., nominal predicates), and those I have treated as 'complex VPs' - e.g., *want to give* in (3) is treated as a single VP, as is the VP in (4), *may have given*.[5]

(2)   *(When you went there), did (you) (see) (the accussed)?*
       Adjunct   subj verb   object

(3)   *I want to give him flowers.*

(4)   *I may have given him flowers.*

The results in Table 1 reveal the distributions of each of the five degrees of givenness across the four major syntactic categories (all given in their canonical positions) and across adjuncts which were split according their actual placements (nominal and verbal predicates are not distinguised in this table).

In total, only 23.1% of all phrasal information uttered is completely given information to the discourse space (i.e., is repeated across turns), but also only 20.9% is completely new (i.e., first mention during the trial). Firstly, the wave-distribution of new information (given in solid black) shows that although new information predominates in verb/post-verb region of contributions, it also occurs in every other syntactic position. Secondly, the distributions of given and accessible information (at the top of each column) illustrate that while highly given information clearly favours subject position (60% given and 30% accessible, but only 4% new), it very definitely is not confined to it.

These results support a popular view that subjects are primary candidates for conveying the topic of conversation which is generally given information (cf. Keenan 1976, Givón 1984; Chafe 1994). Similarly, van Oosten (1986) argues that criteria such as given information, *aboutness* (or *theme*), and *focus* together with the semantic notion of *agent*, are prototypical features of subjects that together organize around it. This ordering of functional units that places previously known information early in a sentential string, would facilitate the conceptual process of grounding on-line information into a developing representation of discourse. In effect, it makes sense that grounding mechanisms should occur early in contributions, as that would enable the user's attention systems to find in conceptual space what is talked about, before adding the new or noteworthy

---

[5] This is in contrast with standard grammars that would treat infinitive constructions as two separate clauses: S1=*I want*; and S2=(*I*) *give him flowers*.

information to that element. However, the distributions illustrated in Table 1 also show that much reference to given and accessible information occurs later in sentential strings - i.e., 46.2% of objects contain given and accessible information, while across adjuncts the proportions are between 37% (initial adjuncts) and 43% (final adjuncts). Hence, givenness is also prevalent toward the end of utterances where grounding would not be expected.

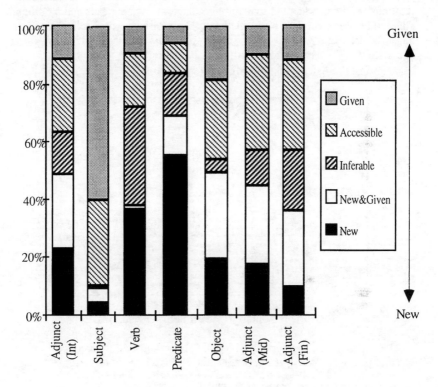

TABLE 1. Sentence Function BY Degree of Newness.

Courtroom discourse is a highly goal-directed discourse and so it ought be assumed that all information has a purpose. I put forward the view that such grounding references toward the end of strings function as further instructions to hearers about how to integrate on-line information into their developing conceptual structure of the trial. Because I assume that there is an interplay between hearers choosing focal information from the speech-stream, and speakers making that information accessible, the analyst needs to isolate those linguistic mechanisms by which this claim could be true. The linguistic pattern that I've isolated in my work is called the head + post-modifier or 'x prep y' pattern.

4   'x prep y' (Head + postmodifier) Pattern

The 'x prep y' pattern includes syntactic elements and the phrases or clauses that act as modifiers of those elements. In all cases, the y component is a postmodifier that holds a dependency relation to the x element. Dependency relations are most evident in standard tree-diagrams where heads and modifiers share that same mother node in the tree. Similarly, this relationship is captured in Figure 1. It is my claim that this syntactic structure both specifies what is new or noteworthy and points to that information expected to be part of the listener's knowledge representation.[6]

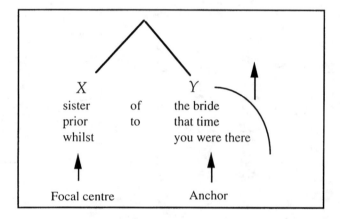

FIGURE 1. 'x prep y': Head-modifier relations.

For example, the utterance given in (5) contains two (embedded) 'x prep y' patterns: *a girlfriend of the deceased*, and *the deceased in this matter*.

(5)   *and were you in 1986 a girlfriend of the deceased in this matter?*

a girlfriend (Head)	*of*	*the deceased* (Modifier)
the deceased (Head)	*in*	*this matter* (Modifier)

Hence, the y modifier component identifies the relevant node in the developing discourse structure to which on-line testimony is to be attached,

---

[6] Patterns like: *when you were there* were included as 'x prep y' patterns as they were seen to work in the same way - i.e., the y component (a declarative phrase/clause) points to either given or presupposed information (= anchor to earlier discourse information); while the head defines the spatial configuration of that reaccessed discourse information.

and the x head component is the focal centre which adds new or noteworthy information to the reaccessed concept in the hearer's representation of the crime narrative (cf. 'the figure' against the 'the ground' - Langacker 1987, 1991).[7] Example (5) - illustrated in Figure 2 - shows how modifiers relate a quality or property x to an existing element in the developing schema of discourse, referred to in y.

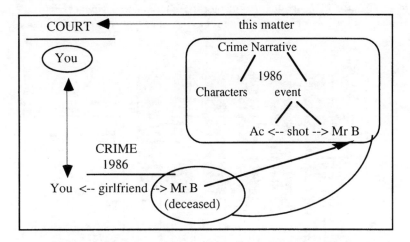

FIGURE 2. Adding information to given knowledge structures.

In example (5), the immediate predicate, *a girlfriend*, is the focal head of the 'x prep y' pattern *a girlfriend of the deceased*, and *the deceased* anchors that structure to the developing narrative; that is, at this point in the discourse all hearers know about the deceased, but not that this witness was his girlfriend. Hence, the property *girlfriend* is attributed to the accessible entity *the deceased, Mr B*, which is retrievable from prior discourse. Similarly, *the deceased* is further anchored by the prepositional phrase *in this matter.* This places *the death of Mr B* in the entire crime narrative of the trial. In effect, the second y component *this matter* serves to anchor the events of the crime narrative into the here-and-now, which reminds all on-lookers of why they are in court.

The kind of rippling out of increased givenness of information (or increased grounding references) from the main clause nucleus elements - as evidenced by these multiply embedded 'x prep y' patterns - is compatible with the distributions shown earlier in Table 1, insofar as new information was shown to predominate in the verb/predicate region of main clauses, and a

---

[7] The data set of 3701 contributions (and 11,167 phrases) revealed a total of 6388 'x prep y' patterns (2543 occurred in non-verbal constructions).

relatively high proportion of final sentential elements were shown to convey given and accessible information.

To further support the validity of the 'x prep y' pattern as a reliable grounding instruction to hearers, heads and modifiers were also compared in terms of the degree of newness hierarchy offered earlier - see Table 2 (and Table 3 in Appendix).[8] These results show that in general modifiers are more given than their heads. The extent of variation from the norm is (in general) only 11%, while 27% of modifiers have equal newness with their heads, and 62% of all modifiers having a lessor degree of newness

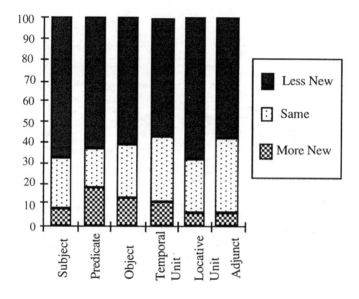

TABLE 2. 'x prep y': Heads & Modifiers BY Degree of Newness

---

[8] These tables only show the distributions across non-verbal 'x prep y' patterns. The results for verbal patterns is of course less strong, as would be predicted by the relatively high incidence of new (and new&given) information conveyed by sentence objects (21% new and 29% new&given = 50% to some extent new). The results for these patterns are: Verb + PP: 31.7% modifiers are more new; 31% same degree of newness; and 37.3% of modifiers are less new than their heads; VP + Object: 55.6% modifiers are more new; 28.7% same degree of newness; and 15.7% of modifiers are less new than their heads.

than their heads.[9] Furthermore, this likelihood is much greater for both subjects (sentence initial) and the more peripheral elements (i.e., adjuncts) that may also occur sentence finally.[10]

Hence, this is a structure of 'grounding in reverse' where the anchor to foregone discourse follows the new or noteworthy element. In this way, this (often cross-phrasal) structure provides explicit instructions about how to integrate on-line information into a developing (schematic) representation of discourse information.

5 Wider concerns (Topic-based computational models)

The result of this argument is that the anchoring function is far more pervasive than a topic-based approach to discourse processing would predict or achieve. This has direct implications for computational approaches to discourse (e.g., Polanyi 1988; Grosz 1986; Allen 1987), which process information from left-to-right as is compatible with a subject=topic approach to discourse information - i.e., with each speaker contribution, the hearer will identify the topic and attach all other information to that reaccessed node. As a consequence, a major problem for these approaches is that incoming information is only attachable to an open right-most node on the tree; hence preventing backtracking to suspended topics and also preventing mappings to other related issues raised in an utterance. Such an approach is convenient for two-dimensional, linear representations, but cannot cope with general discourse situations where multiple narrated actions are performed simultaneously.

For example, (6) - illustrated in figure 3 - shows that a single utterance may contain any number of references to elements already known to discourse participants. In this example, the modifier elements of each 'x prep y' pattern (listed under (6)) had been given in earlier discourse. This

---

[9] Because analysis did not separate first from subsequent 'x prep y' patterns in multiple embedded strings, the statistics is weaker than it otherwise could have been. For example, in a string like *girlfriend of the deceased in this matter*, the accessible modifier of the first pattern (*the deceased*) is also the head of the subsequent pattern (*deceased in this matter*); therefore, even though the difference in degree of newness is borne out in the first pattern, it is not true of the second. Hence, counting all patterns in whatever position has diluted the statistics.

[10] The remaining 11% is very interesting and is dealt with in another paper (Luchjenbroers 1995, in submission). Essentially the tactic of putting new or noteworthy information into a non-focal (modifier) position enables speakers to 'smuggle' information into discourse. In my trial data this was shown to be potentially ominous - e.g., when a witness was asked about the accused (who was on trial for shooting a person to death), *Did he tell you of his love of duckshooting?*

phenomenon is not easily captured by topic-based approaches that attribute all incoming information to the topic (i.e., right-most) node.

(6)   *Now, was anything said to you during this interchange about the security gates or the parking of the car in the courtyard area, or to Mr B at the time?*   [W2E:114]

- *during*		*this interchange*	HPP
- *(said)*	*about*	*the security gates*	VPP
- *(said)*	*about*	*the parking ...*	VPP
- *the parking*	*of*	*the car*	HPP
- *the parking*	*in*	*the courtyard area*	HPP

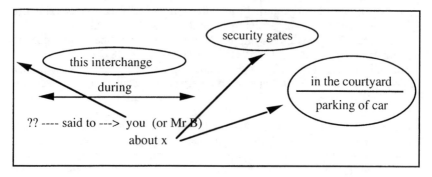

FIGURE 3. Interconnectedness within single contributions.

Although the above could be represented in tree fashion with subsequent modifiers pointing to higher points in the tree, the anchoring phrases designate different (albeit related) points in physical space and may serve to create links in discourse and schematic structure where they previously had not been. As a result, anchoring structures are not necessarily relevant a sentence level, but rather function at the more local phrasal (and cross-phrasal) level.

6   Conclusions

In conclusion, the results of this study show the '*x* prep *y*' pattern to encompass both the means to locate an earlier point in discourse and give some new or noteworthy information about that reaccessed point. At the introduction of each new witness and each discourse topic (i.e., who/what each discourse participant is talking about), Jurors must decide where to integrate such information into their developing schema of the crime narrative. Hence, they must search in memory for those parts of their developing crime narrative to attach on-line testimony. To this end, the '*x* prep *y*' pattern functions as a very specific instruction to hearers about where to attach on-line focused information into their developing schematic representation, and how to link already presented information together; hence, also providing speakers with some measure of control over the process of mutual ground construction. Although the data for these analyses was taken from a very rigid discourse type, it seems to me unlikely that these strategies would only be true of courtroom discourse. However, future studies on other kinds of discourse data are needed to establish the generalizability of these findings to other forms of discourse.

Acknowledgements:
The research drawn upon in this paper was supported by an Australian Postgraduate Research Grant with La Trobe University, Australia. Many thanks to: Edith Bavin (PhD supervisor); Aaron Cicourel and Gilles Fauconnier for their insights during my stay at CogSci UCSD in 1991; and Eve Sweetser, Leslie Stirling (dissertation examiners), Adele Goldberg and Wallace Chafe for their helpful comments on my work. Thanks also to the anonymous reviewers of this paper for their helpful comments. Of course all oversights are my own.

This paper was written during a two-year contract with the HK Polytechnic Univ., Hung Hom, Kowloon, HONG KONG. The author's current address is c/- C.L.T.R. Univ of Queensland, Brisbane Qld. 4072. Australia.

APPENDIX

	More New	Same	Less New
Subject	7.9%	23.9%	68.2%
Predicate	17.1%	19.3%	63.6%
Object	12.7%	25.5%	61.8%
Temporal Unit	10.8%	31.7%	57.5%
Locative Unit	6.0%	25.0%	69.0%
Adjunct	6.6%	35.1%	58.3%
AVERAGE	11.05%	27.15%	61.8%

TABLE 3. HPP: Head-Modifier relations in terms of the head.

REFERENCES

Allen, James. 1987. *Natural Language Processing*. Benjamin/ Cummings Publ.

Chafe, Wallace 1994. *Discourse, consciousness and time: The flow and displacement of conscious experience in speaking and writing*. Chicago: Univ of Chicago Press.

Clark, Herbert. & Carlson, T.B. 1982. Speech acts and hearer's beliefs. In: N.V. Smith (ed.). *Mutual Knowledge*. London: Academic Press. 1-36.

Clark, Herbert. & Schaeffer, E.F. 1987. Collaborating on contributions to conversation. *Language and Cognitive Processes* 2: 1-23.

Fauconnier, Gilles 1985. *Mental Spaces*. Cambridge, Mass.: MIT Press.

_____ 1990. Domains and connections. *Cognitive Linguistics* 11: 151-174.

Givón, Talmy. 1984. Syntax: A Functional-Typological Introduction. A'dam: Benjamins.

Grosz, Barbara J. 1986. The representation and use of focus in a system for understanding dialogs. In: B.J. Grosz, K.S. Jones & B.L. Webber (eds.) *Readings in Natural Language Processing*. Los Altos, California: Morgan Kaufmann Publ. 353-362.

Johnson-Laird, P.N. 1980. Mental models in cognitive science. *Cognitive Science* 4: 71-115.

Keenan, E.L. 1976. Towards a universal definition of "subject". In: C. Li (ed.). Subject and topic. New York: Academic Press.

Langacker, Ronald.W. 1991. *On of and of-Periphrasis*. Paper presented at the 5th Annual Cognitive Linguistics Workshop. University California, San Diego.

Luchjenbroers, June. 1990. *The Narrative structure of Courtroom Interaction*. 24th Annual ALS Conference - Language & the law Workshop. Macquary Univeristy, Australia.(ms).

_____ 1991, Discourse Dynamics in the Courtroom: some methodological issues for discourse analysis. *La Trobe University Working Papers in Linguistics* 4: 85-109.

_____ 1993. *Pragmatic Inference in Language Processing*. Unpublished PhD Dissertation. La Trobe Univeristy, Melbourne Australia.

_____ 1995. *Barrister talk vs. Witness talk: Who's smuggling What?* First Annual Intern.Conf. on Crime and Justice: Email conference. Univ of Arkansas, Little Rock.

Mandler, George. 1985. *Cognitive Psychology: An Essay in Cognitive Science*. Hillsdale, N.J.: Lawrence Erlbaum.

Oosten, J. van. 1986. *The Nature of Subjects, Topics and Agents: A cognitive explanation*. Bloomington: Indiana Univ. Linguistics Club.

Polanyi, Livia. 1988. A formal model of the structure of discourse. *Journal of Pragmatics* 12: 601-638.

Rosch, E.H. 1973. Natural categories. *Cognitive Psychology* 4: 328-350.

_____ 1977. Human Categorization. In: N. Warren (ed.).*Studies in cross-cutlural psychology,* Vol. I. London: Academic Press. 1-49.

Sperber, Dan & Wilson, Deirdre. 1982. Mutual knowledge and relevance in theories of comprehension. In: N.V. Smith (ed.). *Mutual knowledge*. London: Academic Press. 61-87.

_____ 1986. *Relevance: communication and cognition*. Oxford: Blackwell.

Talmy, Leonard. 1983. *How language structures space*. Berkeley Cognitive Science Report No. 4. UC Berkeley.

How Abstract is Subjective Motion? A Comparison of Coverage Path Expressions and Access Path Expressions

YO MATSUMOTO

Meijigakuin University

1 Subjective Motion

In this paper[1] I will discuss the nature of expressions involving subjective or fictive motion (e.g., Langacker 1986, 1987, 1990, 1992, Talmy 1983, 1989, to appear, Matsumoto to appear a). Two types of subjective motion expressions will be discussed, and they are exemplified in (1) and in (2). Those in (1) are what Talmy calls *coverage path expressions* (see Dowty 1979, Talmy 1983, 1989, Langacker 1986, 1987, 1990, Levin 1993, Honda 1994, Matsumoto to appear a), and those in (2) are *access path expressions* (see Bennet 1975, Lindkvist 1976, Brugman 1981, Jackendoff 1983, Hawkins 1984, Lakoff & Brugman 1986, Lakoff 1987, Langacker 1987, 1990, 1992, Taylor 1993, Talmy 1989, to appear).

(1) Coverage Path Expressions
    a. The highway goes from Los Angeles to New York.
    b. The mountain range goes from Canada to Mexico.   (Talmy 1989)

(2) Access Path Expressions
    a. The bike is parked across the street.
    b. There is a lake through the forest.

---

[1]This paper is a revised version of the paper presented at the Conference on Conceptual Structure, Discoruse, and Language, held at UCSD in November, 1994. I would like to thank several participants in that conference for some important suggestions that I was able to include in this version. I would also like to thank Mary Dalrymple and Mille Surber for helping me with data. Any errors in this paper should of course be attributed to me. E-mail address: yomatsum@ltr.meijigakuin.ac.jp.

Those sentences do not express a real motion of the subject NP. However, it has been argued that these sentences involve some sort of implicit motion subjectively evoked in the mind of a conceptualizer who mentally traces the path described in those sentences, with an image of a moving entity often projected onto such tracing (see Talmy 1983, 1989, Langacker 1986, 1987, 1990, Matsumoto to appear a).

The issue that I will take up particularly in this paper concerns the difference in the nature of the motion implicit in these two types of expressions. Differences among different types of subjective motion expressions have not been discussed much in the literature. One notable exception is Talmy's (1989, to appear) recent work focusing on "emanation path" expressions, in which he posits such parameters of variation as the reality of motion and an object in motion as well as the nature of an observer and a moving entity. In this paper, I will look at the nature of coverage path expressions and access path expressions from a perspective different from Talmy's: namely, how abstract or specified the motion in these two expressions is.

A real, objective motion event is composed of different components -- path, manner, a moving entity, etc. (Talmy 1985), which can be fully specified linguistically in describing it. I will point out that coverage path expressions and access path expressions do not allow all such components of motion to be linguistically specified, and that the two expressions differ in the specifiable components of motion. I will argue that such differences reflect the differences in the cognitive and functional motivations for the two expressions as well as grammatical differences of the forms employed to describe subjective motion.

2 Coverage Path Expressions

First, let us look at coverage path expressions. Coverage path expressions are used to represent the configuration or the extent of a spatially extended entity referred to by the subject of the sentence.

In Matsumoto (to appear a) I have distinguished two different types of those expressions. Type I coverage path expression is exemplified in (3) and Type II, in (4).

(3) Type I   (non-actual motion)
    a. The mountain range goes from Canada to Mexico.
                                            (mental tracing only)
    b. The highway enters California there.　　(hypothetical motion)

(4) Type II   (actual motion)
    a. The road went up the hill (as we proceeded).
    b. This highway will enter California soon.　　(uttered by the driver)

Type I coverage motion expressions are based on non-actual motion, i.e., either purely subjective motion (mental tracing), as in (3a), or the hypothetical motion of an arbitrary moving entity at an arbitrary time, as in (3b). Such expressions are static descriptions of an object represented in the subject NP. Type II coverage path expressions are based on the actual motion of a particular moving entity at a particular time. Such expressions represent the described entity as experienced by a particular mover. These different types of coverage path expressions exhibit somewhat different properties as I will point out.

2.1 Path of Motion

First, consider how the path of motion is specified in coverage path expressions. Coverage path expressions *must* specify the path of motion (Matsumoto to appear a). Path can be specified either in a prepositional phrase (PP), as in (3a) and (4a), or as a part of a verb meaning, as in (3b) and (4b). (In (3a) and (4a) the verb *go* also codes some deictic property of path.) An interesting phenomenon is the case like (5a).

(5) a. The road began to run *(along the shore).
    b. He began to run (along the shore).

In this case, path is not specified in the meaning of the verb *run*. In such a case a prepositional phrase representing an aspect of path *must* be used. (5a) is unacceptable without such a phrase. Compare this with (5b), which represents a real motion. In this case, a prepositional phrase indicating a path is optional. This shows that path must be specified in coverage path expressions even when the verb does not require it grammatically.

2.2 Manner of Motion

How about the manner of motion? Manner of motion cannot be specified in coverage path expressions unless it is used to describe a related path feature (Matsumoto to appear a). Consider the sentences in (6).

(6) a. * The road {walks / speeds / hurries / strides} through the park.
    b. * The road runs {angrily / happily / desperately / slowly} through the forest.
    c. * The road runs through the forest {by car / on foot}.

(6) show that manner in these sentences is excluded whether it is specified in a verb meaning, as in (6a), or in an adjunct, as in (6b) and (6c).

Note here that manner specification is not possible even in Type II coverage path expressions, in which a specific manner of motion can be known, as shown in (7).

(7) * The highway (I was driving on) {speeded / drove / hurried} along the
river.

When manner-of-motion verbs or manner adverbs can in fact be used in
coverage path expressions, they describe a related path feature. Thus, the
verbs *ramble* and *wander* in (8a) are used to indicate the shape of a path, and
slowly in (8b) describes the steepness of the described slope, rather than the
manner with which a moving entity moves along the path.

(8) a. The road {rambles / wanders} though the forest.
    b. The road descends slowly.

The only exception that cannot be explained this way is *run* (cf. (5a)). This
verb is very general in the manners that it describes, and it appears that only
such general manner-of-motion verb can be used to represent subjective
motion, suppressing the manner information that it could carry (Matsumoto
to appear a).

2.3 Duration of Motion

How about the duration of motion? In Matsumoto (to appear a) I have
pointed out that duration can be specified in coverage path expressions. A
closer examination has revealed that the specifiability of duration varies
according to the types of motion involved. Type I expressions involving
mental tracing only do not allow any duration to be specified, as in (9).

(9) * The mountain range goes along the coast for some time.

Type I expressions involving hypothetical motion do allow duration to
be specified, as in (10) (Matsumoto to appear a).

(10) a. The highway runs along the river for a while.
     b. How long does the highway run along the river?

In (10a), the temporal phrase *for a while* is used to indicate the duration of
motion along the river. This duration is metonymically correlated with the
length of the relevant section of the highway, which it is used to describe.
The acceptability of (10b) confirms the temporal nature of this duration
phrase.

There is a restriction on the precision of such duration that can be
expressed in such examples. Consider (11).

(11) a. ? The highway goes along the river for 3 minutes.
     b. ?? The footpath goes along the river for 15 minutes.
     c. The highway goes along the river for 3 miles.

In contrast to (10a), sentences (11a) and (11b) sound rather odd (though some speakers find them somewhat better when the speaker and the hearer share an assumption about the speed with which an imagined person moves). This suggests that a PP conveying precise information about duration is not totally compatible with Type I expressions involving hypothetical motion. Grammatically speaking, there is nothing wrong about sentences like (11a) and (11b). The restriction is clearly semantic. Note, in contrast, that distance can be precisely specified, as in (11c).

Type II coverage path expressions present a different picture. Consider (12).

(12) a. The road (I was driving on) went along the river for 3 minutes.
     b. This highway will enter California {soon / in a few minutes / in 3 minutes}.
     c. This highway will go through this tunnel in 3 minutes.

In contrast to (11a) and (11b), these sentences are more acceptable, showing that Type II expressions allow relatively precise specifications of duration. In fact, as far as temporality is concerned, motion in Type II expressions is essentially no different from a real motion, and it is a process in Langacker's (1987) sense: it evolves over a conceived time (time at which a conceived event takes place).

2.4 Moving Entity

Finally, consider the moving entity. Coverage path expressions do not allow a moving entity to be expressed linguistically as an argument or adjunct of the motion verb. For example, sentences like (13a) are not possible. This is also true of Type II expressions like (13b) in which a specific moving person can be known.

(13) a. * The road ran from Los Angeles to New York by drivers.
     b. * The highway will enter California soon by us.

In this respect, coverage path sentences are similar to middle verbs, which do not allow agent to be expressed.

Also, consider the nature of this unexpressed moving entity. Type I expressions do not require the unexpressed moving entity to be a specific human being or any other entity. As I have pointed out, it can be simply the focus of attention or a hypothetical, arbitrary entity.

On the other hand, Type II expressions necessarily involve a specific human or other concrete moving entity. Thus, the objects that cannot be conceived as a canonical travel path cannot be described as Type II expressions, as shown by the unacceptability of (14).

(14)   * The mountain range will enter California soon.

2.5 Summary

(15) is a summary of the findings so far. Coverage path expressions involving mental tracing only are especially less specifiable than those involving hypothetical motion, which in turn are less specifiable than those involving actual motion. In this sense, the subjective motion involved in these different types differs in how abstract it is.

(15)   Coverage Path Expressions

aspects of motion	specification
path	necessary
manner	specifiable only to describe a path feature
duration	
(mental tracing only)	unspecifiable
(hypothetical motion)	roughly specifiable (to describe a path feature)
(actual motion)	precisely specifiable (to describe a path feature)
moving entity	inexpressible
(mental tracing only)	focus of attention
(hypothetical motion)	concrete, arbitrary
(actual motion)	concrete, specific

There appear to be some correlations between different properties given in (15). For example, manner of motion is usually a property of a moving person (cf. Talmy 1985). Thus, the exclusion of manner is related to the exclusion of a moving entity. The manners that are *not* excluded are precisely those which are not properties of a moving person but of a path. Also, the possibility for duration specification is correlated to the concreteness and specificity of a moving entity.

3   Access Path Expressions

Let us now move on to access path expressions exemplified again in (16).

(16) a.   The bike is across the street.
     b.   His store is down this street.
     c.   There is a gas station toward the end of the street.

In these sentences, the location of an entity is indicated in terms of a PP representing the path of access to the object whose location is indicated. In this kind of expression, an entity whose location is indicated ('located entity') and an entity which is supposed to be moving ('moving entity') are different entities. In this respect, this kind of expression must be carefully distinguished from sentences like (17).

(17)   The horse is now over the fence.

In the most natural interpretation of this sentence, the subject NP is a located entity as well as a moving entity (see Lindkvist 1976, Taylor 1993).

3.1 Path of Motion

Let us now look at which aspects of motion can be linguistically specified in access path expressions.

Access path expressions require path to be expressed, just as coverage path expressions do. In fact, access path is described in terms of path prepositions, and therefore path is necessarily specified. However, one might entertain an alternative view on the nature of path prepositions in these expressions: namely, such path prepositions might in fact be simple locative expressions. For example, *across* in (16a) might simply indicate a location corresponding to the end point of the path represented by this preposition in its normal use, a use which has allegedly resulted from an image-schema transformation (cf. Brugman 1983, Lakoff 1987, Taylor 1993, Dewell 1994).

However, there is some evidence suggesting that *across* in (16a) is not a simple end-point locative preposition. Evidence comes from the possibility of sentences like (18).

(18)   There is a lake {halfway / twenty miles} across the desert.

This sentence indicates that the located entity is situated at an intermediate point in the overall path represented by *across the desert*.

Another evidence comes from the possibility of a sequence of PPs, as exemplified in (19). Such a sequence of PPs define one continuous path, in a spatial sequence that matches the order of PPs. If a PP in access path expressions is simply locative, then this cannot be explained.

(19)   There is a beautiful chapel across the river, through the meadow, and
        (then) over the hill.

The source or the initial point of the path can also be specified, as in (20a), as has been noted by Hawkins (1984), Taylor (1993), and others.

(20) a.   The chapel is across the river from us.
      b. * The chapel is from us across the river.
      c.   From us, the chapel is across the river.

This source PP has a special status, in that it is not a part of a sequence of PPs; it does not respect the temporal ordering, as shown in (20b), and also it can appear at the beginning of the sentence independently of the other PPs, as shown in (20c).

3.2 Duration of Motion

How about the duration of motion? This is a difficult issue. Motion implicit in access path expressions *does* appear to have temporality: it is an event that occurs over a period of time. The temporality can be seen in the temporal order of sequential PPs in a sentence like (19) above. Note that in (19) a temporal expression *then* can be added on the last PP in a sequence.

The temporal nature of motion can also be seen in (21).

(21) a.   His house is halfway through the increasingly dense forest.
      b. ? His house is somewhere in the increasingly dense forest.

In (21a), the adjective phrase *increasingly dense* indicates a change that is noted over the time during which a motion occurs. The unacceptability of (21b) suggests that such a reading is not so natural with a purely locative, non-motional expression, at least without adequate contextual support.[2]

Thus, motion implicit in access path expressions does seem to have temporality. This observation is important in considering the nature of access path expressions; it is another evidence against a simple locative analysis of access path expressions.

Given the temporality of motion in access path expressions, how can the actual duration of motion be specified? Duration can be specified as a part of the specifier of a preposition. Spatial prepositions like *across* can take a distance phrase as their specifier, as in (22a). A duration phrase can be used in this position, as in (22b), to define the location of the located entity.

(22) a. The city lies many miles across the desert.
      b. The city lies many hours across the desert.

Such a duration phrase is a substitute for a distance specifier. This can be exemplified by the unacceptability of *how long* in (23b) as opposed to the acceptability of *how far* in (23a).

(23) a.   How far across the desert does the city lie?
      b. * How long across the desert does the city lie?

In spite of the fact that grammar requires this specifier to be a distance phrase and not really a duration phrase, a highly precise value of duration can

---

[2]One context that makes this possible is the one in which the sentence is uttered by a moving person. Thus, (i) is possible when uttered by a traveller.

(i)   His house is somewhere in this increasingly dense forest.

be specified in this way to define the location of the located entity. This is exemplified in (24).

(24) a. There is a village 25 minutes through the forest.
    b. The hotel is only three minutes down the road.
    c. There is a bridge 15 minutes down the footpath.

This contrasts with coverage path expressions involving hypothetical motion seen earlier. In both cases, duration phrase can be used to indicate distance, with an assumption about the speed with which an imagined person moves. However, there is a clear difference in the possibility for precise specification of duration.

3.3 Manner of Motion

How about manner? Manner of motion can also be specified to the extent that it defines the location of a located entity. It can be expressed in terms of an adjunct PP, as in (25a), or as a part of a specifier, as in (25b).

(25) a. The hotel is 15 minutes down the road {by car / on foot / at that speed}.
    b. The hotel is a 15-minute {drive / walk / run} down the road.

Manner cannot be specified if it does not help to define the location of the located entity. This accounts for the difference between (26a) and (26b) below. In (26a), *fast* and *slow* are used to define the location of the hotel in combination with a temporal specification *15-minute*. In contrast, *careful* and *careless* cannot be used, as shown in (26b); these adjectives indicate the unexpressed mover's properties, and does not help to identify the location of the hotel. The adjective *careful* sounds a little better than *careless* for some speakers, presumably because carefulness of driving can be correlated with a slow speed, and hence indirectly helps to identify the location of the located entity. Note also that various adjectives can be used in this position in the specifier to indicate the properties of the access path assumed, as in (26c) and (26d).[3]

(26) a. The hotel is a 15-minute {fast / slow} drive down the road.
    b. The hotel is a 15-minute {??careful / *careless} drive down the road.
    c. The hotel is a 15-minute {dangerous / zigzagy} drive down the road.
    d. Richmond is a scenic and interesting two hour ride along the shore.

---

[3] I would like to thank George Lakoff and Eve Sweetser for clarifying this point.

Also consider examples in (27). (27a) is good but (27b) is not. This is because the phrase *by car* helps to define a location when it occurs with a duration phrase like *five minutes*, but it doesn't without such a phrase. Note also that *by car* can occur with a distance specifier like *five miles* only when the addition of this phrase helps to define the location of the located entity; it is acceptable only when the length of access path is different for car drivers and, say, hikers.

(27) a.   The motel is five minutes through the forest by car.
    b. * The motel is through the forest by car.
    c.   The motel is five miles through the forest by car.

3.4 Moving Entity

Finally, the access path expressions does not allow a moving entity to be expressed, as in coverage path expressions.

This unexpressed moving entity must be a human being or at least a concrete entity. In other words, access path expressions describe the position of the located entity in terms of how someone can go there, and not how you can move your focus of attention to identify the location.

This point can be supported by a phenomenon noted by Brugman (1981). She has noted that (28a) is not possible because one cannot go over the valley to cross it. She has also noted the difference between (28b) and (28c). While you can usually cross a city wall through a gate, you had to climb the Berlin Wall to go to the other side. She argues that this is why (28b) is bad but (28c) is good.

(28) a. * The village is over the valley from us.
    b. ?? The town lies over that wall.
    c.   The free world [was] (just) over the Berlin Wall.

This is not limited to the case of *over*. For example, sentence (29a) is acceptable, while (29b) is not normally acceptable. This is because a garden fence can be easily crossed, while a wall separating offices usually cannot. Note further that even (29b) would be good for a Superman, who can break through a wall easily, which supports the present analysis.

(29) a.   His garden is across the fence.
    b. */OK His office is {across / through} this wall.[4]

Note also the use of *through* in (30). This sentence is normally unacceptable, given that one cannot usually go through a mountain.

---

[4]There seem to be relatively a few speakers who accept this sentence under normal circumstances.

However, this sentence gets relatively acceptable if there is a tunnel through the mountain.

(30)   */? Through the mountain was a beautiful city.

These phenomena suggest that a moving entity in access path expressions must be a concrete entity.

3.5 Summary

(31) is a summary of our findings about access path expressions.

(31)   Access Path Expressions

aspects of motion	specification
path	necessary
manner	specifiable to the extent it defines a location
duration	precisely specifiable to define a location (spatialized)
moving entity	inexpressible; necessarily concrete

This suggests that access path expressions are less abstract than Type I coverage path expressions (involving mental tracing or hypothetical motion) and roughly as abstract as Type II coverage path expressions (involving actual motion).

4   Comparison

A comparison of (31) and (15) suggests a few difference between coverage path expressions and access path expressions. First, coverage path expressions can have a non-concrete moving entity, and specifiability of duration also varies in accordance with the types of moving entity assumed. Second, the role of specifiable manner and duration is different: manner and duration are allowed when they define a location in access path expressions, while they are allowed when they describe a path feature in coverage path expressions. Third, the nature of duration specification is different: it is spatialized in access path expressions, while it is purely temporal in coverage path expressions.

What are the sources of those differences? One possible source of the differences is the grammatical difference between prepositions in which access path is coded and verbs in which coverage path can be coded. Hawkins (1984) and Langacker (1987, 1990, 1992) point out that a verb profiles a process (an event evolving over a conceived time), while prepositions cannot profile a process as such but they treat the sequence of states in a process holistically, in a summary fashion (the case of 'complex atemporal relation'), if it does treat a sequence of states. Prepositions in access path expressions seem to encode temporality in this way. This might account for why duration is spatialized (de-temporalized) in access path expressions.

However, this grammatical difference does not seem to explain the other two differences concerning the concreteness of a moving entity and the role (and specificity) of manner and duration specification. The concreteness of a moving entity has nothing to do with the distinction between verbs and prepositions. In addition, subjective motion expressions do not accept manner and duration specifications even if they are sanctioned by grammar, if they are not sanctioned by their semantics (defining a location, etc.). (The importance of a semantic factor over a grammatical one can also be seen in the obligatoriness of a path PP with coverage path verbs that do not necessarily subcategorize for a path PP; see (5))

These differences between the two kinds of expressions come from cognitive and functional motivations for the use of these expressions. Coverage path expressions are motivated by the need to scan the length of a spatially extended entity to compute its configuration or extent, and they describe such an entity as a path over which such motion takes place. Therefore path is a necessary part of this expression, and other aspects of motion can be specified only when it helps to describe a path. Also, the possibility of mental scanning means that the moving entity does not have to be concrete, and if not concrete, specific duration of motion cannot be easily imagined.

Access path expressions are motivated by the need to compute a location of an entity in terms of the path that one can take to get there (cf. Klein 1982, Wunderlich & Reinelt 1982). Therefore, an unexpressed moving entity must be a concrete entity, and when manner and duration are specified, they are to define the location of the located entity.

Both coverage path and access path expressions are conservative in allowing manner and duration of motion to be expressed: they are specified only when they match the cognitive and functional motivations for these expressions. In this sense, motion in these expressions is necessarily abstract.

One issue that might be considered here is whether or not such linguistic specifiability of manner and duration is purely cognitive in nature. A cross-linguistic comparison of coverage path expressions suggests that there is some room for conventionalization in different languages. Japanese, for example, does not seem to allow Type I coverage path expressions involving hypothetical motion to express duration of even a minimum specificity when so-called the *-te iru* form is used, as suggested by the unacceptability of (32a). Type II expressions do allow such specification, as in (32b).

(32) a. # Sono michi wa shibaraku mori no naka o tootte iru.
       the   road Top for.a.while forest Gen inside Acc go.through Asp

    "The road goes through a forest for a while." (intended)

b. Kono michi wa shibaraku mori no   naka o   tooru
    this road Top for.a.while forest Gen inside Acc go.through
    "This road will go through a forest for a while."

Coverage path expressions and access path expressions are only two of the several different kinds of subjective motion expressions. Comparisons of more different types of subjective path expressions would reveal different manifestation of subjective motion in language. Each type of subjective motion expression seems to accept different kinds of specifications in accordance with different cognitive and functional motivations for their use. Consider now briefly what Talmy (to appear) calls orientation path expressions, exemplified in (33). Talmy has argued such sentences involve an emanation of an imaginary, invisible force, which is evoked to compute the direction expressed in these sentences.

(33) Orientation path expressions (Jackendoff 1983, Talmy to appear)
      a. He turned his face toward Mecca.
      b. The arrow pointed toward the town.

Talmy observes that path in examples like (33) can pass through obstacles. In (33a), for example, a path connecting his face and Mecca can cross any walls. This contrasts sharply with access path expressions, in which a moving entity must be concrete and therefore it cannot pass through obstacles untraversable by a concrete entity. A full examination of this and other types of subjective motion expressions is, however, beyond the scope of this paper.

5 Concluding Remarks

In this paper, I have pointed out that different types of subjective motion expressions allow different aspects of motion to be specified in accordance with the grammatical properties of the forms used and cognitive and functional motivations for their use. Such constraints based on cognitive and functional motivation are strong linguistic evidence for the cognitive reality of subjective motion. The grammatical restrictions on the other hand testify to the fact that the subjective motion expressions are linguistically conventionalized realizations of underlying cognitive processes (Matsumoto to appear a, b).

References

Bennet, David. 1975. *Spatial and Temporal Uses of English Prepositions*. London: Longman.
Brugman, Claudia. 1981. *The Story of Over*. M.A. Thesis, University of California, Berkeley. [Distributed by the Indiana University Linguistics Club].

Dewell, Robert B. *Over* again: Image-schema transformation in semantic analysis. *Cognitive Linguistics* 5: 351-380.

Dowty, R. David. 1979. *Word Meaning and Montague Grammar*. Dordrecht: Reidel.

Hawkins, Bruce. 1984. *The Semantics of English Spatial Prepositions*. Ph. D. Dissertation. University of California, San Diego.

Honda, Akira. 1994. From spatial cognition to semantic structure: The role of subjective motion in cognition and language. *English Linguistics* 11: 197-219.

Jackendoff, Ray. 1983. *Semantics and Cognition*. Cambridge: MIT Press.

Klein, Wolfgang. 1982. Lexical deixis in route description. In R. J. Jarvella & W. Klein, eds., *Speech, Place, and Action: Studies in Deixis and Related Topics*. Chichester: John Wiley.

Lakoff, George. 1987. *Women, Fire and Dangerous Things*. Chicago: University of Chicago Press.

_____ and Claudia Brugman. 1986. Argument forms in lexical semantics. *Proceedings of the Twelfth Annual Meeting of Berkeley Linguistics Society*, 442-454.

Langacker, Ronald. 1986. Abstract motion. *Proceedings of the Twelfth Annual Meeting of Berkeley Linguistics Society*, 455-471.

_____. 1987. *Foundations of Cognitive Grammar*. vol. 1. Stanford: Stanford University Press.

_____. 1990. Subjectification. *Cognitive Linguistics* 1: 5-38.

_____. 1992. Prepositions as grammatical(izing) elements. *Leuvense Bijdragen* 81: 287-309.

Levin, Beth. 1993. *English Verb Classes and Alternations: A Preliminary Investigation*. Chicago: University of Chicago Press.

Lindkvist, Karl-Gunnar. 1979. *A Comprehensive Study of Conceptions of Locality in Which English Prepositions Occur*. Stockholm: Almqvist & Wiksell.

Matsumoto, Yo. to appear a. Subjective motion and the English and Japanese verbs. To appear in *Cognitive Linguistics*.

_____. to appear b. Subjective change expressions in Japanese and their cognitive and linguistic bases. In Gilles Fauconnier & Eve Sweetser, eds., *Mental Space, Grammar, and Discourse*. Chicago: University of Chicago Press.

Talmy, Leonard. 1983. How language structures space. In Herbert L. Pick, Jr. and Linda P. Acredolo, eds., *Spatial Orientation: Theory, Research and Application*. New York: Plenum Press.

_____. 1985. Lexicalization patterns: Semantic structure in lexical forms. In Tim Shopen, ed., *Language Typology and Syntactic Description*, vol. 3, *Grammatical Categories and the Lexicon*. London: Cambridge University Press.

_____. 1989. Fictive motion in language and perception. A paper presented at the Conference on Meaning and Perception, 5/89 French Canadian Assn. for the Advancement of Science, University of Quebec, Montreal

_____. to appear. Fictive motion in language and 'ception': The emanation type.

Taylor, John R. 1993. Prepositions: patterns of polysemization and strategies of disambiguation. In Cornelia Zelinsky-Wibbet, ed., *The Semantics of Prepositions: From Mental Processing to Natural Language Processing*, 151-175. Berlin: Mouton de Gruyter.

Wunderlich, D., & Reinelt, R. 1982. How to get there from here. In R. J. Jarvella & W. Klein, eds., *Speech, Place, and Action: Studies in Deixis and Related Topics*, 183-201. Chichester: John Wiley.

The Exclamative Sentence Type in English

LAURA A. MICHAELIS & KNUD LAMBRECHT

University of Colorado, Boulder & University of Texas, Austin

0. Introduction.[1] We say that a sentence type exists when a certain communicative function is conventionally associated with a particular grammatical structure. Traditionally recognized sentence types include declaratives, imperatives and questions. The notion that various illocutionary forces receive distinct formal coding is referred to by Levinson (1983) as the Literal Force Hypothesis (LFH). Levinson casts doubt on the tenability of the LFH. In particular, he shows that it is manifestly inadequate when we attempt to account for indirect speech acts. He looks at findings in conversational analysis which indicate that "the functions that utterances perform are in large part due to the place they occupy within specific conversational (or interactional) sequences" (p. 279).

König (1986) raises further questions about the reliability of the form-function fit. He looks at examples of formal overlap involving the adverbial constructions concessive, concessive conditional and conditional. He points out that even though these three categories are typically associated with distinct formal properties, they may also be formally indistinguishable. For example, he observes that in interrogative contexts like (1a), conditionals are interpreted as concessive conditionals. He also shows that in contexts like (1b), a concessive conditional may be interpreted as a concessive:

(1)   a.   Will you take the car if it is snowing? (= even if it is snowing)
      b.   He looked at me kindly if somewhat skeptically. (= although somewhat...)

The issue that concerns us here is whether we can identify an exclamative sentence type for English once we confront the great variety of forms to which someone could intuitively assign an exclamative function. The expressions in (2) show the heterogeneous character of the class of exclamative sentences:

(2)   a.   It's amazing how much you can get in the TRUNK.
      b.   It's amazing the DIFFERENCE! (Fixodent commercial)
      c.   You wouldn't believe the BICKERING that goes on. ('For Better or for Worse' 8/15/94)

---

[1]   For inspiration and input, we wish to thank: George Lakoff, Charles Fillmore, Paul Kay, Jean-Pierre Koenig and Adele Goldberg.

d. GOD my feet hurt.
e. What a DAY (I had).
f. The things I DO for that boy!
g. Are YOU in for it!
h. I'm amazed at how much TIME it took.
i. It's so HOT in here!

At the very least, it seems to be a misnomer to speak of a unitary exclamative sentence type in English. The data in (2) illustrate a further difficulty inherent in presuming a form-function fit in the realm of exclamatives: sometimes there's not much form to pin a function on. In the case of (2f), for example, we find only an NP, pronounced emphatically. How can this form be related to the far more elaborate form in (2c)? It's difficult to decide what an exclamative should look like. According to Sadock and Zwicky (1985), exclamatives are closely related to declaratives, and therefore closely resemble declaratives in form. However, examples (2e) and (f) do not look like declarative sentences.

We will argue that it is possible to maintain the LFH in the case of exclamatives. In other words, we will claim that all of the constructions in (2) represent conventional means of performing an exclamative speech act. Given the variety of forms involved, we cannot presume that form is in any way predictable on the basis of the illocutionary force involved. The problem is one of the motivation: how does a learner organize the knowledge that each of the forms in (2) is dedicated to the exclamative function? We postulate that the form-meaning pairs in (2) are motivated though relations of INHERITANCE.

Inheritance networks provide a way of representing formal and semantic correspondences among constructions (Fillmore and Kay 1993, Lakoff 1987, Goldberg 1992). These inheritance networks invoke the connectionist model of memory. According to Pinker and Prince (1991:232) this model is "both associative and superpositional: individual [linguistic] items are dissolved into sets of features, and similar items...overlap in their physical representations, sharing representational real estate". Rather than invoking the superimposition metaphor, we will describe structure sharing by means of inheritance LINKS (Lakoff 1987). In the case of (2), we will claim that each of these exclamative subtypes inherits its semantic and pragmatic properties from an abstract superconstruction: the ABSTRACT EXCLAMATIVE CONSTRUCTION (AEC). This construction interacts with four templates which are independently licensed by the grammar. These are: EXTRAPOSITION, the BARE COMPLEMENT QUESTION CONSTRUCTION, the INVERTED CLAUSE CONSTRUCTION, and the SUBJECT-PREDICATE CONSTRUCTION. Our analysis of these four familiar constructions is taken from Fillmore and Kay (1993). The Extraposition construction licenses sentences like (3). The Complement Question Construction licenses indirect questions, as in the italicized portion of (4). The Inverted Clause Construction licenses main-clause questions like (5):

(3)   It's obvious why he didn't come.
(4)   I wonder *who saw me there*.
(5)   Did you ask about it?

The network of exclamative constructions will feature several instances of MULTIPLE INHERITANCE. As Goldberg points out (1995), multiple inheritance "allows us to capture the fact that some construction types seem to resist being uniquely categorized in a natural way". Notice for example sentence (2a): *It's amazing how much you can get in the trunk*. This sentence appears to instantiate two constructions: the extraposition construction and a construction which Milner (1978) refers to as an INDIRECT EXCLAMATIVE. This label suggests an analogy with indirect questions: an indirect exclamative consists of a verb which governs a clausal complement introduced by a *wh*-word. In fact, we will claim that the indirect exclamative subsumes the Bare Complement Question construction instantiated in (4).

Another instance of multiple inheritance to be found in our network involves a construction that is uniquely dedicated to the expression of exclamative semantics: the METONYMIC NP CONSTRUCTION. This construction licenses a reading of a definite NP in which a definite NP 'stands for' a proposition that invokes some degree of a scalar property. Notice, for example, sentence (2b): *It's amazing the difference*. The definite NP *the difference* can be said to stand for the propositional function "There is X degree of difference". The Metonymic NP construction is instantiated by several of our exclamative examples. By invoking this construction, we account for the paraphrase relationship shown in (6):

(6)   a.   I can't believe the money I spent on clothes last summer.
       b.   I can't believe how much money I spent on clothes last summer.

The rest of our paper will be structured in the following way. In the next section, we will look at the semantic and pragmatic components of the Abstract Exclamative Construction. In the third section we will demonstrate that the inheritance approach provides a way of taming the considerable syntactic variety found in the domain of exclamative constructions. We will conclude with some thoughts about the relevance of this approach for syntactic theories like Construction Grammar, which treat sentence types as a crucial basis for grammar.

1. The Abstract Exclamative Construction (AEC). The AEC, as we see it, has a grammatical status like that of the Left Isolate construction discussed by Fillmore and Kay (1993). LI is a clausal construction which licenses long-distance dependencies like *wh*-questions and topicalization. Fillmore and Kay say that the LI construction "is really a family of constructions, or better an abstract construction whose properties are inherited by a number of more detailed constructions" (p. 11.4). The LI construction contains only very general syntactic and semantic constraints. A complement is instantiated to the left of a maximal verb, which may or may not have a subject. The valence slot that the 'extracted' complement fills is embedded at an undefined depth within the maximal verb. Any structure which is formed in accordance with the LI template must satisfy the general constraints associated with the abstract constuction. The idea underlying the AEC is much the same. However, in the case of the AEC we find no formal constraints other than a general requirement that all components of the semantico-pragmatic frame receive expression. Certain of these components can be realized through metonymic construal or through a type of pragmatic construal similar to that found in instances of null complementation (Fillmore 1986).

Let's now look at the semantic and pragmatic components of exclamations. A word of caution is in order here: we are not looking at all expressions of English that could conceivably be labeled exclamations. In particular, we are excluding expressions like the ones in (7):

(7)   a.   Damn!
      b.   It's a beech tree!
      c.   There we were in some remote part of Bali and who did we see but Joel and Dina.

Example (7a) represents an interjection rather than an exclamation. An interjection is like an exclamation in that it expresses the speaker's emotional stance toward some situation. An interjection is unlike an exclamation in that it has no recoverable propositional content. What about sentences (7b-c)? These are exclamative in that they express an affective stance toward some propositional content. What's more, the stance is one of surprise, as in our original examples. We will exclude exclamatives like (7b-c) because they do not involve the notion of DEGREE. All of the exclamatives that we will consider involve a scalar property (say, amount). The notion of surprise or expectation contravention comes into play because the exclamative utterance counts as an assertion that the degree of the scalar property in question is unusually high. The semantic and pragmatic properties shared by the exclamative examples in (1) are listed in (8):

(8)   *Semantico-Pragmatic Properties of the Abstract Exclamative Construction*

      a.   Presupposed Open Proposition
      b.   Scalar Extent
      c.   Assertion of Affective Stance: Expectation Contravention
      d.   Identifiability of Described Referent
      e.   Deixis

Let's look at properties (a)-(c) together. We'll take the sentence in (9) as our example:

(9)   I can't believe how much he's GROWN!

The presupposed open proposition contains a variable in place of a particular degree specification: *He has grown to X extent.* The person uttering (9) presupposes that the person referred to has grown to some extent. The quantity expression *much* invokes a scale whose origin is some minimal amount. The open proposition places the individual at some point on the scale of ascending quantity for growth. The entire utterance expresses the speaker's judgement that the proposition is surprising, and the surprise stems from the fact that the degree in question is higher than the speaker had expected. In example (9), the main clause *I can't believe* expresses the speaker's affective stance.

A property related to presupposition of the open proposition is that of referent identifiability (8d): the entity of whom the scalar property is predicated must be identifiable.[2] An identifiable referent is one for which a shared representation exists in the minds of speaker and hearer at speech time (Lambrecht 1994). Identifiable referents surface as pronominal or definite NPs. Notice, for example, the anomaly of the sentences in (10):

(10)   a.   *What a nice guy someone is.
        b.   *It's amazing a difference.
        c.   ??Someone is so messy.

Thus far, our analysis resembles that of Sadock and Zwicky (1985), who distinguish exclamations from declaratives in the following way:

---

[2]   It is difficult to determine whether this property is a constraint on the AEC or a general constraint on property attribution: when a speaker attributes a property to something, the speaker necessarily presupposes that the entity in question can be identified by the hearer. The authors have previously employed the more general explanation for the anomaly of sentences like (10) (Michaelis and Lambrecht 1994). There, we invoked sentences like those in (a) and (b):

(a)   ??Someone is a really nice person.
(b)   ??A car is a Volvo.

Problems with the property-attribution constraint surface when we look at sentences like (c), which have an inferential quality:

(c)   Someone is a Fellini fan. (said upon seeing movie poster in an unfamiliar home)

...exclamations are intended to be expressive whereas declaratives are intended to be informative. Both represent a proposition as being true, but in an exclamation, the speaker emphasizes his strong emotional reaction to what he takes to be a fact, whereas in a declarative, the speaker emphasizes his intellectual appraisal that the proposition is true. (p. 162)

We depart from Sadock and Zwicky in emphasizing the importance of scalarity. Another crucial property for us is that of DEICTIC ANCHORING. Exclamatives involve personal and temporal deixis. The notion of affective stance entails the presence of someone making a judgement, and the speaker is the judge by default. The speaker's status as judge may be explicit, as in (9), where the main-clause predicator has a first-person subject. It may also be implicit, as in (11):

(11)   It's amazing how fast the WEATHER can change.

Sentence (11) can be paraphrased as: "I find it amazing how fast the weather can change". In some cases, however, the speaker invites the hearer to do the judging, as in (12):

(12)   a.   You wouldn't believe how much he's grown.
        b.   You won't believe how much he's grown.

Exclamatives in which the hearer is the judge have a marked status. This is shown by the fact that sentences like (12) require a subjunctive or futurate main verb. The sentences in (12) have a conditional flavor; they convey the message: "You would find the situation remarkable if you were in the position to judge". This conditional flavor seems to be crucial; sentence (13) does not count as an exclamative:

(13)   You can't believe how much he's grown.

The sentences in (14) don't count as exclamatives either, because the judgement predicates are not deictically anchored:

(14)   a.   They wouldn't believe how much he's grown.
        b.   My mom can't believe how much he's grown.

With respect to temporal deixis, it appears that the affect evoked by the main-clause predicator must hold at speech time, whether or not the denoted situation also holds at speech time. Therefore, sentence (15a) is exclamative, but sentence (15b) is merely a recollection:

(15)   a.   I can't believe how much we spent.

b.   I couldn't believe how much we spent.

We've just argued that sentences which lack deictic anchoring do not count as exclamatives. This argument doesn't quite go through, because the sentences in (14) and the past-tense sentence in (15b) have a formal feature that is unique to exclamatives. Only the AEC licenses a valence frame in which the verb *believe* takes a complement introduced by a *wh*-word. When *believe* has this valence structure, it must be negated. Notice the anomaly of (16):

(16)   a.   *I believe how much money you spent.
        b.   *I believe what a jerk he is.

The negation requirement is motivated by the fact that asserting lack of belief counts as a judgement of expectation contravention, as required by the AEC. Therefore, it is apparent that sentences like *My mom couldn't believe how much money we spent* are formed in accordance with the general exclamative template, even though they lack the characteristic deictic anchors. We will analyze sentences like this as instances of PERSPECTIVAL SHIFT (Fillmore 1982). Sentences like (14) and (15b) move the identity of the judge and/or the time of the judgement away from the speech scene. This type of transfer invites the hearer to empathize with the response of a third-person judge or the speaker at some point in the past.[3]

Thus, while deictic anchoring is not a necessary property of the AEC, the encoding of an affective judgement is. This claim might seem controversial, since there are exclamative types which do not require a predicate evoking expectation contravention. Notice (17a) as against (17b):

(17)   a.   What a jerk he is.
        b.   I can't believe what a jerk he is.

We want to claim that sentences like (17a) require the interpreter to infer the presence of an affective judgement. If such a judgement were lacking, the sentence would not count as an exclamative. To see this, notice

---

[3]   One puzzle that presents itself when we look at this type of perspectival shift is illustrated by the contrast between (a) and (b):

(a)   I don't believe how much this is costing me.

(b)   I $\left\{ \begin{array}{l} \text{??didn't} \\ \text{couldn't} \end{array} \right\}$ believe how much it was costing me.

If (b) is simply the shifted version of (a), why isn't the auxiliary *do* permitted?

that the *what a* complement is licensed by predicates which do not code an affective stance toward the proposition expressed by that complement. In particular, we find examples like (18), involving factive main verbs:

(18)   a.   They don't realize what a jerk he is.
       b.   We all know what a jerk he is.

Like (17b), the sentences in (18) signal that the referent of the pronoun has achieved some value on the jerk scale, and that this value is above the norm. Intuitively, however, the sentences in (18) do not count as exclamations. This is because they do not encode the speaker's judgement that the scalar degree exceeds expectation. Therefore, the affective judgement is a necessary ingredient. Where it is not explicitly encoded, as in (17a), the interpreter must reconstruct it. Where this reconstruction is preempted by the presence of a factive verb like *realize*, the sentence does not represent an exclamation.

A word is in order on the information structure of exclamatives. Some exclamatives represent predicate focus, or topic-comment, sentences and some represent sentence-focus structures (in terms of Lambrecht 1994). We maintain that exclamatives involving extraposition are sentence-focus structures, while exclamatives like the indirect exclamative are predicate-focus structures. Therefore, when we talk about the semantico-pragmatic properties of the AEC, we leave aside the issue of information structure.

Let us now look more closely at the individual exclamative constructions. We will argue that these constructions instantiate the AEC and certain other independently motivated constructions. Some of the exclamative subtypes also subsume the Metonymic NP construction. As required, each exclamative subtype realizes, in some way or another, the semantico-pragmatic properties of the AEC.

2. **The Inheritance Network.** We will now consider each of the relevant exclamative subtypes in turn, looking in particular at those properties which can be motivated in terms of inheritance links. We will give informal rather than formal analyses of the various constructions.

2.1. *The Indirect Exclamative.* This construction is exemplified in (19):

(19)   a.   I'm amazed at how much I spent.
       b.   I can't believe who they hired.

The Indirect Exclamative construction represents an instance of the AEC. It is also linked to the Bare Complement Question construction by a subsumption link. As we mentioned, the Bare Complement Question construction licenses indirect questions, as in (20):

(20) a.   I wonder how much I spent.
        b.   I wonder who they hired.

Indirect questions, like direct questions, can be represented as open propositions: *I spent X amount, they hired X*. The open proposition represents the presupposed material. In (20a), for example, the speaker presupposes that she spent some amount. The main clause signals that the speaker wishes to determine this amount. The *wh*-complement in the case of the indirect exclamative (19a) can be given the same analysis. Again, the complement evokes the presupposition *I spent X amount*. The difference between (19a) and (20a) lies in the contribution of the main predicator. Sentence (19a), which contains a predicate denoting expectation contravention, asserts that this amount is remarkably high. Therefore, (19a) instantiates all components of the AEC: it evokes a scale (of amount), it contains a predicate expressing the speaker's epistemic stance, and it contains a presupposed open proposition.

Sentence (19b) is a somewhat complicated case. The presupposed open proposition *They hired X* does not obviously evoke a scale. Nevertheless, the sentence is not easily taken to mean: they hired a certain person, and this surprises me. Instead, the sentence does seem to evoke a scale. In accordance with Fillmore, Kay and O'Connor 1988, we assume that individuals may be assigned positions on property scales. Sentence (19b) presupposes or rather creates the presupposition that the person hired deserves to be ranked on the scale of incompetence. The sentence asserts that this ranking is remarkably high.

2.2. *The Extraposed Indirect Exclamative.* This construction is exemplified in (21):

(21)   It's amazing how much he's GROWN.

This construction subsumes the Bare Complement Question construction. It is an instance of the AEC and the Extraposition construction. What about the information structure of (21)? We have established that sentences like (21) assert a judgement relative to some presupposed situation. The presupposed information is represented as the open proposition *He has grown to X extent*. Although this proposition is known information, it is focal rather than topical. Sentence (21) could not be an answer to a question like: "Tell me something about how much he's grown". Formally speaking, sentence-final elements which bear accent represent focal elements. Therefore, we say that both the predicate and the open proposition are in focus, and (21) counts as a sentence-focus sentence.

2.3. *The Inversion Exclamative.* This construction is exemplified in (22):

(22)   God, am I LATE!

This construction is linked via instance links to both the AEC construction and the Inverted Clause construction. The inversion construction licenses constructs like those in (23):

(23)   a.   Am I late?
        b.   Had I known...
        c.   So did she.
        d.   Not only did he refuse the application...
        e.   And into the room walks Harry.

All of the constructions in (23) are also instances of more specific constructions, like the main-clause yes-no question, the negative adverb preposing construction, etc. By looking at the pragmatic properties of these constructions, we can make one generalization about the pragmatics of the inversion construction: inversion signals a departure from the canonical topic-comment or predicate-focus information structure. For example, sentence (23c) represents a narrow-focus construction. Sentence (23e) represents a sentence-focus construction. At the level of the speech-act type, inversion can also signal that the speech-act in question is not a declarative. Questions are not declaratives and neither are exclamatives, as Sadock and Zwicky point out.

In the case of (22), in particular, the inverted clause receives a scalar, factive interpretation: I am late to some degree. This interpretation is licensed by the AEC, Likewise, the expletive *God* represents the affective judgement: the degree is remarkably high. Since inversion is a main-clause phenomenon, the affective judgement cannot be coded by a complement-taking prediate like *amaze* or negated *believe*. Notice the anomaly of (24):

(24)   *I can't believe am I late!

2.4. *The Antitopic Exclamative*. Examples of this construction are given in (25):

(25)   a.   JESUS it's cold out there.
        b.   GOD that boy can talk.

The Antitopic Exclamative is an instance of the AEC. It also subsumes the subject-predicate construction. The affective stance is coded by an expletive, while the presupposed scalar proposition is coded by the clause to the right. The remarkable property of this construction is its prosody: the expletive receives the sentence accent; the rest of the sentence bears no accent. This prosodic feature makes the Antitopic Exclamative look like the antitiopic construction found in (26):

(26)   It's OUTRAGEOUS, what he's asking.

Sentence (26) is an instance of right dislocation. The headless relative *what he's asking* is an ANTITOPIC. An antitopic is a de-accented resumptive element which appears to the right of the focus domain. Antitopics, like topics, are referential elements which are ACTIVE or ACCESSIBLE in the discourse context. So, (25a) signals that the proposition *It's cold out there* is not only known but also active.

   2.5. *The What-a Exclamative*. This construction is exemplified in (27):

(27)   a.   What a good TIME we had.
        b.   What a QUESTION!
        c.   JESUS, what an IDIOT (I am).
        d.   I can't believe what an IDIOT I am.
        e.   They're such IDIOTS.

   In this construction, the scalar degree is encoded by the nominal modifier *what* or *such*. When the modifier is *what*, there is inversion syntax, since a *wh*-element must be placed in the CP-specifier position. When the modifier is *such*, there is canonical syntax. Both modifiers select for an indefinite NP, whether singular or plural. The predicate nominal modified by *what* or *such* codes the type of entity considered. The scalar property may be encoded by a prenominal adjective, like *good* in (27a). The scalar property may also be inferred, as in (27b). A priori, we don't know whether the question at issue was particularly incisive, inappropriate or obtuse. In the case of (27c), the predicate nominal *idiot* is itself scalar, and so no adjective has to be inferred. The inverted subject, like the noninverted subject in (27e), is topical, and when the main verb is copular, both the verb and the inverted subject have the potential for null realization. For example, in (27c) the copula and the subject may be deleted.
   The affective judgement may be expressed by a subordinating predicator like *I can't believe* or by an expletive like *Jesus*. The affective judgement may also be inferred, as in (27a) and (b). What-a exclamatives closely resemble indirect exclamatives. They contain *wh*-syntax and they presuppose that a particular degree of some property has been attained. In addition, what-a clauses, like indirect questions, can be tied to nonexclamative, factive matrix verbs, as in (18a): *They don't realize what a jerk he is*.
   2.6. *The Degree-Adverb Exclamative*. This construction is exemplified in (28):

(28)   GOD, I'm so TIRED of this (that I want to SCREAM).

This construction is an instance of the AEC and the subject-predicate construction. It invokes anaphoric degree word modification, which Zwicky (1994b) distinguishes from the degree modification performed by adverbs like *very*. As an anaphor, *so* differs from *very* in that it accepts a CONSECUTIVECLAUSE like *that I want to scream*. *So* also differs from *very* in that the latter is not compatible with exclamative semantics. Sentence (29) is not an instance of the Degree-Adverb Exclamative:

(29)   I'm very ANNOYED with him.

We say that (29) is not a degree-word exclamation because it is not compatible with an expletive encoding the affective judgement. Notice the oddness of (30):

(30)   GOD, I'm very ANNOYEDwith him.

It seems to be no accident that the Degree-Adverb Exclamative requires the anaphoric degree word *so*. This adverb is invoked by a correlative construction which presupposes the attainment of a particular degree: the consecutive-clause construction. The clause denoting the consequence is new information; the fact that I am tired to some degree is presupposed. Thus, with or without a consecutive clause, sentences like (28) presuppose the attainment of a given scalar degree, as required by the AEC.

2.7. *The NP-Complement Exclamative*. This construction is exemplified in (31):

(31)   a.   I can't believe the TIME I spent on this.
        b.   I'm amazed at the PEOPLE you know.
        c.   I can't believe the NERVE of some people.

In this construction, an epistemic predicate denoting the affective stance takes a definite-NP complement. This NP can be paraphrased by a *wh*-exclamative clause. For example, (31a) is synonymous with (32):

(32)   I can't believe how much time I spent on this.

We propose that the NP-Complement Exclamative, in addition to being an instance of the AEC, also subsumes the Metonymic NP Construction. The Metonymic NP Construction licenses a reading of a definite NP in which the NP evokes a particular scalar extent. Notice that the NP itself need not explicitly evoke a scalar amount or degree (as it does in, e.g., *I am amazed at the degree of progress.*). Definite NPs like *the nerve* do not explicitly encode an amount or degree. By positing the Metonymic NP construction, we account for the paraphrase relation between (31a) and the indirect exclamative (32).

We said earlier that the Metonymic NP Construction is uniquely devoted to the expression of exclamative meaning. This claim requires some justification, particularly in light of (33):

(33) a.   I realize the pressure you're under.
        b.   I now know the magnitude of that catastrophe.

The definite NPs in (33) can be paraphrased as, respectively, *how much pressure I'm under* and *how great the catastrophe was*. Thus, it seems clear that a definite NP can invoke a scalar extent whether it appears in an exclamative construction or complements a factive verb like *know* or *realize*. Notice, however, that NP complements of factive verbs are constrained in a way that the NP complements in (31) are not:

(34) a.   ??I realize the people she knows.
        b.   ??I now know the nerve of some people.

The examples in (34) suggest that factive verbs *know* and *realize* do not welcome NP complements which do not have intrinsic scalar meaning. The absence of this constraint in examples like (31) indicates that the principle of nominal interpretation involved in (31) is particular to exclamative constructions.

2.8. ***Nominal Extraposition.*** This construction, which is analyzed in some detail in Michaelis and Lambrecht (1994), is exemplified in (35):

(35) a.   It's amazing the DIFFERENCE!
        b.   It's amazing the PEOPLE she knows.
        c.   It's astonishing the BOOKS that can pile up.

In our earlier paper, we demonstrated that NE is distinct from right dislocation. For example, we find no number agreement between the pronominal subject and the extraposed NP, as shown in (35b). In addition, the extraposed NP lacks the deaccentuation of antitopic constituents that is characteristic of right dislocated NPs. We also showed that NE has an exclamative function: it licenses predicates denoting expectation contravention and it has a scalar interpretation. Our observations so far make it easy to see how NE fits into the family of exclamative constructions. It is an instance of the AEC, it is an instance of Extraposition, and it subsumes the Metonymic NP construction. We refer the reader to our 1994 paper for further discussion of this construction.

2.9. ***The Bare-NP Exclamative.*** This construction is exemplified in (36):

(36) a.   The things I put UP with around here.

    b.   The NERVE of that man!

It is tempting to regard (36b), for example, as an elliptical instance of either (37a) or (37b):

(37) a.   I can't BELIEVE the NERVE of that man!
       b.   It's INCREDIBLE the NERVE of that man!

The problem is that we then have two potential sources for (36b). A simpler option, which doesn't have the taint of a deletion transformation, is simply to regard (36b) as an instance of an elliptical construction, where the affective judgement is pragmatically inferred.

3.0. **Conclusion.** In conclusion, we will cite Zwicky's recent prolegomenon to a theory of grammatical constructions (1994a). Says Zwicky, "Like a morpheme or a lexical item..., a construction is neither pure form nor pure meaning, but a Saussurean sign, a pairing of the two". Zwicky points out that "there is a very great latitude in the way in which formal conditions are associated with semantics". To this we add pragmatics: different constructions, with different formal conditions and different information-structure articulations, can be associated with the same complex of semantic and illocutionary properties. Where does this leave us with respect to our question concerning the form-function fit? By positing an inheritance network, we discover regularities that enable us to see a diverse array of forms as a paradigm. Given an emic level, that of the AEC, and an etic level, that of the nine exclamative types, we find that the relevant question is not: is there a form-function fit in this domain? The relevant question is: what conditions determine speaker choice in this domain? Constraints of information structure will be relevant here. We leave this problem for another paper.

References

Fillmore, Charles. 1982. "Toward a Descriptive Framework for Spatial Deixis". In J. Jarvella and W. Klein, eds., Speech, Place and Action. London: J. Wiley and Sons.

Fillmore, Charles. 1986. "Pragmatically Controlled Zero Anaphora". In K. Nikiforidou, et al., eds., BLS 12. Berkeley: BLS, Inc.

Fillmore, Charles and Paul Kay. 1993. Construction Grammar. Unpublished ms., UC Berkeley.

Fillmore, Charles, Paul Kay and M.C. O'Connor. 1988. "Regularity and Idiomaticity in Grammatical Constructions". Language 64: 501-538.

Goldberg, Adele. 1995. Constructions: A Construction Grammar Approach to Argument Structure. Chicago: University of Chicago Press.

König, Ekkehard. 1986. "Conditionals, Concessive Conditionals and Concessives: Areas of Constrast, Neutralization and Overlap". In E. Traugott et al., eds., On Conditionals. Cambridge: Cambridge University Press.

Lakoff, George. 1987. Women, Fire and Dangerous Things: What Categories Reveal about the Mind. Chicago: Chicago University Press.

Lambrecht, Knud. 1994. Information Structure and Sentence Form. Cambridge: Cambridge University Press.

Levinson, Stephen. 1983. Pragmatics. Cambridge: Cambridge University Press.

Michaelis, Laura and Knud Lambrecht. 1994. "Nominal Extraposition: A Constructional Analysis". In S. Gahl, et al., eds., BLS 20. Berkeley: BLS, Inc.

Milner, Jean-Claude. 1978. De la syntaxe à l'interpretation. Paris: Editions du Seuil.

Pinker, Steven and Alan Prince. 1991. "Regular and Irregular Morphology and the Psychological Status of Rules of Grammar". In L. Sutton, et al., eds., BLS 17. Berkeley: BLS, Inc.

Sadock, Jerrold and Arnold Zwicky. 1985. "Speech Act Distinctions in Syntax". In T. Shopen, ed., Language Typology and Syntactic Description, vol 1. Cambridge: Cambridge University Press.

Zwicky, Arnold. 1994a. "Dealing out Meaning: Fundamentals of Grammatical Constructions". In S. Gahl et al., eds., BLS 20. Berkeley: BLS, Inc.

Zwicky, Arnold. 1994b. "Exceptional Degree Markers: A Puzzle in Internal and External Syntax". Unpublished ms., Ohio State University and Stanford University.

The Dynamic Nature of Conceptual Structure Building: Evidence from Conversation [1]

TSUYOSHI ONO & SANDRA A. THOMPSON

University of Arizona & University of California, Santa Barbara

1.   In this paper we will examine the implications for our understanding of conceptual structures of a frequent type of conversational
phenomenon. Langacker (1986) suggests:

Meaning is equated with conceptualization. Linguistic semantics must therefore
attempt the structural analysis and explicit description of abstract entities like
thoughts and concepts. The term conceptualization is interpreted quite broadly:
it encompasses novel conceptions as well as fixed concepts; sensory,
kinesthetic, and emotive experience; recognition of the immediate context
(social, physical, and linguistic); and so on. Because conceptualization resides
in cognitive processing, our ultimate objective must be to characterize the types
of cognitive events whose occurrence constitutes a given mental experience.
The remoteness of this goal is not a valid argument for denying the conceptual
basis of meaning. (Langacker 1986:3)

Our aim in this paper is to begin implementing this program by examining live discourse in which actual on-line cognitive processing can be
most easily observed.

2.   In order to focus on the phenomenon we wish to investigate, we
begin with the data that triggered our fascination with this problem,
which is given in example (1). In all the examples, the transcription
system follows Du Bois 1991 and Du Bois et al. 1993. A brief outline of
the transcription conventions can be found in the APPENDIX. Each line
represents one prosodic unit, which we call an 'intonation unit' following
Chafe 1987, 1994, Du Bois 1991, and Du Bois et al. 1993, with a
comma indicating a continuing intonation contour and a period or
question mark indicating a final intonation contour. Square brackets
indicate overlap.

---

[1] We are indebted to John Du Bois and the Corpus of Spoken
American English for the conversational data upon which this paper is based.
We also thank Michael Ewing and the audience at the CSDL meeting for
valuable feedback on earlier versions.

391

(1) Lam 26[2]. Miles and Janie are discussing the heavy flirting at a
     dancing hall called Bahia frequented by Miles.

     1   *Miles: you don't do that with- --*
     2   *Janie: this is all [at Bahia]?*
     3   *Miles: [strangers].*
     4   *Janie: all this stuff happens at [Bahia].*
     5   *Miles: [yeah].*
     6   *Janie: hunh?*
--> *7 Miles:*   *... to %other people I mean.*
     8   ALL BURST INTO LAUGHTER FOR 8 SECONDS

What Miles has done at the arrow is of great interest syntactically,
interactionally, and conceptually. Miles has 'added' a prepositional
phrase to something based on what Janie has said. Thus it might appear
that Miles and Janie are 'co-constructing' an instantiation of a
constructional schema (as discussed in Lerner 1991 and Ono and
Thompson to appear). But what he has added it TO is not explicitly
present in the conversation.

    We could say that what Miles has added his prepositional phrase
to is Janie's *all this stuff happens at Bahia, hunh?* in lines 4 and 6. But on
further inspection we see that he can't have added it to what she has
said in line 4, since her utterance is accompanied by a tag *hunh?* and it
wouldn't make interactional sense to add a prepositional phrase to an
utterance ending with such a tag.

    So perhaps a better analysis is that Miles has added his
prepositional phrase to the proposition which underlies Janie's utterance
in line 4. But from an interactional point of view, this would also be
unacceptable, since his prepositional phrase is accompanied by a
discourse marker *I mean*, which can only be said by a speaker who is
amending his/her OWN utterance.

    This suggests that what Miles has added his prepositional phrase
to is the proposition underlying his own *yeah*, namely *all this stuff
happens at Bahia*, to which it is appropriate to add a qualifying
prepositional phrase - *to other people I mean*. But crucially, in so doing,
he has effected a change in the way the participants understand that
proposition. That is, when he says *yeah* in line 5, responding to Janie's
queries, he is confirming the location at which the flirting activities
occur. Even though Janie's utterance *all this stuff happens at Bahia* does
not specify whether Miles is part of these activities or not, his *to other
people I mean*, by explicitly denying that he is a part of them, also
retrospectively attributes the implication that he might be part of them
to the proposition *all this stuff happens at Bahia*. The speakers of the

---

2 The notation after the example number is a label referring to the
conversation from which the example is drawn.

conversation recognize this shift in interpretation and burst into laughter.

We will use the term 'conceptual structure' to refer to this kind of implication, following Langacker 1987, 1991. With this terminology we could then say that when Miles adds the prepositional phrase *to other people I mean* in line 7, a new conceptual structure is created, in which a new contrast is created between the flirting activities, 'all this stuff' that 'happens at Bahia', and the fact that they don't happen to HIM. It is this shift in meaning that makes everyone laugh.

These shifts in conceptual structure occur frequently in conversation. Not all of them are sources of humor; in fact, some of them are quite prosaic. Consider example (2):

(2)　Car 1.　George and David are discussing David's new car.

> *1 George:　that's an expensive car,*
> *2　　　　　.. and then you got to get the tags on it.*
> *3　　　　　right%?*
> *4 David:　.. I got everything.*
> *5 George:　.. you got everything?*
> *6 David:　... I got everything taken care of.*
> *7　　　　　I got insurance on it too.*
> *8 George:　[how much <X it X>] --*
--> *9 David:　[under my] name.*
> *10　　　　　... eleven hundred a year.*
> *11 George:　eleven hundred.*
> *12 David:　three hundred [dollars down],*
> *13 George:　[that's cheap] man,*

In example (2), in line 9 David adds new material to what he has already said, just as Miles did in (1). And just as in (1), this 'addition' results in a shift in the conceptual structure. When David says *under my name* in line 9, he does not mean that insurance is one of the things he got under his name. Rather, in line 7 he first presents buying insurance as one of several car-related activities (that's why he says *I got insurance on it TOO*), and then in line 9 he specifies this insurance-purchasing with respect to who the policy-holder is. We thus see David highlighting different facets of the same activity. This is again nicely captured as a change in conceptual structure based on the proposition underlying line 7 *I got insurance on it too*. The conceptual structure corresponding to that proposition involves his car-buying activities, while the conceptual structure corresponding to the new proposition resulting from David's addition of *under my name* involves who the policy-holder is. In the context of the conversation, this change is significant, since David has just broken up with his girlfriend and is trying to re-establish himself as a single person. This example, then, could be seen as a less dramatic instance of the phenomenon that caused the laughter in (1).

Before we discuss what these examples tell us about language, cognition, and social interaction, let's look at one more example, given in (3). In (3) the @-sign indicates laughter.

(3)   Lam 23.   Miles has been describing the suggestive behavior of two people at the same dancing hall as in (1), whom he had assumed did not know each other.

```
      1 Miles:     .. I figured,
      2 Janie:     [oo=].
      3 Miles:     [oh,
      4             they must know each] other.
      5 Janie:     ... oo=.
-->   6 Harold:    .. very well.
      7            <@ in fact @>.
```

In line 6 and 7 Harold adds something to what Miles has said in line 4. What Harold is doing here is 'upgrading' the characterization that Miles has given of the relationship between the two people - it's not just that they 'must know each other', as Miles has said, but that they must know each other 'very well, in fact'.

Notice here that Miles's utterance *they must know each other* is presented as what came to his mind when he watched the couple's behavior, as a quote of his own thought. Then Harold's *very well, in fact* is his assessment of the relationship as a participant in the present conversation. That is, these two utterances not only belong to two different speakers but to two different worlds. Miles's suspicion is first reported, and then Harold takes its basic proposition and re-presents it together with his stronger assessment based on what he has just been told.

Once again, in adding this adverbial phrase to Miles's utterance, Harold has changed the conceptual structure from one involving Miles's suspicion that the two people on the dance floor were not strangers to each other to one involving a stronger conviction that their inappropriate behavior would cause anyone to think they knew each other VERY WELL.

3.   Now, in order to say what we think these examples show, we need to propose two theoretical concepts first.

As we said at the beginning of this paper, we see our project as taking off from certain ideas of Langacker, as outlined in several works, including Langacker 1986, 1987, and 1991; if "conceptualization resides in cognitive processing, our ultimate objective must be to characterize the types of cognitive events whose occurrence constitutes a given mental experience" (Langacker 1986:3). We believe we can most easily observe actual cognitive processing of conceptualization in on-line discourse.

Our notions of 'conceptual structure' and 'proposition' are similar to Langacker's (1987 and 1991). That is, the term 'conceptual structure' is applied broadly to thoughts, concepts, perceptions, and mental experience. A 'proposition' is then a conceptual structure that functions as the 'semantic pole' of a clause. A 'conceptual structure' is a broader, more inclusive category, of which 'propositions' are one type. These conceptual structures have many of the same properties of the 'mental spaces' of Fauconnier 1985. What our data show is that an understanding of how these 'conceptual structures' work can be gained by considering the actual behavior of conversational participants.

4.   How, then, should we account for the examples we have just considered? The answer is that there is one feature which our three examples have in common. Namely, the 'additions' in each case come after the unit to which they are added is complete. For example, in example (3), Miles's clause in line 4, *they must know each other*, has a period indicating final intonation, and is a grammatically and semantically complete clause. Such points of intonational, grammatical, and semantic completion are termed 'transition-relevance places' by researchers in Conversation Analysis, and are critical points in conversational interaction, because they are precisely the points where turn transition is most likely, as has been shown in a number of works, including Sacks et al. 1974, Oreström 1983, Ford 1993, and Ford and Thompson to appear.

There is also evidence from the processing literature to suggest that these transition-relevance places might be points of major closure for the construction of semantic - or conceptual - structures (Bever et al. 1973, Caplan 1972, Jarvella 1979, Fodor et al. 1974).

If extensions are added to a clause which has already been completed, both intonationally and grammatically, and if such completion points are important points of signalling and interpreting interactional closure, then we can begin to understand why these examples can change the conceptual structure rather dramatically: it's because participants have to 're-open', as it were, the conceptual structure which they had already taken as complete. In such cases, very often the just-constructed conceptual structure has to be totally abandoned and a new conceptual structure has to be constructed, as in example (1), where the dramatic change brings about the laughter. Sometimes the just-constructed conceptual structure simply needs to be 'updated', so to speak, or made more specific, as in example (2), where a rather general conceptual structure involving buying insurance needs to be narrowed to one specifying whose name the insurance is purchased under, or as in (3), where a mild suspicion upon a single viewing of the scene is 'upgraded' to a strong conviction derived from more synthesized views presented in a conversation about it.

This process of re-designing conceptual structures happens all the time in conversation, as speakers contribute their turns, and most of the time we don't notice it. What is significant about examples (1) - (3), however, is, as we have said, that more material is 'added' to something which is already completed. What this means is that a conceptual structure which has been completed has to be RE-designed or OPENED UP for restructuring and re-interpretation AFTER it has been completed. This is manifested most clearly in examples like (1), where the proposition underlying Miles's *yeah* is that Bahia is the place where 'all this stuff' happens. But the new conceptual structure invoked by Miles's prepositional phrase *to other people I mean* is that 'all this stuff' doesn't happen to HIM.

5.   As a final example to illustrate our point, consider example (4).

(4)   Lam 6. Harold and Janie (a married couple) are joking about the poor quality of their audio system speakers.

1 Harold:	*these are like,*
2 Janie:	*the [world's worst] speakers.*
3 Miles:	*[where is the other one].*
4 Harold:	*these are the [shittiest] ..*
	speakers on earth.
5 Janie:	*[over here].*
--> *6*	*... besides the ones in the kitchen.*

In example (4), there are two superlative claims about the speakers, one in lines 1-2, *these are like the world's worst speakers.*, co-constructed by Harold and Janie, and one in line 4, *these are the shittiest speakers on earth.*, said by Harold. The end of each of these intonation units is a transition-relevance place, since it is complete intonationally, semantically, and grammatically.

Thus, in line 6, when Janie jokingly adds the prepositional phrase *besides the ones in the kitchen*, a new conceptual structure has to be built. And this new conceptual structure conflicts with those already available from the two superlative statements. That is, from the claims that Harold and Janie's speakers are 'the world's worst speakers' and 'the shittiest speakers on earth', the standard inference is that there ARE NO OTHER speakers that are that bad.

But Janie's 'addition' in line 6 creates a new conceptual structure, namely *these are the shittiest speakers on earth, besides the ones in the kitchen*, that is, that there is a pair of speakers that is even worse.

6.   In conclusion, what we have tried to do in this paper is to begin to implement the approach to conceptual structure in cognitive processing advocated by Langacker 1986. Our data show that when people talk, conceptual structure building can be seen to be very much a joint

activity, constantly changing as the actual interaction proceeds. We have focused on a particular type of interaction, where a clause comes to completion at a transition-relevance place, and then more syntactic material is added. We suggest that in such cases the conceptual structure has to be RE-built with the addition of the new grammatical material. Sometimes the result is totally unremarkable, as in example (2) about the car insurance. But sometimes, the resulting clash between the old conceptual structure and the new one is remarkable, and is remarked on and noticed by the participants, as in (1), where the new conceptual structure conveys the understanding that all the flirting at Bahia only happens to other people, but not to him.

We suggest that a cognitive model of language must include a way of accounting for the remarkable ability of speakers to perform the kinds of activities exhibited in these examples, where syntactic material is apparently 'added' to something which has come to closure in the conversation, and further, where such 'additions' cause radical re-building of conceptual structures in the interaction.

APPENDIX: SYMBOLS FOR DISCOURSE TRANSCRIPTION

adapted from Du Bois et al. 1993

UNITS
    Intonation unit   `{carriage return}`
    Truncated intonation unit   `--`
    Word   `{space}`
    Truncated word   `-`

SPEAKERS
    Speaker identity/turn start   `:`
    Speech overlap   `[ ]`

TRANSITIONAL CONTINUITY
    Final   `.`
    Continuing   `,`
    Appeal   `?`

LENGTHENING
    Lengthening   `=`

PAUSE
    Long   `. . .`
    Short   `. .`

VOCAL NOISES
    Vocal noises   `( )`
    Glottal stop   `%`
    Laughter   `@`

QUALITY
    Quality   `<Y Y>`
    Laugh quality   `<@ @>`

TRANSCRIBER'S PERSPECTIVE
    Uncertain hearing   `<X X>`

REFERENCES

Bever, T. G., M. F. Garrett, and R. Hurtig. 1973. The Interaction of Perceptual Processes and Ambiguous Sentences. *Memory and Cognition* 1:277-286.

Caplan, D. 1972. Clause Boundaries and Recognition Latencies for Words in Sentences. *Perception and Psychophysics* 12:73-76.

Chafe, Wallace. 1987. Cognitive Constraints on Information Flow. In Tomlin, Russell, ed., *Coherence and Grounding in Discourse*. Amsterdam: Benjamins.

Chafe, Wallace. 1994. *Discourse, Consciousness, and Time: the Flow and Displacement of Conscious Experience in Speaking and Writing*. Chicago: University of Chicago Press.

Du Bois, John. 1991. Transcription Design Principles for Spoken Discourse Research. *Pragmatics* 1:71-106.

Du Bois, John, Stephan Schuetze-Coburn, Danae Paolino, and Susanna Cumming. 1993. Outline of Discourse Transcription. In Jane A. Edwards and Martin D. Lampert, eds., *Talking Data: Transcription and Coding Methods for Language Research*, 45-89. Hillsdale, NJ: Lawrence Erlbaum.

Fauconnier, Gilles. 1985. *Mental Spaces*. Cambridge, MA: MIT Press.

Fodor, J. A., T. G. Bever, and M. F. Garrett. 1974. *The Psychology of Language: An Introduction to Psycholinguistics and Generative Grammar*. New York: McGraw-Hill.

Ford, Cecilia E. 1993. *Grammar in Interaction: Adverbial Clauses in American English Conversations*. Cambridge: Cambridge University Press.

Ford, Cecilia and Sandra A. Thompson. To appear. Interactional Units in Conversation: Syntactic, Intonational, and Pragmatic Resources for the Projection of Turn Completion. In Ochs, Elinor, Emanuel Schegloff, and Sandra A. Thompson, eds., *Interaction and Grammar*. Cambridge: Cambridge University Press.

Jarvella, R. J. 1979. Immediate Memory and Discourse Processing. In G. H. Bower, ed., *The Psychology of Learning and Motivation* 13. New York: Academic Press.

Langacker, Ronald W. 1986. An Introduction to Cognitive Grammar. *Cognitive Science* 10:1-40.

Langacker, Ronald W. 1987. *Foundations of Cognitive Grammar*, Vol. 1. Stanford: Stanford University Press.

Langacker, Ronald W. 1991. *Foundations of Cognitive Grammar*, Vol. 2. Stanford: Stanford University Press.

Lerner, Gene. 1991. On the Syntax of Sentences-in-progress. *Language in Society* 20:441-458.

Ono, Tsuyoshi and Sandra A. Thompson. To appear. Interaction and Syntax in the Structure of Conversational Discourse. In Eduard Hovy and Donia Scott, eds., *Discourse Processing: an Interdicsiplinary Perspective*. Heidelberg: Springer-Verlag.

Oreström, Bengt. 1983. *Turn-taking in English Conversation*. (Lund Studies in English 66.) Lund: CWK Gleerup.

Sacks, Harvey, Emanuel Schegloff, and Gail Jefferson. 1974. A Simplest Systematics for the Organization of Turn-taking for Conversation. *Language* 50.4:696-735.

Situation Perspective: On the Relations of Thematic Roles, Discourse Categories, and Grammatical Relations to Figure and Ground

MARIA POLINSKY
University of Southern California

1.1 Perspective-dependent Notions

Situation perspective is often described in terms of the contrast between Figure and Ground (Talmy 1978; 1985) or trajector and landmark (Langacker 1987; 1990).[1] This contrast allows us to account for the semantic differences between sentences (a) and (b) in (1) and (2), where the Figure is put in perspective, and the Ground is assumed as a reference point.

(1) a. Dr. Jekyll (Figure) is next to Mr. Hyde (Ground)
     b. Mr. Hyde (Figure) is next to Dr. Jekyll (Ground)
(2) a. The hill (Figure) is above the forest (Ground)
     b. The forest (Figure) is beneath the hill (Ground)

The F-G contrast is generally accepted as playing a role in the choice between sentences such as (a) and (b) above. Structural corollaries of this contrast in English have also been described (Jackendoff 1976: 96-8;

This study was supported in part by the NSF grant SBR-9220219. I am indebted to Ramazan Rajabov for Tsez data and to Bernard Comrie, Leonid Iomdin, Ed Keenan, Ron Langacker, Paul Parshin, Jakov Testelets for the discussion of this paper. All errors are my sole responsibility.

Abbreviations: ABS - Absolutive; AD - proximal *-xo*; APUD - proximal *-de*; COM - Comitative; DAT - Dative; ERG - Ergative; ESS - Essive; F - Figure; G - Ground; GER - Gerund; IMP - Imperative; LAT - Lative; PASTEV - Past Evidential; PASTNEV - Past Non-evidential; RES - Resultative; # - infelicitous, % - marginally felicitous. Roman numerals indicate grammatical class.

[1]For other terms referring to perspective-dependent notions, see (Fillmore 1975: 16-27; 1977; Talmy 1978; Lang 1989; Dowty 1991: 563). In this paper, I will use *Figure* and *Ground* as general terminology.

1990: 91-3, 159-63), but the status of perspective-oriented notions vis-à-vis thematic roles, grammatical relations, and discourse categories such as topic and focus remains unclear. Dowty (1991: 562-4) discusses this issue and presents some arguments against the (often implicit) identification of F and G with thematic roles. In a nutshell, his arguments against such an identification are as follows. "[A]ll putative instances of perspective-dependent" contrasts can be accounted for as semantic correlates of the hierarchy of grammatical relations: F can be described as a semantic correlate of the subject, and G corresponds to a lower grammatical relation.

This paper presents empirical evidence supporting Dowty's general claim that F and G do not belong with other accepted thematic roles. The main argument against the identification of perspective-dependent notions with thematic roles is that the F-G contrast—which is generally assumed as characteristic of stative predicates—has repercussions in different types of constructions as well as in various sets of thematic roles. Contrary to Dowty's claim, I also argue that the F-G contrast cannot be reduced to the opposition of grammatical relations and/or discourse categories.

Where then do perspective-dependent notions belong? The argument advanced here is that they operate at the interface between the conceptual structure and the semantico-syntactic structure. This type of interface has been studied less than other language modules, and the analysis proposed here is only tentative. My hypothesis is that the F-G contrast determines the choice of a construction, therefore preceding the assignment of thematic roles, grammatical relations, and topic-focus functions.

Of course, the conclusions reached in this paper will be preliminary as they will be established on the basis of a single language, Tsez.

1.2   Tsez: General Information

Tsez belongs to the Nakh-Daghestanian family and is spoken by 8,000 people in the NE Caucasus. In order to follow the discussion below, the reader should be aware of several grammatical features of Tsez. Tsez is a V-final language; however, V-medial structures are also possible when motivated by discourse factors. There are no articles, though adjectives are marked for definiteness (the so-called restrictive adjective). The language is ergative, and the verb agrees in grammatical class with the absolutive argument (intransitive subject or direct object). In complex constructions, a distinction is made between medial (non-finite) verb forms and the final (finite) verb, cf. (12a, b) below.

In addition to the absolutive and ergative, the language also has the dative, genitive, instrumental, and a number of locative cases.[2] All locative formations are serial: each locative form includes a localization marker denoting the positional characteristic of the reference point ('on', 'in',

---

[2]To avoid ambiguity, I will be using the term *locative* to refer to actual language forms and *spatial* to denote the relevant relational meaning.

'under', 'above', etc.) followed by a locative case marker expressing orientation towards that reference point, for example:[3]

(3)   Hon-Ło-Ror
        mountain-LOCALIZATION 'ON'-DIRECTIVE CASE
        'up into the mountains'

Locative forms can have both a spatial and a non-spatial meanings. As most localization markers have developed non-spatial meanings, postpositions are often used to clarify the meaning of an otherwise ambiguous suffix, for example:

(4)   a. R'utku-ø   Hon-xo-ø   igo   joł
          house-ABS   mountain-AD-ESS near is
          'The house is near the mountain.'
      b. Hon-xo-ø   igo   R'utku-ø   joł
          mountain-AD-ESS near   house-ABS   is
          'There is a house near the mountain.'

In this paper, I will examine two proximal markers: -de and -xo, which have both a spatial and a comitative interpretation (see Polinsky and Rajabov 1994 for details). My principal goal is to establish whether there are any content-based constraints that determine F-G relationships in Tsez.

1.3   Acceptability and Felicity

The discussion below will rely heavily on the identification of certain constructions as felicitous or infelicitous according to the intuition of a native Tsez speaker. It is important to distinguish acceptability, a grammatical judgment, from felicity which indicates the pragmatically-based judgment of constructions as appropriate, marginal (%), or inappropriate (#).
At first glance, it seems that the difference between acceptability and felicity is straightforward: the former is responsible for the unacceptability of such things as *teached, and the latter is responsible for such things as #like son, like father. Informally, then, unacceptable are those things that violate finite and explicable rules of grammar, and infelicitous are things that tend not to occur. For infelicitous sequences, one can often think of a context where they could occur but this very context is specialized and does not immediately come to mind. Thus, acceptability is a more fixed category than felicity. At a closer look, however, the line

---

[3]For more details on locative formations, see Polinsky and Rajabov (1994); Comrie *et al.* (forthcoming).

between the two categories is quite fuzzy. What about numerous linguistic examples such as (5) and (6) which, in linguistic literature, appear with a star, or a question mark, or a percentage sign? These may be judged unacceptable or infelicitous depending on a variety of factors: individual idiolect, comparison with other examples, or even the goals of a linguistic study they are used in.

(5)   ?*%The snake climbed down the tree (Jackendoff 1990: 35)
(6)   ?*%Fellowships are easy to award physicists.

The fuzzy line between the grammatical and pragmatic will not be resolved in this work but I will explain the strategy of distinguishing felicitous from grammatically acceptable which I adopted here; hopefully, this strategy could be adopted in other studies as well. Acceptability is a binary category: acceptable and unacceptable are polar entities. Felicity is a scalar category, obeying a set of preference rules or conditions (Jackendoff 1985; 1990: 36-7, 283): constructions can be judged more or less felicitous depending on how many preferential rules they satisfy.

2   Figure and Ground in Stative Situations

In a number of instances, though the main predicate of a construction is dynamic, some of its arguments remain in a stative relationship one to another. As a result, I prefer to speak of *stative situations* rather than *stative predicates*. For example, the process/action of seeing or finding something subsumes the existence or location of the entity (entities) seen or found (Jackendoff 1990: 167, 202-4, 208). If two entities are found, one of the entities can be described in relationship to another, and this relationship can be that of F and G.

2.1   Stative Situations: X Is Near Y

This subsection considers only those constructions which have no existential interpretation: the examples below describe the relationship between two referents whose existence is presupposed (though the referents are not necessarily definite, cf. (9) and (10) below).

1) Size. The first constraint on the F-G relationship in Tsez concerns the relative size of F and G: a smaller entity (F) has to be described in relationship to the larger one (G), not vice versa. This is obvious from the comparison of (4a) above, where G (mountain) is significantly larger than F (house), and the infelicitous (7a, b), where F is larger than G:[4]

---

[4]Note that in English and English-like languages, the equivalent of (4a) above is felicitous in a wider array of contexts than the equivalents of (7a, b). Still, contexts in which the latter would be appropriate in English are easy to imagine,

(7) a. #Hon-ø   R'utko-x-ø   igo   joɬ

          mountain-ABS   house-AD-ESS   near   is

          'The mountain is near the house.'

    b. #R'utko-x-ø   igo   Hon-ø

          house-AD-ESS   near   mountain-ABS

          j-oq-no   joɬ

          II-be-GER   is

          'The mountain is near the house.'

That only the relative size of F vis-à-vis G is relevant is confirmed by (8a, b), where both entities are small. Nevertheless, a mushroom can serve as reference point (G) for a berry (8a), but the opposite is infelicitous (8b):

(8) a. dā-r   eɬu-ø   zik'u-de-ø

          1SG-DAT   blackberry-ABS   mushroom-APUD-ESS

          igo   j-esu-s

          near   II-find-PASTEV

          'I found a blackberry branch near a/the mushroom.'

    b. #dā-r   zik'u-ø

          1SG-DAT   mushroom-ABS

          eɬu-de-ø   igo   j-esu-s

          blackberry-APUD-ESS   near   II-find-PASTEV

          'I found a mushroom near a/the blackberry branch.'

Commensurate size is also relevant for animate entities: a larger one can serve as G for a small one (9a) but the opposite is infelicitous (9b):

(9) a. dā-r   k'et'u-ø   ʕomoj-de-ø   igo

          1SG-DAT   cat-ABS   donkey-APUD-ESS   near

          b-ikwaj-si

          III-see-PASTEV

          'I saw the/a cat next to the/a donkey.'

---

e.g., as the answer to the question "Where is that mountain where you go skiing?".

    b. #dā-r   ʕomoj-ø   k'et'u-de-ø

        1SG-DAT   donkey-ABS   cat-APUD-ESS

        igo   b-ikwaj-si

        near   III-see-PASTEV

        'I saw the/a donkey next to the/a cat.'

     If two entities located in relation to one another are commensurate in size, other factors determine the F-G assignment.

     2) Mobility. The next constraint on F-G assignment becomes clear from the comparison between the felicitous (10a) and the infelicitous (10b):

(10)   a. dā-r   bikori-ø   mašu-de-ø

        1SG-DAT snake-ABS   pipe-APUD-ESS

        igo   b-ikwaj-si

        near   III-see-PASTEV

        'I saw the/a snake next to a/the pipe.'

    b. %dā-r   mašu-ø   bikori-de-ø

        1SG-DAT   pipe-ABS   snake-APUD-ESS

        igo   r-ikwaj-si

        near   IV-see-PASTEV

        'I saw the/a pipe next to the/a snake.'

The contrast between (10a) and (10b) indicates that, if two entities are commensurate in size, the (more) stationary one is a better G than the more mobile one. Intuitively, this seems to be a plausible condition; the stationary entity makes a better reference point precisely because its coordinates are fixed, and it is easier to think of such an entity as a stable point of departure for describing something that is not fixed in time or space. In English and English-like languages, the difference between examples similar to (10a) and (10b) is a matter of frequency; examples such as (10a) are more frequent, probably because they better satisfy preferential rules for structuring and processing information.

     3) Conventional value. Conventional value is a reflection of the rank occupied by a given entity in a particular culture's view of what is important in the world around us. The relevance of conventional value (prototypical status) for one type of construction in English—conjoined elements—has been described by Cooper and Ross (1975: 64-70, 100-103). One can expect conventional value to have multiple repercussions in the

structure of a language, and I will not be able to expose all of these repercussions in Tsez.

The role of conventional value becomes apparent from the contrast between the felicitous (11a) and the infelicitous (11b). Despite the arguably commensurate size, a person can serve as reference point (G) for locating an animal but an animal cannot be the reference point for locating a human being. Since there are no indications of a grammatical contrast between human names and names of animals, this asymmetry can be explained by the higher pragmatic or conventional value assigned to humans in society.[5] Further, not all humans are equal: adults are apparently assigned a higher conventional value than children (see (12a, b)).

(11)   a.   pat'imat-de-r   dej meši-ø   b-oq-no

          Fatima-APUD-LAT   my calf-ABS   III-be-GER

          b-ičā-si

          III-be-RES

          'My calf is where Fatima is/with Fatima.'

       b.   #dej meši-de-r   pat'imat-ø   j-oq-no

            my calf-APUD-LAT   Fatima-ABS   II-be-GER

          j-ičā-si

          II-be-RES

          'Fatima is where my calf is/with my calf.'

In some instances, conventional value may outweigh the size factor. Thus, in (12a), the shepherd serves as G for the cattle herd, but the cattle herd cannot be located in reference to a boy, whose conventional value is lower than that of a shepherd, hence the infelicitous (12b).

(12)   a.   dandi sis   aHo-de-ø   posur-ø

          only   one   shepherd-APUD-ESS   cattle-ABS

          r-oq-zaŁ   zej-ā   sis   zija-ø

          IIPL-be-because   bear-ERG one   cow-ABS

          b-ok'ek'-no

          III-steal-PASTNEV

          'Since the cattle herd was tended for only by one shepherd, a bear stole a cow.'

---

[5]I will use the term *conventional* below to avoid discourse-related connotations of the term *pragmatic*.

b. #dandi　　　sis　　　uži-de-ø　　　　　posur-ø

only　　　one　　　boy-APUD-ESS　　　cattle-ABS

r-oq-zaŁ　　　　zej-ā　　　sis　　　zija-ø

IIPL-be-because　bear-ERG　one　　cow-ABS

b-ok'ek'-no

III-steal-PASTNEV

'Since the cattle herd was tended for only by a boy, a bear stole a cow.'

So far, the examples suggest that the F-G assignment in Tsez is sensitive to several cognitive characteristics of the referents: their relative size, mobility, and conventional value. The concomitant question is whether these three criteria can be ranked; however, their ranking falls outside the scope of this paper and I will treat them below as independent characteristics.

2.2   Existential Constructions[6]

All the cases discussed so far have situations in which F and G are equal or comparable in definiteness. One might expect that fewer restrictions should apply if G is definite and F indefinite, for instance, if F is introduced as a new entity in the existential construction. However, the examination of Tsez existential constructions reveals that the constraints discussed above remain valid.

Comparing example (4b) above with the infelicitous (13), we see that in existential clauses also, a smaller entity must be located in reference to the larger one:

(13)　　　#Rutko-x-ø　　　igo　　Hon-ø　　　　jo4

house-AD-ESS　　near　　mountain-ABS　　is

'There is a mountain near the house.'

The effect of mobility on F-G assignment is as follows: if of two otherwise comparable entities one is less mobile/more stationary than the

---

[6]The difference between existential and non-existential constructions in Tsez needs some explaining. Both constructions can include the existential verb *jo4*, but in the non-existential construction this predicate can be preceded by a non-finite form of another stative verb ('become', 'stay'), as in (7b). If no such non-finite form is used, the two readings are distinguished by the relative order of the stative Theme and Location; in the non-existential construction, the Theme precedes the Location, as in (4a), and in the existential construction the Theme follows the Location, as in (4b) above.

other, the more stationary entity serves as G. In (14), the situation involves two insects, both of which are mobile, a worm and a flying insect. The worm is a better reference point: compare (14a), where a worm serves as G, and the infelicitous (14b) where the configuration is reversed:

(14)   a.   acurjo-de-ø   igo   t'ut'-ø   joɬ

               worm-APUD-ESS   near   small insect-ABS is

               'There is a fly/bee near the worm.'

    b.   #t'ut'-de-ø   igo   acurjo-ø   joɬ

               small insect-APUD-ESS near   worm-ABS   is

               'There is a worm near the fly/bee.'

The effect of conventional value is illustrated in (15), where a beggar can be located in reference to the king (15a), but it is awkward to locate the socially more important king in reference to the beggar.

(15)   a.   xan-de-ø   igo   netin

               king-APUD-ESS   near   always

               esirnok'u-ø   joɬ

               beggar-ABS   is

               'There is always a beggar near a/the king.'

    b.   #esirnok'u-de-ø   igo   netin

               beggar-APUD-ESS near   always

               xan-ø   joɬ

               king-ABS is

               'There is always a king near the beggar.'

Overall, these examples indicate that the relative size, mobility, and conventional value of two participants affect the choice of perspective: the participant that is larger, more stationary, or of a higher conventional value is preferred as G.

2.3   The Linear Ordering of Figure and Ground

There have been suggestions that the nature of F-G orderings may lie in the basic or dominant order of a language; for example, it has been argued that, in Japanese, at some level of derivation existential sentences have the G-before-F ordering (Kuno 1973: 351-402). As a V-final language, Tsez too, has the G-before-F ordering in existential constructions, cf. (4b), (14a),

(15a). Meanwhile, in other constructions, the F-G ordering may vary, depending on discourse factors. For example, in (16a), where F (worm) precedes G (snake), both referents are viewed as new and relatively salient in the discourse (hence the suitability of the indefinite article in the English translation). If the snake is viewed as a given entity, and therefore more topic-oriented, it is likely to be named first, as in (16b).

(16)   a.   dā-r   acurjo-ø   bikori-de-ø

             1SG-DAT   worm-ABS   snake-APUD

             igo   b-ikwaj-si

             near   III-see-PASTEV

             'I saw the/a worm next to the/a snake.'

       b.   dā-r   bikori-de-ø   igo   acurjo-ø

             1SG-DAT   snake-APUD   near   worm-ABS

             b-ikwaj-si

             III-see-PASTEV

             'I saw a/the worm next to the snake.'

The comparison between 16a) and (16b) indicates that, all other factors being equal, the F-G ordering is determined by discourse factors. This suggests that the contrast between perspective-dependent notions is independent of discourse-dependent contrasts and, therefore, it cannot be reduced to the latter. This does not exclude the correlation between F and the topic of discourse (Dowty 1991: 563) observed in English, but this correlation is not entirely rigid. Cross-linguistically, one instance in which it is violated is the existential construction, where G is normally a given entity and/or topic, while F is focus. Thus, G-before-F in the existential construction can be predicted as a frequent ordering (but not as the only one, which allows for languages with existential expletives) in those languages where topic precedes focus. Such languages include the SOV type but they can also include other types. Similarly, languages with focus-before-topic orders (for example, VOS) can be expected to have the F-before-G ordering in the existential construction, thus, in Malagasy (VOS):

(17)   m-isy   ankizy   ø-ao   an-tsekoly

        PRES-be   children   PRES-in   OBL-school

        'There are children at school.'

3   Figure and Ground in Comitatives

So far, the F-G distinction has been observed in precisely those situations where it might be expected: a stative Theme (F) is positioned with respect to the Location (G). In this section, we will see that the F-G contrast has repercussions in comitative constructions as well.

As was stated above, the markers -*de* and -*xo* can encode the comitative function—that of one participant accompanying another participant in an event.[7] For instance, (18) allows the spatial and the comitative interpretation. Under the comitative interpretation, the man is viewed as a more central participant, who is then accompanied by the father. Given that the verb in (18) is stative, 'this man' is the stative Theme, and 'the father' is the comitative.

(18)   obij-de-r   ejda   žek'u-ø   ø-oq-no

          father-APUD-LAT   this   man-ABS   I-be-GER

          ø-ičā-si

          I-be-RES

          'This man is with the father/at the father's.'

I will first examine the constraints on comitatives and then show that comitatives cannot be analyzed as metaphorical statives. Note that the role of mobility distinctions is obscured in comitatives because both participants are comparable in an active situation.

1) Size. As with statives, a larger entity can be marked as the comitative in relation to a smaller one, but not otherwise. Compare the felicitous (19a) and the infelicitous (19b):

(19)   a.   kaRat-ø   sumka-zā-de-ø   cadaq

                letter-ABS   bag-PL-APUD-ESS   with

                j-is-o

                II-take-IMP

                'Take the letter (F) with the luggage (G).'

          b.   #sumka-zā-bi-ø   kaRata-de-ø   cadaq

                bag-PL-ABS   letter-APUD-ESS   with

                r-is-o

                IIPL-take-IMP

                'Take the luggage (F) with the letter (G).'

---

[7] In Tsez, abstract nouns cannot appear as comitatives, hence the impossibility of such comitatives as 'with enthusiasm.'

2) Conventional value. The relevance of conventional value is illustrated by the contrast between (20a), where the man is assumed as reference point for the donkey, and the infelicitous (20b), where the donkey is the reference point for the man. Note that in both examples the comitative nominal occupies the topic position, which indicates once more that the F-G contrast is independent of the topic-focus contrast.

(20)   a.   ejda   žek'u-de-ø   ʕomoj-ø   b-egir

            this   man-APUD-ESS   donkey-ABS III-send/IMP

            'Send the donkey (F) with this man (G).'

       b.   #ʕomoj-de-ø   ejda   žek'u-ø   ø-egir

            donkey-APUD-ESS   this   man-ABS I-send/IMP

            'Send this man (F) with the donkey (G).'

In the Tsez view of the world, children and adults are clearly assigned different conventional values (note the contrast between (12a) and (12b) above). This difference in conventional value is reflected in the felicity of comitatives: compare the infelicitous (20b), where the man accompanies the donkey, and the felicitous (21), where the boy accompanies the donkey:

(21)   ʕomoj-de-ø   ejda   uži-ø   ø-egir

       donkey-APUD-ESS   this   boy-ABS   I-send/IMP

       'Send this boy (F) with the donkey (G).'

These examples show that, in Tsez, the main argument and the comitative obey the same constraints as Theme and Location with statives. It is plausible to account for the similarity of constraints by identifying the comitative nominal with G and the main participant with F.

However, Tsez restrictions on the size or conventional value of the comitative are more difficult to imagine since they tend to contradict the well-known observation that cross-linguistically, human beings are considered better agents and topics than inanimate entities or even animals (Silverstein 1976; Comrie 1989: 57-62; Dowty 1991: 577-9), probably because they are fit the description of "the prototypical speaker" (Cooper and Ross 1975: 65-7). On the basis of this observation, one would expect felicity judgments for (20a,b) to be just the opposite of what can actually be observed. In my view, this shows that anthropocentric linguistics—which identifies human referents with agents, subjects, and topics—reflects only one of several coexisting dimensions of human referents. Indeed, though human referents are distinguished from referents of other natural classes, this difference can take various linguistic realizations.

On the one hand, assuming that the definition of an agent involves the ability to begin, continue or terminate the situation at will, humans are the best prototypical agents because they have free will and mobility. Prototypical agentivity is, in turn, correlated to topicality and subjecthood; these features are more typical of F than of G. On the other hand, assuming the same the anthropocentric view of the world, humans (and the first person in particular) make the best reference points to which everything else can be related, hence the Me First principle (Cooper and Ross 1975: 67). Accordingly, it can be argued that humans provide a better G than other referents. In Tsez, it is the latter generalization that forms the basis of comitative constructions; in English-like languages, it is the former.

This shows that universalizing explanations of various conceptual hierarchies are not without limitations, simply because they capture only some of the relevant aspects of an otherwise modular system. In a number of instances, these hierarchies agree, thereby yielding harmonious results. However, as is shown here, such agreement is not universal.

To recapitulate, examples (19)-(21) show that the main participant and the comitative are subject to similar constraints as F and G in statives. One might argue that the comitative is simply an extension of the spatial function of the respective locative marker and that there is no need to posit the comitative as a special function. Though this is a plausible diachronic explanation, there are clear disadvantages to accepting this as an adequate synchronic account.

First, assuming that the comitative function is simply an extension of the stative function, one would expect the comitative to occur only as a stative participant, inactively accompanying another participant. That this is not true is confirmed by examples such as (22), which is ambiguous precisely because the comitative can be interpreted as accompanying either the more active or the more passive participant:

(22) dā-r   MoHama-ø   Irbahin-de-ø

      1SG-DAT   Muhammed-ABS   Ibrahim-APUD-ESS

      ø-ikwaj-si

      I-see-PASTEV

'I saw Mohammed with Ibrahim.'
or: 'I, together with Ibrahim, saw Muhammed.'

Next, Tsez has special morphology for expressing those comitatives which are totally inactive, and the relevant marker (-q) is totally unrelated to the -de and -xo markers. All of this indicates that synchronically the comitative function cannot be treated as a simple extension of the spatial function.

4.1 Conjoined Elements

Constraints on the linkage of nominals in English have been studied extensively by Cooper and Ross (1975),[8] who conclude that "ordering relations among conjuncts" are determined by the semantic categorization of a prototypical speaker. The first nominal of a fixed conjoined phrase obeys, among others, the following semantically important features: 'solid', 'agentive', 'animate', 'adult', 'male'. For the purposes of this description, the first feature is related to size, the second and third are related to mobility, and the two latter features can be subsumed under conventional value.

Without undermining the value of the Me First Principle, I would like to argue that this principle represents a particular case of the G-F ordering, where the prototypical speaker is assumed as the reference point, therefore, as G. As we compare the factors that determine the ordering of elements in free conjoined phrases in Tsez to the factors that determine the structure of Tsez statives and comitatives, the similarity becomes apparent.

In Tsez, each nominal of a conjoined nominal phrase is marked by the suffix *-n(o)* 'and'. The order of nominals in conjoined phrases is sensitive to the size, conventional value, and mobility of the two nominals: the nominal that can be identified as G precedes. For example, (23a) is felicitous and (23b) is not, because a mother is viewed as having a higher conventional value than a daughter:

(23)   a. enij-no   kid-no   b. #kid-no   enij-no

       mother-and girl-and   girl-and   mother-and
           'mother and daughter'

Similarly, in linking pronouns, it is felicitous to start with the first person.[9] Speakers normally view themselves as the main reference point, the main point of empathy; the other entity is located in reference to the speaker, which accounts for the infelicity of (24b), where the other person is taken as the reference point.

(24)   a. di-n   žedi-n   b. #žedi-n   di-n

       1SG-and 3PL-and   3PL-and   1SG-and
           'I and they'

---

[8]Note though that Cooper and Ross focus their attention on fixed conjuncts (freezes), whereas most of the Tsez examples in this section involve "free" conjuncts, which prove not to be free after all.

[9]In Tsez, both 'I and you' and 'you and I' are felicitous in the linking of first and second person pronouns.

Likewise, in (25), the two entities differ in size, and it is typical for Tsez to assume the larger one as G, which explains why (25a), where G precedes F, is felicitous:

(25)   a. Hon-no   ažom-no   b. #ažom-no Hon-no

        mountain-and tree-and   tree-and mountain-and

        'a/the mountain and a/the tree'

Consider (26a), where the name of the stationary entity is taken as G and thus precedes the name of the moving entity (F); (26b) is infelicitous:

(26)   a. ažom-no   gut'-no   b. #gut'-no   ažom-no

        tree-and   cloud-and   cloud-and   tree-and

        'a/the tree and a/the cloud'

Thus, the ordering of the conjoined nominals is not arbitrary and is determined by the relative size, mobility, and/or conventional value of the referents. Overall, the name of the reference point (G) precedes the other nominal (F). Assuming that in a V-final language topics are located in the leftmost position, the element identified with G is in a more topical position than the F element. Meanwhile, the assumption seems to be that F, not G, should correlate with topic. This suggests once again that the F-G distinction is orthogonal to discourse-dependent distinctions, e.g., between topic and focus or between given and new. Thus, while it is more common to associate F with topic, in several constructions G can be a more likely topic (for example, in existentials), and the examination of Tsez conjoined phrases suggests that the order G-before-F may even be grammaticized.

4.2   Partially Symmetric Predicates

A predicate is considered symmetric if for two of its arguments, x and y, $P(x, y) = P(y, x)$ (Lakoff and Peters 1969; Dowty 1991: 583-6). In a number of cases, the relationship between the two arguments can be shown to be just partially symmetric, and this asymmetry cuts across different thematic roles (Dowty 1991: 584-5). In Tsez, the most common construction involving a presumably symmetric predicate links the two arguments of that predicate, as in (27). In this linking, the order of the conjoined nominals follows the felicity principles discussed in 4.1.

(27)   enij-ø-no   kid-ø-no   r-iHanaj-xo

        mother-ABS-and girl-ABS-and IIPL-quarrel-PRES

        'The mother and the daughter are quarreling.'

However, there are several predicates for which the truth-conditional asymmetry of the arguments is reflected in the asymmetry of the linguistic construction. Compare (28a), where the word for the masculine pronoun appears in the proximal locative and is identified as G, and the word for the girl is F. The reversal of perspective in this construction is impossible, hence (28b) is not only infelicitous, but ungrammatical.

(28)   a.   kid-ø   žā-x-ø   j-egir-si

                girl-ABS   he-AD-ESS   II-send-PASTEV

                'The girl was married to him.'

    b.   *že   kidbe-x-ø   ø-egir-si

                he/ABS   girl-AD-ESS   I-send-PASTEV

                'He was married to the girl.'

Since in a traditional Tsez culture the active role in marriage belongs to a man, only the man can be viewed as the reference point (G) in the description of a wedding or marriage. Again, as was already discussed in section 3, the identification of the man with G apparently contradicts its identification with the agentive participant, suggesting that the two types of identification are independent of one another.

The relevance of size parameter in the choice of situation perspective becomes obvious if we turn to the construction 'X is almost equal to Y', where X can be identified with F and Y with G. Along with the conjoined phrase construction, illustrated in (29), the asymmetric construction is possible, but only if X is numerically less than Y, hence, (30a) is felicitous, and (30b) is not:[10]

(29)   oc'ino-n   biƚno-n   sistow   joƚ

                ten-and   eight-and   similar   is

                'Ten and eight are almost the same.'

(30)   a.   biƚno-ø   oc'inora-de-ø   igo   joƚ

                eight-ABS   ten-APUD-ESS   near   is

                'Eight is close to ten.'

    b.   #oc'ino-ø   biƚnora-de-ø   igo   joƚ

                 ten-ABS   eight-APUD-ESS   near   is

                'Ten is close to eight.'

---

[10]In English, felicity contrasts are essentially the same in this case.

In Tsez, some evidence in favor of distinguishing between F and G in symmetric predicate constructions can be found in the morphology of one of the arguments, which is marked by the proximal locative -*xo*. However, even in the absence of such morphology, the analysis of symmetric predicate constructions becomes more compact if we assume the F-G contrast; despite the differences between the thematic roles selected by individual symmetric predicates, the two arguments can be uniformly distinguished as F and G (see also Dowty 1991: 584-5). For Tsez then, the selection of G is determined by the criteria of relative size, mobility, and conventional value.

5   Conclusion

In this paper I have discussed the relationship between two referents in stative constructions (locative and existential), comitative constructions, conjoined constructions, and (partially) symmetric predicate constructions. For all these constructions, it has been argued that perspective-dependent notions (F and G) play a crucial role in the differentiation of the two arguments, regardless of their thematic roles. Furthermore, the parameters for determining which referent is put in perspective and which referent is assumed as (part of) the background remain the same for all the constructions discussed here. Specifically, it has been shown that the referent that is larger, is more stationary, and/or has a higher conventional value is assumed as the reference point for locating another referent; in other words, the former element is identified with G, the latter with F.

These findings have two theoretical implications. First, the F-G contrast is valid outside the realm of stative constructions—where perspective-dependent notions have traditionally been viewed as relevant. Concomitantly, the F-G distinction is independent of thematic roles and should be treated as separate from them. Furthermore, not only are perspective-dependent notions orthogonal to thematic roles, but moreover the principles of identifying F and G may contradict the well-known principles of assigning thematic roles based on prototypical agenthood and thematicity.

The next conclusion is that perspective-dependent notions are orthogonal to discourse categories and to grammatical relations. Though Tsez displays a frequent correlation between topic and F, this correlation is not obligatory. A number of examples above ((4b), (11a), (12a), (14a), (15a)) show that the nominal identified as G may appear in the topic position and that the F-G linear ordering can vary depending on discourse factors. The data suggest that the F-G distinction is independent of grammatical relations. True, there is a cross-linguistic correlation between F and a higher grammatical relation (in particular, subject) and between G and a lower grammatical relation (Dowty 1991: 563-4). In Tsez, this correlation is evident in stative and comitative constructions but it is irrelevant in existential constructions, where the existential Theme (F) can be shown to lack any subject properties whatsoever (Comrie *et al.*, forthcoming).

These conclusions are negative; perspective-dependent notions cannot be identified with those categories with which they have often been identified in the relevant literature. Naturally, the question arises: what is the proper place for perspective-dependent notions? In my view, the answer to this question lies in the further study of individual languages; however, two suggestions for further investigation are appropriate here. In a general and preliminary way, this paper has attempted to argue that perspective-dependent notions serve as a link between the conceptual structure and the semantic and syntactic structure. Knowledge about how particular participants are positioned in actual or mental space with respect to each other contributes to the representation of functional relations that determine the order of linguistic elements and the choice of actual linguistic marking. Thus, the F-G contrast precedes and is crucial to the assignment of thematic roles, grammatical relations, and communicative functions. To further such an account, it would be useful to determine whether situation perspective will emerge as a language characteristic similar to animacy in that it has repercussions in various language domains and is superimposed on various language constructions. In such an analysis, situation perspective may subsume the Me First Principle (Cooper and Ross 1975) and empathy (Kuno and Kaburaki 1977) as particular cases. Second, it is important to determine whether or not perspective-dependent notions should be treated as primitives. Given that the selection of F and G is determined by several parameters, such as those discussed in this paper, the answer will probably be negative, but the question remains open.

References

Comrie, Bernard. 1989. *Language Universals and Linguistic Typology: Syntax and Morphology.* 2nd ed. Chicago: University of Chicago Press.

Comrie, Bernard, Maria Polinsky, and Ramazan Rajabov, forthcoming. Tsezian. In Alice Harris and Rieks Smeets, eds. *Languages of the Caucasus: The Indigenous Languages and Their Speakers.*

Cooper, William E., and John Robert Ross. 1975. World Order. In Robin E. Grossman, L. James San, and Timothy J. Vance, eds. *Papers from the Parasession on Functionalism*, 63-111. Chicago: Chicago Linguistic Society.

Dowty, David. 1991. Thematic Proto-roles and Argument Selection. *Language* 67: 547-619.

Fillmore, Charles. 1975. *Santa Cruz Lectures on Deixis, 1971.* Bloomington: Indiana University Linguistics Club.

Fillmore, Charles. 1977. The Case for Case Reopened. In Peter Cole and Jerrold Sadock, eds. *Syntax and Semantics 8: Grammatical Relations*, 59-82. New York: Academic Press.

Jackendoff, Ray. 1976. Towards an Explanatory Semantic Representation. *Linguistic Inquiry* 7: 89-150.

Jackendoff, Ray. 1985. Multiple Subcategorizations and the θ-Criterion: The

Case of *Climb*. *Natural Language and Linguistic Theory* 3: 271-95.

Jackendoff, Ray. 1990. *Semantic Structures*. Cambridge, Mass.: MIT Press.

Kuno, Susumu. 1973. *The Structure of the Japanese Language*. Cambridge, Mass.: MIT Press.

Kuno, Susumu, and E. Kaburaki. 1977. Empathy and Syntax. *Linguistic Inquiry* 8: 627-72.

Lakoff, George, and Stanley Peters. 1969. Phrasal Conjunction and Symmetric Predicates. In David Reibel and Sanford Shane, eds. *Modern Studies in English*, 113-40. Englewood Cliffs: Prentice Hall.

Lang, Ewald. 1989. The Semantics of Dimensional Designation of Spatial Objects. In Manfred Bierwisch and Ewald Lang, eds. *Dimensional Adjectives. Grammatical Structure and Conceptual Interpretations*, 263-417. Berlin: Springer.

Langacker, Ronald W. 1987. *Foundations of Cognitive Grammar*, vol. 1: *Theoretical Prerequisites*. Stanford: Stanford University Press.

Langacker, Ronald W. 1990. *Concept, Image, and Symbol: The Cognitive Basis of Grammar*. Berlin: Mouton.

Polinsky, Maria, and Ramazan Rajabov. 1994. At, By or With? Quasi-Synonymous Locative Series in Tsez. Paper Presented at the 1994 Annual Meeting of the LSA, Boston.

Silverstein, Michael. 1976. Hierarchy of Features and Ergativity. In Robert M. W. Dixon, ed. *Grammatical Categories in Australian Languages*, 112-74. Canberra: Australian National University Press.

Talmy, Leonard. 1978. Figure and Ground in Complex Sentences. In Joseph Greenberg, ed. *Universals of Human Language*, vol. 4: *Syntax*, 625-49. Stanford: Stanford University Press.

Talmy, Leonard. 1985. Figure and Ground as Thematic roles. Paper Presented at the 1985 Annual Meeting of the LSA, Seattle.

Manipulation of Discourse Spaces in American Sign Language

CHRISTINE POULIN
Stanford University

1.1 Introduction

Focusing on the pronominal reference system and drawing on the theory of mental spaces (as defined in Fauconnier 1985), van Hoek (1988, 1992, in press) discusses how it is possible in American Sign Language (ASL) "to distinguish between [discourse] contexts ... by the choice of pronominal form" (1988:9), and claims that for a number of constructions, sign space is used to represent mental space. Building on her work, I show that referential shift is one of these constructions and present some further instances of discourse spaces and their linguistic representation.

1.2 Spatial Referential Framework

The use of space and spatial contrasts in ASL is crucial at all levels of linguistic organization, but the most striking is its role in syntax and discourse, especially in marking coreference. A number of ASL constructions rely on the establishment of links between points in the signing space and referents in the discourse. When introduced into the discourse, the referent of a nominal is associated with a particular point in the signing space, termed *referential locus* (Padden 1983, Lillo-Martin 1986, Liddell 1990). One way of establishing a referent is to sign a nominal and then point to some locus in the signing space. This is referred to as *indexing* (Kegl 1977). Pronominal reference is then realized by pointing to the locus associated with the intended referent. An important group of ASL verbs (agreeing verbs) make use of this association and move between specific loci to indicate grammatical relations. Typically,

Conceptual Structure, Discourse, and Language.
Edited by Adele Goldberg.

the verb-sign begins at the locus of the subject and ends at the locus of the object (e.g., ASK, GIVE).[1]

The arrangement of loci associated with their referents has been termed *frame of reference* by Lillo-Martin and Klima (1990). In discourse, the frame of reference can shift. When this referential shift takes place, the referent of a third person locus is reassociated to a first person locus. The shift is indicated by modifications in the signer's facial expression and body position, i.e., in the orientation of the shoulders, the head and/or the eyes. The breaking of eye contact with the addressee is the most consistent change to indicate that the signer has entered a referential shift (Loew 1984). Figure 1, where semicircles represent the signing space in front of the signer, illustrates a referential shift.

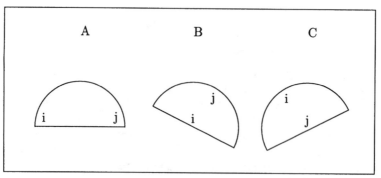

FIGURE 1   Use of space and referential shift.[2]

In A, the signer locates i to the left and j to the right in the signing space. In B, the signer shifts toward the locus of i and i interacts with j. In C, the signer shifts toward the locus of j and j interacts with i.

Sign language researchers have commonly described referential shift as being comparable to direct quotation in spoken languages, that is, when signers report the words of a third person. However, its use is not limited to reported speech as the examples in (1) show. The signer can also report actions ((1a), (1b)), states (1c) or thoughts (e.g., Engberg-Pedersen 1995, Loew 1984, Padden 1990, Lillo-Martin 1995, Lillo-Martin and Klima 1990, Meier 1990, Poulin 1994).[3]

---

[1] The approximate English meaning of a sign is conveyed through an upper case English word. When a gloss needs more than one English word, these words are hyphenated.
[2] Adapted from Lillo-Martin and Klima (1990).
[3] In the transcriptions, the referential shift is indicated by a line above the glosses. The letters IX stand for INDEX. The index following 'shift' indicates the referent whose

(1)   a.

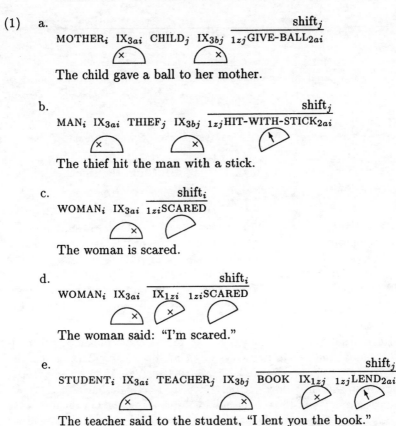

$$\text{shift}_j$$
MOTHER$_i$ IX$_{3ai}$ CHILD$_j$ IX$_{3bj}$ $_{1zj}$GIVE-BALL$_{2ai}$

The child gave a ball to her mother.

   b.

$$\text{shift}_j$$
MAN$_i$ IX$_{3ai}$ THIEF$_j$ IX$_{3bj}$ $_{1zj}$HIT-WITH-STICK$_{2ai}$

The thief hit the man with a stick.

   c.

$$\text{shift}_i$$
WOMAN$_i$ IX$_{3ai}$ $_{1zi}$SCARED

The woman is scared.

   d.

$$\text{shift}_i$$
WOMAN$_i$ IX$_{3ai}$ IX$_{1zi}$ $_{1zi}$SCARED

The woman said: "I'm scared."

   e.

$$\text{shift}_j$$
STUDENT$_i$ IX$_{3ai}$ TEACHER$_j$ IX$_{3bj}$ BOOK   IX$_{1zj}$ $_{1zj}$LEND$_{2ai}$

The teacher said to the student, "I lent you the book."

Referential shift is clearly used to report speech, thoughts, actions or states, but more generally it is used as a perspective or point of view marker. This is illustrated by the contrast between sentences like (2a) and (2b). Both sentences describe the same event but (2a) uses a shift and (2b) does not.

---

locus has been reassociated. The numbers *1, 2, 3* represent pragmatic indices, and they mark person agreement with respect to the point of view adopted by the signer. They correspond roughly to grammatical first, second and third person. The letters *a, b* and *z* are spatial indices that mark location in space: *z* represents the body of the signer and *a, b* represent locations other than the signer's body. The letters *i* and *j* are referential indices in the traditional sense of the term. Following van Hoek's notation system, underneath some of the glosses are semicircles representing the spatial plane in front of the signer used for pronominal reference and verb agreement. Within these semicircles, an arrow represents the direction of movement of the verb-sign (when there is movement), and an *x* indicates the locus where the NP has been established. A shifted semicircle represents a referential shift. The base of the semicircle is rotated toward the location of the referent whose locus has been reassociated.

(2) a.

$$\text{MAN}_i \ \text{IX}_{3ai} \ \text{THIEF}_j \ \text{IX}_{3bj} \ \overline{\phantom{\text{IX}}}^{\ \text{shift}_j}_{1zj}\text{HIT-WITH-STICK}_{2ai}$$

The thief hit the man with a stick (from the thief's point of view).

b. $\text{MAN}_i \ \text{IX}_{3ai} \ \text{THIEF}_j \ \text{IX}_{3bj} \ _{3bj}\text{HIT-WITH-STICK}_{3ai}$

The thief hit the man with a stick (from the signer's point of view).

The difference in meaning between the two sentences lies in the point of view adopted by the signer to describe the event. In (a), the signer identifies herself with one of the discourse actants, the thief, whereas in (b) the signer describes the event from her own point of view. The difference between the two forms is thus between internal point of view (i.e., that of the actant) and external point of view (i.e., that of the signer).

Referential loci are sometimes analyzed as overt phonological manifestations of the semantic indices associated with referents in the discourse (e.g., Lillo-Martin and Klima 1990). Van Hoek (1988, 1992) shows that referential loci not only identify referents, but also carry information relative to the conceptual location of referents in the discourse space. "Each referential locus may be associated with both a referent and a conceived situation or setting involving the referent, so that a particular locus used for pronominal reference or verb agreement may invoke not only the conception of a referent, but the conception of the situation in which the referent is involved" (van Hoek 1992:185). To illustrate her point, van Hoek examines contexts in which a single referent is associated with two distinct loci in the signing space, such as that in (3).[4] In (3), the referent he_i is first associated with the spatial locus a, which is associated with the room (i.e., he in the room). Then, the same referent he_i is reassociated with the spatial locus b, which is associated with the yard (i.e., he in the yard). The example in (3) shows that a single referent can be associated with different points in the signing space, providing different conceptions of that referent.

---

[4] van Hoek's (in press) example (1). I have added the indices.

(3)　NIGHT, WE-TWO TALK IX-THERE$_a$ HIS$_{ai}$ ROOM$_a$.

IX$_{3ai}$ BAWL-OUT. I TELL I SORRY. IX$_{3ai}$ FORGIVE ME.

MORNING, I GO OUT Y-A-R-D$_n$, SEE IX$_{3bi}$ AGAIN.

BAWL-OUT AGAIN. STRANGE. BEFORE, IX$_{3ai}$ TELL

IX$_{3ai}$ FORGIVE ME; MORNING, IX$_{3bi}$ ANGRY AGAIN.

In the evening, we talked, in his room. He bawled me out. I told him I was sorry, and he forgave me. In the morning, I went out to the yard, and saw him again. He bawled me out again. It was strange. Before, he told me he forgave me, but in the morning, he was angry again.

Van Hoek argues that this shift between loci can be accounted for if we think of referential loci as elements embedded within conceptual frames in the discourse. She proposes that the frame of reference is the overt representation of the contents of a particular mental space, the Current Discourse Space (CDS), which is the speaker/signer and addressee's representation of the discourse context (see also Langacker 1991) — the CDS is a mental space and other mental spaces can be embedded within it as they are introduced in the discourse. The referential use of space in ASL would then involve setting up a spatialized representation of the CDS. The arrangement of referential loci in the signing space reflects the relations among entities in the CDS including its subspaces.

1.3 Discourse Spaces

According to van Hoek (in press), the CDS is invoked by a first person pronoun designating the signer. The second person designates the addressee and the third person designates any other entities contained in the CDS or in a mental space embedded within the CDS. The choice of a particular locus for pronominal reference indicates the location of the referent. Under the view that the spatial frame of reference in ASL represents some of the concepts introduced into the discourse and the relationships between these concepts, a specific pronominal locus in the

frame of reference represents a specific point in that network of relationships. These relationships can be described in terms of mental spaces
set up in the discourse, and the entities within them. Thus, the use of
two distinct loci to refer to a sole entity overtly shows that the referent
is involved in two distinct mental spaces. The shift from one locus to
the other corresponds to a shift in *focus space* (van Hoek in press). The
focus space corresponds to the space defined by the immediate context
for a given utterance in the discourse, and it shifts as the discourse unfolds. The sequence in (3) is an example of this. In (3) the signer shifts
between describing the event in the room and describing the event in the
yard. The selection of a locus for pronominal reference in each clause
thus indicates the focus space in which that clause is contextualized.

The choice of a spatial locus to refer to an entity depends on the
specific focus space in which the pronoun is embedded. The choice of
pronominal form thus makes it possible to distinguish between different
subspaces within the CDS. In much the same way, referential shift allows
one to distinguish between different focus spaces, and this is what I will
describe now in more detail.

Building on the work of van Hoek (1988, 1992, in press) and Poulin
and Miller (1995), I propose that utterances containing a shift involve
different discourse spaces. The *main discourse space* is a permanent
frame of reference where the elements are referentially located in space
and time. It resembles the CDS proposed by Langacker and van Hoek.
This space corresponds to the point of view of the signer. From this main
discourse space, the signer can decide to shift the frame of reference
in order to express the point of view of a particular discourse actant.
This creates a new discourse space whose interpretation depends on the
establishment of the referents in the main discourse space. I use the
term *perspective space* to refer to a space invoked by a shift. This is
illustrated in (4):

(4)

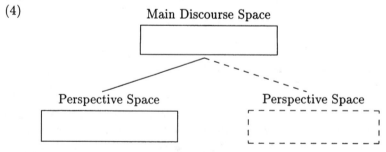

The main discourse space establishes the base referential domain of
the discourse. In this permanent frame of reference, the elements are

referentially located in time and space, and the different indices (spatial, referential and pragmatic) are associated with their referent. In (4) for instance, the actants are located in the main frame of reference where they are associated with a specific locus in the signing space. The main discourse space corresponds to the narrator's point of view, whereas the perspective spaces represent the actants' point of view. Within the discourse, the signer can decide to move between the different spaces in order to express the point of view of a particular actant. Consequently, the interpretation of the perspective space depends on the establishment of the referents in the main discourse space. The signer can then refer to the different actants of the discourse by shifting between their respective perspective space.

For example, sentence (1a), reproduced here in (5), where the signer adopts the point of view of the thief, would be represented as in (6):

(5)

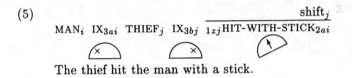

$$\text{MAN}_i \ \text{IX}_{3ai} \ \text{THIEF}_j \ \text{IX}_{3bj} \ \overline{\text{1}_{zj}\text{HIT-WITH-STICK}_{2ai}}^{\text{shift}_j}$$

The thief hit the man with a stick.

(6)

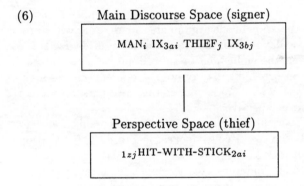

Main Discourse Space (signer)

$$\text{MAN}_i \ \text{IX}_{3ai} \ \text{THIEF}_j \ \text{IX}_{3bj}$$

Perspective Space (thief)

$$\text{1}_{zj}\text{HIT-WITH-STICK}_{2ai}$$

The two actants, MAN and THIEF, are set up in the main discourse space. Then the signer shifts to the thief's perspective (i.e., the thief's third person locus is reassociated to a first person locus), invoking the thief's perspective space. Although the interpretation of the new mental space depends on the establishment of the referents in the main discourse space, the two spaces are not mutually accessible. The shift creates a new reference setting, and the signer must comply with this new set of relationships as long as he or she is within that space. It follows that overt third person pronouns referring to the actant whose point of view is expressed through the shift are unacceptable within the shift because of the clash in the loci referring to that actant as in (7). However, non-overt pronouns are acceptable, and present the point of view of the first person within the shift as shown in (8).

(7)

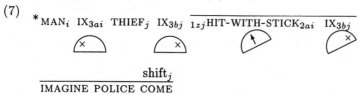

$$\text{*MAN}_i \ \text{IX}_{3ai} \ \text{THIEF}_j \ \text{IX}_{3bj} \ _{1zj}\text{HIT-WITH-STICK}_{2ai} \ \text{IX}_{3bj}$$

$$\underline{\hspace{3cm} \text{shift}_j}$$
IMAGINE POLICE COME

The thief hit the man with a stick. He was scared the police would arrive.

(8)

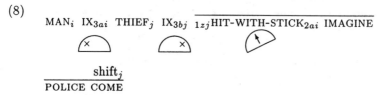

$$\text{MAN}_i \ \text{IX}_{3ai} \ \text{THIEF}_j \ \text{IX}_{3bj} \ _{1zj}\text{HIT-WITH-STICK}_{2ai} \ \text{IMAGINE}$$

$$\underline{\hspace{2cm} \text{shift}_j}$$
POLICE COME

The thief hit the man with a stick. He was scared the police would arrive.

In each case, the expression of the arguments as null, or as overt pronouns, requires a particular relation between the main discourse space (frame of reference) and the embedded or subordinate spaces. Specifically, overt third person pronouns may only take referents in the main discourse space; this is why only (7) is bad, as the third person pronoun (IX_{3bj}) is in the shifted perspective space.

When there is an overt first person pronoun within a shift, another particular relation between the discourse spaces is forced. This situation necessarily involves the notion of a speaker/signer, and the discourse segment within the shift must be interpreted as embedded direct discourse as discussed in Poulin (1994). This is illustrated in (9).

(9)

$$\text{MAN}_i \ \text{IX}_{3ai} \ \text{THIEF}_j \ \text{IX}_{3bj} \ _{1zj}\text{HIT-WITH-STICK}_{2ai} \ \text{IX}_{1zj}$$

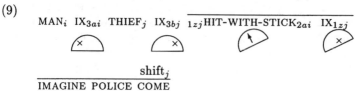

$$\underline{\hspace{3cm} \text{shift}_j}$$
IMAGINE POLICE COME

The thief hit the man with a stick and said, "I'm scared the police will come."

The first person pronoun IX$_{1zj}$ (the English "I") appears as the subject of IMAGINE. "I" within a described discourse refers to the speaker of that discourse. It follows that the referential shift in (9) must be the result of speech by the third person whose point of view is expressed by the shift. Formally, we can think of referential shift as functioning like a higher verb of saying, the referent of IX$_1$ being the subject of the saying.

The example in (9) can be represented as in (10):

(10)

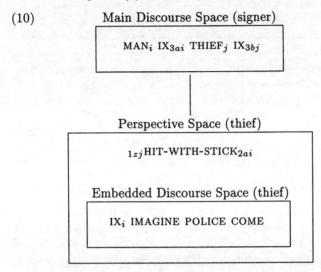

Main Discourse Space (signer)

MAN$_i$ IX$_{3ai}$ THIEF$_j$ IX$_{3bj}$

Perspective Space (thief)

$_{1zj}$HIT-WITH-STICK$_{2ai}$

Embedded Discourse Space (thief)

IX$_i$ IMAGINE POLICE COME

The reference shift invokes a perspective space, and the first person pronoun invokes a new discourse space whose subject is the actant whose point of view is expressed through the shift. Since the shift creates a new reference setting which must be respected as long as the signer is within it, any discourse subsequent to the shift must be contained within the perspective space.

For some signers however, the shift itself triggers the reported speech interpretation and there is no need for an overt first person pronoun. It follows that for these signers, the shift will always generate simultaneously both the perspective space and an embedded discourse space. Sentence (11a) is an example of this. It is contrasted here with (11b). (11a) would be represented as in (10) and (11b) as in (6).

(11) a.

$$\overline{\text{shift}_j}$$
MOTHER$_i$ IX$_{3ai}$ CHILD$_j$ IX$_{3bj}$ $_{1zj}$GIVE-BALL$_{2ai}$

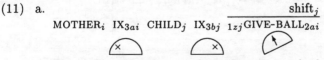

The child said to her mother, "I gave you the ball".

b.

$$\overline{\text{shift}_j}$$

MOTHER$_i$ IX$_{3ai}$ CHILD$_j$ IX$_{3bj}$ $_{1zj}$GIVE-BALL$_{2ai}$

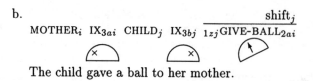

The child gave a ball to her mother.

The conditions under which the referential shift functions like a higher verb of saying as opposed to just a perspective marker are yet to be defined. In Poulin (1992) I have noted that in Quebec Sign Language (LSQ), factors such as oralization seem to play a role in the expression of reported speech. This might also be true for ASL.

The next utterance in (12) offers a compelling example of how different discourse spaces can be manipulated. It is particularly interesting as it shows how it is possible in ASL to bring two spaces together.

(12)

$$\overline{\text{shift}_i}$$

TEACHER$_i$ $_{3ai}$LOOK-AT$_{1zj}$ - - - - - - ▶ LATER IX$_{1zi}$ $_{1zi}$TALK$_{2aj}$

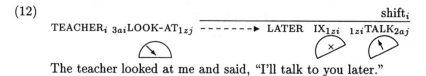

The teacher looked at me and said, "I'll talk to you later."

In (12), the signer signs $_{3ai}$LOOK-AT$_{1zj}$ (she looked at me), holds this sign, and simultaneously enters a referential shift, identifying herself with the teacher. Although there is an apparent clash of indices (3a vs 1z) the example is good (in contrast with (7)). This is crucial evidence that referential shift involves different discourse spaces and that they can be manipulated, as represented in (13a):

(13) a.

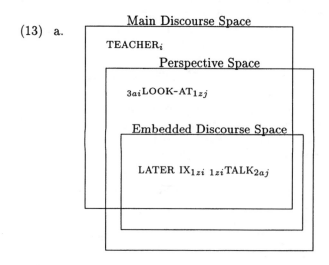

Main Discourse Space

TEACHER$_i$

Perspective Space

$_{3ai}$LOOK-AT$_{1zj}$

Embedded Discourse Space

LATER IX$_{1zi}$ $_{1zi}$TALK$_{2aj}$

b.   Main Discourse Space (signer)

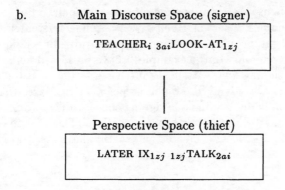

TEACHER$_i$ $_{3ai}$LOOK-AT$_{1zj}$

Perspective Space (thief)

LATER IX$_{1zj}$ $_{1zj}$TALK$_{2ai}$

The example in (12) is good because both the main frame and the shifted frame share the same space, the overlap in (13a). But when considered separately, as in (13b), within each space, each index is associated with a single referent and there is no incompatible doubling of the indices like that in (7); the third person space is just held into the shifted space. So, the essential difference between (7) and (12) is that in (12), the main discourse space overlaps with the perspective space as a result of $_{3ai}$LOOK-AT$_{1zj}$, which is associated with the main discourse space, being maintained through the shift. In (7) there is no overlapping of the different spaces, which results in the clash between the indices referring to the thief.

1.4 Conclusion

In this paper, I have shown that referential shift is another instance of sign space being used to represent mental space. The establishment of referents in the signing space invokes the main discourse space. From that main space, the signer can shift to adopt the point of view of any discourse actant. This invokes a new mental space, the perspective space, whose interpretation depends on the interpretation of the main discourse space. However, the two spaces are not mutually accessible, as subsequent discourse is interpreted in one or the other, and the form of the sign indicates which.

Further, the interpretation of null and overt arguments within the shift seems to manipulate the different discourse spaces. Thus, an overt first person pronoun necessarily triggers the reported speech interpretation and generates a new discourse space within the perspective space. This contrasts with nonovert pronominal signs which have no such restrictions (Poulin 1994).

The referential shift examples support van Hoek's claim that sign space overtly represents mental space. In fact, we see that there are two ways in which ASL uses its spatial modality to manipulate linguistic spaces: in the examples that van Hoek gives, a single referent is associated with different points in the signing space, providing different conceptions of that referent. In the examples I have presented here, the orientation of the signing space itself is shifted while the locus of the referent is kept constant, giving the different perspective spaces that I have described. Finally, by holding one signing space while shifting into another, a signer may bring the two spaces together. These, then, are some of the ways in which ASL creates and manipulates its discourse spaces.

Acknowledgements

Many thanks to Bonita Ewan, Cathy Haas, Brett Kessler, Steve McCullough, Rachel Nordlinger, Peter Sells and Linda Uyechi for help, comments, suggestions and language consultation.

References

Engberg-Pedersen, Elizabeth. 1995. Point of view expressed through shifters. In *Language, Gesture and Space*, ed. Karen Emmorey and Judy Reilly. Hillsdale, NJ: Lawrence Erlbaum Assoc.

Fauconnier, Gilles. 1985. *Mental Spaces*. Cambridge, Mass.: MIT Press.

Kegl, Judy. 1977. Research in progress and proposed research. Unpublished manuscript, MIT, Cambridge, Mass.

Langacker, Ronald. 1991. *Foundations of Cognitive Grammar, Volume II: Descriptive Application*. Stanford, California: Stanford University Press.

Liddell, Scott. 1990. Four functions for a locus: Reexamining the structure of Space in ASL. In *Sign Language Research: Theoretical Issues*, ed. Ceil Lucas. 176–201. Washington, DC: Gallaudet University Press.

Lillo-Martin, Diane. 1986. Two kinds of null arguments in American Sign Language. *Natural Language and Linguistic Theory* 4:415–444.

Lillo-Martin, Diane. 1995. The point of view predicate in American Sign Language. In *Language, Gesture and Space*, ed. Karen Emmorey and Judy Reilly. Hillsdale, NJ: Lawrence Erlbaum Assoc.

Lillo-Martin, Diane, and Edward Klima. 1990. Pointing out differences: ASL pronouns in syntactic theory. In *Theoretical Issues in Sign Lan-*

guage Research I: Linguistics, ed. Susan Fischer and Patricia Siple. 191–210. Chicago: University of Chicago Press.

Loew, Ruth. 1984. *Roles and References in American Sign Language: A Developmental Perspective*. Doctoral dissertation, University of Minnesota.

Meier, Richard. 1990. Person deixis in American Sign Language. In *Theoretical Issues in Sign Language Research I: Linguistics*, ed. Susan Fischer and Patricia Siple. 175–190. Chicago: University of Chicago Press.

Padden, Carol. 1983. *Interaction of Morphology and Syntax in American Sign Language*. Doctoral dissertation, University of California, San Diego.

Padden, Carol. 1990. The relation between space and grammar in ASL morphology. In *Sign Language Research: Theoretical Issues*, ed. Ceil Lucas. 83–102. Washington, DC: Gallaudet University Press.

Poulin, Christine. 1992. Le jeu de rôle en langue des signes québécoise: une question de point de vue. MA thesis, Université du Québec à Montréal.

Poulin, Christine. 1994. Null arguments and referential shift in American Sign Language. Paper presented at the Sixth Student Conference in Linguistics, Rochester, NY, May 8–9. To appear in *MIT Working Papers in Linguistics* 23:257–271.

Poulin, Christine, and Christopher Miller. 1995. On narrative discourse and point of view in Quebec Sign Language. In *Language, Gesture and Space*, ed. Karen Emmorey and Judy Reilly. Hillsdale, NJ: Lawrence Erlbaum Assoc.

van Hoek, Karen. 1988. Mental space and sign space. Paper presented at the Annual Meeting of the LSA, New Orleans, Louisiana.

van Hoek, Karen. 1992. Conceptual spaces and pronominal reference in American Sign Language. *Nordic Journal of Linguistics* 15:183–199.

van Hoek, Karen. in press. Conceptual location for reference in American Sign Language. To appear in E. Sweetser and G. Fauconnier (Eds.), *Spaces, Worlds and Grammars*. Chicago: University of Chicago Press.

Roles, Values, and Possessives: Deictic Adjectives in the Noun Phrase

RONALD E. SHEFFER, JR.
University of California, San Diego

1. Introduction

In this paper I am going to consider a class of adjectives that I will term *deictic adjectives* and some of the grammatical problems associated with these adjectives. I hope to show that understanding how these adjectives combine with nouns semantically will allow us to account for some of their grammatical peculiarities.

Generally, deictics may only be combined with nouns as determiners or postnominally, as the examples in (1) show. They may not appear inside the noun phrase as we see in (2), though in some dialects of English the examples in (3), where a deictic is used as an extension of the determiner, may be permissible.

(1)   a. this house
        b. the house here

(2)   a. *the this/here house
        b. *a this/now president

(3)   a. this here house
        b. that there book

There is, however, a class of adjectives relating to temporal instantiation that do appear in attributive adjective position as exemplified in (4). I will term these *deictic adjectives*. Members of this class of adjectives are listed in (5).

(4)   a. the *former* mayor of Cardiff
        b. Fred's *previous* wife

(5) | **Past** | **Present** | **Future** |
        |----------|-------------|------------|
        | former | present | future |
        | old | current | next |
        | past | new | coming |
        | last | | |
        | previous | | |
        | prior | | |
        | earlier | | |

In section 2 I will present some facts about deictic adjectives and show how they contrast with other adjectives. In section 3 I will review some basic facts about nouns, noun phrases, and prototypical adjectives based on Langacker's theory of Cognitive Grammar. In section 4, we will return to the problems discussed in section 2 and I will suggest solutions to these problems. I will conclude in section 5.

2.0 Facts about Deictic Adjectives

Deictic adjectives have three grammatical problems associated with them which I will discuss in this paper, namely: 1) the selectional restriction problem, 2) the grammatical frame problem, and 3) the semantic substitutability problem. Let us consider each of these phenomena in turn.

2.1 The Selectional Restriction Problem

Deictic adjectives may not be used with just any noun and determiner, as the examples in (6) show (note that all of these examples are grammatical without the deictic adjective):

(6)   a. *He threw away the former book.
         b. *She stopped reading every former magazine.
         c. *A current parent sat in on her child's class.
         d. *The recent water flowed into the pond.

However, there are two seemingly divergent environments where these adjectives may felicitously be used.

First, these adjectives may be used with nouns denoting occupations, religions, or societal offices. We may also observe that when these adjectives are used with this type of noun, they may appear with any determiner. These facts are illustrated in (7).

(7)   a. the former plumber/Lutheran/President
         b. all former presidents, every former president, the former president, a former president, etc.

The second environment where these adjectives may felicitously be used is when there is some overt possessive marking, as we see in (8). Note that *car, house,* and *husband* may not appear with the deictic adjective *former* and the determiner *the*. But, if we put a possessive into the NP, either as a determiner or as a possessive *of-*phrase, then these NPs are grammatical.

(8)   a. *the former car/house/husband
         b. Ethyl's former car/husband/house/etc.
         c. a former car/house/husband of Lucy's

One of the questions we will be attempting to answer in this paper is: what do these two environments have in common? Why should it be possible to use deictic adjectives with nouns designating occupations, religions, and societal offices on the one hand and with other nouns only in case there is some overt marking of possession?

2.2 The Grammatical Frame Problem

The class of deictic adjectives is very restricted in terms of syntactic distribution. These adjectives may only appear in attributive adjective position, at least with their deictic meaning (some of these adjectives also have nondeictic meanings, eg., *old*). They may not appear as predicate adjectives or postnominally, even if we control for the selectional restrictions discussed above. This is shown in (9) and (10)[1].

(9)   a. the former president walked into the room.
     b. *the president who was former walked into the room.
     c. *the president is former.
     d. *the president former walked into the room.

---

[1] This contextual problem is, of course, not unique to deictic adjectives. Many adjectives are restricted to one or another of the positions discussed here. In the following we see that *tall* may occur attributively or predicatively, but not postnominally. *Navigable* may occur in any of the three positions. *Selected* may occur attributively or postnominally, but not predicatively.

(i)   The tall building is where the Merces live.
     The building which is tall is where the Merces live.
     The building where the Merces live is tall.
     *The building tall is where the Merces live.

(ii) A navigable river is hard to find.
     A river which is navigable is a good place to go.
     Most rivers are navigable.
     A river navigable is hard to miss.

(iii) The selected book was later thrown out the window.
     The book which was selected is on the ground.
     *The book on the ground is selected.
     The book selected was later thrown out the window.

(10) a. Ricky's last bicycle is in the swamp.
   b. *Ricky's bicycle which is last is in the swamp.
   c. *Ricky's bicycle is last.
   d. *Ricky's bicycle last is in the swamp.

Our second question will be to ask why deictic adjectives may only be found in attributive adjective position.

2.3 The Substitutability Problem

The final problem I will deal with only arises in contrast to other attributive adjectives. Most attributive adjectives may be seen as restricting the class of referents and thus, the noun by itself may generally be substituted for the adjective + noun combination, with no conflict in meaning (i.e., no necessary difference in designation or truth conditions), but the converse is not true. Consider (11) and (12) for example.

(11) a. The Cuban singer is very talented.
   b. The singer is very talented.

(12) a. The Siamese cat is on the table.
   b. The cat is on the table.

Cuban singers are a subset of the class of all singers, though singers are not a subset of Cuban singers. If (11a) may be said of a situation, then (11b) is also true of that situation. *Singer* is a more schematic variant of *Cuban singer*; it doesn't contain information about the origins of the singer, but it also doesn't conflict with this information. Similarly, *cat* may refer to a Siamese cat, because Siamese cats are a subset of the larger set of all cats. We see in these examples that the more general non-modified noun may be substituted for the modified noun, but not vice versa.

With deictic adjectives, a non-modified noun may not be substituted for a modified one:

(13) a. The former president talked to Lucy.
   b. The president talked to Lucy.

(14) a. We talked to a former Mormon.
   b. We talked to a Mormon.

If we assume the date of this paper as the reference time for such sentences, then in (13) *the former president* will refer to Bush, while *the president* must refer to Clinton. These noun phrases refer to different people. The facts are similar in the second example where, at a particular time, *Mormon* and *former Mormon* cannot be used to designate the same person.

So, the third question I will be addressing is why the bare noun may not be substituted for a deictic adjective + noun compound.

3. Theoretical Constructs

To gain some insights into the problems discussed above and the nature of deictic adjectives in general, I will turn to Langacker's (1987, 1991) theory of Cognitive Grammar and discuss some facts about prototypical adjective + noun combinations.

3.1 Nouns, Noun Phrases, and Adjectives

Two facts about the semantics of nouns and adjectives are crucial to our understanding of deictic adjectives. First, we must recognize a difference between noun types and noun instances. Second, we must understand how a prototypical adjective such as *red* fits into this distinction.

In Langacker's (1991) discussion of the difference between a noun and a noun phrase, he shows that we must distinguish a noun *type* from a noun *instance*. That is, a bare noun stem designates a type of thing, abstracted away from any actual manifestation of that thing. The only overt types we find in English are noun-noun compounds and possibly certain noun-verb compounds. In compounds such as *cat lover* or *babysit* for example, no conceptualization of a particular cat or baby is necessary. In fact, we are necessarily abstracting away from any particular instance of the cat or baby categories.

In the English noun phrase we are generally not referring to a type *per se*, but to a particular instance of that type. We use the abstract type to pick out a concrete referent in a particular situation. If I say *a/the cat walked into the room*, I am in fact conceptualizing a manifestation of the cat type.

When a prototypical adjective combines with a noun, it creates a more elaborate type. That is, it creates a new type that is more specific than the noun by itself. This new type may then be instantiated in a full noun phrase. Let us consider how adjectives and nouns combine in more detail within the framework of Cognitive Grammar.

In this theory, all linguistic constructs are said to consist of symbolic units, comprised of the conventional pairing of a semantic and a phonological component (or pole). This model of grammar is considered to be valid at the morphemic, word, and syntactic levels, which vary only in terms of their complexity.

Symbolic units are combined via their semantic or phonological compatibilities. That is, aspects of the meaning of two conceptual structures which overlap in their semantic (or phonological) poles will permit them to be combined. This process is termed *integration* and in general one component is said to *elaborate* another. In figure 1, I have shown how the adjective *red* combines with the noun *book*.

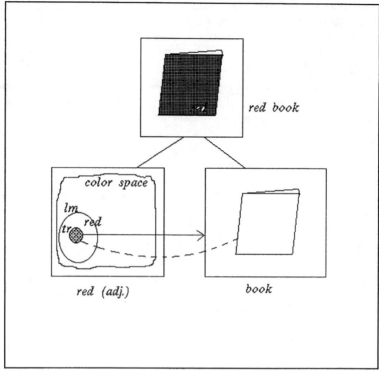

Figure 1

Adjectives are relational, profiling the relation between a landmark and a trajector. In the representation giving in figure 1, the landmark (lm) designates a region in color space. The trajector (tr) in this relation is an elaboration site. It must be elaborated by a noun, in this case the noun *book*, to form the composite structure *red book*.

For my purposes, it is crucial to note that elaboration is seldom a one-way street. While *book* elaborates the trajector of *red*, we must also note that *red* elaborates a particular aspect of the meaning of *book*. In this example, we understand *red* to be an elaboration of the outer surface of the book[2]. Elaboration of an *internal*

---

[2] This is the default meaning, but context can easily override this default, as, for example, if speaker and hearer are talking about the color of book pages. This in no way diminishes the point being made, however. What is at issue is not what aspect of the noun type is being modified, but how, in the prototypical case, elaboration of

aspect of the semantics of a type such as *book* creates a new type that is more specific than the type designated by the noun by itself. If I use the NP *the red book*, I am conceptualizing an instance of the *red book* type.

4 Addressing the Problems Found with Deictic Adjectives

We will now return to the problems discussed in section 2 with respect to deictic adjectives, namely the selectional restriction problem (4.1), the attributive adjective problem (4.2) and the substitutability problem (4.3).

4.1 Selectional Restrictions

We noted in section 2 that deictic adjectives combine with nouns denoting occupations, religions and societal offices. What do these environments have in common? With nouns such as these we recognize a special relationship between the noun type and the noun instance (the particular referent designated). I will refer to these special noun types and instances as *roles* and *values*, respectively[3]. Roles are not just abstractions away from particular instances but can be seen as constant and independent entities within elaborate frames, the particular values of which change over time. *President*, for example, is a very prototypical role noun and as a type designates a societal office which exists continually and independently of any particular person who holds the office.

What aspects of the semantics of role nouns do deictic adjectives modify? Most adjectives elaborate an aspect of the internal semantics of the nouns they combine with, as we saw with *red book*. Deictic adjectives, on the other hand, do not modify the internal semantics of the nouns they combine with but, rather, the relationship between the role and the particular values it takes. They specify that an association between a role and a value exists at a particular point in time. A schematic representation of this is given in figure 2.In this diagram we see that the instantiation of the role by a particular value exists at time t2, but that no such association exists at t1 or t3. Choice of deictic adjective depends on where we locate reference time. That is, if reference time is understood to be t3, then we are discussing an association between the role and a particular value that existed in the past and we may use deictic adjectives referring to past instantiations, like *former, past, last*, etc. Similarly, if RT is taken to be t2, then we may use deictic adjectives that situate the instantiation in the present, and if RT is taken to be t1, then the instantiative

---

some facet of the noun type creates a more specific type.

[3] Though I will not specifically invoke the theory of Mental Spaces it should be noted that much of the following analysis is inspired by Fauconnier's work on roles and values (Fauconnier 1985).

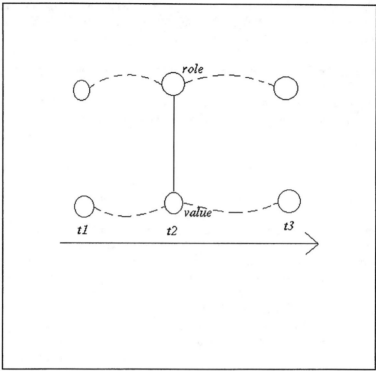

Figure 2

relationship in the future and we may say, for example, the *future/next* president.

I will hypothesize that the nouns deictic adjectives may be used with have two specific properties:

1) the type and the instance must be conceptually independent, i.e., they are roles and values.

2) the association between the type and the instance must be temporally bounded (i.e., it must be temporary).

In all of the environments where we find deictic adjectives, we also find these conditions. It is easiest to see this with role nouns denoting occupations, religions and societal offices, as in the case of *president*. I will now turn to possessive constructions and attempt to explain how these also satisfy these conditions. In (15), a number of examples of various possessives are given.

(15)   my watch; her cousin; your foot; the baby's bib; his rook; our host; their group; Sara's office; the book's weight; your anxiety; our neighborhood; its location; my quandary; Lincoln's assassination; Booth's assassination; their candidate; my bus

It is crucial to note that the actual semantic relations between the possessor and the possessee differ a great deal. Langacker has characterized the commonality among various possessive relations in terms of the Reference Point Model (RPM), represented in figure 3.

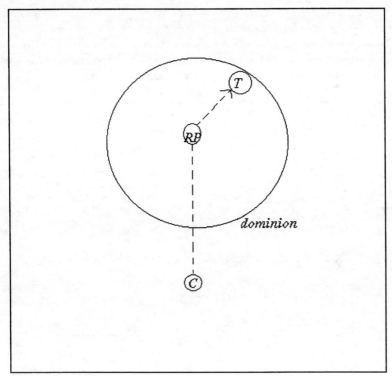

Figure 3

In the Reference Point Model, a conceptualizer (C) traces a mental path through a reference point (RP) to a target (T), which is in the dominion of the reference point. That is, it is in "the conceptual region (or set of entities) to which a particular reference point affords direct access".

Using the reference point model, let us now return to the two properties of nouns that permit them to be used with deictic adjectives to see how the possessives that may be used with deictic adjectives also exhibit them.

First, the relationship between the possessor and the possessee must be temporally bounded. In (16), we see examples that do not work with deictic adjectives because the relationship is not temporally bounded. These are examples of inalienable possession.

(16)   a. *my former leg
        b. *my current uncle

It must be noted that contexts in which these relationships can be seen as temporary will result in grammaticality. We can imagine the bionic man, for example, referring to *his former leg* because it is possible for him to switch legs. And, in my own family, where marital relations are often temporary and change rapidly, there is nothing unusual about saying *my current uncle*. Figure 4 represents the dynamic nature of possessives which deictic adjectives make use of.

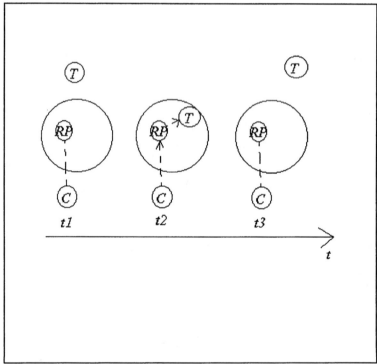

Figure 4

Second, as we would expect, a temporary relationship between the possessor and the possessee is not quite enough. We must also recognize the possessed entity as a kind of role, i.e., an independent slot in people's lives that is filled by various values over time. The examples in (17)-(19) are intended to illustrate this.

(17)   *our future pizza/watch/rook

(18)   Ethyl's former car/husband/house/etc.

(19)   my current toothpaste/bus

The examples in (17) are anomalous because we do not recognize these as stereotypical roles in people's lives. That is, there *only* a temporary association between the possessor and the possessee but we do not recognize pizza, watches, and rooks as roles that are constant and distinct from the values they may take.

The nouns in (18), in contrast, are not just temporary parts of people's lives, but are elevated to the status of roles in people's lives. The particular values may change but we generally expect some form of a car, husband, or house to be a constant part of someone's life.

The role construal of a noun is more striking in the case of *my current toothpaste* or *bus*. Toothpaste can only be understood as a role if we think of it in terms of brands of toothpaste, and buses in terms of bus routes. This contrast shows up in (20) and (21). The predicate in (20a) doesn't necessarily refer to a role and is ungrammatical, while (20b) highlights the role construal of *toothpaste* (and a particular value it may take). Similarly, buses, as roles, may not be late, but they may be instantiated by particular routes.

(20)   a. *My current toothpaste is gone
         b. My current toothpaste is Crest.

(21)   a. *My current bus is late
         b. My current bus is route 301.

4.2 The Grammatical Frame Problem

We now return to the grammatical frame problem. Attributive adjective position is crucial for modifying or delimiting instantiation and adjectives that are limited to this position are restricted to this sort of modification. This observation was first made by Bolinger (1967) who distinguished *reference modification* (typically found in attributive adjective position) from *referent modification* (typically found in predicate adjective position). He gives the examples reproduced in (22)-(26) to show that adjectives that may only be found in attributive position modify the reference. Some of these adjectives may be found in other positions but with significant meaning differences. Bolinger's classification of three classes of reference modifying adjectives is given with the examples below.

    1) "Adjectives that identify the reference of the noun with itself."
        (22)   a. a regular policeman
                  b. a true poet
                  c. a sheer fraud

    2) "Adjectives that modify the determiner *the*."
      a) "*The* in the sense 'already determined'":
        (23)   a. the very man
                  b. the particular spot
                  c. the precise reason

      b) "*The* in the sense of importance":
        (24)   a. their main faults
                  b. the prime suspect
                  c. the sole survivors

      c) "*The* in the sense 'recognized'":
        (25)   a. the lawful heir
                  b. the rightful owner
                  c. the true king
                  d. the right/wrong book

    3) "Adjectives that seem to qualify the tense of the verb in some underlying structure":
        (26)   a. the future king
                  b. a sure winner
                  c. my old school
                  d. our late President

    I won't discuss all of these examples, but it's easy to see that cases such as *regular policeman, true poet*, in (22), and *the rightful owner, the true king, the right book*, in (25) all specify the extent to which the type/role designation is applicable to a particular referent.
    If my analysis is correct, that deictic adjectives temporally locate the relationship between the role and the value, then we would only expect them to appear attributively and, indeed, this is exactly what we find.

4.3 The Substitutability Problem
    The solution to the substitutability problem also follows directly from my

analysis. Most adjectives elaborate a facet of the internal semantics of the nouns they combine with. The non-modified noun may be substituted for the modified noun because it is more schematic[4]. Deictic adjectives do not create more specific types, they serve a different function in nominal modification, namely locating the relationship between the role and the value in the temporal realm. For this reason we should have no expectations about substitutability.

5. Conclusion

I hope the preceding has shown how one class of adjectives combine in a non-prototypical way with nouns, as well as some of the differences between this class of adjectives and more prototypical adjectives. We have seen how three grammatical problems can be seen as the direct consequence of the way these adjectives combine semantically with nouns.

References

Bolinger, Dwight. 1967. Adjectives in English: Attribution and Predication. *Lingua* 18. 1-34.

Fauconnier, Gilles. 1985. *Mental Spaces: Aspects of Meaning Construction in Natural Language*. Cambridge, MA and London: MIT Press/Bradford.

Haegeman, Liliane. 1991. *Introduction to Government and Binding Theory*. Cambridge, Massachusetts: Basil Blackwell, Inc.

Langacker, Ronald W. 1987. *Foundations of Cognitive Grammar, vol. I: Theoretical Prerequisites*. Stanford: Stanford University Press.

Langacker, Ronald W. 1991. *Foundations of Cognitive Grammar, vol. II: Descriptive Application*. Stanford: Stanford University Press.

---

[4] *Red book* and the other examples contrasted with deictic adjective usage in this paper are very prototypical in this regard and allow substitutability. There are other adjectives which are not deictic but which are also not substitutable in this way, e.g., *fake guns* are definitely not a subset of *guns*, *a partial story* is not substitutable by *story*, *nonexistent house* is not a subset of *house*. It is beyond the scope of this paper to consider how these adjectives differ from more prototypical adjectives like *red*.

How Productive are Metaphors? A Close Look at the Participation of a Few Verbs in the STATES ARE LOCATIONS Metaphor (and Others).

SARAH TAUB
University of California, Berkeley

Though we feel we have good evidence for a general conceptual metaphor STATES ARE LOCATIONS, which includes as a submapping CHANGE IS MOTION, we find that individual verbs of motion have unique and idiosyncratic patterns of participation in that metaphor. That is, one might expect that all verbs that describe a change of location would be equally able to describe metaphorically a change of state, but this is not the case.

This paper has three purposes: first, to present a number of additions to STATES ARE LOCATIONS that explain many of the verbs' usage patterns; second, to explore a set of idiosyncracies that metaphor theory in its current form does not address; and third, to suggest some ways metaphor theory might expand to handle these idiosyncrasies.

1 A puzzle

The major project of metaphor theory (as described in Lakoff 1993 and elsewhere) has been to use linguistic evidence to find systematic sets of correspondences (known as *mappings*) between two domains of thought. One extremely widespread mapping is that from the domain of physical locations, movements, and forces to the domain of states, changes, and causes. This metaphor, known as STATES ARE LOCATIONS, is well-documented and pervasive in English (Espenson 1991; Lakoff 1993; Taub 1994); it has also been found in languages as diverse as English, Uighur,

449

Japanese, and Hebrew. One might expect that such a common and familiar metaphor would be regular and productive in how it uses vocabulary from the domain of locations to describe the domain of states. It turns out, however, that this is not so.

Consider the ways that individual verbs of motion are used in STATES ARE LOCATIONS. There are a number of idiosyncrasies such as the following:

(1) a. The water *came* to a boil.
   b. The water *reached* a boil.
   c. The heat *brought* the water to a boil.
   d. *The heat *drove* the water to a boil.

(2) a. *Temperatures *came* to record heights.
   b. Temperatures *reached* record heights.
   c. The heat wave *brought* temperatures to record heights.
   d. The heat wave *drove* temperatures to record heights.

Nothing in earlier mappings of this metaphor (e.g., Espenson 1991, Lakoff 1993) explained why some verbs could be used to describe certain changes and other verbs could not; why, for example, water could *come* to a boil but temperatures could not *come* to record heights. Some of these idiosyncrasies could be explained by additions to the mapping (that is, by mechanisms already approved by metaphor theory) and some could not (that is, metaphor theory has no means to deal with them). This paper will give details on both the new mappings and the anomalies which remain.

2 Phenomena that fit into metaphor theory

This investigation includes the following verbs of motion and of caused motion: the causative verbs *bring, take, send, push, lead, guide, throw, drive, put, move, remove, drag, set,* and *plunge*; and the noncausatives *come, go, reach, arrive, leave, return, enter, exit, move, run, hurry, fly, burst,* and *break*. Each of these verbs can be used to describe many different examples of caused changes of state (e.g., *flipping a switch causes the room to become dark; damp weather causes the grain to rot*). The type of state, change, and causation in each event, and the lexical semantics of each verb provide evidence for a few new metaphorical correspondences. These findings are summarized here, followed by a revised mapping.

2.1 Additions to STATES ARE LOCATIONS

First of all, more features of the source domain, CAUSED CHANGE OF LOCATION, are mapped. Let us review some of the elements of that domain which were previously mapped (Lakoff 1993): there is an entity which moves; there is a starting location, a final location, and a path between them; and there is some force which acts on the entity to make it move. To these we must add at least the following: *deixis*---the distinction between co-location with the speaker (HERE) and location elsewhere (THERE) (cf. Emanatian 1991); the *willfulness* of the thing that is moving---its resistance to or compliance with the force acting on it; and the *abruptness of causation*---whether the force acts on the object for only a brief time (e.g., throwing or kicking a ball), or whether it continues to act on the object as it travels (e.g., pushing a stalled car).

Second, since these verbs are highly polysemous, we need to specify the particular source-domain sense that is being mapped. For example, the verb *send* is not necessarily deictic in the source domain---I can *send* a package to a friend in New York, or he can *send* one to me---but the sense that gets mapped to the target domain involves caused motion from HERE to THERE (basically the opposite of *bring*). As evidence for this, consider examples (3)a-d, which also invoke the previously-established mapping NORMAL MENTAL STATES ARE HERE (Lakoff 1993).

(3) a. I *sent* her *into* a trance.
   b. *I *brought* her *into* a trance.
   c. I *brought* her *out of* a trance.
   d. *I *sent* her *out of* a trance.

A trance is not a normal mental state, and thus gets mapped as having distal deixis; since *send* is only used for changes from normal to abnormal states, we can assume that the deictic sense is the one being mapped.

Third, we need to recognize that parts of STATES ARE LOCATIONS can optionally combine with other deictic and directional metaphors to form different *constellations* (in the sense of Grady, Taub, and Morgan, same volume). In other words, some metaphorical expressions that use correspondences from STATES ARE LOCATIONS will also incorporate correspondences from other mappings, and some will not. For example, examples (3)a-d combine CHANGE IS MOTION (from STATES ARE LOCATIONS) and NORMAL MENTAL STATES ARE HERE. Other metaphors that can be brought in are GOOD IS UP, THE END STATE OF A LONG PROCESS IS HERE, and

CURRENT STATES ARE HERE. The last two metaphors are new, and will be discussed further later on.

2.2 A revised mapping for STATES ARE LOCATIONS

Table 1 presents a revised mapping for STATES ARE LOCATIONS which incorporates these changes; each correspondence is justified by at least one example. The new material, correspondences 4-7, appears in *italics*.

There are some additional points to be made about the new correspondences. For (4), MANNER OF CAUSING CHANGE IS MANNER OF INDUCING MOTION, note the contrast between *throw* and *bring*: *throwing* involves a brief, forceful transfer of momentum to an object, which maps onto causation by a rapid single event; *bringing* involves accompanying an object along a path, which maps onto causation that takes a longer period of time.

The sense of *drive* mapped in (5), ENTITY'S ATTITUDE TOWARD CHANGE IS ENTITY'S ATTITUDE TOWARD MOTION, is like that in *driving cattle*: forcing an unwilling entity to move; this is mapped to forcing an entity to an undesired state. Conversely, *guide* implies that the entity is being taken to a place where it wishes to go; this maps onto willing change of state.

In (6), SPEED OF CHANGE IS SPEED OF MOTION, *flying,* a rapid type of motion, is mapped onto a rapid change of state.

Finally, in (7), ABRUPTNESS OF CHANGE IS ABRUPTNESS OF MOTION, *plunge* entails a sudden descent, often into some kind of fluid; the abruptness of the transition maps onto an abrupt change of state. A special case of abrupt motion is what happens when an entity suddenly breaks through a barrier; this is mapped to particularly sudden and dramatic changes of state.

Table 1: A Revised Mapping for STATES ARE LOCATIONS

SOURCE DOMAIN	==>	TARGET DOMAIN

---

1. PLACES   ==>   STATES

I'm *in* a depression.

2. MOVEMENT FROM PLACE   ==>   CHANGE FROM ONE STATE
    TO PLACE   TO ANOTHER

He *went from* fat *to* slim in a matter of weeks.

3. CAUSING AN ENTITY TO MOVE ==> CAUSING AN ENTITY TO CHANGE
    FROM ONE PLACE TO ANOTHER   FROM ONE STATE TO ANOTHER

The solar eclipse *sent* the world *into* darkness.

4. *MANNER OF INDUCING MOTION*   ==> *MANNER OF CAUSING CHANGE*
    A. *"PROPULSIVE" MANNER*   ==> *CAUSATION BY A QUICK SINGLE
                                              EVENT*

The home run *threw* the crowd *into* a frenzy.

    B. *"ENTRAINING" MANNER*   ==>   *CAUSATION BY A PROLONGED
                                              EVENT OR SERIES OF EVENTS*

John *brought* the water *to* a boil.

5. *ENTITY'S ATTITUDE TOWARD*   ==>   *ENTITY'S ATTITUDE TOWARD
    MOTION*   CHANGE*
    A. *RESISTED MOTION*   ==>   *RESISTED CHANGE*

Hunger *drove* Jane *to* desperate measures.

    B. *WILLING MOTION*   ==>   *WILLING CHANGE*

Over the years, the chef *guided* his student *to* mastery.

6. *SPEED OF MOTION*   ==>   *SPEED OF CHANGE*

Mark *flew into* a rage.

7. *ABRUPTNESS OF MOTION*   ==> *ABRUPTNESS OF CHANGE*

The room was *plunged into* darkness.
    A. *BREAKING THROUGH A*   ==> *ABRUPT CHANGE*
       BARRIER

The tree *burst into* flame.

2.3 Optional additional mappings

Table 2 presents four more mappings which sometimes join with STATES
ARE LOCATIONS correspondences in motivating metaphorical expressions.
Note that in I, III, and IV, the additional correspondence gives a different
metaphorical meaning to proximal (and usually distal) deixis; this meaning
motivates the choice of the deictic verbs *come, go, bring,* and *send.*

Table 2: Four mappings that sometimes combine with STATES ARE
LOCATIONS.

I. NORMAL STATES ARE HERE (Lakoff 1993)
1. HERE   ==> NORMAL STATES
He quickly *came to* his senses.
The doctor *brought* her *back to* life.
2. AWAY/THERE   ==> ABNORMAL STATES
Lisa *went out of* her mind.
A rare February thaw *sent* the fruit trees *into* bloom.
The solar eclipse *sent* the world *into* darkness.

II. GOOD IS UP (Lakoff & Johnson 1980)
1. UP   ==> GOOD STATES
2. DOWN   ==> BAD STATES
One bee sting was enough to *plunge* her *into* shock.

III. *THE END STATE OF A LONG PROCESS IS HERE*
HERE   ==> *NATURAL END-POINT OF*
                                   PROCESS / EXPECTED STATE
Susan *brought* the water *to* a boil.
The marble *came to* a stop outside the circle.
John *brought* his story *to* an end.

IV. *CURRENT STATES ARE HERE*
HERE   ==> *CURRENT STATES*
How did the water *come to* be red?
What *brought* you *to* study linguistics?

Mappings I and II in Table 2 have been discussed in previous
publications (e.g., Lakoff & Johnson 1980; Lakoff 1993), though the way

they combine with STATES ARE LOCATIONS in deictic and directional verbs of motion has not been given explicit attention.

Mappings III and IV have not been previously proposed, though Espenson (1991) analyzes IV's data as EXISTENCE IS HERE, and Emanatian (1991) conflates IV with THE PRESENT MOMENT IS HERE. The present analysis is unusual in two respects; one is that the mappings' main supporting evidence is the internal semantics of the deictic verbs given above. The other is that they seem to have only one correspondence; (4)a-b below show that distal deixis appears not to be mapped.

(4) a. *He unexpectedly *sent* the water *to* a boil.
   b. **Away from us*, the water will be clear again.

More time ought to be spent in deciding whether the single correspondence and the small set of supporting examples justify the existence of III and IV. Nevertheless, these metaphors as stated here fit well with the analysis of metaphorical verbs of motion presented in this paper.

2.4 Some puzzles resolved

We can now resolve some apparent contradictions in the STATES ARE LOCATIONS system. For example, the following pairs of sentences have verbs with opposite deixis, yet the sentences' meanings are nearly the same. The explanation for this is that members of the pairs invoke different optional mappings.

(5) a. He *came to* a bad end.
      (EXPECTED FINAL STATES ARE HERE)
   b. The house *went to* wrack and ruin.
      (ABNORMAL STATES ARE AWAY)

(6) a. Communism *brought* the USSR *into* chaos.
      (EXPECTED FINAL STATES ARE HERE)
      (LONG-TERM CAUSATION IS ACCOMPANIMENT WHILE CAUSING
      MOTION)
   b. Communism *sent* the USSR *into* chaos.
      (ABNORMAL STATES ARE AWAY)
      (ABRUPT CAUSATION IS PROPULSIVE CAUSATION OF MOTION)

All four sentences describe the end state of a process (metaphorically HERE) that produced a bad or abnormal result (metaphorically AWAY); thus, in each case, the speaker could choose to represent the final state using either metaphorical proximal or distal deixis, by choosing which optional mappings to include. In particular, the (a) sentences use EXPECTED FINAL STATES ARE HERE, while the (b) sentences use ABNORMAL STATES ARE AWAY. Note that all the sentences also use STATES ARE LOCATIONS mappings such as CHANGE IS MOTION and MANNER OF CAUSATION IS MANNER OF CAUSING MOTION.

3 Phenomena that stretch metaphor theory

The rest of this paper will be devoted to a discussion of some idiosyncratic phenomena that metaphor theory does not explain; these include constructions, idioms, and other anomalies that are tied to specific lexical items. I will first discuss data from the STATES ARE LOCATIONS mapping, and then show that other metaphors have similar lexical anomalies. We will see that in addition to the broad, highly productive conceptual mappings, languages have metaphor-based idioms and constructions that are frozen at every level of productivity, from completely productive to not productive at all.

3.1 Anomalies in STATES ARE LOCATIONS

Let us first consider *idioms*: as noted by Lakoff and Turner (1989) and others, these phrases often seem to use source-to-target mappings identical to larger, more "free" mappings. Yet the words in an idiom are usually completely frozen, with no substitutions allowed. The following idioms fit quite well with the mapping presented in the first half of this paper: *flying* => changing abruptly; *dragging* => forcing someone to change unwillingly; and so on:

(7) a. She *flew off* the handle.
    b. I was *dragged* kicking and screaming *into* doing it.
    c. His reaction *threw* me for a loop.
    d. It *came to* pass that...

Clearly, however, the broad mapping given in section 2.2 does not explain or predict the existence of these fixed phrases, or the additional vivid images they contain.

The second group of phenomena can be loosely termed *constructions*: some verbs can require particular (and often peculiar) syntactic frames in their metaphorical senses. For example, metaphorical *go* can take at least two syntactic patterns that nonmetaphorical *go* cannot, and each pattern specifies a particular shade of meaning. *Go* followed by an adjective means 'change to an unexpected or unwanted state described by the adjective': *He went crazy; The room went dark.* On the other hand, *go* followed by *from* adjective$_1$ *to* adjective$_2$ means 'change from state described by adjective$_1$ to state described by adjective$_2$': *The situation went from bad to worse; The water went from hot to cold in a matter of minutes.* Note how the first pattern conventionally incorporates the mapping ABNORMAL STATES ARE AWAY, while the second does not.

As further examples, note that *break*, when used metaphorically to mean 'abruptly begin an action', requires the action to take the grammatical form of a action nominal: *She broke into a run* and *She broke into song* are acceptable, while **She broke into singing* is not. *Burst*, in the same context, can take two syntactic frames: *out* followed by a gerund, as in *He burst out crying*; or *into* followed by an action nominal, as in *She burst into tears*.

The third group of phenomena might be called *lexical preference*: certain lexical items are conventionally used metaphorically to refer to particular types of causation. For example, *push* is used to refer to exhortation by a human (cf. *pushy*).

(8) a. ?Hunger *pushed* him *to* find new solutions.
    b. Hunger *drove* him *to* find new solutions.
    c. Jim *pushed* her *to* find new solutions.
    d. Jim *drove* her *to* find new solutions.

Push is questionable when used to describe an unpleasant circumstance which motivates someone to change; *drive* fits much better in that context. Similarly, *push,* when its subject is human, must refer to an act of urging, while *drive* may be used when the subject is simply being obnoxious. Other examples of lexical preference are that we usually speak of *setting* fires or *setting* things on fire; *putting* people or animals into unconscious states; and *moving* people to different emotional states.

Finally, there are *lexical gaps*: some motion verbs are never used metaphorically to describe changes, although all their semantic components are mapped. For example, the verb *toss* involves propulsive causation of motion and slow motion from one place to another, both of which are represented in the mapping in 2.2. But unlike the similar verb *throw*, *toss* is not used to express metaphorical meanings via STATES ARE LOCATIONS.

(9) a. The wet weather *threw* their plans *into* disarray.

    b. *The wet weather *tossed* their plans *into* disarray.

Another example is the non-use of *arrive at* to describe the onset of a final state, as in *The story arrived at an end.* Verbs such as *reach* or *come to* are used instead, though the semantic difference is only slight and all of *arrive's* internal semantics is in fact mapped by the metaphor.

3.2 Anomalies from other metaphors

The lexical anomalies given above are all limits on the productivity of the STATES ARE LOCATIONS metaphor. Space does not permit a detailed consideration of other metaphors, but a cursory glance will show that many exhibit the same types of anomalies. For example, the metaphor LIGHT IS A FLUID, where light is described as *flowing, seeping,* etc., and illumined areas are described as bodies of fluid, clearly shows lexical gaps: we can speak of a *pool* of light, but not a *pond, puddle,* or *lake* of light. In another example, *I've got him wrapped around my finger,* a fixed-phrase idiom, is clearly in line with the productive mapping CONTROL IS MANIPULATION WITH THE HANDS.

On the other hand, the newly-formed metaphor THE INTERNET IS A SUPERHIGHWAY SYSTEM seems to have unlimited productivity: *traffic, cops, on-ramps, roadblocks,* and *roadmaps* have all been used in this metaphor, and new words and concepts are mapped almost daily. It may be that because this metaphor is so new, and because the target domain (the INTERNET) is not yet commonly understood, there is an awareness that people are still playing with the mapping and looking for useful correspondences. If this metaphor is still conscious and deliberate in the minds of those who use it, there is no reason for them not to fill in lexical gaps and smooth out other anomalies. It would seem that these lexical anomalies are a feature of older, conceptually and grammatically entrenched metaphors.

3.3 Expanding metaphor theory: the descriptive task

Given the existence of these lexical and constructional particularities, how could we expand conceptual metaphor theory to handle them? Clearly, the old slogan, metaphors *motivate but do not predict* the existence of expressions, is not the final solution; it may be true, but we can find additional generalizations on many levels. In expanding metaphor theory, we have two tasks to address: first, we need a mechanism to *describe* how metaphor interacts with the uses of particular lexical items; and second, we need to find ways to *explain* why certain lexical items develop irregularities.

The descriptive task is very much in the spirit of Fillmore and Kay's Construction Grammar, and may facilitate links between the theories. According to them,

"The aim of a construction grammar is to account for the generalizations of a language without distorting the particularities ... [it] embraces ... the explicit recording of the generalizations implicit in each language; it adds to this goal that of accounting within the same formal system for the partial regularities and the exceptional structures that make up most of what gets said." (Fillmore & Kay, 1987)

In a system like theirs, each lexical item, idiom, and syntactic pattern receives its own description; the descriptive elements are shared and make up the basic building blocks of the grammar. The broad conceptual mappings that make up metaphors like STATES ARE LOCATIONS could become yet another element with which to capture the properties of words and syntactic patterns; each pattern that involves a metaphor could have that metaphor specified in its semantic description. Since Construction Grammar can handle patterns at every level of productivity, it could no doubt be adapted to represent the whole range of metaphor phenomena, from broad and productive to idiomatic and frozen.

3.4 Expanding metaphor theory: the explanatory task

If we wish to go beyond description of the present metaphor system to an explanation of why the system exists, we need to start asking questions such as the following ones. Do only particular types of metaphors display these lexical and constructional complexities? If so, why? Which comes first, the general conceptual mapping or the particular constructions, idioms, and so on? Does one motivate the other, or do both result from a third process? How exactly *do* metaphorical mappings arise? In short, we will need to look closely at the origins and development of metaphorical expressions and mappings. There are many possible directions to go in looking for answers to these questions; I will present here a brief example of one strategy: looking to earlier meanings of lexical items to explain present anomalies in their metaphorical uses.

The example in question is Joseph Grady's (pers. comm.) analysis of the proposed metaphor ACTIONS ARE OBJECTS. The mapping of this metaphor is as follows: *objects* map onto *actions*; *holding or possessing an object* maps onto *performing an action*; *not holding an object* maps onto *not performing an action*. This mapping, however, is unusually low in productivity: it has very few lexical items which participate, and all belong to highly conventionalized constructions; also, related source-domain concepts (e.g., *giving* and *receiving*) are not mapped.

(10) a. He *kept* running.
    b. *He *possessed* running.
    c. *He *had* running.
    d. *He *owned* running.
    e. He *left off* running.
      f. *He *dropped* running. (in the sense that he stopped a particular instance of running)
      g. *She *gave* him running. (in the sense that she caused him to run)

As the examples in (10) show, *keep* is the only POSSESSION verb that can be used, and *leave off* the only CESSATION OF POSSESSION verb. Clearly, ACTIONS ARE OBJECTS as a mapping is only weakly supported by the data.

Grady noted that all the verbs that participate have earlier *locational* meanings (e.g. *keep* 'stay at a place', as in *keep one's room*). He argues that the mapping ACTIONS ARE OBJECTS does not exist, and that all the putative examples derive from a different, much more productive metaphor, ACTIONS ARE LOCATIONS (Taub 1994). According to his analysis, the verbs in question developed their particular ACTION-related constructions while they still had locational meanings, under the influence of the ACTIONS ARE LOCATIONS mapping. Later shifts in meaning then obscured the origins of these phrases.

I do not mean to claim that Grady has had the final word on the status of ACTIONS ARE OBJECTS; his reasoning and data are given here as an example of how and where we might find explanations for unusual phenomena linked to particular lexical items. In general, earlier meanings of words still influence the way they are used in specific constructions (see, e.g., Traugott 1993, Sweetser 1990, Emanatian 1992).

Another possible source of explanations is the large body of work on *grammaticalization,* which (in part) tries to account for how individual lexical items undergo metaphor-like meaning shifts. For example, English *going to* followed by a verb has turned into a marker of future tense; this shift bears some resemblance to the STATES ARE LOCATIONS and ACTIONS ARE LOCATIONS mappings cited in this work, in that a motion verb is being used to describe a change of state or action (cf. Emanatian 1991, Taub

1994). Explanations for such phenomena in the grammaticalization literature invoke such processes as *contextual spreading* (e.g., Traugott 1982), *pragmatic reinterpretation* (e.g., Traugott 1982), and *changes in frequency* of the lexical item in question (Tabor 1994). The grammaticalized items in question are much like the idioms, constructions, and other lexical particularities which pervade metaphors such as STATES ARE LOCATIONS; we ought to test whether these processes can explain the metaphor phenomena.

4 Conclusions

This paper has argued for several points. First, one can deduce metaphorical correspondences from the lexical semantics of verbs; there are a number of additions to STATES ARE LOCATIONS which were found using this method. Second, along with broad, productive metaphorical mappings, languages have metaphor-related constructions, idioms, lexical gaps, and lexical preferences: that is, there is a cline of productivity in metaphor from completely productive patterns to completely frozen ones. Last, metaphor theory must expand to handle these different levels of productivity; describing them may involve mechanisms like those of Construction Grammar, while explaining them could bring in theories of metaphor genesis, data from the histories of constructions, and processes of grammaticalization.

Acknowledgements

Special thanks to Joe Grady, Pam Morgan, George Lakoff, and Eve Sweetser, for many useful conversations.

References

Fillmore, Charles J., and Paul Kay. 1987. Construction Grammar Lecture. Paper presented at the Linguistics Society of America Summer Institute. Stanford University.

Emanatian, Michele. 1992. Chagga 'Come' and 'Go': Metaphor and the Development of Tense-Aspect. *Studies in Language* 16-1:1-33.

Espenson, Jane. 1991. The Structure of the System of Causation Metaphors. Ms. University of California, Berkeley.

Grady, Joseph, Sarah Taub, and Pamela Morgan. Same volume. A "Constellation" Proposal for Metaphor Theory.

Lakoff, George. 1993. The Contemporary Theory of Metaphor. In Andrew Ortony, ed., *Metaphor and Thought,* 2nd ed., 202-51. Cambridge: Cambridge University Press.

Lakoff, George, and Mark Johnson. 1980. *Metaphors We Live By.* Chicago: University of Chicago Press.

Lakoff, George, and Mark Turner. 1989. *More than Cool Reason.* Chicago: University of Chicago Press.

Sweetser, Eve. 1990. *From Etymology to Pragmatics: Metaphorical and Cultural Aspects of Semantic Structure.* Cambridge: Cambridge University Press.

Tabor, Whitney. 1994. *Syntactic Innovation: A Connectionist Model.* Unpublished doctoral dissertation. Stanford University.

Talmy, Leonard. 1985. Lexicalization Patterns: Semantic Structure in Lexical Forms. In T. Shopen, ed., *Language Typology and Syntactic Description, Vol. 3: Grammatical Categories and the Lexicon,* 57-148. Cambridge: Cambridge University Press.

Taub, Sarah. 1994. Event Structure Metaphors and Grammaticalization: Preliminary Data from English and Uighur. Ms. University of California, Berkeley.

Traugott, Elizabeth Closs. 1982. From Propositional to Textual and Expressive Meanings: Some Semantic-Pragmatic Effects of Grammaticalization. In W. Lehmann and Y. Malkiel, eds., *Perspectives on Historical Linguistics,* 245-71. Amsterdam: John Benjamins.

Traugott, Elizabeth Closs. 1993. The Conflict *Promises/Threatens* to Escalate into War. In Joshua S. Guenter, Barbara A. Kaiser, and Cheryl C. Zoll, eds., *Proceedings of the Nineteenth Annual Meeting of the Berkeley Linguistics Society,* 348-60. Berkeley Linguistics Society, University of California, Berkeley.

On the Discourse Function of Rightward Movement in English*

GREGORY WARD & BETTY BIRNER

Northwestern University & University of Pennsylvania

While much work has been done on the discourse functions of individual constructions, little has been done to develop generalizations concerning classes of syntactic constructions. Previous work by Ward & Birner (1994b) shows that leftward movement in general serves to front 'given' information, although the type of givenness involved varies from construction to construction. In this paper we examine three constructions which have been analyzed as rightward-moving (Stowell 1981, Safir 1985, inter alia; cf. Rochemont & Culicover 1990): inversion, existential *there*-insertion, and presentational *there*-insertion. Based on an extensive study of naturally-occurring data, our analysis reveals that these three constructions are all sensitive to a similar pragmatic constraint: that the postverbal NP represent information that is unfamiliar, either within the discourse or in the hearer's (inferred) knowledge store. Thus, we show that as a class, rightward-moving constructions postpose unfamiliar information (Horn 1986); moreover, this property is not shared by right-dislocation, a superficially similar but non-rightward-moving construction.

1 Inversion

As demonstrated in Birner 1994, felicitous inversion in English is crucially dependent on the 'discourse-familiarity' of the information represented by the preposed and postposed constituents, where discourse-familiarity is determined by prior evocation in the discourse, inferrability based on the prior discourse, and recency of mention within the discourse. The first two factors determine whether information is old

*For helpful discussions about some of the syntactic issues raised in this work, we thank Beatrice Santorini. For supplying us with some of the naturally-occurring data used in this study, we thank Beth Levin, Mari Olsen, Claude Steinberg and David Yarowsky. This research was supported by NIDCD Grant R01-DC01240 (Ward) and NSF Science and Technology Center Grant SBR93-47355 A03 (Birner).

or new with respect to the discourse; information that has been evoked in the prior discourse or is inferrable based on the prior discourse is discourse-old, while information that has not been evoked and is not inferrable is discourse-new (Prince 1992). Among discourse-old information, that which has been mentioned more recently in general is treated as more familiar, in the sense of being more salient, than that which has been mentioned less recently.

In the study reported in Birner 1994, an examination of a corpus of 1778 naturally-occurring inversions revealed that in 78% of the tokens, the preposed constituent represented discourse-old information while the postposed constituent represented discourse-new information, as in (1):

(1)   We have complimentary soft drinks, coffee, Sanka, tea, and milk. *Also complimentary is red and white wine.* We have cocktails available for $2.00.
        [Flight attendant on Midway Airlines]

Here, the preposed AdjP *also complimentary* represents information previosly evoked in the discourse, while the postposed *red and white wine* is new to the discourse. There were no tokens in which the situation was reversed; that is, in no case did a preposed discourse-new element appear in combination with a postposed discourse-old element. Moreover, information that had not been evoked in the prior discourse yet was inferrable in context (Prince 1981c) behaved as discourse-old, occurring in exactly the same range of contexts as did explicitly evoked information.

Of the two constituents in question, it is the postposed constituent that will be most relevant for the purposes of this paper. Consequently, it should be noted that of 1290 applicable tokens in the corpus (excluding incomplete tokens and those lacking sufficient context), in 1149, or 89%, the postposed constituent represented discourse-new information. These cases included not only tokens containing preposed discourse-old information, but also 141 tokens (11%) whose preposed and postposed constituents were both discourse-new.

It is not the case, however, that the postposed constituent need always be discourse-new. In 11% of the tokens in the corpus, both the preposed and the postposed constituents represented discourse-old information. Interestingly, however, of those cases in which the preposed and postposed elements had both been explicitly evoked, but at different points in the prior discourse, in 91.3% of the cases the preposed element was the more recently mentioned (and hence more salient) of the two, as in (2):

(2)   Each of the characters is the centerpiece of a book, doll and clothing collection. The story of each character is told in a series of six slim books, each $12.95 hardcover and $5.95 in paperback, and in bookstores and libraries across the country. More than 1 million copies have been sold; and in late 1989 a series of activity kits was introduced for retail sale. *Complementing the relatively affordable books are the dolls, one for each fictional heroine and each with a comparably pricey historically accurate wardrobe and accessories....*
[Chicago Tribune]

Here, although the dolls have been evoked in the prior discourse, they have been evoked less recently, and are thus arguably less salient within the discourse, than the books. For this reason, switching the preposed and postposed constituents in the inversion results in infelicity:

(3)   Each of the characters is the centerpiece of a book, doll and clothing collection. The story of each character is told in a series of six slim books, each $12.95 hardcover and $5.95 in paperback, and in bookstores and libraries across the country. More than 1 million copies have been sold; and in late 1989 a series of activity kits was introduced for retail sale. #*Complementing the relatively affordable dolls are the books, one for each fictional heroine....*

Here, placing the less recently mentioned dolls in preposed position results in infelicity. Thus, even in cases where both constituents have been previously evoked, the postposed constituent nonetheless represents less familiar information, where familiarity is defined by prior evocation, inferrability, and recency of mention. The results from the corpus study indicate that the postposed constituent in an inversion tends to represent, but need not always represent, discourse-new information; moreover, when it represents discourse-old information, this information is still less familiar within the discourse than that represented by the preposed constituent. Thus, what is relevant for the felicity of inversion in discourse is the relative discourse-familiarity of the information represented by these two constituents.

2 There-Insertion

The felicitous use of *there*-insertion is also sensitive to the information status of the postverbal NP (Erdmann 1976; Rando & Napoli 1978; Ziv 1982; Penhallurick 1984; Holmback 1984; Lumsden 1988; Prince 1992;

McNally 1992; Abbott 1992, 1993; Ward & Birner 1994a; inter alia). However, previous studies have generally focused on *there*-insertion with main verb *be*. Others (Aissen 1975, Larson 1988, Rochemont & Culicover 1990, inter alia) have argued that there are two structurally distinct types of *there*-insertion: 'existential' *there*, restricted to main verb *be*, and 'presentational' *there*, restricted to verbs of 'appearance' or 'emergence' (Levin 1993). The two types are illustrated in (4a) and (4b), respectively:

(4) a. There's a problem with our analysis.
         [BB to GW in conversation]

     b. Daniel told me me that shortly after Grumman arrived at Wideview Chalet there arrived also a man named Sleeman.
         [Upfield, A.W. The Devil's Steps. 1987:246]

We will argue that, notwithstanding any structural differences that may exist between them, the two types of *there*-insertion are pragmatically distinct with respect to the information status of the NP in postverbal position. We begin with existential *there*.

2.1 Existential There-Insertion

Unlike inversion, existential *there*-insertion is sensitive not to DISCOURSE-familiarity, but rather to HEARER-familiarity. That is, as first noted in Prince 1988, 1992, the postverbal NP (henceforth PVNP) of existential *there*-insertion is required to represent information that the speaker believes is not already familiar to the hearer. Such information is typically, although not necessarily, represented by morphologically indefinite NPs, as illustrated above in (4a). This correlation has led some researchers to go so far as to claim that definites are grammatically and categorically excluded from the postverbal position of this construction. However, as we have argued in earlier work (Ward & Birner 1994a), it is not only possible but quite common for definite NPs to appear in this position just in case they represent hearer-new information. In Ward & Birner 1994a we discuss five such types of PVNP; these are listed in (5).

(5)   Types of definite PVNP in existential *there*-insertion:

        I   Hearer-old entities marked as hearer-new
        II Hearer-new tokens of hearer-old types
        III Hearer-old entities newly instantiating a variable
        IV Hearer-new entities with unique descriptions
        V   False definites

Type I consists of hearer-old entities marked as hearer-new. This category includes the 'reminder' *there*-insertion noted by, inter alia, Bolinger (1977), Hannay (1985), Lakoff (1987), and Abbott (1993), as illustrated in (6):

(6)   Almanzo liked haying-time. From dawn till long after dark every day he was busy, always doing different things. It was like play, and morning and afternoon *there was the cold egg-nog*. [Wilder, L.I. Farmer Boy. 1933:232]

Although the entity represented by the PVNP here (*the cold egg-nog*) is evoked two pages earlier, there are sufficient grounds for the writer to believe that the entity has been (temporarily) forgotten by the reader, thus licensing her to reintroduce it and treat it as hearer-new (see Lakoff 1987).

Examples of Type II, in which the PVNP represents a new instance of a known type, are well attested in the literature (Jenkins 1975, Erdmann 1976, Ziv 1982, Woisetschlaeger 1983, Hannay 1985, Lakoff 1987, Lumsden 1988, Prince 1992, Abbott 1993, inter alia); these include PVNPs with adjectives indicating an instance of a known or inferrable type (e.g., *same, usual, obligatory, ideal, perfect, necessary*), as in (7):

(7)   CP: We had another one of our delightful faculty meetings today.
        GW: My God, what do you have? Three a week?
        CP: I know. And they're always the same. *Today there was the usual bickering...*
        [CP to GW in conversation]

Here, the PVNP has dual reference, both to a type and a token. The definite is licensed by the unique identifiability of the (hearer-old) type (Hawkins 1978, 1991), while the *there*-insertion is licensed by the hearer-new status of the current instantiation of that type. Thus, the bickering evoked in (7) is presumed to be familiar; what is hearer-new is the newly instantiated bickering that held of the particular faculty meeting in question.

The third class of definite PVNP corresponds to the so-called 'list' interpretation that has been widely acknowledged to tolerate definite NPs in *there*-insertion (Milsark 1974, 1977; Rando & Napoli 1978; Lakoff 1987; Lumsden 1988; Abbott 1992, 1993; inter alia). It consists of one or more hearer-old entities newly instantiating a variable, as in (8):

(8)   [Khalili] joined the staff of the Rehabilitation Institute of Chicago, a nationally prominent 20-story medical facility, which at the time was just a handful of doctors working in a former warehouse at Ohio Street and McClurg Court. "At times, *there were just the two of us,* and he and I had to see all the patients," recalled Dr. Henry Betts, the institute's medical director and chief executive officer.
        [Chicago Tribune]

Here, the definite NP specifies the uniquely identifiable set of two individuals evoked in the prior discourse. However, this set of individuals also constitutes a hearer-new instantiation of the variable in the salient open proposition 'X-many doctors were at the Rehabilitation Institute of Chicago' (see Prince 1981b, Ward 1988, Prince 1986, inter alia, for details).

Unlike the first three types, the fourth type of definite PVNP does not depend on the prior context for its felicity. Consider the example in (9):

(9)   In addition to interest-rate risk, there is the added risk that when interest rates fall, mortgages will be prepaid, thereby reducing the Portfolio's future income stream.
        [Vanguard Financial Center Newsletter]

Here, although this particular risk constitutes new information for the hearer, the description provided in the NP is sufficient to fully and uniquely identify the risk in question, hence the felicity of the definite (cf. Holmback 1984).

The last type of definite PVNP is what we call 'false definites'. As Prince (1981a) notes, the demonstrative *this* can be felicitously used to non-deictically introduce a hearer-new entity, as in (10):

(10)   There once was this sharp Chicago alderman who also happened to be a crook.
        [Mike Royko, Chicago Tribune]

While most uses of demonstratives require that the speaker assume the hearer is in a position to identify the referent, the use of *this* exemplified in (10) assumes the hearer is not in such a position; and, as we would expect, NPs that represent such hearer-new entities are fully felicitous in the PVNP position of existential *there*-insertion. We use the term *false definite* to refer to formal definites used to represent entities not assumed to be uniquely identifiable to the hearer.

Thus, postverbal position in existential *there*-insertion may felicitously be occupied by exactly those definite NPs that are construable as hearer-new. Given this, there is no reason to appeal to the so-called 'definiteness effect' (Milsark 1974, Safir 1985, Reuland & ter Meulen 1987, inter alia). More importantly, these results demonstrate that what is relevant for the felicitous use of existential *there*-insertion is not discourse-familiarity, but rather hearer-familiarity. That is, it is not sufficient for the PVNP to be merely discourse-new; it must in fact be hearer-new for the felicitous use of existential *there* in discourse.

2.2 Presentational There-Insertion

The other class of *there*-insertion in English contains main verbs other than *be*. Based upon an analysis of a corpus of 428 naturally-occurring tokens, we found that the PVNP of presentational *there*, like that of existential *there*, is felicitous when the NP represents hearer-new information, regardless of the morphological definiteness of the PVNP. However, unlike existential *there*, presentational *there* is not limited to PVNPs representing hearer-new entities; hearer-old entities are also possible, provided they are discourse-new.

First, note that morphologically definite PVNPs may occur with presentational *there*-insertion when they represent hearer-new information, as in (11):

(11)   a.   The first to be seen of the Wirragatta homestead by anyone following the creek track from the Broken Hill road were the stockyards; and then, as he swung round a sharp bend in what had become the Wirragatta River, *there came into view the trade ships, the men's quarters, then the office-store building, and finally the large bungalow surrounded by orange-trees, which in turn were confined by a white-painted wicket fence.*
[Upfield, A.W. Winds of Evil. 1937:55]

       b.   The visitors here are a doctor who keeps zapping himself with a burglar-fighting stun gun, and Moon Unit's best friend, a lovable flake played by Bess Meyer. The two women like to wear goofy hats. The credits say that three writers were required to create this tableau.

Okay, but it has only one good line. The line is: "So?"
There remains the burning question of whether the Zap-
pas, offspring of rock star Frank Zappa and occasional
guest veejays on MTV, can act.
[AP Newswire 1990]

In (11a), the PVNP represents a hearer-new instantiation of a variable
(a Type III PVNP). The open proposition 'X came into view' is licensed
by the preceding description of what could be seen from various vantage
points. Although the various things that came into view are themselves
familiar to the reader, the identification of those items as instantiations
of the variable constitutes hearer-new information. Example (11b) is
an example of a Type IV PVNP. In this case, the burning question is
uniquely identifiable by virtue of having been explicitly and completely
identified within the NP. Nonetheless, the question is assumed to be
new to the reader and thus may appear felicitously as the PVNP.

However, while both types of *there*-insertion permit PVNPs that
represent hearer-new information, presentational *there* is less restrictive
than existential *there*, in that it allows PVNPs representing hearer-
old information as well; however, presentational *there*-insertion requires
that this NP represent information that is discourse-new. Consider the
examples in (12):

(12)   a.   There appeared before the committee your good friend
            Jim Alterman.

       b.   There stood behind him the Vice President.

       c.   Suddenly there ran out of the woods the man we had
            seen at the picnic.
            [=Aissen 1975:2, ex. 12]

In these examples, the referent of the PVNP represents information that
is presumably familiar to the hearer. Thus, presentational *there* is less
constrained than existential *there* in allowing the PVNP to represent
hearer-old information, as long as that information is NEW WITHIN
THE DISCOURSE.[1]

However, both types of *there*-insertion disallow PVNPs representing
discourse-old information. Consider (13)-(14):

(13)   a.   A: Hey, have you heard from Jim Alterman lately? I
            haven't seen him for years.
            B: Yes, actually. #There appeared before the commit-
            tee today Jim Alterman.

---

[1] See Prince 1988 for an analysis of a construction in Yiddish that appears to be
subject to the same constraint.

      b.   President Clinton appeared at the podium accompanied by three senators and the Vice President. #There stood behind him the Vice President.

(14)   a.   A: Hey, have you heard from Jim Alterman lately? I haven't seen him for years.
B: Yes, actually. #There was before the committee today Jim Alterman.

      b.   President Clinton appeared at the podium accompanied by three senators and the Vice President. #There was behind him the Vice President.

The PVNPs in these examples represent discourse-old information, and hence are infelicitous in either presentational or existential *there*-insertion. Presentational *there*-insertion, then, shares with inversion the property of backing discourse-new information; however, it shares with existential *there*-insertion the property of being sensitive to absolute (rather than relative) information status.

3   Right-Dislocation

In contrast to inversion and the two types of *there*-insertion, right-dislocation does NOT require that the clause-final NP represent new information. Consider the right-dislocations in (15):

(15)   a.   Below the waterfall (and this was the most astonishing sight of all), a whole mass of enormous glass pipes were dangling down into the river from somewhere high up in the ceiling! *They really were* ENORMOUS, *those pipes.* There must have been a dozen of them at least, and they were sucking up the brownish muddy water from the river and carrying it away to goodness knows where. [Dahl, R. Charlie and the Chocolate Factory. 1964:74-75]

      b.   Can't write much, as I've been away from here for a week and have to keep up appearances, but did Diana mention the desk drama? Dad took your old desk over to her house to have it sent out, but he didn't check to see what was in it, and forgot that I had been keeping all my vital documents in there – like my tax returns and paystubs and bank statements. Luckily Diana thought "that stuff looked important" so she took it out before

> giving the desk over to the movers. Phew! *She's a smart cookie, that Diana.*
> [personal letter]

In each of these examples, the sentence-final constituent (*those pipes* in (15a) and *that Diana* in (15b)) represents information that has been explicitly evoked in the immediately prior discourse. Since this information is both hearer-old and discourse-old, right-dislocation cannot be viewed as marking new material; on the contrary, this construction appears to disallow new information in dislocated position, as illustrated in (16):

(16)   a.   Below the waterfall (and this was the most astonishing sight of all), a whole mass of enormous glass pipes were dangling down into the river from somewhere high up in the ceiling! #*They really were* ENORMOUS, *some of the boulders in the river.* Nonetheless, they were sucked up into the pipes along with the brownish muddy water.

        b.   [...] Some of the boulders in the river really were enormous. Nonetheless, they were sucked up into the pipes along with the brownish muddy water.

Here, the presentation of new information in dislocated position renders the utterance infelicitous, although its canonical non-dislocated variant (16b) is felicitous in the same context.

The functions posited by previous researchers for right-dislocation, in fact, generally assume that the dislocated NP represents information that is to some extent given or inferrable within the discourse. For example, Davison (1984) argues that right-dislocation marks the referent of the dislocated NP as a topic, and thus also as having a 'discourse antecedent' (1984:802). Tomlin (1986), on the other hand, maintains that right-dislocation's primary function is "to self-correct potentially defective texts" (1986:62), with the speaker initially believing that the pronoun will be sufficient for the hearer to identify the referent, but then anticipating a possible communicative breakdown and providing a more explicit referring expression. Similarly, Geluykens (1987) argues that right-dislocations (in his terminology, 'tails') represent a repair mechanism for self-initiated correction of a potentially unclear reference (see also Givón 1976). However, in cases like those in (15) above, it is not plausible to consider the right-dislocation to be correcting for a possible reference failure. In (15a), for example, the identity of the referent of *they* in the right-dislocation is clear; not only do the pipes represent the only entity realized by a plural in the previous sentence, but they are also presumably the most salient entity in the discourse at the time the pronoun is uttered. Similarly, in (15b), Diana is the only female mentioned in the prior discourse, and thus the only available referent for the pronoun *she*. Geluykens suggests that such cases may be functionally distinct from right-dislocations used for repair purposes; he does not, however, offer an account of such cases, but rather maintains that the majority of right-dislocations serve as repairs.

Ziv & Grosz (1994), on the other hand, draw a sharp distinction between right-dislocations and repairs, or 'afterthoughts', on the basis of distinct syntactic and intonational properties. For example, afterthoughts are characterized by a pause before the final NP, while right-dislocations consist of a single intonation contour with no such pause. Similarly, they note that the two have different functions as well. Whereas the function of afterthoughts is corrective, the function of right-dislocation, they argue, is organizational. In right-dislocation, according to Ziv & Grosz, an entity which has previously been situationally or textually evoked (Prince 1981c) is brought to the top of the 'Cf list' (Grosz, Joshi, and Weinstein 1983); that is, it becomes the most salient entity available for subsequent reference. Following Lambrecht (1981), they argue that right-dislocation instructs the hearer to search the context for the intended referent. They state that "if the immediately preceding utterance includes a reference to the entity in question right-dislocation is not felicitous" (1994:190), except when (a) the entity is merely inferrable from, but has not been explicitly evoked in, the prior utterance, or (b) the dislocated NP is predicative rather than purely referential (e.g., when it expresses additional descriptive or emotive content). However, as we have seen in (15), the dislocated NP may in fact felicitously represent information that is immediately accessible and currently topical, even when it has been explicitly mentioned in the prior utterance and expresses no further descriptive or emotive content.

Crucially, this information status is exactly the one that is disallowed by all of the other three constructions we have considered thus far: In no case may the postposed NP of inversion or either type of *there*-insertion represent the most recently evoked, or most topical, information in the discourse. Moreover, what all of the above accounts of right-dislocation share is a prohibition on the appearance of brand-new information in dislocated position, where 'brand-new' refers to information that has not been evoked either textually or situationally, is not inferrable from the prior discourse, and is not believed to be otherwise within the hearer's knowledge store (Prince 1981c). And this, importantly, is also precisely the one information status that is not only allowed, but is in fact prototypical, in postposed position for inversion and both types of *there*-insertion (which differ from each other only in terms of the nature of the newness on which their felicity depends). Thus, despite the current lack of consensus regarding the discourse function of right-dislocation, it is clear that the functional restriction on the dislocated NP in right-dislocation differs radically from that imposed on the PVNP in inversion and *there*-insertion.

4   The Function of Rightward Movement

Our corpora-based study of four constructions – inversion, existential *there*-insertion, presentational *there*-insertion, and right-dislocation – reveals that each is sensitive to different constraints on the information status of the NP in marked position. However, the pragmatic constraints to which these constructions are sensitive do pattern in such a way that significant generalizations across constructions can be drawn. Our findings are summarized in Table 1.

Table 1. Constraints on Information Status of the PVNP
in Four Constructions

CONSTRUCTION	INFORMATION STATUS OF PVNP
inversion	relatively new in the discourse
existential *there*	hearer-new
presentational *there*	discourse-new
right-dislocation	discourse-old

First, note that our analysis predicts different distributions for the four constructions in question. For example, in contexts where the information represented by the PVNP is familiar to the hearer yet new to the discourse, inversion should be felicitous but the corresponding existential *there*-insertion should not (contra Hartvigson & Jakobsen 1974, Erdmann 1976, Breivik 1981, Penhallurick 1984, Freeze 1992, inter alia). This prediction is borne out, as evidenced in (17):

(17)   a.   Mary didn't know why she had been called out of class, but she hurried to the principal's office and went in. Standing in the corner holding a fat red folder was the algebra teacher.

     b.   [...] #Standing in the corner holding a fat red folder there was the algebra teacher.

Similarly, although existential *there*-insertion disallows hearer-old, discourse-new information in postverbal position, presentational *there*-insertion does not, as seen in (18):

(18) a.   There appeared before the committee your good friend Jim Alterman. [=(12a)]

b.   #There was before the committee your good friend Jim Alterman.

Here, the PVNP constitutes hearer-old information and, as such, is disallowed in existential *there*-insertion yet is felicitous in presentational *there*-insertion.

Second, notice that three of the four constructions under investigation – inversion and the two types of *there*-insertion – share an important function, namely the postposing of information that is unfamiliar, either within the discourse or within the hearer's knowledge store. Interestingly, this property is shared by precisely those constructions that have been argued to involve rightward movement of the PVNP (Stowell 1981, Safir 1985, inter alia; however, cf. Rochemont & Culicover 1990). Thus, we can hypothesize that rightward-movement in English is characterized by the postposing of unfamiliar information.

Crucially, this function does not apply to right-dislocation, a superficially similar construction which involves no movement to PVNP position. With right-dislocation, in addition to the dislocated PVNP, there is necessarily a pronoun within the same sentence that is interpretable as coreferential with the dislocated NP. In the case of inversion and *there*-insertion, on the other hand, the PVNP appears in postverbal position as a result of movement, leaving behind no coreferential pronoun, but rather the hallmark of syntactic movement: a gap, or trace, that is subject to various independently motivated constraints on movement and extraction. Thus, we assume that the 'dislocated' NP of right-dislocation is simply base-generated in postverbal position.[2]

---

[2] Ziv & Grosz (1994) invoke the notion of subjacency to rule out non-afterthought examples of right-dislocation, and thus commit themselves to a movement account of RD. Consider (i):

(i) *The story that he told us was very interesting, Bill. [=Ziv & Grosz 1994:185, ex. 5]

Ziv & Grosz maintain that the pronoun in (i) cannot be interpreted as coreferential with *Bill* because it occurs within a complex NP, resulting in ungrammaticality. However, consider the following (constructed) example:

(ii) One thing he'll never be is motivated, that guy.

The grammaticality of this example suggests that the deviance of (i) is pragmatic rather than syntactic, and that no subjacency violation is involved. Rather, the possibility of a coreferential interpretation in (ii) is consistent with the non-movement analysis of right-dislocation that we are assuming in this study.

And corresponding to the syntactic difference between right-dislo-cation and the other constructions that do involve rightward move-ment, we find that right-dislocation is subject to an entirely different pragmatic constraint. Unlike NPs that occur in postverbal position as the result of movement, the dislocated NP of right-dislocation is con-strained to constitute familiar, discourse-old information in context. Thus, we propose that rightward movement in English always restricts the familiarity of the referent of the moved NP.

5   Conclusion

It is argued in Horn 1986 that leftward movement in general serves to prepose 'thematic' or familiar information, whereas rightward move-ment serves to postpose nonthematic or unfamiliar information. Previ-ous work (e.g., Ward & Birner 1994b) has shown that leftward move-ment does indeed serve to front familiar information, although the type of familiarity involved varies from construction to construction. In this paper we have examined three constructions which have been an-alyzed by syntacticians as rightward-moving, and have found that all three postpose information that is unfamiliar, either within the dis-course or in the hearer's knowledge store. In the case of inversion, the PVNP is required to represent information that is less familiar in the discourse than that represented by the preposed constituent. Pre-sentational *there*-insertion is similarly sensitive to discourse-familiarity, but requires that the PVNP represent information that is absolutely, rather than relatively, new within the discourse. Finally, existential *there*-insertion requires that the PVNP represent information that is not only new to the discourse, but also (presumed to be) new to the hearer.

Thus, these constructions share the property of postposing infor-mation which is 'new' in some sense. Moreover, this property is not shared by right-dislocation, a superficially similar but non-rightward-moving construction. These findings, in combination with those noted above for leftward movement, support the proposal that in general, left-ward movement in English preposes information that is familiar while rightward movement postposes information that is not.

References

Abbott, Barbara. 1992. Definiteness, Existentials, and the 'List' Interpretation. In Chris Barker and David Dowty, eds., *Proceedings of SALT II*. Columbus, Ohio.

Abbott, Barbara. 1993. A Pragmatic Account of the Definiteness Effect in Existential Sentences. *Journal of Pragmatics* 19.39-55.

Aissen, Judith. 1975. Presentational-There Insertion: A Cyclic Root Transformation. In *Papers from the Eleventh Regional Meeting, Chicago Linguistic Society*, 1-14. Chicago Linguistic Society, University of Chicago.

Birner, Betty. 1994. Information Status and Word Order: An Analysis of English Inversion. *Language* 70.233-259.

Breivik, Leiv E. 1981. On the Interpretation of Existential *There*. *Language* 57.1-25.

Bolinger, Dwight. 1977. *Meaning and Form*. London: Longman.

Davison, Alice. 1984. Syntactic Markedness and the Definition of Sentence Topic. *Language* 60.797-846.

Erdmann, Peter. 1976. *There Sentences in English*. Munich: Tuduv.

Freeze, Ray. 1992. Existentials and Other Locatives. *Language* 68.553-595.

Geluykens Ronald. 1987. Tails (Right Dislocations) as a Repair Mechanism in English Conversations. In Jan Nuyts and G. de Schutter, eds., *Getting One's Words into Line: On Word Order and Functional Grammar*. Dordrecht: Foris. 119-130.

Givón, Talmy. 1976. Topic, pronoun, and grammatical agreement. In Charles Li, ed., *Subject and Topic*. NY: Academic Press. 149-58.

Grosz, Barbara, Aravind Joshi, and Scott Weinstein. 1983. Providing a Unified Account of Definite Noun Phrases in Discourse. In *Proceedings of the 21st Annual Meeting of the Association for Computational Linguistics*, 44-50.

Hannay, Michael. 1985. *English Existentials in Functional Grammar*. Dordrecht: Foris.

Hartvigson, Hans, and Leif Jakobsen. 1974. *Inversion in Present-Day English*. Odense: Odense University Press.

Hawkins, John A. 1978. *Definiteness and Indefiniteness*. Atlantic Highlands, NJ: Humanities Press.

Hawkins, John A. 1991. On (In)definite Articles: Implicatures and (Un)grammaticality Prediction. *Journal of Linguistics* 27.405-442.

Holmback, Heather. 1984. An Interpretive Solution to the Definiteness Effect Problem. *Linguistic Analysis* 13.195-215.

Horn, Laurence R. 1986. Presupposition, Theme and Variations. In *Papers from the Parasession on Pragmatics and Grammatical Theory, Chicago Linguistic Society*, 168-92. Chicago Linguistic Society, University of Chicago.

Jenkins, Lyle. 1975. *The English Existential*. Tübingen: Niemeyer.

Lakoff, George. 1987. *Women, Fire, and Dangerous Things*. Chicago: University of Chicago Press.

Lambrecht, Knud. 1981. Topic, Anti-Topic and Verb Agreement in Non-Standard French. In *Pragmatics and Beyond* II,6. Amsterdam: John Benjamins.

Larson, Richard. 1988. Light Predicate Raising. *Lexicon Project Working Papers* 27. MIT: Center for Cognitive Science.

Levin, Beth. 1993. *English Verb Classes and Alternations: A Preliminary Investigation*. Chicago: University of Chicago Press.

Lumsden, Michael. 1988. *Existential Sentences: Their Structure and Meaning*. London: Croom Helm.

McNally, Louise. 1992. *An Interpretation for the English Existential Construction*. Doctoral dissertation, University of California at Santa Cruz.

Milsark, Gary. 1974. *Existential Sentences in English*. Doctoral dissertation, MIT.

Milsark, Gary. 1977. Toward an Explanation of Certain Peculiarities of the Existential Construction in English. *Linguistic Analysis* 3.1-30.

Penhallurick, John. 1984. Full-Verb Inversion in English. *Australian Journal of Linguistics* 4.33-56.

Prince, Ellen F. 1981a. On the Inferencing of Indefinite-*This* NPs. In Aravind Joshi, Bonnie Webber, and Ivan Sag, eds., *Elements of Discourse Understanding*. Cambridge: Cambridge University Press. 231-50.

Prince, Ellen F. 1981b. Topicalization, Focus-Movement, and Yiddish-Movement: A Pragmatic Differentiation. In *Papers from the Seventh Annual Meeting, Berkeley Linguistics Society*, 249-64. Berkeley Linguistics Society, University of California.

Prince, Ellen F. 1981c. Toward a Taxonomy of Given/New Information. In Peter Cole, ed., *Radical Pragmatics*. NY: Academic Press. 223-54.

Prince, Ellen F. 1986. On the Syntactic Marking of Presupposed Open Propositions. In *Papers from the Parasession on Pragmatics and Grammatical Theory, Chicago Linguistic Society*, 208-22. Chicago Linguistic Society, University of Chicago.

Prince, Ellen F. 1988. The Discourse Functions of Yiddish Expletive *Es* + Subject-Postposing. *Papers in Pragmatics* 2.176-94.

Prince, Ellen F. 1992. The ZPG Letter: Subjects, Definiteness, and Information-Status. In Sandra Thompson and William Mann, eds., *Discourse Description: Diverse Analyses of a Fundraising Text*. Amsterdam: John Benjamins. 295-325.

Rando, Emily N., and Donna Jo Napoli. 1978. Definites in *There*-Sentences. *Language* 54.300-13.

Reuland, Eric, and Alice ter Meulen. 1987. *The Representation of (In)-definiteness*. Cambridge, MA: MIT Press.

Rochemont, Michael, and Peter Culicover. 1990. *English Focus Constructions and the Theory of Grammar*. Cambridge: Cambridge University Press.

Safir, Kenneth. 1985. *Syntactic Chains*. Cambridge: Cambridge University Press.

Stowell, Tim. 1981. *Origins of Phrase Structure*. Doctoral dissertation, MIT.

Tomlin, Russell. 1986. *Basic Word Order: Functional Principles*. London: Croom Helm.

Ward, Gregory. 1988. *The Semantics and Pragmatics of Preposing*. New York: Garland.

Ward, Gregory, and Betty Birner. 1994a. English *There*-Sentences and Information Status. In *Proceedings of the Ninth Annual Conference and of the Workshop on Discourse*, 165-83. The Israeli Association for Theoretical Linguistics.

Ward, Gregory, and Betty Birner. 1994b. A Unified Account of English Fronting Constructions. In *Penn Working Papers in Linguistics, Vol. 1*, 159-65. University of Pennsylvania Department of Linguistics.

Woisetschlaeger, Erich. 1983. On the Question of Definiteness in "An old man's book". *Linguistic Inquiry* 14.137-154.

Ziv, Yael. 1982. Another Look at Definites in Existentials. *Journal of Linguistics* 18.73-88.

Ziv, Yael, and Barbara Grosz. 1994. Right Dislocation and Attentional State. In *Proceedings of the Ninth Annual Conference and of the Workshop on Discourse*, 184-99. The Israeli Association for Theoretical Linguistics.

Deontic and Epistemic Modals in ASL: A Discourse Analysis

PHYLLIS PERRIN WILCOX
University of New Mexico

When American Sign Language words are used to represent mental designata, there is an isomorphic relationship existing between the two–not only at the lexical level but at the pragmatic/discourse level. This visual/gestural language follows George Lakoff's Spatialization of Form Hypothesis (1987) in which there is a prediction of an association between grammar and such cognitive abilities as object recognition, spatial structure, and body awareness grounded in immediate bodily experience of physical objects.

Eve Sweetser (1990) argues that the language of the external world is applied to the internal mental world, thus metaphorically structuring an extension from root-modal meanings to epistemic domains. Metaphorical mapping of the more abstract domains of our understanding in terms of more concrete domains motivates semantic connections which lead to further understanding in terms of our everyday discourse structures.

Sweetser (1990: 49) found evidence that there is a "crosslinguistic tendency for lexical items to be ambiguous between the root and the epistemic senses." She demonstrates that many unrelated languages are alike in having some set of predicate which carry both root and epistemic modal meanings, as the English language does, i.e. *may* or *must*. Sweetser proposes a force-dynamic analysis of modality in which, for example, *must* indicates either a real-world force that is imposed on the speaker to do the action or "an epistemic force applied by some body of premises, which compels the speaker (or people in general) to reach the conclusion embodied in the sentence." (64). The two deontic and epistemic senses in this example (*must*) and many others, can naturally and regularly represent both of these different meanings.

In Wilcox and Wilcox (1995) it was shown that the root and the epistemic forms (See Figures 1–3) found in ASL are not necessarily always the same. However, this paper will demonstrate that MUST[1] can assume an epistemic sense as well as the deontic sense, and that both the modals MUST and MAYBE are semantically affected by the iconic forces pervading ASL.

It is difficult to document evidence for phonological change in ASL since there were few photographs or videotapes of signed languages until relatively

---

1. Following conventional procedure, ASL words are capitalized in this article.

recent times, and earlier written texts did not always contain explicit descriptions of the signs. But in the case of the etymological relationship between MUST and SHOULD, Long (1918: 26) offers the following descriptions:

> **Should, Ought,** indicating duty.— Press the crooked forefinger of the right "G" hand against the lips and then move toward side and downward as in "must" (see below). Or,

> (2) Indicate by the signs "better" and "must." Better is signed as follows: Place the end of the right open hand pointing toward the left, palm against the mouth; draw away toward the side, assuming the position of "A" and lifting it to a level with the head. "Must," see below.

> **Must, Need, Have to.**—Crook the forefinger of the right "G" hand, pointing it downward, and press the hand down some distance with more or less force. Sometimes the motion is repeated several times.

The forms described by Long for SHOULD are no longer used. While MUST is essentially unchanged from this earlier form, SHOULD is now made with reduplicated flexion and extension of the wrist. This phonological relationship (single, punctual movement versus reduplicated, cyclic movement) will reappear in other modals (cf. Humphries et al., 1980; Wilcox & Wilcox, 1995).

Wilcox & Wilcox (1995) argue that strong obligation in ASL can be expressed with the lexical modal MUST (Figure 1a).[2] Weak obligation is expressed with the lexical modal SHOULD (Figure 1b).

Epistemic possibility can be indicated in ASL with the lexical items POSSIBLE (Figure 2a) and MAYBE (Figure 2b). Long (1918) related the word MAYBE ('may,' 'maybe,' or 'perhaps') to the physical act of comparing weights by using the hands as a balance scale. POSSIBLE is related to CAN; the phonological relationship parallels that of MUST and SHOULD. MUST and CAN are articulated with strong, single movements; POSSIBLE and SHOULD are articulated with weaker, reduplicated movements.

Ferreira Brito (1990: 255) comments on the same relationship between deontic and epistemic modals in Brazilian Cities Sign Language (BCSL). Deontic modals are expressed with "simple and energetic movements" which, she suggests, is related to an underlying metaphor of obligation for something to be done as actions or events in the real world. Epistemics are distinguished by nonenergetic movement of the hands.

---

2. All figures in this article are taken from *A Basic Course in American Sign Language* (O'Rourke, et.al., 1980).

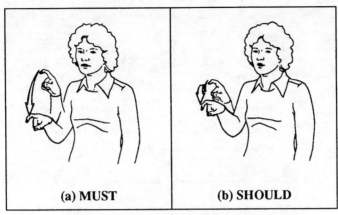

Figure 1: Modals of Obligation

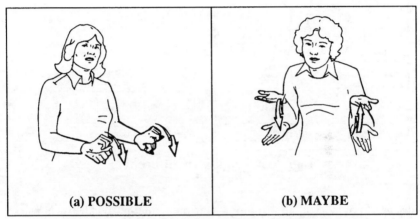

Figure 2: Modals of Weak Inference

Epistemic modalities in ASL are also expressed with lexical items such as FEEL, SEEM and OBVIOUS (Figure 3)[3], in other constructions such as questions, and with particular non-manual markings (NMSs).[4]

A number of facts about the expression of modality lend themselves to a

---

3. Figure 3c is actually a representation for the word BRIGHT; OBVIOUS is made with reduced movement.
4. A discussion of non-manual grammatical markings which can accompany modals is found in Wilcox & Wilcox (1995).

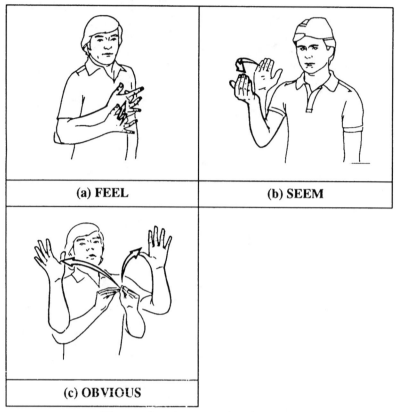

(a) FEEL	**(b) SEEM**

(c) OBVIOUS

Figure 3: Modals of Inference

discussion of iconicity in ASL. First, note the formal relation between pairs of related words: MUST and SHOULD (Figure 1), CAN and POSSIBLE (Figure 2a). MUST is stressed and unreduplicated; SHOULD is unstressed and reduplicated. The same holds true for CAN and POSSIBLE. Other words discussed above also take part in this relationship: FEEL, SEEM, OBVIOUS, and MAYBE. The relationship can be described in terms of stress and reduplication.[5]

For FEEL, the relevant feature for the present discussion is reduplication. When FEEL is produced using a single, upward movement it refers to the physical sense of feeling. When it is produced with multiple, reduplicated

---

5. Wilbur & Schick (1987) describe several features associated with stress, including non-manual behaviors, sharp sign boundaries, higher placement in the signing space, faster movement, and repetition.

movements (and the appropriate NMSs) it acquires an epistemic reading.

OBVIOUS is related to the ASL word BRIGHT ('bright' or 'light'). Compared to BRIGHT it is made with less stressed, reduced movement. In its epistemic sense it appears in constructions such as:

(1)   HE RICH, OBVIOUS

"He must be rich."

SEEM is historically related to the words MIRROR and COMPARE, words related to physical resemblance. SEEM is more complex than FEEL when it takes on epistemic readings. Consider the following: In a discussion of which of two possible translations would be more appropriate for a particular ASL utterance, the following conversation took place:

(2)   Speaker A: "Which do you think she said, this [indexi] or that [indexj]?"
        Speaker B: SEEM++ INDEXi
        "She probably said this ..."
        (The two study the videotape of the utterance under discussion some more.)
        Speaker B: SEEM INDEXi!
        "Yes, this has to be what she said."

In example (2), the first occurrence of SEEM is slowly reduplicated; the second is signed once with emphatic stress. The first expresses weak epistemic probability, the second stronger epistemic certainty. The iconicity principle in operation here seems to be:

(A)   In epistemics, possibility is expressed with reduced gestural substance; probability or certainty is expressed with strong gestural substance.[6]

The iconicity principle (A) appears to be confirmed by the fact that the same relationship holds between other related forms in ASL. Thus, MAYBE may be signed with slow, unstressed, long movements or with stressed, faster, shorter movements. The former means 'maybe, but barely possible'; the latter means 'maybe, probably true'.[7]

Wilcox and Wilcox (1995) note that all of the above epistemic modals are related to ASL words which denote physical activity and perception:

(1) physical strength (POSSIBLE)

---

6. Wilcox & Wilcox (1995) believe that this is an instance of the iconic expression of force-dynamics in ASL modals (cf. Talmy 1985).

7. This discussion on FEEL, SEEM and OBVIOUS epistemics was taken from Wilcox & Wilcox (1995).

(2) judging the physical weight of an object (MAYBE)

(3) the physical sense of feeling (FEEL)

(4) physical resemblance, as reflected in a mirror (SEEM)

(5) the bright light needed for clear visual perception (OBVIOUS)

This relationship has been noted by others (Sweetser, 1990), and clearly relies on a metaphorical mapping between embodied, physically-grounded source domains and mental, abstract target domains.

It should be pointed out that the deontic modals MUST and SHOULD are not commonly used epistemically in ASL. Thus, the sentence:

(3)   *YOU MUST TIRED YOU

does not mean "You must be tired" in the epistemic sense. Likewise, the sentence, "We should be finished by 4 PM" in ASL would not use the lexical item SHOULD.

Sweetser (1990: 64) reminds us that in English "the same (syntactic as well as lexical) form can naturally and regularly represent both" deontic and epistemic readings. In ASL, we find the same form (i.e., MUST/SHOULD or CAN/POSSIBLE), with slightly different reduplication movements. However, both pairs are demonstrating deontic readings of either strong or weaker obligation (Wilcox & Wilcox, 1995).

Until recently, formal linguistics has maintained that to the extent that a communication system exhibits iconicity, it is less a *human language*. Givón (1984, 1989) and Haiman (1984) argue against this position for spoken languages, suggesting instead that linguistic form is often motivated by iconic principles. Although it is difficult to deny the existence of iconicity in signed languages, few signed language linguists ascribe the deeply significant role to iconicity that functional and cognitive linguists have in spoken languages. Many ASL linguists have, in fact, attempted to "explain away" iconicity in ASL. However, ASL is not dualistically separated from its physical realization, but deeply rooted in its bodily basis.[8] Neither is grammar independent of meaning. Such a view is compatible with cognitive or functional theories of language developed in works such as Bybee (1985), Deane (1991, 1993), Givón (1989), Lakoff (1987), and Langacker (1987, 1991).

ASL demonstrates that there is additional complexity to how metaphors are mapped. The mapping revealed in ASL deals not only with the iconicity prevalent in spoken languages (Bybee, 1985; Fleischman, 1982; Fauconnier, 1985; Givon, 1991; Haiman, 1984; Langacker, 1991; Talmy, 1983) but with the actual use of handshape icons (and their corresponding movements and locations) that add their own visual images to the linguistic spectrum.

---

8. This view is more fully described in a work on the gestural origin of language by Armstrong, Stokoe, and Wilcox (1995).

ASL phonemes and morphemes can be isomorphic, with their corresponding handshapes having the same appearance of form. Although the phonological and morphological components of ASL may, at times, be one and the same, it is important to recognize the difference between iconic and metaphorical conceptual relationships. Prior research has systematically confounded the issue of iconicity in ASL. For further information on distinguishing iconicity from metaphoricity when analyzing ASL words, see P. Wilcox, (1993).

For this paper, the data elicitation was originally designed to explore the hypothesis that ASL exhibits metaphorical mapping in the language and thought domains. In the original study were many questions that lent themselves exceptionally well to the expression of modals. For example, throughout the research interviews, inquiry dealing with the function of a word or parameter was interjected. Questions were used to explore the reasoning behind the selection of certain phonological (verb stem) handshapes, specific locations, and path movements that the native informants used when producing their signed replies. If an informant expressed strong probability of accepting a particular sign articulation as a legitimate word in ASL, the interviewer would then shift the location of the sign production and ask if the movement represented a semantic change, or if the word could still be accepted into the ASL lexicon, even with the new parameter shift.

Analysis for this paper centered on two modals, MAYBE and MUST.

In normal discourse, the modal MAYBE is produced with closed fingers, and a steady symmetrical balancing motion (See Figure 2b). However, when an informant responded to an inquiry by answering with a hypothetical situation, or attempted to suggest an extremely remote possibility, the fingers producing MAYBE often opened slightly and the movement of the co-occurring symmetrical hands slowed down, or stopped completely.

One informant was asked if the sign used for ESP (extrasensory perception) occurring between two people could be moved from the standard location near the forehead, to an unorthodox location near the mouth. His response showed extreme wariness of this possibility, since the change in location created a semantic change in the word itself (from a verbal ESP, to a sign similar but not identical to, the verb, TO-TATTLE). However, he attempted to formulate a possible situation in which that new verb might occur:

(4)   MAYBE {no balancing movement occurring, both hands totally still; fingers on both hands opened loosely}. FUNNY. MAYBE {standard sign used here} I TATTLE, YOU TATTLE. (I) TATTLE (You) TATTLE. MAYBE (slow balancing of hands, slight loosening of fingers, head tilted back and pulled away from the hands to create a sense of distancing). [Loose translation: "Although extremely unlikely, perhaps. It might be odd, but perhaps if I initi-

ated tattling on you *to you*, and then you subsequently began to tattle on me *to me*, and we continued like this back and forth for a
while until all of a sudden we both seemed to tattle *on one another*
at the same exact moment, then that particular sign might occur and
be understood and accepted in content."]

As the above segment illustrates, the more hypothetical the created situation, the slower the movement of the hands and the more opened the fingers
are. One MAYBE modal, the first, did not even create movement in the form
of balancing possibilities. The hand produced a resembling phonological
shape, but remained perfectly still.

The epistemic sense–as the deontic–can be strong or weak, as evidenced
by the above example. In ASL, MAYBE is not a strong epistemic since no
one conclusion is determined. However, we see that the standard use of
MAYBE can be stronger than the even more hypothetical and rarer MAYBE
modal that is called upon when showing a very extreme possibility. The standard MAYBE uses closed fingers, indicating that in the possibility presenting
itself there are at least alternatives that can be comfortably held up, and metaphorically, weighed and balanced. The more vigorous the balancing motion,
the more confident the mental activity. On the other hand, opened fingers can,
metaphorically, "hold" no ideas. The possible ideas or beliefs fall through the
fingers, leaving nothing to be balanced.

Bybee (1994:201) states, "Metaphorical change involves a shift to a different domain–in this case [when an epistemic use of *must* arises in contexts
with aspectual interpretations distinct from the obligation uses] from the domain of social obligations and physical necessities applied to an agent, to the
epistemic domain that speaks of the necessary conditions under which a proposition can be true." She also claims that the mechanism of change involving
metaphorical extension occurs more readily with words that are less grammaticalized–such as the English word *must*.

In ASL, the meaning of MUST is also less eroded than that of SHOULD,
and more closely resembles a lexical item, conditions lending themselves to
metaphorical extension in modals, according to Bybee. This corresponds with
Sweeter's (1990:58) claim that the "polysemy of modals, then, may lie rather
in the presence or absence of a metaphorical mapping than in the presence or
absence of a single feature making the sense more specific." In other words,
separate formal-semantic structures for root and epistemic modals are not
necessarily relevant to the analysis of modality.

Most modals glossed as MUST are designated as either strong or weak
deontic readings. They are usually signed close to the body, with a relatively
strong physical thrust, depending on the deontic reading. It is rarer that a signer will use MUST epistemically. However, MUST can take on epistemic
readings on occasion and under typical epistemic conditions. One excellent

example discovered clearly exhibits an epistemic MUST.[9]

One Deaf person was giving a lecture on Deaf Culture and related to the audience of Deaf people an interesting incidence that had occurred to her. It happened that a Deaf friend asked her a question, to which she gave a knowledgable reply. At a later time, she noticed the friend asking a hearing person the identical question. The lecturer confronted the Deaf friend, and asked why he had sought to verify her answer by asking a hearing person. The friend nonchalantly responded that he had decided to check with the hearing person just to "make sure" it was the correct answer. The lecturer, after retelling this anecdote, faced her Deaf audience and said:

(5)   HEARING MUST KNOW, MUST.

"Hearing people must know everything."

People who are aware of the long-term oppression of Deaf people by the dominant majority group, hearing people, can appreciate the lecturer's demonstration of peeved chagrin when her fellow Deaf friend sought the assurance of a hearing person's knowledge over her own. Until recently, when the new technological advents because available to the Deaf community, hearing people were often "ahead" of what was happening in the world. Yet, even though her friend's behavior might have caused some annoyance, this lecturer recognized it as a cultural phenomenon exemplified through her epistemic statement.

Sweetser (1990) claims that an epistemic force applies some body of premises that compels the speaker to reach the conclusion embodied in a statement. She (1990:64) notes that the "epistemic force is the counterpart, in the epistemic domain, of a forceful obligation in the sociophysical domain." The use of the above modal, MUST, does not indicate a root-modal meaning involving force or obligation. It is not an indication of a social rule, in which hearing people are commanded to go out and learn everything to be known. It is the result of a culturally made conclusion draw from premises: "We don't trust Deaf people to know the latest information, since they often are the last ones to be provided with technological communication resources; therefore, we *conclude* that hearing people know the answer and Deaf people don't."

Langacker (1991) discusses subjectification as a semantic shift or extension in which an entity originally construed objectively comes to receive a more subjective construal. On the other hand, objectivity implies that a conception makes no reference to the conceptualizer. The iconic principle is rooted in the production of the epistemic modal above and exemplifies itself objectively through the physical fully extended arm that changed the obligation from internally imposed to externally imposed. The physical distance of

9. My appreciation to MJ Bienvenu for allowing analysis of the above epistemic MUST in this paper.

the sign MUST from the signer (arm fully extended) results in a mental distancing effect. The sociophysical idea that we have of distance spatialization creates an objectification of the modal MUST, implying that an obligation of an individual is compelled by forces or authority outside of oneself, rather than personal, internal obligations of the signer. It contrasts with the internally imposed force of the reading of the more commonly used modal, deontic MUST, which is produced closer to the body of the signer and applies a stronger physical downward thrust.

In conclusion, American Sign Language is not dualistically separated from its physical realization but has an experiential bodily basis, which is motivated by metaphorical and iconic principals. Bybee (1994:195), in her cross-linguistic research, found that epistemic senses develop later than, and out of, the agent-oriented senses. The initial, tentative, evidence found in ASL modality research tends to support this extension from the basic root sense to the epistemic sense. The analysis of discourse through diachronic procession can lead to an understanding of the grammaticalization of ASL modals, and the profound affect that iconicity has on the entire process.

References

Armstrong, D.F., Stokoe, W.C., and S. E. Wilcox. 1995. *Gesture and the nature of language*. Cambridge: Cambridge University Press.

Brito, Ferreira L. 1990. Epistemic, alethic, and deontic modalities in a Brazilian sign language. In S.D. Fischer & P. Siple (Eds.), *Theoretical issues in sign language research*. Chicago: University of Chicago Press.

Bybee, J.L. 1985. *Morphology: A study of the relation between meaning and form*. Amsterdam: John Benjamins.

Bybee, J., Perkins, W.D. & W. Pagliuca. 1994. *The evolution of grammar: Tense, aspect and modality in the languages of the world*. Chicago: University of Chicago Press.

Deane, P.D. 1991. Syntax and the brain: Neurological evidence for the spatialization of form hypothesis. *Cognitive Linguistics, 2(4)*, 361–367.

Deane, P.D. 1993. *Grammar in mind and brain: Explorations in cognitive syntax*. Berlin/New York: Mouton de Gruyter.

Fleischman, S. 1982. *The future in thought and language: Diachronic evidence from Romance*. Cambridge: Cambridge University Press.

Fauconnier, G. 1985. *Mental spaces*. Cambridge, MA: MIT.

Givón, T. 1984. *Syntax: A functional–typological introduction volume I*. Amsterdam: John Benjamins.

Givón, T. 1989. *Mind, code and context: Essays in Pragmatics*. Hillsdale, NJ: Lawrence Erlbaum.

Givon, T. 1991. Isomorphism in the grammatical code: Cognitive and biological considerations. *Studies in Language, 15(1)*, 85–114.

Haiman, J. 1984. *Iconicity in syntax*. Amsterdam: John Benjamins.

Humphries, T., Padden, C. & T.J. O'Rourke. 1980. *A basic course in American Sign Language*. Silver Spring, MD: TJ Publishers.

Lakoff, G. 1987. *Women, fire, and dangerous things: What categories reveal about the mind*. Chicago: University of Chicago Press.

Langacker, R. 1987. *Foundations of cognitive grammar volume I: Theoretical prerequisites*. Stanford: Stanford University Press.

Langacker, R. 1991. *Foundations of cognitive grammar volume II*. Stanford: Stanford University Press.

Long, J.S. 1918. *The sign language: A manual of signs*. Washington, DC: Gallaudet College Press.

O'Rourke, T., Humphries, T. & C. Padden. 1980. *A Basic Course in American Sign Language*. Silver Spring, MD: T.J. Publishers, Inc.

Sweetser, E. 1990. *From etymology to pragmatics: Metaphorical and cultural aspects of semantic structure*. Cambridge: Cambridge University Press.

Talmy, L. 1983. How language structures space. In H. Peck, & L. Acredolo (Eds.), *Spatial orientation: Theory, research, and application*. New York, NY: Plenum Press.

Talmy, L. 1985. Force dynamics in language and thought. In *Papers from the Parasession on causitives and agentivity*, 1, 293–337. Chicago: Chicago Linguistic Society.

Wilbur, R.B. & B.S. Schick. 1987. The effects of linguistic stress on ASL signs. *Language and Speech, 30(4)*, 301–323.

Wilcox, P. 1993. Metaphorical Mapping in American Sign Language. Unpublished dissertation, University of New Mexico.

Wilcox, S. & P. Wilcox. 1995. The Gestural Expression of Modality in ASL. In J. Bybee & S. Fleischman (Eds.), *Mood and Modality*. Amsterdam: John Benjamins. pp. 135-162.

Author Index

Subject Index